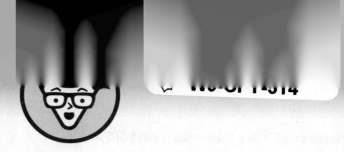

Nonprofit Kit

6th Edition

by Dr. Beverly A. Browning, Stan Hutton, and Frances N. Phillips

for dummies®

A Wiley Brand

Nonprofit Kit For Dummies®, 6th Edition

Published by: **John Wiley & Sons, Inc.**, 111 River Street, Hoboken, NJ 07030-5774, www.wiley.com

Copyright © 2022 by John Wiley & Sons, Inc., Hoboken, New Jersey

Media and software compilation copyright © 2022 by John Wiley & Sons, Inc. All rights reserved.

Published simultaneously in Canada

For general information on our other products and services, please contact our Customer Care Department within the U.S. at 877-762-2974, outside the U.S. at 317-572-3993, or fax 317-572-4002. For technical support, please visit https://hub.wiley.com/community/support/dummies.

Wiley publishes in a variety of print and electronic formats and by print-on-demand. Some material included with standard print versions of this book may not be included in e-books or in print-on-demand. If this book refers to media such as a CD or DVD that is not included in the version you purchased, you may download this material at http://booksupport.wiley.com. For more information about Wiley products, visit www.wiley.com.

Library of Congress Control Number: 2021946367

ISBN: 978-1-119-83572-1

ISBN 978-1-119-83574-5 (pbk); ISBN 978-1-119-83573-8 (ebk)

SKY10038399_111422

Contents at a Glance

Table of Contents

CHAPTER 9: **Evaluating Your Work: Are You Meeting Your Goals?** 147

CHAPTER 10: **You Can Count on Me! Working with Volunteers** 161

CHAPTER 11: **Working with Paid Staff and Contractors** 179

Introduction

t may sound corny, but we feel a certain sense of mission when it comes to nonprofits. We've started them, directed them, raised funds for them, consulted for them, volunteered for them, given money to them, and written about them. We've worked with nonprofits in one way or another for more years than we care to remember.

Why have we continued to work for nonprofit organizations? Yes, we care about others and want to see the world become a better place — our values are important to us. But, to be honest, that's not the only reason we've worked for nonprofit organizations for so many years. We believe the reason is that we can't think of anything more interesting or more challenging to do.

Starting a new program is exciting. Securing your first grant is thrilling. Working with the multifaceted personalities that come together on a board of directors is fascinating. Learning a new skill because no one else is there to do it is fun. Seeing the faces of satisfied clients, walking along a restored lakeshore, hearing the applause of audiences — all are gratifying.

That's why we do it.

About This Book

We try to cover the gamut in this book — everything you need to know to start and manage a charitable organization, from applying for your tax exemption to raising money to pay for your programs. We include supplemental information at Dummies.com, including forms to help you create a budget, examples of grant proposals, and links to websites where you can find more help.

We also attempt to give you a bird's-eye view of the economy's nonprofit sector. When you look at financial resources, for example, nonprofits are much like the rest of the world: Most of the wealth is held by relatively few nonprofit organizations, a certain number of them are in the middle, and many, many more struggle to make ends meet.

Note: When we refer to nonprofit organizations, unless we say otherwise, we're talking about organizations that have been recognized as 501(c)(3) nonprofits and are considered public charities by the IRS.

We try to be honest about the difficulties you'll sometimes face. You probably won't be able to achieve everything you set out to accomplish, and you'll always wish you had more resources to do more things. Still, we can't imagine doing anything else. Maybe you'll feel the same way after you jump into the nonprofit world.

As you're reading, you may note that some web addresses break across two lines of text. If you're reading this book in print and want to visit one of these web pages, simply key in the web address exactly as it's noted in the text, pretending the line break doesn't exist. If you're reading this as an e-book, you've got it easy — just click the web address to be taken directly to the web page.

To make the content more accessible, we divided it into five parts:

>> **Part 1:** Getting Familiar with the Nonprofit Framework

>> **Part 2:** Bringing Your A-Game to Nonprofit Management

>> **Part 3:** Raising Funds Successfully

>> **Part 4:** The Part of Tens

>> **Part 5:** Appendixes

Foolish Assumptions

When writing this book, we made some assumptions about who may be interested in reading it. Here are some of the readers we imagined:

>> You have an idea that will help solve a problem in your community, and you believe that starting a nonprofit organization is the best way to put your idea into action.

>> You serve on a board of directors and wonder what you're supposed to be doing.

>> You work for a nonprofit and need some ideas about fundraising, managing your organization, or working with your board of directors.

>> You're simply curious about the nonprofit sector and want to find out more about it.

If you're one of these people, we're confident that this book will answer your questions and give you the information you're seeking.

Icons Used in This Book

We use the following icons throughout the book to flag particularly important or helpful information.

REMEMBER

The Remember icon emphasizes important information that you should be ready to put into practice.

TECHNICAL STUFF

You may not need this technical stuff today (and can skip over it), but — who knows? It may be invaluable tomorrow.

TIP

This icon is posted next to little hints and suggestions gleaned from our experience over the years. Put these ideas to good use to save yourself some time, energy, or money.

WARNING

Warnings are just what you think they may be. We alert you to information that can help you avoid problematic situations.

Beyond the Book

In addition to the material in the print or e-book you're reading right now, this product also comes with some access-anywhere goodies on the web. Check out the free Cheat Sheet for a list of steps that are necessary for securing nonprofit status from the IRS, a rundown of the roles and responsibilities of people who sit on the board of directors for a nonprofit organization, and ideas for raising money for your nonprofit organization. To get this Cheat Sheet, simply go to www.dummies. com and type **Nonprofit Kit For Dummies Cheat Sheet** in the Search box.

You can also go to www.wiley.com/go/nonprofitkitfd6e for samples, forms, and lists of helpful websites. We mention many of these files within the chapters; we also include a file of web resources for most chapters. All digital files are labeled with the chapter number and the order in which the element appears in the chapter. For instance, the first digital file in Chapter 2 is labeled File 2-1. For a complete list of digital files, turn to Appendix B, at the back of this book.

Where to Go from Here

One of many handy features about this book is that it's modular, which means you can start reading anywhere you like! If you're new to the nonprofit world, we suggest beginning with Chapter 1, where you find fundamental information to get you moving in the right direction. If you're familiar with nonprofits already but want to better understand your responsibilities as a board member, you can find the answers you need in Chapter 7. If you're a new board member and want to understand the organization's finances when spreadsheets are passed out at board meetings, we provide guidance about making a budget *and* understanding financial statements in Chapter 12. If you need help to publicize and market your programs, we offer some suggestions in Chapter 13.

If you're like many nonprofit workers or volunteers, you want to know how to find and obtain money for your organization. Part 3 covers this topic, so those chapters are good places to begin.

Whether you're new to the nonprofit world or a seasoned professional, we think you'll find helpful and valuable information in this book to get you started or continue your good work.

1

Getting Familiar with the Nonprofit Framework

Peek inside the structure of a nonprofit organization and how nonprofits compare to for-profits.

Get an inside glimpse at what it takes to start a nonprofit organization.

Learn why building your board of directors is the first priority.

See what goes into a mission statement and vision statement and follow some pointers on how to write these two upfront organization-driving documents.

Discover what you need to do to incorporate your new nonprofit. After that task is completed, apply for tax-exempt status from the IRS.

Make sure you maintain your nonprofit status by filing the required IRS reports.

» **Getting started with a nonprofit**

» **Encouraging volunteerism**

» **Acquiring the resources your nonprofit needs**

Chapter **1**

Journeying into the World of Nonprofit Organizations

I t's a typical day in your hometown. Your alarm wakes you from a restful sleep and you switch on your radio to hear the latest news from your local public radio station. You hear that a research institute's study reports that economic indicators are on the rise and that a health clinic across town is testing a new regimen for arthritis. Plato, your golden retriever/Labrador mix, adopted from the animal shelter when he was 5 months old, bounds onto your bed to let you know it's time for breakfast and a walk. Plato is followed by Cynthia, your 4-year-old daughter, who wants to help you walk Plato before she's dropped off at her preschool housed in the community center. You remember that you promised to bring canned goods to the food bank that's next-door to Cynthia's school. You haven't even had coffee yet, but already your morning is filled with news and services provided by nonprofit organizations.

You know that your public radio station is a nonprofit because you hear its pledge drives three or four times a year and you volunteer a few hours each month for the food bank, so clearly it's a nonprofit. But you may not know that the research institute is probably a nonprofit organization, just like the health clinic where the arthritis research is being tested and the animal shelter where you found Plato. Cynthia's preschool and the community center where the preschool rents its space are likely nonprofit organizations. Whether you realize it or not, all of us — rich, poor, or somewhere in between — benefit from the work of nonprofit organizations every day.

Nonprofits find revenue from a variety of sources in order to provide services. Because most nonprofits serve a need in the community, tax-deductible donations are an important revenue source. Sometimes nonprofits charge a fee for the service they provide or the work they do. Other nonprofits may sign contracts with your city or county to provide services to residents. Usually, nonprofit organizations scrounge up their income from a combination of all these revenue sources.

The nonprofit sector isn't a distinct place — it isn't some plaza or district that you come upon suddenly as you weave your way through the day. It's more like a thread of a common color that's laced throughout the economy and people's lives. No matter where people live or what they do, it's not easy to reach the end of a day without being affected by the work of a nonprofit organization.

Perhaps your lifelong goal is to find a way to help others in your community, your state, your country, or the world. (If this statement is true of you, thank you, kind citizen.) You think about your options every day, but you haven't the foggiest notion about the next steps to take to help you reach this admirable goal. You have so many topics to research and tasks to determine how to complete — and so much necessary funding to nail down to help you get started. Think of this chapter as the beginning of the journey. Here we help you understand exactly what a nonprofit organization is and how to start and manage one.

Check out File 1-1 at www.wiley.com/go/nonprofitkitfd6e for a list of web resources related to the topics we cover in this chapter.

What Is a Nonprofit Organization?

People hear the term *nonprofit* and picture a different type of business where the owner isn't allowed, by tax law, to make a profit or draw a paycheck. But, in fact, some nonprofit organizations end their fiscal year with a profit, and that's good because surplus cash (also referred to as *reserves*) keeps a nonprofit operating in the black versus the red.

Comparing for-profits to nonprofits

REMEMBER

The main difference between a for-profit corporation and a nonprofit corporation is what happens to the profit. In a for-profit company like Amazon, Google, United Parcel Service, or your favorite fast-food chain, profits are distributed to the owners (or shareholders). But a nonprofit can't do that. Any profit remaining after the bills are paid has to be plowed back into the organization's service programs, spent to strengthen the nonprofit's infrastructure, or stored in reserve for a rainy day. Profit can't be distributed to individuals, such as the organization's board of directors.

What about shareholders — do nonprofits have any shareholders to pay off? Not in terms of a monetary payoff, like a stock dividend. Rather than shareholders, nonprofit organizations have *stakeholders* — they're the people who benefit from the nonprofit's mission and services to their target population (those in need, from animals to humans). These people are often called *stakeholders* because they're committed to the success of the nonprofit, such as board members, volunteers, community partners, and the people whom the nonprofit serves directly and indirectly.

Introducing the coveted 501(c)(3) status for nonprofits

When we use the term *nonprofit organization* in this book, for the most part we're talking about an organization that has been *incorporated* (or organized formally) under the laws of its state and that the Internal Revenue Service (IRS) has classified as a 501(c)(3) and determined to be a public charity. If the term *501(c)(3)* is new to you, add it to your vocabulary with pride. In no time, "five-oh-one-see-three" will roll off your tongue as if you're a nonprofit expert.

TECHNICAL STUFF

Private foundations also have the 501(c)(3) classification, but they aren't *public charities.* They operate under different regulations, and we don't cover them in this book.

Other kinds of nonprofit organizations *do* exist; they're formed to benefit their members, to influence legislation, or to fulfill other purposes. They receive exemption from federal income taxes and sometimes relief from property taxes at the local level. (Chapter 2 discusses these organizations in greater detail.)

Nonprofit organizations classified as 501(c)(3) receive extra privileges under the law. They are, with minor exceptions, the only group of tax-exempt organizations that can receive contributions that are tax-deductible for their donors.

The Internal Revenue Code describes the allowable purposes of 501(c)(3) nonprofit organizations, which include serving religious, educational, charitable, scientific, and literary ends.

TIP

Check out File 1-2 at www.wiley.com/go/nonprofitkitfd6e for a more-detailed list of the activities that 501(c)(3) nonprofits take on.

REMEMBER

Being a nonprofit organization doesn't mean that an entity is exempt from paying all taxes. Nonprofit organizations pay employment taxes, employee salaries, and wages just like for-profit businesses do. In some states, but not all, nonprofits are exempt from paying sales tax and property tax, so be sure that you're familiar with your jurisdiction's laws and nonprofit reporting requirements. Also, check with the appropriate office in your state to see whether you're required to apply for a state tax exemption or a license to solicit funds.

A SECTOR BY ANY OTHER NAME

Not everyone thinks that *nonprofit sector* is the best name. That's because of the array of organizations with different types of nonprofit status. Some of these organizations are formed to benefit their members — such as fraternities and labor unions — and don't share a broad public-serving intent. Another reason *nonprofit sector* may not be the best choice of terms is its negative connotation. After all, what's worse than not making a profit? But, as we point out earlier, and we remind you again in later chapters, not making a profit isn't the determining factor. Here are some alternative terms you may hear:

- **Voluntary sector:** This term emphasizes the presence of volunteer board members and the significance of voluntary contributions and services to the work of 501(c)(3) organizations. In this definition, the organizations alone don't represent the meaning of *nonprofit;* the definition includes the vast web of supporters who participate as volunteers and donors.

- **Independent sector:** This term emphasizes the public-serving mission of these organizations and their volunteers and their independence from government. (Independent Sector is also the name of a nonprofit organization that provides research, advocacy, and public programs for and about the nonprofit sector.)

- **Charitable sector:** This term emphasizes the charitable donations these organizations receive from individuals and institutions.

- **Third sector:** This term emphasizes the sector's important role alongside government and the for-profit business economy.

We use the term *nonprofit sector* throughout this book, but we want you to understand its limitations and be familiar with other commonly used terms.

Knowing Your Mission Before Entering the Nonprofit World

People form nonprofit organizations in order to work toward changing some condition in the world, either for a specific group of people or for society in general. The overall goal or purpose of a nonprofit is known as its *mission*. Taking the time needed to clearly outline a nonprofit's mission is time well spent because the mission guides the activities of the organization, helps the nonprofit's directors decide how to allocate resources wisely, and serves as a measure for evaluating the accomplishments of the group. We think developing a mission statement is so important that we devote an entire chapter (see Chapter 4) to guiding you through this process.

You must also examine your personal mission before launching a nonprofit. You're creating a legal entity that has responsibilities for reporting to both the state and federal governments. If the organization grows to the point where you must hire employees, you're responsible for paying regular salaries and providing adequate benefits. And although you can be compensated for your work as a nonprofit staff member, you can't develop equity in the organization or take away any profits at the end of the year. Chapter 2 has more information to help you make this important decision.

Setting up a nonprofit

Nearly all nonprofit organizations are established as corporations under the laws of a particular state. If you're located in Iowa and you plan to do most of your work in that state, you follow the laws in Iowa to set up the basic legal structure of a nonprofit corporation. Although you'll find some differences from state to state, in general, the process requires writing and submitting articles of incorporation to the state and developing *bylaws*, the rules under which the corporation will operate.

After your nonprofit is established under your state laws, the next step is applying for 501(c)(3) status from the IRS. This step requires completing and submitting IRS Form 1023 or Form 1023-EZ. If you submit Form 1023, you will need to specify in some detail the proposed activities of the new organization, and you're asked for projected revenue and expenses for the year in which you apply and two years into the future. To be honest, you can't complete this form in one afternoon. It requires substantial time and thought to develop the necessary material and should be reviewed by an accountant and legal representative before filing. We discuss the incorporation and IRS application process in Chapter 5.

Making plans and being flexible

After you start managing a nonprofit organization, you'll discover that planning is your best friend. Every task from budgeting to grant-writing requires that you make plans for the future. This continuous planning process for nonprofit leaders (founders and board members) is called *strategic planning.* And you need to do a substantial amount of strategic planning before you're ready to send in your IRS application for tax exemption.

Don't be frightened by this recommendation to plan strategically early on in the nonprofit formation process. The act of strategic planning fundamentally comes down to thinking through what you're going to do as well as how and when you're going to do it and writing it down. Your strategic plan becomes the map that guides you toward achieving your nonprofit's mission, vision, and goals. Strategic planning is something you should pay attention to every day.

REMEMBER

You should always begin with a strategic plan, but that doesn't mean that the original plans shouldn't be altered when the situation calls for it. Circumstances change; flexibility and adaptability are good traits to nurture if you're running a nonprofit organization. Chapters 8 and 12 cover strategic planning and budgeting. Chapter 9 addresses how to evaluate your work and know whether your plans are achieving the results you want to see. Chapters 13 and 14 discuss planning for marketing and fundraising.

BIGGER THAN A BREAD BOX

The nonprofit sector is larger than many people realize. Here are some figures from the National Center for Charitable Statistics, based on IRS data, and the Independent Sector, regarding 501(c)(3) public charities in the United States:

- Nearly 1.6 million organizations were registered as public charities with the IRS in 2020.

- Assets held by these groups in 2020 totaled more than $3.79 trillion.

- Nearly 30 percent of public charities that reported to the IRS in 2019 had annual expenses of less than $100,000.

Embracing and Sharing Your Inspiration

The nonprofit sector is exciting. It encourages individuals with ideas about solving social problems or enhancing arts, culture, the environment, or education to act on those ideas. It creates a viable place within our society and economy for worthy activities that have little chance of commercial success. Nonprofit organizations combine the best of the business world with the best of government social-service programs, bringing together the creativity, zeal, and problem-solving from the business side with the call to public service from the government side.

Speaking from experience, volunteerism is inspiring. Everyone has heard stories of tightly knit communities where neighbors gather to rebuild a home that was lost to a fire or a hurricane. That spirit of pitching in to help is the best part of living in a community in which people share values and ideas.

Communities have become more diverse and are populated with neighbors who come from a wide variety of places and cultures. The nonprofit sector provides institutions and opportunities where everyone can come together to work toward the common good. Volunteerism gives everyone the chance to pitch in to rebuild "the house and make it a home again."

Applying the term *voluntary sector* to nonprofit organizations came about for a good reason. The US Census Bureau reported that 77.3 million people volunteered at least once in 2020.

When you're working in a nonprofit, you'll likely be supervising volunteers — and they'll likely supervise you. What we mean is that (with few exceptions) nonprofit boards of directors serve as unpaid volunteers. And if you're the executive director, your supervisors are the trustees or board members of the organization. At the same time, you likely depend on volunteers to carry out some or all of the activities of the organization. You may serve as a volunteer yourself.

REMEMBER

The word *supervision* sounds harsh, and we don't mean to suggest that nonprofits are or should be run with an iron hand. The board of directors does have ultimate responsibility, however, for the finances and actions of a nonprofit organization, and, therefore, people serving in that capacity have a real duty to make sure that the organization has sufficient resources to carry out its activities and that it's doing what it's supposed to be doing.

We prefer to think of nonprofits as organized group activities. You need to depend on others to reach your goals, and they need to depend on you. We talk about boards of directors in Chapter 7 and working with volunteers in Chapter 10. If your nonprofit employs paid staff or hopes to someday, Chapter 11 provides some guidance in hiring and managing employees.

CURIOSITY REWARDED THIS CAT

Here's a story about a nonprofit dreamer, perhaps much like yourself, who (spoiler alert!) started her own nonprofit and made it sustainable with hard work, self-investment, and resourcefulness.

I (Bev) had worked in the corporate sector of small- to midsize businesses for decades. My supervisors and their demeanor set the tone for each workday. There were good days and not-so-good days in my multiple workplaces. One day, I was approached by a nonprofit executive director who invited me to attend a board meeting. Somewhat perplexed at the invitation to attend a meeting for an organization that I was unfamiliar with seemed an overstretch given my business employment experiences. Yet, out of a wee bit of curiosity, I decided to attend.

I was greeted by the board of directors and the executive director (the source of my invitation to attend the meeting). Everyone seemed genuinely interested in getting to know me. I was asked if I had ever done any volunteer work or served on a board. I shared my longtime volunteer experiences with other agencies and my time as a foster parent. There were lots of smiles around the boardroom table. A board member asked me if I would stay for the entire meeting and listen to their updates on policies, programs, and processes for the Voluntary Action Center of Genesee and Shiawassee counties. At the end of the board meeting, I was invited to join the board of this well-established nonprofit organization. Guess what? I did! Thus began my learning process about nonprofit organizations, how they operate, their mission and vision statements, and clarification on ownership. It was that first experience, which lasted for two years, that made me start to dream about starting my own nonprofit organization. Yes, you read this right! I went on to form two successful nonprofit organizations.

Finding the Resources to Do the Job

One distinctive feature of the nonprofit sector is its dependency on contributions. We devote many pages of this book — most of Part 3 — to advice about getting contributions from fundraising.

Gifts from individuals of money, goods, services, time, and property make up the largest portion of that voluntary support. This portion, which is also the oldest of the voluntary traditions in the United States, dates back to colonial times. Since the late 19th century, private philanthropic foundations have emerged as another source of support, and more recently — particularly after World War II — the federal government and corporations have become important income sources. Earned income from fees for service, ticket sales, and tuition charges also is an important revenue source for many nonprofits; in fact, in 2013 nearly three-quarters of the revenues for public charities was earned.

Who is giving to nonprofit organizations?

Among private, nongovernmental sources of support, gifts from living individuals — as opposed to bequests from people who have died — have always represented a large portion of total giving, but philanthropic giving by foundations and corporations has been growing. According to the Giving USA Foundation, in 2019 corporations represented the largest portion of total giving and the COVID-19 pandemic is furthering this trend. This resulted in corporations giving the largest share of nonprofit sponsorships and grants. For new nonprofit organizations, the best fundraising strategy is to take a balanced approach that includes multiple forms of contributions.

Supporting your mission with fundraising

Nearly every nonprofit organization depends on generous donors for the cash it needs to pay its bills and provide its services. Even if you have income from ticket sales, admission charges, or contracted services, you'll find that raising additional money is necessary to keep your organization alive and thriving.

Corporate contributions are the largest source of contributed income to nonprofit organizations. But you can't just sit and wait by the mailbox for the donations to begin arriving. How will contributors even know that your new nonprofit is up and running, providing services? Two basic rules of fundraising are that potential funders need to be asked for donations and thanked after giving one. Chapter 15 focuses on raising money from individuals, Chapter 16 covers raising money with special events, and Chapter 19 discusses campaign fundraising, which is used when you need to raise extra money for your building or your endowment.

Grants from foundations and corporations make up a smaller percentage of giving to nonprofits, but their support can be invaluable for start-up project costs, equipment, technical support, and sometimes general operating costs. Some organizations get most of their income from foundation grants; others get very little. Chapter 17 introduces you to resources to help you find potential grant sources. Chapter 18 walks you through the process of crafting a grant proposal.

Fundraising works better if people know you exist. That knowledge also helps draw people to your theater or to sign up for your programs. Here's where marketing and public relations enter the picture. Chapter 13 helps you figure out what your message should be and how to circulate it to the world.

REMEMBER

Make no mistake about it: Fundraising is hard work. But if you approach the task with a positive attitude and make your case well, you can find the resources you need.

» Starting your nonprofit the right way

» Embracing the understanding of nonprofit ownership

» Surveying the different types of nonprofit organizations

» Knowing the difference between nonprofit and for-profit corporations

» Enlisting a fiscal sponsor to help you provide a service or complete a project

Chapter **2**

Understanding What It Takes to Start a Nonprofit

Maybe you've been thinking for years about starting a nonprofit organization, or maybe an idea to solve a social problem or provide a needed service has just popped into your head. It might be time to make your idea a reality. But before you file the incorporation papers, you need to consider the positive and not-so-positive factors that can make or break your new organization. As with opening any business, starting and managing a nonprofit organization isn't a simple matter.

Take a look at the economy around you. Are existing nonprofit organizations in your community thriving, or are they struggling to find financial and volunteer support? In addition, are you equipped to manage money and raise funds — which isn't an easy task even when business is booming — and can you inspire others to work with you whether they're board members, staff, or volunteers?

In this chapter, we pose some questions that you should think about (and answer) before you begin the process of incorporating and applying for tax exemption. If some of your answers point to the conclusion that your idea is worth pursuing but you want to test the idea first, we suggest that you consider using a fiscal sponsor. As we point out later in this chapter, the benefits of fiscal sponsorship are many.

REMEMBER

A *nonprofit,* in this book, refers to a type of corporation that has been recognized by the Internal Revenue Service (IRS) as exempt under section 501(c)(3) of the IRS Tax Code and is described as a public charity. Later in this chapter, you can read about other kinds of nonprofits, to nail down the distinct attributes of these 501(c)(3) tax-exempt public charities.

TIP

Check out File 2-1 at www.wiley.com/go/nonprofitkitfd6e for a list of web resources related to the topics we cover in this chapter.

Weighing the Pros and Cons of Starting a Nonprofit

Before you jump headfirst into making your nonprofit dream a reality, you need to absorb some basic facts about nonprofit organizations. Let's begin with some pros: You will

>> Receive exemption from taxes on most income to the nonprofit

>> Be able to receive, for most nonprofits formed under Section 501(c)(3) of the IRS Tax Code, contributions that are deductible for the donor

>> Have the opportunity to receive grants from foundations, corporations, and government agencies

>> Get to feel that you're contributing to the solution of a problem or to the improvement of society. As the founder, your vision is unfolding for the greater good.

Just about everyone would consider these facts to be positive, but they don't tell the whole story. If you're thinking of starting a nonprofit to get rich or to avoid paying taxes, consider this list of cons:

>> **Paying employment taxes:** Nonprofit employees' salaries are subject to income tax, like all other types of compensation. Tax-exempt doesn't include payroll tax — it must be withheld, matched by the nonprofit, and deposited with the IRS on time every month (usually on the 15th day unless the 15th falls on a weekend or federal holiday).

>> **Sharing the decision-making process with a board of directors:** Even though you have the vision to form a nonprofit organization, the IRS requires it to have a board of directors. The board makes the decisions and is responsible for financial, management, legal, and operational oversight. Any decisions made by the founder or executive director must be approved by the board. (See Chapter 3 for more about the board's role.)

>> **Filing an annual report with the IRS:** The complexity of the report increases as your nonprofit income increases. (See Chapter 6 for more information about reporting requirements.)

>> **Competing with others for funding:** Competition for grants from foundations, corporations, and government agencies is tough, and so is garnering donations from individuals. You'll compete with more-established nonprofits that have successful track records.

>> **Being unable to take any assets with you if you leave:** If you decide to move on to other pursuits down the road, for example, you can't take with you any assets accumulated by the organization you've built. Others will continue running the nonprofit, or else it will need to be dissolved and the assets given to another nonprofit. (See Chapter 20 for more about the process for closing a nonprofit.)

REMEMBER

A nonprofit organization is given special privileges because it's formed to benefit the public, not specific individuals. Think carefully about your motivation for launching one.

Doing Your Homework First

Beyond thinking about the challenges you face in starting and running a nonprofit organization, you need to apply some common sense. Nonprofits don't operate in a vacuum, and neither should you. Personal commitment and inspiration can take your organization far, but you also need to find out how your community will receive your particular idea. Before going full steam ahead, investigate your competition, garner community support, recruit the right board members, choose how to fund your organization, determine whether you're truly ready to run a nonprofit, and develop a game plan. Read on to find out how to get your nonprofit off to a great start.

Analyzing the competition

Just as though you were starting a for-profit business, you should analyze your competition before starting a nonprofit organization. If you want to open a grocery store, you don't choose a location next to a successful supermarket, because the market can bear only so much trade. This principle holds true for nonprofits, too. You may have the best idea in the world, but if someone else in your community is already doing it well, don't try to duplicate it.

On the other hand, if your area has no similar program, ask yourself why. Maybe your community lacks a sufficient number of potential clients or audience members to support the project. Or maybe funders don't perceive the same needs in the community as you do.

TIP

Assessing the needs of your area is a good way to evaluate the potential market for your nonprofit's services. You may want to use some or all of the following methods to determine your community's needs:

» **Online surveys or written questionnaires** to a random sample of residents in your community

» **Interviews** with local foundation program staff and civic officials

» **Focus groups** with people who are likely to benefit from the organization

» **Recent community needs assessments** (from researching and reading) to look for gaps in services

For more details on assessing your community's needs, see Chapter 8.

Identifying the right people to help you

Your chances of success increase if you begin with support from others, and the more help you have, the better. Sure, you can probably find an example of a single-minded visionary who battles alone through all sorts of adversity to establish a thriving nonprofit, but starting and running a nonprofit organization is essentially a group stakeholder activity.

When starting a nonprofit, find people, known as *stakeholders,* who will serve on the board of directors and support your efforts with donations of money and volunteer time. The first people you usually identify as supporters are family and friends. How can they turn you down? In the long run, however, you need to expand your group of supporters to others who believe in the organization's mission (and not because you personally created it) and can give substantial financial contributions to a new nonprofit.

TIP

Identify and select the *right* people to join you in your mission. Some people hesitate to share their idea with others, because they believe that someone may steal it. We think this fear is largely unfounded. No matter what your idea is, you're better off inviting others to join you in making it a reality.

To find people to help you and support your organization, take every opportunity to speak about your idea before civic groups, religious groups, and service clubs. You can pass out fliers or set up a booth at a volunteer fair. Set up Facebook and LinkedIn profile pages and invite your contacts to spread the word. Talk to your friends and coworkers. Put on your salesperson's cap and convince the community that it needs your program and that you need their volunteer and financial support.

WARNING

If you're having a difficult time drumming up support, it may be a sign that you need to refine your idea or that others view it as impractical. You may need to go back to the drawing board. Ask yourself, "Is this something that I would pull out my wallet for and donate to support its mission?"

Figuring out how you'll survive financially

Funding your nonprofit organization is a big issue. Even if you begin as a volunteer-run organization and work from a home office, you still need funds for securing a website, assigning a dedicated telephone number, and purchasing technology, Internet access, supplies, postage, and insurance. You also have to pay filing fees for your state incorporation and IRS tax-exemption application. Many nonprofit start-ups are funded by the founder in the beginning. Are you able to pay all start-up expenses before revenues start flowing to your new nonprofit?

MY STORY: A CALCULATED RISK

What are you willing to do to create a financially sound nonprofit organization? I (Bev) am a baby boomer (born between 1946 and 1964 — I'll leave it at that), and I started my own nonprofit organization knowing that surviving the start-up process and securing early-on funding would not be easy. So, I decided to live off my monthly social security income for two years and not burden the new nonprofit with a salary expense. I'm happy to report that the nonprofit is still in operation and financially stable and that it has created a reserve bank account for rainy days ahead. You may not need to go without a paycheck for months or years, like I did, in order to get your nonprofit off the ground, but it's important to consider salaries when you're planning your first-year operating budget with the board of directors.

Putting together a budget can help you determine whether the start-up expenses are manageable for you. You'll create lots of budgets sooner or later, so you may as well get an early start. Flip to Chapter 12 for details on budgeting and other financial issues.

If you can't fund the operation by yourself in the early months, you need to make a compelling case that your new organization will provide an important service to the community and then convince donors that you have the knowledge and experience to provide it. You can solicit contributions from individuals before the IRS grants the organization tax-exempt status, as long as you reveal that your exemption is pending (and will be deductible to the donor if the exemption is granted) and you have met state charitable solicitation registration requirements. These contributions become deductible to the donor if you file for your tax exemption within 27 months of the date you incorporated and receive tax-exempt status.

If your exemption is denied, the contributions aren't deductible, and you may be liable for income tax on the money you've received. Start-up grants from foundations or corporations are rare and next-to-impossible to obtain before the IRS recognizes your organization's tax-exempt status, so don't plan to receive any grants from outside organizations.

TIP

New organizations can avoid the awkward period between starting up and receiving tax-exempt status, by beginning as a sponsored program of an existing nonprofit organization. We discuss this arrangement, known as *fiscal sponsorship*, in detail later in this chapter.

You also can try out your program on a small scale before filing for tax-exempt status by partnering with an existing nonprofit organization to test the success and need of your idea. For example, if you want to start a summer arts program for low-income children, talk to a local church or community center that serves that population and ask whether you can teach an art class one day a week for a month. Then you can try out your idea, demonstrate the need, and set up benchmarks for success.

Acknowledging the reality of what's ahead

Ask yourself whether you're the right person to start a nonprofit organization — and try to answer honestly. Undertaking this endeavor requires both a heart (for helping) and a head (for helping efficiently and effectively). If your organization offers a service, especially in the health and social-service fields, do you have the educational background, qualifications, or license necessary to provide those services? In addition to being professionally qualified, you need to consider whether you feel confident about your management, fundraising, and communication skills.

When starting and working in a new nonprofit organization, you need to be able to stretch yourself across many different skill areas. You may be dressed to the nines one day to pitch your project to the mayor or to a corporate executive, and the next day you may be sweeping the floor of your office or unplugging a clogged toilet. In other words, you need to be versatile and willing to take on just about any task that needs to be done. Nonprofit founders work from the boiler room to the boardroom. Visionaries do whatever it takes to start and manage a nonprofit organization.

REMEMBER

When potential donors are evaluating grant proposals, they certainly look to see whether the organization's leadership has the background, experience, and knowledge necessary to carry out the proposed program. This doesn't necessarily mean that you need to be an experienced nonprofit manager, but try to assess your background to see how you can apply your experience to the nonprofit you hope to start.

Planning, plotting, and projecting

If there was ever a time to plan, this is it. Planning is what turns your initial idea into a doable project. Planning is also a good way to find potential holes in your thinking. For example, you may believe that your community lacks adequate animal rescue services. You may be right, but when you begin to break down the idea of starting an animal shelter, you may find that the project costs more money or requires more staff or facilities than you first imagined. When armed with that knowledge, you can adjust your plan as necessary or scrap the idea altogether.

To begin planning, write a 1- or 2-page synopsis of your nonprofit idea. In your synopsis, include

>> Why your organization should exist

>> What you're trying to do

>> How you plan to do it

Outline both short-term and long-term goals and the resources needed to meet those goals. The list of resources should include money, volunteers, and an appropriate space to carry out your activities. After you've prepared your synopsis and list of resources, talk to as many people as you can about your idea, asking for help and honest feedback about your project. The purpose of this strategic planning process is to think through your nonprofit idea step-by-step. (If you need help in the planning process, take a look at Chapter 8.) The planning process involves thinking strategically, plotting ideas on paper, and projecting the needed ingredients for operational success and sustainability.

Understanding Nonprofit Ownership

We (Stan and Frances) once received a telephone call from a man who was shopping for a nonprofit to purchase. "Do you know if there are any nonprofits for sale in New Hampshire?" he asked. Although this question doesn't come to us often, it illustrates a misconception about the status of nonprofit organizations. No single person or group of people can *own* a nonprofit organization. You don't see nonprofit shares traded on stock exchanges, and any "equity" in a nonprofit organization belongs to the organization itself, not to the board of directors or the staff. IRS regulations allow the assets of nonprofits to be sold, but the proceeds of the sale must benefit the organization, not private parties.

If you start a nonprofit and decide at some point that you no longer want to manage it, you have to walk away and leave the running of the organization to someone else. Or, if the time has come to close the doors for good, any assets the organization owns must be distributed to other nonprofits fulfilling a similar mission. You need to follow the laws of the IRS and your state to close the nonprofit organization, including selection of an appropriate and, in some cases, approved nonprofit that will receive the assets.

REMEMBER

When nonprofit managers and consultants talk about *ownership* of a nonprofit organization, they're using the word metaphorically to make the point that board members, staff, clients, and the community (your stakeholders) all have a stake in the organization's future success and its ability to provide needed programs.

Benefiting the public for the greater good

People form nonprofit organizations to create a public benefit for the greater good of all. In fact, nonprofit corporations are sometimes referred to as *public benefit corporations.* A nonprofit organization can't be created to help a particular individual or family, for example. If that were possible, we'd all have our separate nonprofit organizations. You can start a nonprofit to aid a specific group or class of individuals — everyone suffering from diabetes, for example, or chronically homeless individuals — but you can't create a nonprofit for individual benefit or gain.

REMEMBER

Just because you're working for the public's benefit doesn't mean you can't receive a reasonable salary for your work when your revenues are stable and the drawing of your salary won't result in a budget deficit. And despite the name *nonprofit,* such an organization can have surplus funds — essentially, a profit — at the end of the year. In a for-profit business, the surplus money can be distributed to employees, shareholders, and the board of directors; however, in a nonprofit organization, the surplus funds are used to strengthen the organization or are held in reserve by the organization to respond to emergency needs or invest in future programming.

Being accountable and transparent

Although nonprofit organizations aren't public entities like government agencies and departments, their tax-exempt status — and the fact that contributions are tax-deductible — require them to be more accountable and transparent to the public than a privately owned business is.

It takes only a few media reports about excessive salaries or concerns about how a nonprofit has spent donated funds to prompt donors, legislators, or the general public to begin asking questions regarding the nonprofit's finances and management. An IRS tax-exempt, 501(c)(3) nonprofit organization is required to be transparent and open in all of its operations and transactions.

A few nonprofit organizations have taken on the task of collecting information about other nonprofits and sometimes rating them in various categories so that prospective donors can use this information to help them choose which organizations to support. Charity Navigator (www.charitynavigator.org), CharityWatch (www.charitywatch.org), GuideStar by Candid (www.guidestar.org), and the Better Business Bureau Wise Giving Alliance (www.give.org) are four prominent organizations providing information about domestic (US-based) nonprofit organizations. If you're just starting out and your nonprofit is small, your organization us unlikely to be evaluated by one of these organizations; however, a new nonprofit should definitely create a profile on GuideStar by Candid. For small, early-on funding requests, foundation and corporate grant makers will look for your profile on this website. Be sure to update it annually.

REMEMBER

The degree of operational transparency, financial stability, and program results in your organization can be put under scrutiny by anyone or any entity. The more transparent your nonprofit, the more likely it is to receive initial and ongoing funding support.

We discuss nonprofit disclosure requirements in more detail in Chapter 6, but at minimum, federal law requires that nonprofits file a report (Form 990, 990-N, or 990-EZ) every year with the IRS. The amount of detail required in the report depends on the size of the nonprofit organization. States have their own reporting requirements, so contact your appropriate state office to learn what's required.

TECHNICAL STUFF

Most nonprofits with annual gross receipts equal to or less than $50,000 can file the 990-N; nonprofits with gross receipts less than $200,000 and assets less than $500,000 can file the 990-EZ. Nonprofits with gross receipts equal to or greater than $200,000 or assets equal to or greater than $500,000 must file the long form 990.

A WORD ABOUT EXCESSIVE COMPENSATION

Although nonprofit employees have no dollar limit on the amount of compensation they can earn, the IRS does have the authority to penalize individuals (and organizations) who receive (or pay) excessive compensation. Whether the IRS considers benefits excessive depends on the situation. For instance, a staff member earning $100,000 annually from an organization with a budget of $125,000 may need to worry, but someone earning $100,000 from a nonprofit with a $5 million budget probably doesn't.

An employee who's found to be receiving excessive compensation may be required to return a portion of his compensation and to pay an excise tax, and, in dire cases, the nonprofit organization may lose its tax-exempt status. Chapter 6 offers more information on excessive compensation.

So, when setting your nonprofit's executive director's salary (or your own), make sure the amount of compensation is justified by salary surveys of similar organizations. Also factor in the local cost of living, the size of the nonprofit's budget, and the type of services being provided. Community foundations and nonprofit consulting firms can offer salary guidelines to aid in the compensation decision. Also, many states have a statewide nonprofit organization that collects information about, and provides information to, other nonprofits.

Federal law also requires nonprofits to make their three most recent 990 reports, as well as their application for tax exemption and supporting documents, available for public inspection. State and local laws in your area may require additional disclosures. Posting your 990 reports and other required documents on the web is an acceptable way to meet disclosure requirements.

TIP

To become familiar with the 990 report, download a copy of it from the IRS website at www.irs.gov. You also can view completed 990 forms from other nonprofit organizations at GuideStar by Candid (www.guidestar.org).

Looking at the Many Varieties of Nonprofits

The words *nonprofit* and *charity* go together in most people's minds, but remember that not all nonprofits are charitable organizations. The most common examples are business and trade associations, social welfare organizations, labor organizations, political advocacy groups, fraternal societies, and social clubs. Although these non-profits enjoy exemption from corporate income taxes, people who donate to them can't claim a tax deduction for their contributions.

Most nonprofits, charitable or not, are incorporated organizations that are formed under the laws of the state in which they're created. Some nonprofits have other legal structures, such as associations or trusts, but these are in the minority. The IRS grants tax-exempt status to a nonprofit after reviewing its stated purpose. (See Chapter 5 for information about incorporating and applying for a tax exemption.) Nonprofit types are identified by the section of the IRS Code under which they qualify for tax-exempt status.

In this section, we provide an overview of the types of nonprofit organizations and some of the rules and regulations that you'll be subject to if you decide to incorporate and seek tax-exempt status from the IRS. You may discover, for example, that your idea will have a better chance for success if you create a social welfare organization — a 501(c)(4) — or a for-profit business.

Identifying nonprofits by their numbers

Nonprofit organizations can be formed under the IRS code for many reasons other than charitable ones. To give you a taste of the variety of these organizations, the following list summarizes various classes of nonprofit organizations:

>> **501(c)(3):** Formed for educational, scientific, literary, charitable, or religious pursuits and also to test for public safety and to prevent cruelty to children and animals, nonprofits in this category may be classified as public charities or private foundations — the source of support for the organization usually determines the classification. Foundations are subject to additional rules and reporting requirements. This book focuses on 501(c)(3) organizations that are classified as public charities. Contributions to these organizations are tax-deductible for their donors. Public charities may engage in limited lobbying. You can find more information about lobbying in the following section.

>> **501(c)(4):** These organizations are known as *social welfare organizations* because they're formed for the improvement of general welfare and the common good of the people. Advocacy groups tend to fall into this category because organizations with this classification are allowed more leeway to lobby legislators as a part of their mission to improve the general welfare. Contributions to these organizations aren't deductible for the donor.

>> **501(c)(5):** Labor unions and agriculture and horticulture organizations formed to improve conditions for workers are in this category. These groups also may lobby for legislation.

>> **501(c)(6):** Business and trade associations that provide services to their members and work toward the betterment of business conditions are placed in this classification. This category includes chambers of commerce and real estate boards, for example. Again, lobbying for legislation is allowed.

>> **501(c)(7):** This section covers social clubs formed for recreation and pleasure. Country clubs and organizations formed around a hobby come under this classification. These organizations must be funded primarily by memberships and dues.

>> **501(c)(9):** This type of nonprofit is an employees' beneficiary association that's created to pay insurance benefits to members and their dependents. It must be voluntary, members must have a common bond via employment or a labor union, and in most cases it must meet nondiscrimination requirements.

Several other 501(c)-type organizations are so specialized in nature that we don't go into them here. One of our favorites is the 501(c)(13), which covers cemetery companies.

Political action committees (PACs) and parties have their own special classification, too. They're recognized under IRS Code section 527 and are organized for the purpose of electing persons to office. They have special reporting requirements and aren't required to be incorporated. Donations to these organizations aren't tax-deductible, and the names of their donors must be disclosed.

TIP

To see the full flavor of the various categories of nonprofit organizations, check out the IRS website (www.irs.gov) or review IRS Publication 557.

Adding rules and regulations to add to your file

Entire volumes have been written about IRS regulations and laws pertaining to nonprofits. But don't worry — we just want to give you an overview of some facts that may help you decide whether starting a 501(c)(3) nonprofit organization is your best choice.

WARNING

IRS regulations can change from year to year, so be sure to look at the most recent version of IRS Publication 557 for the latest information.

Nonprofits and political activities

Nonprofits can't campaign to support or oppose the candidacy of anyone running for an elected office. However, the stipulations on lobbying for specific legislation are less clear. In the following list, we break down the rules so that you know what you can and can't do, depending on which type of nonprofit you set up:

>> **Social welfare organizations and labor unions, 501(c)(4):** These organizations have more leeway when it comes to legislative lobbying than 501(c)(3) organizations do. They can engage in political intervention activity as long as it isn't their primary activity. Groups that lobby must inform their members what percentage of dues they use for lobbying activities, and they can't work toward a candidate's election.

>> **Charitable organizations, or nonprofits that the IRS considers public charities under section 501(c)(3):** These nonprofits may participate in some legislative lobbying if it isn't a "substantial" part of their activities. The IRS doesn't define the term *substantial,* so it determines this question on a case-by-case basis. These nonprofits can generally spend a higher portion of their budgets on lobbying activities if the organization chooses to elect the *501(h) designation* (IRS Form 5768). The IRS allows more expenditures for *direct lobbying* (when members of the nonprofit talk with a legislator about an issue at hand) than for *grassroots lobbying* (encouraging members of the general public to contact legislators to promote an opinion about a piece of legislation).

>> **Private foundations:** Although they, too, are recognized under section 501(c)(3), these organizations may not participate in any legislative lobbying. The only exception to this rule is when pending legislation may have an impact on the foundation's existence, tax-exempt status, powers, or duties, or on the deductibility of its contributions.

Penalties for engaging in too much political activity can include loss of your organization's tax exemption. However, going deeper into the details of these laws and reporting requirements is beyond the scope of this book. So if you're contemplating involving your nonprofit in serious legislative activity, consult an attorney or a tax specialist for advice. One place to find more information is the National Council of Nonprofits. (www.councilofnonprofits.org).

The situation with churches

Churches are in a category all by themselves. The IRS doesn't require them to file for a tax exemption, nor does it require them to file annual reports. Some churches, however, do apply for an exemption because their social-service outreach programs often include anything from preschools to soup kitchens to affordable housing. These programs seek 501(c)(3) status so that they can more easily apply for foundation funding and government grants or contracts to help pay the costs of providing the services.

Churches that haven't been officially recognized as being tax-exempt are highly unlikely to receive foundation grants or government contracts.

Taxes, taxes, taxes

Nonprofit organizations may be subject to *unrelated business income tax*, also known as UBIT. When a nonprofit makes $1,000 a year or more in gross income from a trade or business that's regularly carried on and that's unrelated to its exempt purpose, this income is taxable even if the proceeds support the organization. In addition, some corporate sponsorship funds may be subject to UBIT if they're perceived by the IRS as advertising dollars. IRS Publication 598 tells you all you need to know about this subject; visit www.irs.gov to take a look at this publication.

Some states exempt *some* nonprofits from paying state sales and use taxes. Check the laws in your state to see whether your organization is exempt from paying these taxes. The same is true of property taxes — it depends on your local jurisdiction. Your nearest tax assessor can tell you whether you have to pay property taxes.

Nonprofit employees must, of course, pay income tax on their salaries and other taxable compensation.

Nonprofits owning for-profits

Nonprofits can own for-profit businesses. We don't recommend it, because you'll have enough on your plate, especially when you're starting out, but it is possible. The business is subject to all regular taxes, just like all other for-profit businesses. Profits from the business may be distributed to the nonprofit, and the nonprofit must use them to further its goals and programs.

Very small organizations

If your nonprofit has less than $5,000 in annual revenues, it doesn't need to apply for a tax exemption. You can even go a bit over $5,000 in a year if your average annual income over a 3-year period is less than $5,000. When your income averages more than that amount, however, you have 90 days following the close of your most recent tax year to file for a tax exemption.

WARNING

Even if your organization has revenues under $5,000, you may still need to file the IRS 990-N form. This form can only be filed online. Check the IRS website at www.irs.gov for the latest information about this requirement.

Nonprofit compensation

Nonprofit organizations have one common feature, regardless of their type: No board member, staff member, or other interested party can benefit from the earnings of a nonprofit. Instead, assets are forever dedicated to the purpose of the organization. If the organization dissolves, the nonprofit must transfer the assets to another organization that performs a similar function. Keep in mind that board members cannot be compensated by the nonprofit they govern. This would be considered a conflict of interest and could result in the nonprofit losing its tax-exempt status.

REMEMBER

Just because assets are dedicated to fulfilling an organizational mission doesn't mean that staff are required to work for nonprofit organizations for free. Nonprofits can and should pay reasonable salaries to their staff members, if they have any. But keep in mind the difference between paying a salary and splitting the profits at the end of the year.

Comparing Nonprofits and For-Profits

Believing that nonprofit organizations have special advantages isn't uncommon. And to some extent, it's true. How many for-profit businesses, for example, get help from volunteers and generous donors? On the other hand, the advantages to owning your business exist, too. In this section, we discuss the similarities and differences between nonprofits and for-profits to help you decide which direction you should go.

How they're alike

We start with the similarities between the nonprofits and for-profits because, believe it or not, there are several. For instance, consider the following statements:

>> Sound business practices are important to both organizations.

>> Strong financial oversight, including budgeting for revenue and expenses, is a key factor for both organizations.

>> Good planning based on good information is a critical factor in the success of both nonprofits and for-profits.

>> Management skills, the ability to communicate clearly, and attention to detail make a difference whether you're working in a nonprofit or somewhere else.

>> A little bit of luck doesn't hurt either type of organization.

A final similarity involves the term *entrepreneur,* which usually describes someone who starts a new business. But any person or group that sets out to establish a nonprofit organization is entrepreneurial as well. After all, you're starting out on a path that may lead to great success, and you'll assume some risks along the way. We hope that you won't risk your house or your savings account to get a nonprofit going, but you may have uncertain income for a while.

How they differ

Although for-profits and nonprofits require similar professionalism and dedication from their leaders, they differ when it comes time to interpret their bottom lines and successes.

REMEMBER

The biggest difference between nonprofits and for-profits is the motivation for doing what you do — in other words, the *mission* of the organization. For-profit businesses exist to make money (you know, a *profit*). Nonprofits exist for the greater good of all to provide a public benefit.

Evaluating the success of a for-profit endeavor is easy: Did you make money, and, if so, how much did you make? We're not saying this to cast stones at the capitalist system or to in any way disparage the millions of folks who work for profit-making endeavors. After all, the nonprofit sector depends on profits and wealth from the for-profit sector for its support. And of course, nonprofits have to balance the books, too. Even nonprofits prefer to end the year with more money than they had when they started. They just don't call it *profit*; they call it a *surplus.*

For a nonprofit to be successful, it needs to change some aspect of the human, animal, or ecological condition; it needs to solve a problem, provide education, or build a monument. Because the goals of nonprofits are so lofty and progress toward achieving them is often slow, evaluating nonprofit success is sometimes difficult. See Chapter 9 for information about evaluating the results of your work.

HYBRID CORPORATIONS: NEITHER FISH NOR FOWL?

Some states have passed legislation that allows for the formation of corporations that can earn and distribute profits to shareholders but also must pay attention to the social and public benefits of their business. Efforts to create these new corporate entities, which blend the best of the nonprofit and for-profit worlds, arise largely from the corporate social responsibility movement, which has grown substantially during the past 30 years.

You may have heard the term *double bottom line,* a concept that essentially means businesses should not only try to make profits but also work toward improving the social condition of their workers and customers and the environment in which they operate. To that end, many companies have corporate giving programs that support nonprofit organizations in their communities, as well as programs that encourage employees to volunteer for local charitable groups. In the case of the new hybrids, however, corporate responsibility isn't optional; companies are obliged to consider the social impact of their activities and work toward making the world a better place.

The following three corporate models fall into the hybrid category. As such, they all have one thing in common: In the eyes of the IRS, they're viewed as for-profit entities, and their income is taxable as in any for-profit business. That means if you wanted to make a donation to the work of a hybrid corporation, the IRS wouldn't allow you to claim your contribution as a charitable gift.

- **Low profit limited liability companies (L3Cs):** The L3C model was designed to better attract capital investments from investors seeking a return on their money, as well as program-related investments (PRIs) from foundations. (PRIs are typically loans from foundations, not grants.) Foundations can count the funds used to provide PRIs toward their charitable-spending requirements as long as the charitable purpose of the project furthers the foundations' charitable purposes. The governing documents of the L3C are designed to make this approval easier to receive. So far, the IRS hasn't approved blanket acceptance of all PRIs awarded to L3C companies. Find more information about the L3C hybrid corporation on the Americans for Community Development website (www.americansforcommunitydevelopment.org).

- **B-Corp organizations:** B-Corps must adhere to certain accountability and transparency standards and have positive impacts on society and the environment. The nonprofit organization known as B-Labs (www.bcorporation.net) is leading the B-Corp accountability standards and advocacy efforts toward encouraging state lawmakers to pass legislation establishing this corporate model. B-Labs compares the B-Corp movement to fair trade certification, which ensures that products are produced in an equitable, environmentally sound manner.

- **Flexible purpose corporations (FPCs):** Sometimes called social purpose corporations, this newest form of hybrid corporation is similar to the B-Corp, except that it must have a more specific charitable purpose. Accountability and transparency standards for FPCs are developed internally by the corporations rather than by outside certifying agencies.

Although the notion of doing good in the world while still being allowed to make a profit is attractive, we recommend approaching these new corporate forms with caution. It's still early in this movement, and it's difficult to predict how effective these new hybrid corporations will be. If you're thinking of establishing an L3C or another hybrid organization, consult an attorney who's knowledgeable in this field before moving forward.

Using a Fiscal Sponsor: An Alternative Approach

If you're simply interested in providing a service, maybe you don't want to waste your time with the bureaucratic and legal matters that can complicate a new non-profit start-up. Or maybe you have a project that will end after a year or two, or you simply want to test the viability of an idea. Why bother to establish a new organization if it will close when you finish your project?

You may not need to start a nonprofit to carry out the program you're thinking of starting. Instead, *fiscal sponsorship* may be the best route for you to take. In this approach, your new project becomes a sponsored program of an existing 501(c)(3) nonprofit organization. Contributions earmarked for your project are tax-deductible because they're made to the sponsoring agency.

A fiscal sponsor is sometimes called a *fiscal agent*, but this term doesn't accurately describe the relationship between a fiscal sponsor and the sponsored project. The term *agent* implies that the sponsoring organization is acting on behalf of the project, when instead the project is acting on behalf of the organization. After all, the project is technically a program of the sponsoring nonprofit.

FISCAL SPONSORSHIP AS A FIRST STEP

Using fiscal sponsorship as a temporary solution while establishing a new nonprofit corporation and acquiring a tax exemption can be an effective approach for the following reasons:

- You have an opportunity to test the viability of raising funds for your idea.

- You have time to establish an organizational infrastructure and to create a board of directors in a more leisurely manner.

- You can pay more attention to building your program services in the crucial beginning stages of your project.

- Your fiscal sponsor can provide bookkeeping, human resources, and other types of expertise, enabling you to focus primarily on developing your programs and activities.

- You have time to determine whether your program is effectively meeting the needs you intend and can develop benchmarks to support the organization if and when you pursue your own 501(c)(3) entity.

This distinction may seem nitpicky, but it's an important one to keep in mind because you must satisfy the IRS requirements for this type of relationship. The 501(c)(3) sponsoring organization is responsible to both the funders and the IRS to see that the money is spent as intended and that charitable goals are met.

Examining common details of a fiscal sponsorship relationship

Here are some important points to keep in mind and negotiate if you decide to go the fiscal sponsor route:

>> **The mission of the fiscal sponsor must be in alignment with the project.** In other words, if you have a project to provide free food to the homeless, don't approach your local philharmonic orchestra as a potential sponsor. Find a nonprofit that has similar goals in its mission statement.

>> **The board of directors of the sponsoring organization should approve the sponsorship arrangements or delegate the responsibility to a key executive of the organization.** The sponsoring organization's board and leadership are, after all, ultimately responsible.

>> **Both parties should agree to and sign a contract or memorandum of understanding, detailing the responsibilities of each one.** See File 2-2 at www. wiley.com/go/nonprofitkitfd6e for a sample fiscal sponsorship agreement.

>> **The fiscal sponsor customarily charges a fee for sponsoring a project.** The fee is usually between 5 percent and 15 percent of the project's annual revenues, depending on the services it provides to the project.

>> **Some fiscal sponsors provide additional services.** These might include payroll services, bookkeeping, office space, group insurance coverage, and even management support, if needed. Be sure to ask whether these additional services are included in the fiscal sponsor's fee.

>> **Contributions to the sponsored project should be written to the sponsor.** Add a note instructing that they be used for the project.

Some foundations are reluctant to award grants to fiscally sponsored projects, even announcing in their guidelines that they won't do it. One reason for this reluctance is their concern that the board of the sponsoring organization exercises less oversight toward fiscally sponsored projects than it does toward their agency's other programs. Those foundations also may be concerned that the sponsoring nonprofit is providing convenient access to 501(c)(3) status to entities engaged in activities that don't qualify for that tax status from the IRS. Not all foundations share these prohibitions, however. In fact, some are proponents of fiscal sponsorship as a way of supporting new ideas and timely programs. You can read much more about foundations and grant proposals in Chapters 17 and 18.

Finding a fiscal sponsor

You may be able to find a fiscal sponsor near you by using the Fiscal Sponsor Directory (www.fiscalsponsordirectory.org). Another place to search is at your local community foundation. Community foundations have wide connections in the areas they serve and likely are aware of qualified fiscal sponsors.

TIP

If your area has no community foundation nearby, find another nonprofit in your area that provides referrals and ask for help in finding the right agency to sponsor your project.

You don't want to go with just any fiscal sponsor. You have to do your homework to find one that fits your needs. First determine whether the sponsor's mission covers the type of program you'll be offering. Then do a little research to find out whether the sponsor is trustworthy and financially healthy. For example, you can perform an Internet search for the fiscal sponsor's name. Does its name appear in news stories detailing nonprofit misconduct or other skullduggery? Ask others in your community, including individuals who are knowledgeable about nonprofit activities in your town. While you're at it, read its 990 tax form posted on GuideStar by Candid (www.guidestar.org) to see whether it's financially sound.

When you're vetting a fiscal sponsor, ask the sponsor these questions to determine whether it's a good fit for your project:

>> Do your board of directors and accounting and legal advisors approve of each fiscal sponsorship?

>> Do you charge for specific services, such as access to insurance programs, over and above your basic sponsorship fees? What additional services do you offer?

>> Do you allow sponsored projects to hire salaried employees, and do you provide payroll services and access to health insurance?

>> Do you provide coaching and mentoring in nonprofit management and fundraising?

>> How frequently do you write checks to pay bills? What's the frequency and format of financial reporting for the sponsored program?

>> Do you require projects to maintain a minimum annual income?

>> Do you formally acknowledge gifts and donations?

>> Do you help sponsored projects raise funds through your website?

TIP

The National Network of Fiscal Sponsors (www.fiscalsponsors.org) has developed guidelines for best practices in fiscal sponsorship. If you're considering using a fiscal sponsor, we suggest reviewing these guidelines to help you make a choice about which fiscal sponsor is best for your project.

Chapter **3**

Prioritizing Building Your Board of Directors

Most nonprofit founding visionaries don't prioritize the task of first getting their governing board onboard with their vision. The board isn't formed after the founder has written the mission and vision statements for the new nonprofit — the board needs to be involved in the creation of these two items when members are starting to develop the new nonprofit's first strategic plan document (see Chapter 4).

Here's a story about a nonprofit visionary who did not prioritize building a board of directors upfront. Jeffery decided to create a nonprofit organization — to help women who are single, pregnant, and homeless get off the streets, learn better parenting skills, and enter the workforce by the time their child is old enough to start kindergarten. Working alone, he wrote his mission and vision statements. He also drafted a strategic plan for the new nonprofit. By the time he started trying to recruit board members, he had set the mission, vision, and organizing documents in stone without input from any board members.

What's wrong with this picture? Well, no board member wanted to buy into Jeffrey's dream without having the ability to work as a team to create the mission, vision, and strategic planning documents. Jeffrey forgot that board members are vested stakeholders who should be recruited, trained, and included from day one of a new nonprofit start-up process. He failed to make forming his board of directors, upfront, a priority. Now he faces dealing with a lack of trust and a high degree of animosity between him and his new board, all of which could have been prevented if the board members had been onboard first and involved in the year-one strategic plan for the new organization.

REMEMBER

Having a founder experience tunnel vision by doing all the upfront strategizing alone isn't the route to take for anyone dreaming of starting a new nonprofit organization to benefit the greater good. Though board members may be in disagreement with the founder, everyone needs to plan together and be objective in the development of critical start-up documents that will shape the trajectory of the organization. So, take the time upfront to build a good board, and work with its members to achieve your collectively written mission, vision, and strategic plan.

TIP

Check out File 3-1 at www.wiley.com/go/nonprofitkitfd6e for a list of web resources related to the topics we cover in this chapter.

Appreciating the Duties of a Nonprofit Board of Directors

A *board of directors* (which we refer to simply as *a board* or *governing board*) is a group of people who agree to accept responsibility for a nonprofit organization. The board — which is responsible for ensuring that the nonprofit is fulfilling its mission — makes decisions about the organization, sets policy for the staff or volunteers to implement, and oversees the nonprofit's activities. Raising money for the nonprofit is another important responsibility that many, but not all, boards assume. Board members almost always serve without compensation; they're volunteers who have no financial interest in the nonprofit's business. However, they do bear responsibility for financial oversight and are held accountable for the accounting and financial reporting of the organization.

REMEMBER

Though paid staff members generally may serve as board members, and often do serve in start-up and small nonprofit organizations, check the laws in your state to determine any restrictions on paid staff members. However, if they're being compensated, they're being paid as employees, not as board members. Skip to the later section "Putting Staff Members on Your Board" for details on why it's not recommended to have your staff serve on the board.

In addition, according to the Internal Revenue Service (IRS), a nonprofit generally should not compensate persons for service on the board of directors except to reimburse direct expenses of such service. Nonprofits may pay reasonable compensation for services provided by officers and staff. In determining reasonable compensation, a nonprofit may want to rely on the rebuttable presumption test of Section 4958 of the Internal Revenue Code and Treasury Regulation section of 53.4958-6.

A nonprofit organization has no owners, like a for-profit business does, but a governing board guides and oversees the organization like an owner might. No one owns city, state, or federal governments either, so citizens hand over the responsibility of running the government to elected officials. In turn, they expect those officials to govern the affairs of their city, state, or nation. The job of a nonprofit governing board is similar — in fact, it's referred to as *nonprofit governance*. If you want more information on this type of governance than you find here, grab a copy of *Nonprofit Law and Governance For Dummies* by Jill Gilbert Welytok and Daniel S. Welytok (Wiley).

Primary role: Preserving public trust

A board's primary governance responsibility is *fiduciary* — to uphold the public trust. Laws in the United States give special rights and privileges to nonprofits recognized by the IRS as public charities. Primarily, these nonprofits earn the right to exemption from corporate income tax and the right to receive contributions that are tax-deductible for the donor. The government gives nonprofits this special status because they provide a public benefit. A board's leadership and oversight keep the organization's focus on that public benefit and make sure it doesn't abuse these rights and privileges.

Suppose that a nonprofit begins with a mission to rescue horses that have been neglected or abused. People who support this idea make contributions to the nonprofit with the belief that their money is being spent on programs to help the plight of horses in need of intensive care. But unknown to the donors, the nonprofit begins to spend its money on programs to charter schools. Supporting charter schools is a worthy goal, but it's a long way from the original purpose of helping neglected or abused horses. So, in this example, even though the nonprofit is using its contributions for a good cause, it isn't using them as the donors intended or to fulfill the organization's original purpose. Most importantly, the nonprofit is forgetting its mission, vision, and strategic plan. Either the founder or the governing board appears to have a case of amnesia for heading down an unapproved service road for quite a different target population.

WARNING

A nonprofit that collected funds to help neglected and abused horses but instead used the funds for the personal benefit of the board members and staff would be even worse. This dishonest act is serious and possibly a crime. Aside from potential felony fraud charges, such an activity violates IRS rules and can result in the revocation of the nonprofit's tax-exempt status.

In a for-profit business, the managers can share the net earnings (in other words, profit) at the end of the year among the company's owners or stockholders. If nonprofit board members decide to divide surplus funds among themselves, it's called *inurement*, a big word that basically means personal enrichment, which isn't allowed in the nonprofit world. Board members and staff can't personally benefit from nonprofit funds except for compensation for services provided or for reimbursement of expenses. A board must not only ensure that the nonprofit is doing what it set out to do but also make sure that it spends its funds properly. If a board does nothing else, it must make sure the organization adheres to these standards.

REMEMBER

A board's responsibilities are legal responsibilities. The three main duties that every board must uphold are care, loyalty, and obedience. Although they sound like vows one may take when entering a monastery, they actually describe established legal principles. Here's what these duties entail:

>> **The duty of care:** Refers to the responsibility to act as a prudent board member. In other words, board members must pay attention to what's going on and make decisions based on information that's available with reasonable investigation.

>> **The duty of loyalty:** Means that a board member must put the organization's welfare above other interests when making decisions.

>> **The duty of obedience:** Requires that board members act in accordance with the nonprofit's mission, goals, and bylaws.

TIP

Basic information about board governance is available from BoardSource (www.boardsource.org) without charge. You can access more in-depth material by paying a membership fee.

EX OFFICIO BOARD MEMBERS

Ex officio is a Latin phrase that means "by virtue of an office." For example, if you had the necessary clout, you might have the mayor of your city sitting on your board as an ex officio member. When the current mayor leaves office, that person would be replaced by a successor. Sometimes, in practice, the term is confused with *honorary* or *advisory* by nonprofit organizations that want to honor someone or add a prominent name to their letterhead.

Secondary role: Dealing with planning, hiring, and other board tasks

In addition to the legal and fiduciary responsibilities, a nonprofit board performs other roles, including those described in the following sections.

Providing a guiding strategy

Every nonprofit should have an organizational plan, and every board should play a part in creating and maintaining that plan. Thus, an important role of any board is to guide the overall planning and strategy of its organization. At the most basic level, this job means regularly reviewing the organization's mission statement and goals. Turn to Chapter 8 for more information on planning.

Hiring and working with the executive director

A nonprofit board is expected to hire the organization's executive director. Of course, many nonprofit organizations operate with no paid staff, but if your nonprofit does have employees, finding the right executive director is one of the board's most important tasks. See Chapter 11 for information about hiring paid employees.

A board works with its executive director to set goals and objectives for the year. Board members shouldn't look over the director's shoulder every day, but they should have a good idea of the director's work plan and should ensure that her efforts are in line with the agency's purpose.

Overseeing the organization's finances

A board must make sure the organization has the resources to carry out its goals. As part of this duty, many boards are active in fundraising. But a board also is responsible for reviewing the organization's budget and staying informed of the organization's financial situation. Nothing is more dismal than finding out, for example, that an organization has been ignoring its payroll taxes, and could create personal liability for the directors (check out Chapter 7 for more info about the board's personal liability). A word to the wise: Insist on good financial reporting. At a minimum, have the board treasurer (or perhaps the executive director or bookkeeper, if you have one) prepare monthly financial reports and distribute them to your board for review.

ESTABLISHING AN ADVISORY BOARD

Some organizations form *advisory boards,* which have no governance responsibilities. Advisory boards are optional, and how they operate and relate to the governing board of directors varies widely among different nonprofit organizations. Generally, their role falls into one of the following two categories:

- Members provide advice and guidance because of their professional expertise.
- Prominent names are be listed on the organization's letterhead.

We favor advisory boards that actually give advice (which generally means you have to ask for it) — even if they do so only once a year. Some organizations also use advisory board appointments as a way of getting to know potential board members.

WARNING

Many people join boards because they care about and understand the nature of the service that the organization provides, but they may not be trained in bookkeeping and accounting. These board members must try not to let their eyes glaze over when the financial report is reviewed at the board meeting, because part of a board member's job is to understand finances. If members don't understand the financial fine points, they need to ask questions of staff and other board members until they do understand them. Of course, they also can study Chapter 12 on nonprofit budgets and financial statements.

REMEMBER

Sometimes the problem is more than a lack of comprehension. For instance, the financial information may need to be presented more clearly. If one board member doesn't understand the financial reports, chances are good that other board members don't understand them, either. If your organization uses an outside accountant or bookkeeper to keep track of finances, ask for a brief meeting with that person to explain how they have presented the information. Many nonprofit service organizations offer affordable workshops on nonprofit finances and recordkeeping to assist board and staff members; others have programs that place volunteers from businesses into nonprofits.

Sharing responsibilities among the board, staff, and volunteers

Defining roles causes problems for a number of nonprofit organizations. Should the board of directors be involved in day-to-day management decisions? No, probably not. An executive director and their staff don't need board members to approve every management decision that comes along. The board must trust the staff to run the organization. To put it simply, the board sets the overall goals and policies, and the staff implements them. But (and this is a big *but*) many nonprofits have limited staff or even no staff. What happens when the organization's work is done by the board and other volunteers?

In the case of volunteer-run organizations, board members must wear two hats. Most importantly, they must exercise their fiduciary responsibilities. When they meet as a board of directors, they must see the larger picture and make group decisions that benefit the organization and its programs and clients. But, at the same time, when they have to do the hands-on work needed to provide the services and perform the day-to-day tasks of running a nonprofit, board members must act as if they were employees or volunteer staff members. They may even hold regular, unpaid volunteer jobs with job descriptions and scheduled hours. Confusing, isn't it? Still, anyone who serves as both a board member and a volunteer or staff member needs to keep this distinction in mind.

TIP

In any organization, building practices that create financial checks and balances is a good idea. These practices are particularly important when board members also act as staff. For example, an organization has better financial oversight and control when one person approves bills for payment, a different person signs the checks, and another person reviews the canceled checks and monthly bank statements. You don't *have* to use this system — it's just one way to make sure that funds are used and accounted for properly.

Recruiting the Right People for Your Board

You don't want just anybody to serve on your board. You want to choose the members of your community who believe in what you're doing and who will attend all your meetings, advocate for your programs, provide honest and ethical oversight to the organization, make regular and generous donations, and sweep the floor on weekends.

Perhaps, not surprisingly, you won't find many board members who fit this description. Even so, the following three traits are critical to the success of the organization:

>> Believing in the mission

>> Being a strong advocate on behalf of its programs

>> Serving the organization as a careful and honest board member

Sure, having wealthy members who do the dirty work when needed is nice, but, most importantly, you must find board members who understand and believe deeply in your work. Showing up for board meetings is a nice habit, too.

Think seriously about the skills that board members bring to your organization. Do you need an accountant to set up financial systems? A public relations specialist to help with media campaigns? An attorney to help with legal matters? Yes, you probably do. But don't expect the accountant to do your audit or the attorney to represent you in court. You need a disinterested professional to do that work.

REMEMBER

Your board should reflect your organization's character and mission. A community-organizing group dedicated to collective decision-making may want board members who work well together. A neighborhood development organization clearly wants board members from its neighborhood. A youth leadership organization may want to invest in future leadership by creating positions for youth members on its board. (*Note:* Before adding young people to your board, check whether your state laws allow minors to serve on nonprofit boards. If your state prohibits minors from serving, consider inviting them to serve on advisory committees instead.)

WARNING

Although having a friend or two on the board is fine, be careful about overloading the board with golfing buddies and carpool partners. Boards need diverse opinions and honest feedback from members.

Incorporating diversity, equity, and inclusion in the board's composition

Every governing board should represent the community-at-large that your new nonprofit organization plans to serve. For example, you're planning to locate your new nonprofit in Tucson, Arizona. Before you start recruiting board members, take the time to research the most recent US census demographics for the city, town, village, hamlet, or region where services will be provided. Table 3-1 takes a look at the most recent demographics for what ethnic groups are represented in Tucson's population. *Note:* The board recruitment metrics to meet are calculated based on a 9-member board of directors. The number of board members should always be an odd number so that it's easier to have a board member quorum (majority) in order to start meetings and have a majority of members present to take actions on resolutions.

Recruiting and selecting board members who align with the majority of the population is essential. However, your entire board composition cannot represent the majority. You also have to look at the demographics of the nonmajority groups. In the example I just presented, the two largest population groups are Whites and Hispanic or Latino. Therefore, starting to recruit from these two groups gives you six of the nine planned board members. The remaining three board vacancies should be filed with one member representing Blacks or African Americans, American Indians, and Asians. How would this composition change? It would change if your nonprofit organization weren't serving all of Tucson, but instead was focusing on a census tract or neighborhood where one of the minority groups has the largest number of residents.

TABLE 3-1

Example Demographics for Tucson, Arizona

Population Demographics	2020 Population Estimates*	Board Recruitment Metrics to Meet
Male	48.8%	4
Female	50.2%	5
Total Board Members		9
White	71.2%	4
Black or African American	5.2%	1
American Indian	3.7%	1
Asian	3.2%	1
Hispanic or Latino	43.9%	2

Population estimates, July 1, 2020, US Census Bureau, State and County QuickFacts

REMEMBER

Diversity is often perceived to be about perspective, representation, tough conversation, and supporting inclusion. Inclusion prompts answers about creating environments conducive to feedback, supporting diversity, and being open. Equity is described as fairness, sameness, and valuing diversity and inclusion. This list describes them all:

» **Diversity** incudes all the ways in which people differ, encompassing the different characteristics that make one individual or group (like a nonprofit board) different from another. Though diversity is often used in reference to race, ethnicity, or gender, the definition embraces a broader definition that includes age, national origin, religion, disability, sexual orientation, socioeconomic status, education, marital status, language, and physical appearance.

   Geographic diversity refers to the location(s) of the people you plan to serve. Funders want to know about zip codes, census tracts, specific states, counties, towns, and neighborhoods that will benefit from your services.

» **Equity** is the fair treatment of, access to, opportunity for, and advancement of all people (this applies to your board of directors) while striving to identify and eliminate barriers that have prevented the full participation of some groups. Improving equity involves increasing justice and fairness within the procedures and processes of institutions or systems, including nonprofit organizations.

» **Inclusion** is the creation of environments in which any individual or group (this applies to your board of directors) can be — and can *feel* — welcomed, respected, supported, and valued to fully participate. An inclusive and welcoming climate embraces differences and offers respect in words and actions for all people.

PERSUADING SOMEONE TO JOIN YOUR BOARD

Many people think a board member's primary role is to raise money. In fact, a popular slogan addressed to board members who aren't raising funds is "Give, get, or get off." Harsh, isn't it? Nonprofits can't fulfill their purposes effectively without money, and board members who take an active interest in the organization's financial vitality are important. But a board member's role is broader than fundraising. Other roles include staying well informed about the organization's work, selecting leadership, setting policies, planning, overseeing, and serving as an ambassador for the organization. Many highly skilled volunteers think they shouldn't serve on boards because they aren't wealthy, and this misconception represents a real loss to nonprofit organizations.

Some people are reluctant to serve on boards for other reasons, including personal and financial liability. However, unpaid volunteers who aren't grossly negligent and who act in good faith have some protection under the Volunteer Protection Act of 1997 and may have additional protections under your state's volunteer protection laws. If you need more information about the possible liabilities of board members and other volunteers, we suggest that you get in touch with BoardSource (www.boardsource.org) or your state's association of nonprofit organizations through the National Council of Nonprofits (www.councilofnonprofits.org).

Organizations can protect their boards by purchasing directors' and officers' insurance (see Chapter 22). Generally, the organization's creditors can't come after its board members' personal wealth for payment. An exception is that the IRS can hold board members financially accountable when organizations fail to pay payroll taxes. But even the IRS will work with an organization to develop a payment plan and schedule to catch up on taxes. People are right to take seriously the responsibility of board service, but nonprofit board work also can be fun and satisfying.

Keeping it fresh: Terms of service

Building a board should be a continuing process. Therefore, we highly recommend that your organizational bylaws specify terms of service. Two 3-year terms or three 2-year terms are the most common term lengths for board service. In most cases, bylaws allow reelection to the board after one year's absence. Limiting terms of service helps you maintain a fresh supply of new ideas, which are more likely to come from people who are new to your organization. Plus, limiting terms of service can help you recruit new board members because your potential recruits know their time commitment is of limited duration.

To avoid having all your board members leave in the same year, stagger the years when terms expire. You can allow someone to serve an extra year or ask others to serve shorter terms if necessary and if your bylaws allow it.

If you're thinking about recruiting new board members, create a spreadsheet to help you visualize the skills you need to seek out when you're looking for new members. Along the top of the grid, list the skills you think you need on your board. Along the side, list your current board members and place check marks under the skills they bring to the board.

Check out File 3-2 at www.wiley.com/go/nonprofitkitfd6e for a sample grid for planning board recruitment.

Where do you find new board members? Start with your organization's address book. Whom do you know who may make a good member and be willing to serve? Who benefits from your agency's work? Who are your agency's neighbors? Who is actively involved as a volunteer for your agency? Some cities have nonprofit support organizations that can help in this regard. Consider asking your funders for suggestions and look at former board members of other high-functioning nonprofit organizations with similar missions.

Even if you don't specify board terms, continuously recruiting new board members is important. As time passes, board members' lives may change in ways that draw them away from your organization. Many nonprofit organizations lose vitality when their boards don't refresh themselves with new members.

Big boards or little boards

Opinions differ about the ideal number of board members. One school of thought holds that big boards are better because the members can divide work among more people, consider more diverse viewpoints, and reach into the community more extensively. Other people say that smaller boards are better because maintaining a working relationship with a smaller group is easier and decision-making is better because the board has to consider fewer opinions. Those who support small boards also say that board members can easily become invisible in a large group, meaning that no one will notice if they fail to do their share of the work.

In our opinion, there is no single correct answer to the board-size question. According to a 2010 BoardSource survey of its members, the average size was 16 members and the median size was 15 members. Nonprofits vary widely in size, function, and type, so what works for one nonprofit may not work for another. Nonprofit board size is truly a case where the phrase *one-size-fits-all* doesn't apply.

Consider these points when setting your board's size:

>> **Start-up nonprofits tend to have smaller boards than more mature organizations.** Start-up budgets tend to be smaller, and building a board of directors takes time. State laws generally specify the minimum size required (often, three members).

>> **Boards that are actively engaged in fundraising for major gifts and special events tend to be larger because both fundraising techniques are fueled by personal contacts and friendships.** The more board members you have, the more personalized invitations you can send. Some large cultural institutions have 50 board members or more.

>> **Boards that govern nonprofits funded mostly by grants and contracts tend to have fewer members, perhaps an average of 10 to 16 members.** Board members in these nonprofits usually have fewer fundraising responsibilities for the organization and frequently are representatives of the communities or clients served. They also may have professional experience in the types of service provided by the nonprofit.

Choosing officers and committees

Typical officer positions of most nonprofit boards include president, vice president, secretary, and treasurer. Sometimes the positions of secretary and treasurer are combined into one office. Your state laws may specify which officers are required. Seniority on the board, professional expertise, and skills in negotiating with and listening to others are common traits sought in a board's leaders. Ultimately, however, the board of directors chooses the officers. They're usually elected to 2–year terms. The following list outlines the common responsibilities of board officers:

>> **President (or chairperson):** Presides at board meetings, appoints committee chairpersons, works closely with the executive director to guide the organization, and acts as a public spokesperson for the organization (but also may assign this responsibility to the executive director)

>> **Vice-president (or vice-chairperson):** Presides at board meetings in the president's absence and serves as a committee chairperson as appointed by the president

>> **Secretary:** Maintains the organization's records, records minutes at board meetings, and distributes minutes and announcements of upcoming meetings to board members

>> **Treasurer:** Oversees the organization's financial aspects, makes regular financial reports to the board, and sometimes serves as chairperson of the board finance committee

TIP

Check out File 3-3 at `www.wiley.com/go/nonprofitkitfd6e` for more-detailed job descriptions you can use.

If the board has *standing*, or permanent, committees, the board president may appoint committee chairpersons, or they may be appointed by the board. Typical standing committees are finance, development or fundraising, program, and nominating committees. Other possible committees that may be either standing or *ad hoc* — a temporary committee organized to deal with time-limited projects — are planning, executive search, investment, special events, and facilities. The following list outlines the responsibilities of common standing committees:

>> **Development:** Sets fundraising goals and plans fundraising activities for the organization in consultation with the board president and executive director

>> **Finance:** Assists the treasurer in overseeing financial reports and official tax filings, making budgets, and maintaining relationship with professional accounting firm, if applicable

>> **Nominating:** Recruits new board members and nominates board officers for election to their positions

>> **Program:** Oversees and advises on the program activities of the organization

Board committees make regular reports to the full board about the organization's activities in their particular areas. Board officer terms and the number and type of standing committees should be written into the organization's bylaws.

REMEMBER

If your organization is large enough to conduct an annual financial audit, your board may be legally required to appoint an audit committee. Be sure to check the laws in your state. You may not be permitted to include the board chair or treasurer on the audit committee.

Executive committees are standard groups on some larger boards of directors. Usually the members of the executive committee are the officers of the board, but the committee sometimes also includes the chairs of the standing committees. The executive committee may hold regular meetings to set the agenda for the meetings of the full board and to advise the board president, or it may come together on an as-needed basis. Sometimes an organization's bylaws empower the executive committee to make decisions on behalf of the full board in an emergency or in other special circumstances.

Introducing new and prospective members to the board and the organization

Boards of directors exhibit all the characteristics of small groups, and maybe even families: Friendships develop, alliances form, and disagreements occur. Over time, the group develops routines and habits that help make members feel comfortable with one another and help guide the board's work. When a new member joins the group or when a prospective new member visits, the existing members need to make that person feel comfortable and share with them the collective wisdom they have accumulated.

Invite a prospective board member to observe at least one board meeting before electing them to membership. That way, the new member gets a chance to see how the board operates, and the current members have an opportunity to size up the new person. Encourage the prospective member to ask questions. Also, if your nonprofit provides programs — such as childcare, a health clinic, or a music school — be sure to give your prospective board members a tour of the facilities before they join.

REMEMBER

When asking someone to serve on your board, don't shy away from sharing a clear picture of the work to be done. You may be afraid that your prospect will say no if it seems like too much work. However, keep in mind that being asked is an honor, and contributing good work to a good cause is satisfying. Besides, if the person does decide that you're asking too much, isn't it better to know now rather than later?

TIP

A packet of background materials about the organization and board procedures can help new members get up to speed quickly. The following information is useful for orienting new members:

>> Board job descriptions outlining responsibilities and expectations

>> Board minutes for the past two or three meetings

>> Articles and bylaws

>> Conflict-of-interest policy (if you have one)

>> Calendar of the organization's events and scheduled board meetings

>> Description of programs

>> Financial audit or financial statement

>> Form 990 for the past three years

>> Mission statement

>> Names, addresses, and phone numbers of other board members

>> News clippings about the organization

>> Organizational plan (if one is available)

This information may seem like a lot of reading — and it is. But even if a new board member doesn't read everything from cover to cover, they at least have the reference material when they need it.

We also suggest that the board president or the executive director meet with a new board member soon after the person begins serving on the board, both to welcome them and to answer any questions.

Putting Staff Members on Your Board

As a general rule, we think paid staff shouldn't be board members. The situation can become too complicated. For example, conflict of interest is always a potential problem, especially when board and staff have different priorities, such as when employees want raises but the board says no.

Some exceptions to the rule do exist, though. In fact, many nonprofits have at least one staff member on their boards. In start-up nonprofits, for example, founders frequently serve as both board members and staff members. This situation isn't surprising. Who's better suited to bring the vision and passion needed to create a new organization than the person who formed it in the first place? In many new nonprofits, of course, paying the staff isn't even possible; resources are so limited that all work is done on a volunteer basis.

WARNING

If a founder or another staff member serves on the board, we recommend that they not be elected board president because doing so tends to put all responsibility for vision and leadership in a single person's hands. Sharing that leadership can be an important first step toward broadening an organization's base of support. In addition, the executive director should always be the buffer between the staff and board. This helps keep things cleaner and less complicated.

Laws vary by state, but in many cases, having a paid staff member on your board is permitted. For example, under California nonprofit corporation law, as many as 49 percent of the members of a nonprofit board are allowed to receive compensation from the nonprofit. But the standards of governance set forth by the BBB/Wise Giving Alliance say that a board should include no more than a single compensated member (or 10 percent of members for larger boards). Be sure to check out and follow the nonprofit corporation law in your state.

Using Your Board to Full Capacity

If you spend any time around nonprofit staff, you'll probably hear a few complaints about the board of directors. They may say, "I can't get my board to do anything" or "I can't get them to face hard decisions or raise money." Worst of all, you may hear, "I can't get them to show up to meetings."

Motivating the board is an important part of any nonprofit leader's job. Keeping members well informed so that they can make thoughtful, appropriate recommendations is essential. Sometimes your most important task is gently steering the board's attention back to the organization's mission and immediate needs. Whether or not your nonprofit has paid staff, you can take steps to help the board do its work well.

REMEMBER

The working relationship between the executive director (if you have one) or founder and the board president is a key factor to having an effective board and organization. Ideally, the relationship between these two leaders is one of respect and trust.

Encouraging commitment from board members

Getting members of a board to pull their weight sometimes seems like a problem that you can't solve. Not every board member will contribute equally to the work involved in governing a nonprofit organization. If everyone on your board shows up at every meeting, reads all the materials, studies the financial statements, and contributes to fundraising activities, consider yourself fortunate.

Here are some techniques you can use to encourage full board member participation:

TIP

>> **Board contracts:** Some nonprofits ask new board members to sign an agreement that outlines expectations for board service. The contract may include a commitment to contribute financially to the organization, attend all board meetings, and serve on one or more committees. Although board contracts aren't legally binding, they provide a clear understanding of responsibilities for each board member. With a board contract, no one can say they didn't understand what they were getting into when they joined the board.

Check out File 3-4 at www.wiley.com/go/nonprofitkitfd6e for a sample board contract.

>> **Bylaws:** Organizational bylaws can state the requirements for board partici-pation. For example, a board member may face dismissal from the board after missing three consecutive board meetings.

>> **Job descriptions:** Just like employees, board members often perform better when they know exactly what they're supposed to do. Creating job descrip-tions for officers, committee chairpersons, and individual board members may clarify responsibilities and make them easier to fulfill. If a member isn't pulling their weight, a committee chairperson should speak with that person and remind them of their responsibilities.

>> **Reliance on board members:** Solicit opinions from members between board meetings. Use their expertise and recognize their contributions.

>> **Self-evaluation:** Sometimes, encouraging a board to look at itself motivates board members or encourages those who aren't pulling their weight to resign.

Board members fail to contribute equally to the work of the board because of time constraints, business travel, and just plain laziness. Cut each member some slack. But if a board member's lack of participation impacts the full board, the decision is up to the board president (often, in partnership with the executive director) to ask the member to reconsider their commitment to the organization.

REMEMBER

To a great degree, each board member's work reflects their commitment to the organization's mission. Board members who truly believe in what you're doing will do everything they can to help you succeed.

Holding effective board meetings

Most board work is done in meetings, either with the full board or in committees. The board president is responsible for ensuring that meetings are well organized and begin and end at a scheduled hour. We can't think of anything that damages board effectiveness more than poorly organized meetings that don't stay on topic and that continue late into the night. Nonprofit board members are volunteers; they aren't being paid by the hour.

If the organization has an executive director, the president may delegate some responsibilities for setting up meetings. Ultimately, however, part of the presi-dent's job is to see that board members have the information they need to make good decisions and that they do so in a reasonable amount of time.

Getting the members to show up

Stipulating how often a board of directors should meet is impossible. The only real answer is "as often as it needs to." A meeting schedule depends on the organization's needs and the amount of business conducted at board meetings. The frequency of meetings should be specified in the bylaws. Most nonprofit boards meet more frequently than once a year; some meet quarterly, some meet every other month, and others schedule monthly meetings. Of course, the board president may call a board meeting at any time if the board needs to handle special business.

The advantage of having more frequent board meetings is that board members are more engaged in the governance of the organization. The disadvantage — especially if the agenda doesn't include much business — is that board members may be more tempted to skip meetings.

Some boards schedule meetings at the beginning of the year for the entire year. By entering these dates in their appointment calendars months in advance, board members are less likely to schedule other events on the same days and are more likely to attend the meetings. For example, if you meet monthly, you may schedule your meetings for the second Tuesday of each month. If you aren't this organized, always schedule the next meeting before the end of the present meeting. Doing so is much easier than trying to schedule a meeting by telephone or email.

TIP

Some boards use online collaboration tools to communicate between board meetings and to compile documents in an easily accessible place.

Conducting efficient meetings

If you're looking for some tips to ensure effective board meetings, check out the following ideas:

>> **Schedule a meeting between the executive director and board president before the meeting begins.** This can be done in person or via phone, but it's an important step in determining the agenda and the focus of the upcoming meeting. The meeting also allows the executive director to update the president on staff issues, funding opportunities, and any areas where the executive director needs particular guidance and support from the board.

>> **Ten days to two weeks before a board meeting, send an announcement of the meeting to all board members.** Include the minutes from the last meeting and an agenda for the upcoming meeting. Also include any committee reports, financial statements, or background research that the board will discuss at the meeting.

If the meeting minutes include a list of tasks for board members to complete before the next meeting, try to send members a rough draft of the minutes as soon after the meeting as possible so that they can get started. (File 3-5 at www.wiley.com/go/nonprofitkitfd6e contains an outline of meeting minutes that the board secretary can fill in during the meeting.)

>> **Limit the length of meetings to two hours or less, if possible.** After two hours, especially if you're holding the meeting in the evening, attention begins to wane. If you must go longer than two hours, take a break. Offering refreshments is always a good idea.

>> **Try to find a conference room for the meeting.** Holding a discussion around a conference table is much easier than sitting in someone's living room. The table offers a place to set papers, and people won't argue over who gets the recliner. It also sets the stage and implies that work is to be done.

Avoid holding meetings in restaurants and cafes, if possible. The noise levels are too high to make good discussion possible, and all the activity is a constant distraction. You also have no privacy. Believe us — we've tried it!

>> **Adhere to Robert's Rules of Order.** To adhere to proper board meeting protocol, follow these rules to conduct efficient, effective, and well-documented board meetings. You can download a copy of Robert's Rules for free at https://diphi.web.unc.edu/wp-content/uploads/sites/2645/2012/02/MSG-ROBERTS_RULES_CHEAT_SHEET.pdf, and check out *Robert's Rules For Dummies* by C. Alan Jennings, PRP (Wiley).

>> **Stick to the agenda.** Don't allow people to wander off topic. Some agendas set the time allowed for discussion after each item. You don't have to do this, but if your meetings have been veering off course, setting time limits may help control them. Files 3-6 and 3-7 at www.wiley.com/go/nonprofitkitfd6e are samples of common agenda types you can use as models.

>> **Follow an orderly procedure.** You don't need to be overly formal in your meetings (many board meetings are casual), but having a basic knowledge of when to make a motion and when to call the question is helpful.

>> **Thank your board.** Board members are volunteers who give time and money to your organization. Take every opportunity during meetings to make sure they're appreciated. Mention their names when appropriate in newsletters and media releases. Small gifts are sometimes useful, but don't be extravagant. You don't want to be accused of wasting the organization's money.

Chapter 4

Creating Your Mission Statement and Vision Statement

Every nonprofit needs well-crafted mission and vision statements. A good *mission statement* clearly and succinctly states a nonprofit's reason for existence — including who benefits from its work — and how it works to fulfill that mission from day to day. A *vision statement* is a lengthier statement that looks to the future and describes what you want your nonprofit to achieve in the long run.

The process of developing your mission and vision statements is important. Don't feel like you have to come up with these statements on your own. Instead, we recommend that you take some time to discuss your ideas with your governing board and encourage their input and feedback. Doing so can help you refine your ideas, test them with other people, and inspire those involved in the writing process.

Read on for more guidance about how to create simple yet compelling mission and vision statements.

TIP

Check out File 4-1 at www.wiley.com/go/nonprofitkitfd6e for a list of web resources related to the topics we cover in this chapter.

Honing Your Mission Statement

The mission statement is an organization's heartbeat (see Figure 4-1). In anatomy, your heart is the engine that fuels your entire body. For your nonprofit, the mission conveys the passion in your existence. Your mission statement impacts every stakeholder and is the reason your staff shows up at work. It's the reason your board members work hard to support the nonprofit's work in the community. The mission statement is the driving mantra for your volunteers who show up day after day to roll up their sleeves and carry out their job descriptions. Finally, your mission statement is the living, breathing, *actionable* reason that other organizations in the community want to be partners and step up, when needed, to fill gaps in services. Most importantly, a succinct and compassion-filled mission statement speaks to the hearts (and wallets) of potential donors.

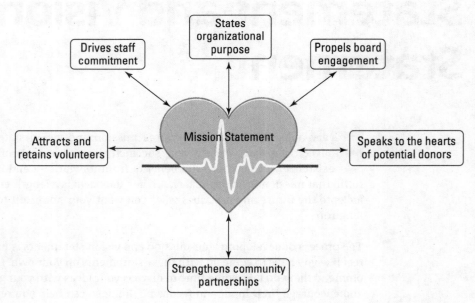

FIGURE 4-1: A strong mission statement is an organization's heartbeat.

REMEMBER

A mission statement should state what the organization's reason for existence is, how the mission will be achieved, and who will benefit from the organization's activities. The mission should be

>> **Memorable:** You want to carry the statement around in your mind — at all times. Stakeholders should be able to remember it with ease and help your organization live it in their daily contributions.

>> **Focused:** You want the statement to be narrow enough to focus on the reason our organization exists but broad enough to support organizational growth and expansion.

>> **Compelling:** You want to communicate the need your organization addresses and the importance of doing something about it. (Bonus points if it also attracts potential board members to want to join your board and be a part of ongoing inspiration and change.)

>> **Easy to read:** Your statement should be written in plain language so that folks don't need a set of footnotes to decipher it. Be sure to limit your use of adjectives, and try to avoid jargon.

After you decide on your organization's mission statement, you can use it as your go-to reference when making decisions about your nonprofit's activities. Add your mission statement to your Form 990 tax report to the IRS, in brochures, and in grant proposals. You may even print it on business cards for your board members and staff.

JARGON IS NOT YOUR FRIEND

Jargon is a term for words that have specialized meaning within an industry or profession. When you're communicating with colleagues, everyone knows the meaning of the specialized words you use. But when you're writing for the general public — the people who are the target of your mission statement — you should use words that have a common meaning for everyone.

For example, if you're an educator, you're probably familiar with the term *scaffolding*. In education, the word is used as shorthand to describe the process of using the skills that students already have to help them learn new skills. If you're a housepainter, it means something entirely different.

Think about the words you use to describe your mission and make sure everyone knows what they mean.

Keeping your mission statement short and sweet

Times have changed from when nonprofit organizations had long, drawn-out mission statements that spanned pages and read like a rambling fact sheet. Instead, we suggest keeping your mission statement short and succinct — aim for one or two memorable sentences that speak about the present and can be easily remembered by your board members, staff, volunteers, and community stakeholders. That way, everyone can remember why your nonprofit organization exists, what it does for the community, and how they can help it stay on focus daily. Save your lengthy writing for the vision statement.

Here's a sample mission statement with the most important words bolded to amplify the nonprofit's reason for existence, intent, and focus.

> The mission of the Grant Writing Training Foundation is to **educate, empower, and enlighten nonprofit staff through affordable professional development training.**

What do your board members need to remember when they're out and about in the community? "We educate, empower, and enlighten your staff through affording training programs." This is short, sweet, and memorable — and it makes sense when the full mission statement is shortened.

TIP

Think of your mission statement as a one-minute elevator speech. You have 60 seconds to describe your organization's purpose and activities. Doing so is easy if you have a clear, short mission statement. Even if you have a longer mission statement, develop a 50- to 75-word spiel that you can recite from memory. Say just enough to capture the attention of listeners. After that, give them a business card with the nonprofit's contact information (on the front) and the full mission statement (on the back).

Stating your mission — the goal for services

When thinking of your organization's reason for existing, think of your desired end result. What would you like to see happen? What would the world (or your community) be like if your organization were to succeed?

To say that you have to have a mission to change lives seems almost too basic. Maybe you're thinking, "*Of course* I have a reason for forming my nonprofit. Why do you think I bought this book? I want to start a nonprofit to [fill in the blank]." We bring up this point because clarifying the reason for your nonprofit's existence is basic to creating your mission statement. Why should your nonprofit exist?

For example, you may know that you love cats and dogs and have always wanted to work with them, but that isn't the same thing as identifying a nonprofit organization's reason for existing. The mission statement for a fictitious humane society might be written this way:

> Friends of Animals provides temporary shelter and medical care for homeless puppies, dogs, kittens, and cats until responsible, loving homes can be found.

This sentence doesn't describe the shelter's facilities or how it recruits and trains volunteers, but it does clearly state which animals it serves and that it doesn't intend to foster them as long as they live but rather to place them in good homes. And if someone visited Friends of Animals with a ferret, a pony, or a tarantula, its staff would know to refer that person to another shelter.

REMEMBER

Knowing and understanding your organization's purpose is essential to making important organizational decisions. It's also a fundamental tool to use when asking for money, recruiting additional board members, hiring and motivating staff, and publicizing your activities. Also, remember that your governing board's input in developing the mission statement is not an option. Buy-in begins with inclusion!

Specifying who will be served by the nonprofit

After you and the governing board have determined the nonprofit's purpose, the primary beneficiaries of its services are documented and included in the mission statement. Their needs — whether they're kittens or refugees — make your mission compelling and achievable. Defining who will benefit from your nonprofit helps to focus your organizational activities and is an essential ingredient in the mission statement.

Some organizations have a more general audience than others. If your nonprofit's focus is preserving historic buildings, the beneficiary of this activity may be current and future residents of a city, a county, or even a state. It may also be the workers you train in the crafts needed to complete the building restorations.

Explaining how you'll accomplish your mission

After you know your organization's mission and its beneficiaries, the next step is deciding how to make it happen. Mission statements usually highlight a phrase describing the methods your nonprofit will use to accomplish its purpose. Think about the activities and programs you'll provide to fulfill your mission. Take a look at these examples:

>> To indicate how it will accomplish its mission, the Friends of Animals' mission statement may say, "Our mission will be accomplished by veterinary professionals and dedicated volunteers who provide temporary shelter for homeless animals."

>> The mission of a human-services nonprofit organization may state, "Our mission will be accomplished by providing juvenile offender reentry recidivism counseling-and-support services for minority probationers exiting the Nassau County Juvenile Detention Center."

REMEMBER

When describing how your organization addresses its purpose, you don't want to be so specific that you have to rewrite its mission statement every time you add a new program. At the same time, you want the mission statement to be concrete enough that people reading it (or hearing you recite it) can picture what your organization does.

Incorporating diversity, equity, and inclusion (DEI) into your mission statement

What does it mean to incorporate diversity, equity, and inclusion (or *DEI*) into your mission statement? Let's look at who's involved and how to add language that is direct and memorable.

Step 1: It takes a village! Involve the founder and/or executive director and the governing board in articulating a brief but striking DEI statement.

Step 2: Remember that adding DEI to your mission statement is core to the organization's values and the way it will conduct business (programs and services).

Step 3: Use positive words like *inclusive, celebrate, grow, freedom, experience,* and *commitment* or *committed.*

Now let's revisit this mission statement and start adding the DEI language:

> Our mission is to provide juvenile offender reentry recidivism counseling-and-support services for minority probationers exiting the Nassau County Juvenile Detention Center by ensuring that our programs are inclusive to all and committed to celebrating diversity, equity, and inclusion for youth and their families during detention and post-detention.

As you can see, not all the parts of DEI have to be included. However, the parts you do include must have an impact on your service population.

DETECTING A WEAK MISSION STATEMENT

Here's an example of a vague, unclear mission statement:

> The Good Food Society works to maximize impact of the utilization of nutritious food groups to beneficially help people in need by proclaiming the good benefits of balanced nutrition.

You probably get the idea that this organization wants people to have better eating habits so that they can enjoy better health. But can it realistically help all people everywhere? Also, try reciting this statement to someone you're trying to convince to contribute to your organization. Can you say *tongue-tied?*

Long, multisyllabic words don't make a mission or vision statement more impressive. If anything, they have the opposite effect. In place of the preceding statement, try this type of wording for your mission statement:

> Believing in the value of good nutrition, the Good Food Society aims to improve public health by providing information about the benefits of a balanced diet to parents of school-age children through public education programs.

Imagining Your Future with a Vision Statement

Simply put, a *vision statement* is your dream — your broadly described aspiration for what your organization can do. Vision statements can describe a future desired condition as a result of the organization's activities, but they're more typically applied to the organization itself. Usually, the statement includes phrases like "the best" or "recognized as a leader."

Table 4-1 provides an example of this future-visioning process.

Capturing your vision statement

A *vision statement* can be long or short. We recommend that you assemble a group of internal stakeholders (founder, board members, staff, and volunteers). Start by spelling out the basic components in a vision statement. Here are the most important aspects a vision statement should convey (or communicate) to the public at-large, including your stakeholders:

>> Project what your nonprofit organization will do over the next five years.

>> Write in future tense.

>> Provide directional language.

>> Be descriptive.

>> Dare to be audacious or bold in your prediction!

TABLE 4-1   **Visioning the future while looking at the present**

Who we are now	Where we see ourselves in 5 years
New nonprofit	One of the best social enterprise nonprofits
Limited financial resources	Endowed
Small footprint in our neighborhood	Recognized statewide as a leader
Hoping to move chronically homeless single mothers with children into Alternative Dwelling Units (ADUs)	Pioneer in changing zoning policies to permit ADUs in multiple residential neighborhoods enabling single-parent homeless families to live in permanent safe housing

Here's an example of a vision statement from a fictitious nonprofit organization serving a Tribal nation in the Pacific Northwest region of the United States:

By 2026, the Native Cultural Food Preservation Institute will encourage Native youth to adapt and embrace the food preservation techniques of their ancestors. Over time, fishing, hunting, and foraging for berries and herbs will result in the restoration of Tribal health-and-wellness practices to reduce obesity, hunger, and debilitating health. The Institute's Native herbal research projects and position statements on American Indian Cultural Food Preservation will be widely circulated to our sister Tribes across the nation and Canada. We will be a conduit for improving Native health. The future of Native health and wellness will be managed via robust education programs, cultural food preservation reclamation initiatives, and an embrace of the ways of our ancestors.

Notice how this vision statement reflects the cultural essence of the organization's purpose and direction.

Asking "Where are we going?" and "Why?"

If your nonprofit organization is small and at this point has only a founder and two or three board members, you can simply convene that small group and ask, "Where are we going and why?" Here are three statements you're likely to hear back in this first round of asking the same question over and over:

"We're going to change the world!"

"We're going to become the largest nonprofit in our state!"

"We're going to be debt-free!"

Don't criticize or belittle your stakeholders. Do you know how many people live for today, and think for today, and never set goals or create a vision for the future? We would have to say that, likely, millions have fallen short of seeing themselves or their nonprofit organizations as sustainable for many years to come. This fear is a common one for new nonprofit founders. Their dreams start out with huge, grandiose ideas — only to have each one of them fizzle at the starting gate. Why? Lack of money, lack of planning, lack of foresight, and lack of appropriate stakeholders at the table on day one of forming their nonprofit organizations. This is why it's important to invite the right people to join your board and lead the organization from a flatline status to a soaring status.

A MISSION LOST IN TRANSITION

You know when you hear about a new nonprofit starting up and you look for their website to find out what they do, you become lost in trying to figure what they actually do. Their extra-long mission statement is lost in transition — it's rambling and unclear.

Here's an example of a rambling vision statement from the Good Food Society:

In the future, the Good Food Society **is** well known throughout the region as a fledging nonprofit that grew to gigantic proportions and increased its service population from a few hundred to hundreds of thousands. Our work **was** recognized by the United Nations and the World Health Organization. We **changed** the eating habits of unhealthy world populations by introducing them to good food choices. Our organization **is** at the forefront of the worldwide health-and-wellness movement. We **accomplished** our goals, **fulfilled** our mission, and **created** a path for other health-and-wellness organizations to follow and replicate. *We are the best of the best!*

(continued)

(continued)

Okay, what's wrong with this vision statement example? Almost *everything*.

Vision Statement Checklist

A projection of where your nonprofit organization will be in five years?	**No:** No year is specified.
Written in the future tense?	**No:** The words in bold font are in the past tense.
Directional?	**No:** The only direction here is backward thinking.
Audacious or bold?	**Yes:** Stating that "we are the best of the best" is a bold but questionable statement. (The "best of the best" at what?)

Here's the revised vision statement for the Good Food Society:

By 2026, the Good Food Society will be well known throughout the world. Our work will be recognized by the United Nations (UN) and the World Health Organization (WHO). We will change the eating habits of an unhealthy world population by introducing them to good food choices. Our organization will be at the forefront of the worldwide health-and-wellness movement. We will accomplish our goals, fulfill our mission, and create a path for other health-and-wellness organizations to follow and replicate. *We will be the best of the best in changing eating habits and restoring health by way of better food choices.*

Can you see the difference between the first and second vision statements? The revised statement may not be perfect, but it incorporates the organization's values, its long-term goals, its targeted beneficiaries, and a general method of accomplishing the goals — all the ingredients of an effective vision statement.

Inviting Stakeholders to the Planning Table

Who are the stakeholders who should be at the planning table for your mission and vision statements? Well, consider who has a vested interest in the creation of your nonprofit organization and its ability to be successful in the community.

>> **Governing board members:** The reason we urge you to form your governing board during the incorporation process is that those folks need to be involved in every step of your nonprofit organization's start-up process — including helping to craft the mission and vision statements.

>> **Staff:** If you bring on staff members early on, via donations or other monetary support, include them in development meetings for the mission and vision statements. The greatest way to attract buy-in to everything about the organization is to invite to the table for inclusion the people who have to carry out the mission and vision.

>> **Volunteers:** Embracing diversity begins with identifying volunteers who have stepped up when you had nothing except a dream. These are the dedicated group of individuals who asked how they could help and then rolled up their sleeves to help raise seed funding by manning yard sale tables and county fair exhibit booths. In all types of weather, these folks stood strong in handing out pamphlets and fliers to hundreds of attendees. Yes, bring them to the planning table. Solicit their input! Show them how much you trust their thoughts and service!

>> **Community partners:** Identify the organizations that opened their doors to you when you were asking for ideas about gaps in services. Remember the executive directors of the nonprofits who stepped up and offered meeting space, office supplies, copies of policies and procedures, and more. Yes, ask them to come to the planning table and participate in developing your mission and vision statements.

>> **Representatives from the target population you plan to serve:** How do you know about a need for your services in the community? Have you spoken to any of your targeted clients or organizations who already serve similar target populations?

Encouraging and embracing stakeholder input

Whether you're working with a newly formed nonprofit or a long-running institution, everyone in your stakeholder's group needs to agree on the mission and vision statements. We recommend holding a meeting to solicit their input. The biggest advantage to this kind of group activity is achieving full buy-in from everyone involved. After all, you want people to believe in and accept the organization's mission and vision statements. If they don't, they likely won't stick around to help uphold that mission and help you achieve your long-term vision statement (or they won't do a good job of upholding it while they're there).

TIP

For groups who are working to establish mission and vision statements for a new nonprofit organization, we recommend that you find an outside facilitator to guide the group through the inevitable discussions about priorities and the direction of the new organization. Finding a neutral person who can bring an outsider's perspective to the group's deliberations is extremely helpful. A facilitator also takes responsibility for managing the group so that you and your colleagues can be full participants in the meeting. If you aren't geographically near a *nonprofit support organization* (a nonprofit that helps other nonprofits with technical assistance), ask other nearby organizations for suggestions.

Bring a few prewritten suggestions to the group meeting. Present them as drafts and ask for feedback. Also, be open-minded to their input and suggested changes to your prewritten suggestions. After an initial discussion among the group, give each member index cards or sticky pads and have all of them write down three ideas they feel strongly about keeping as a part of the mission and vision statements.

After you collect everyone's written ideas, read them all aloud and — as a group — organize them so that similar ideas are grouped together. These notes should identify the key ideas that belong in your mission and vision statements. Also be sure to ask whether anyone thinks an important idea is missing. If not, you're ready to assign someone to draft the mission and vision statements.

Working together to finalize your statements

A group process is essential to identifying the core ideas that belong in the mission and vision statements, but when it comes to putting words on paper, we recommend that you choose two or three of your board members that are the best writers and turn them loose.

We aren't fans of committee-written prose. We've sat in meetings where committees discussed word choices and the placement of commas without apparent end. The result of such efforts is usually murky writing that requires several readings to interpret the meaning. After a draft is on paper, feel free to bring it back to your group for their final thoughts and approval on content, grammar, and word choice.

TIP

When finalizing the wording of your statements, the best advice we can offer is to stay away from jargon and flowery rhetoric. Avoid the buzzwords that are popular in your field. In fact, this is good advice for any kind of writing — grant proposals, memos, letters, and other documents. You don't want your audience scratching their heads and wondering, "What does that mean?"

Living by Your Mission and Staying Fixed on the Vision

You've brainstormed, drafted, and refined a short mission statement and a longer vision statement that clearly identify your organization's present and future focus. Congratulations! Now that you've put considerable thought and time into this exercise, what will you do with it?

You'll use your mission statement in practical ways, of course. For instance, you'll likely

>> Incorporate its description of the organization's purpose in your articles of incorporation (see Chapter 5)

>> Add it to brochures, your website, and other marketing materials (see Chapter 13)

>> Use it to help complete IRS Form 990 — the tax statement you file in one form or another every year (see Chapter 6)

You'll also use your vision statement as a guiding written light to keep your eyes on the organization's future. For instance, you'll likely use it to

>> Establish the ideal state that the leaders of your nonprofit organization want to achieve.

>> Inspire and remind members where you're going as an organization.

>> Keep new and existing staff and volunteers focused on what's ahead.

>> Motivate yourself and others to work hard today to plant the seeds for tomorrow.

Your mission and vision statements also resemble the pin that holds the needle of a compass. You use them to chart your organization's direction. Here are some examples:

>> When you have to make a decision about creating new programs or setting priorities, your mission statement should guide you in whether they're appropriate for your organization. Remember to ask aloud to your stakeholders: "Will this decision help us achieve our vision statement?"

>> When your board and staff sit down to create a new three-year plan, they first need to revisit and commit to the mission statement (the present) and vision statement (the future). All other discussions about setting goals and refining programs should be tested for appropriateness against these statements.

>> When you need to cut your budget and eliminate programs or activities, the mission statement should guide you to protect those programs that are core to your organization's purpose and vision.

» Writing your organization's articles of incorporation

» Applying for an employer identification number (EIN)

» Creating bylaws — the rules of your nonprofit

» Scheduling board meetings

» Applying for IRS tax exemption

Chapter **5**

Incorporating and Applying for Tax-Exemption Status

I f you want to provide programs and services as a nonprofit organization, you must set up the legal structure for your organization and apply for its tax exemption. This process usually consists of forming a nonprofit corporation under the laws of your state and then submitting an online application to the Internal Revenue Service (IRS), requesting that your organization be recognized as tax-exempt. You must take care of these tasks, which require attention to detail and ample planning, before you can begin to fulfill your mission.

REMEMBER

In this chapter, we provide you with a guide to the incorporation-and-exemption process for a 501(c)(3) public charity. We also give you suggestions about where you can go for help. Keep in mind that we aren't attorneys and that the information in this chapter isn't meant to serve as legal advice. Although many nonprofits are formed without the aid of legal counsel, we think that consulting an attorney is a good idea, even if it's only to review your work. After all, you're taking on legal responsibilities. Why not be certain that you've done everything right?

Check out File 5-1 for a list of web resources related to the topics we cover in this chapter. Also, for quick reference, we've put together a checklist for forming a nonprofit organization — check out File 5-2. Both files are available at www.wiley.com/go/nonprofitkitfd6e.

TIP

Creating a New Entity: The Nonprofit Corporation

In almost all cases, the first legal step in creating a nonprofit organization is forming a corporation. A *corporation* is an entity that has legal standing. It's established by a group of individuals — the incorporators — under the laws of the state or territory in which it's formed.

TECHNICAL STUFF

We say the first step is forming a corporation "in almost all cases" because exceptions do exist. In the United States and its territories, for example, associations, trusts, and sometimes limited liability companies (LLCs) can operate as tax-exempt nonprofit organizations. And charitable groups with less than $5,000 in annual revenues, as well as churches, aren't required to apply for tax exemption. In this chapter, we focus on the most common legal structure for nonprofit organizations: the corporation.

One advantage of creating a corporation is that the individuals who govern and work for it are separate from the abstract entity they create. Although board members can be held liable for the corporation's actions if they don't exercise their duties and responsibilities carefully, in most cases, corporations protect individuals from personal liability. So you can think of a corporation as separate from the people who start it, because, well, it is.

REMEMBER

When you establish a corporation, you're creating something that's expected to continue in perpetuity. In other words, the corporation you create goes on living after you decide to do something else or after your death. Corporations can be closed or dissolved, but you must take legal steps to do so. You can't just take down your shingle and walk away.

Following your state's or territory's laws

In the United States and its territories, corporations are created and regulated under the laws of the state or territory in which they're formed. Although the way a corporation is formed from state to state and from territory to territory has more similarities than differences, you do need to create your nonprofit so that it conforms to the peculiarities of your state or territory. Some states and territories, for example, require a minimum of three members on a board of directors; others require only one. (Flip to Chapters 3 and 7 for more information about boards of directors and their roles.)

The best way to find information about incorporating in your state or territory is to do a web search using the phrase *incorporating nonprofit corporation in <your state or territory>*. Usually, the secretary of state's office or the territory's office of public accountability handles incorporations. Some states and territories have an incorporation package that includes samples of the formation documents you need to file. You also can find state and territory contact information on the IRS website at www.irs.gov.

Understanding the required governing documents

Think of a corporation as a tiny government with a constitution and laws. To set down the rules under which the organization will operate, you need to prepare the following important documents:

>> **Articles of incorporation:** The *articles of incorporation* (in some states and territories, called the *certificate of incorporation*) make up the document that creates the organization. It names the organization and describes its reason for existence. In the case of a nonprofit corporation, it specifies that the corporation not be used to create profit for its directors. The articles are signed by the corporation's incorporators — usually, three people — or its initial directors.

>> **Bylaws:** A corporation's *bylaws* typically specify how directors are elected and the length of their terms, the officers and their duties, the number of meetings to be held, whether to have voting or nonvoting members, the rules for director attendance at board meetings, and the process by which the bylaws may be amended. The bylaws also typically specify how many members or directors are required to be in attendance to form a *quorum* (the minimum number of people required to attend a meeting so that official business can be conducted — often, a simple majority of members or directors). The bylaws also may list the standing committees of the board and grant or limit particular powers of the directors.

REMEMBER

As you draft these documents (see the later sections "Writing the Articles of Incorporation" and "Writing Your Organization's Bylaws" for more specific information about writing them), you're creating the legal rules under which your nonprofit will operate. You can change your articles of incorporation and bylaws by following the laws of your state or territory (in the case of articles of incorporation) and, if applicable, the rules described in the bylaws.

Deciding whether to have members in your corporation

Corporations may have members. In fact, they may even have different classes of members — voting and nonvoting, for example. Generally speaking, though, having voting members in your corporation adds responsibilities to the governance of the organization. If you have voting members, for instance, you need to have membership meetings, probably at least one per year, and involve the voting members in choosing directors for the organization.

It's important to determine how new board members join the board. Many times, if the membership votes for board members, it becomes a personality contest with the person who knows the most people winning a board position. It's difficult for the board to recruit members with the needed skills if the members are the ones voting for them. Plus, reverting from a membership organization to one in which the existing board elects their new members is difficult to do with hoops to be jumped through to prove the voting process was legally conducted.

TIP

Depending on state or territory law, you usually have the option to create membership conditions in either the articles or the bylaws. If you have a choice, we recommend adding these conditions to the bylaws, which are easier to amend than the articles of incorporation.

We *don't* advise having voting members, because it adds work and responsibilities to satisfy the obligations to these individuals. However, you may want to involve as many people in your organization as possible, such as a neighborhood-improvement group, and having members is one way to achieve this goal.

REMEMBER

Many nonprofit organizations have members who receive membership cards and special rates on admissions to performances or exhibits. Don't confuse this kind of membership, which is a marketing-and-fundraising strategy, with statutory membership in a corporation. You're free to start a membership program of this type without amending your bylaws or your articles of incorporation. (See Chapter 14 for more information about creating a fundraising plan.)

Finding the best name

Choosing a name for your new corporation may be one of the most important things you do as you set it up. A nonprofit's name is a little like a mission statement. (See Chapter 4 for more on mission statements.) Like the mission statement, your organization's name needs to suggest the types of programs and services you offer and the people you serve.

So, if your programs provide services for homeless people over 65, don't name your nonprofit something generic, like Services for the Elderly. Also stay away from names that are so abstract they have no meaning. A name like The Renewal Society prompts more questions than it answers. What or who is being renewed? How are clients being renewed — and why? Instead, use concrete, descriptive terms.

WARNING

To avoid possible embarrassment, check the acronym that results from your organization's name. The Community Reinvestment Act Program Project, for example, isn't a title you want to abbreviate on your letterhead. After all, we don't know many people who'd want to associate with the CRAPP organization.

Also be careful that you don't select a name that's easily confused with that of another organization. Before you decide on a name, do a web search to see whether any other companies or organizations already have that name. The state or territory agencies that accept your application for incorporation have procedures for ensuring that two corporations in your state or territory don't end up with exactly the same name. However, these procedures can't help you uncover organizations with the same name in other states and territories, or with names that are similar and might be confused with your name. To help ensure that you pick a distinctive name, you may want to include the name of the city or region where your organization is located — Mohave County Transitional Housing Program, for example.

You also can search the Trademark Electronic Search System (TESS) found at www. uspto.gov to determine whether the name you have chosen is trademarked by another organization. If you want, you can register your own trademark with the federal government and with the state or territory in which you incorporate.

If you incorporate your organization under one name and then decide that you aren't happy with it, you can amend the incorporation papers you filed with the state or territory. Often, however, organizations find it easier to register another name as a DBA, or *doing business as*, entity. The original corporate name continues to be your organization's legal name, but you can use the DBA name on your letterhead, annual reports, and press releases — everywhere except legal documents. A county or other local government office usually handles this type of transaction. Check your local laws for more information.

Writing the Articles of Incorporation

For this section, we assume that you have the articles of incorporation papers you need from the appropriate state office. Your state office may even have provided sample articles of incorporation and instructions about how to prepare your own. Pay close attention to the instructions, and follow them step-by-step. The whole process may be as simple as filling in the blanks. Although you can amend articles of incorporation, it requires filing additional forms and paying more fees, so you may as well spend time getting them right the first time.

In this section, we give you some general guidance on drafting your articles. However, note that the sample articles we include here may not coincide exactly with your state's requirements.

TIP

IRS Publication 557 contains information about the language needed in the articles of incorporation, along with some sample articles. You can download this publication from the IRS website at www.irs.gov/pub/irs-pdf/p557.pdf.

Crafting a heading

You must put a heading on your articles so that people can identify them. The heading should read something like this:

Articles of Incorporation of the Paseo Village Workforce Development Initiative, Inc.

Sometimes you're required to add a short paragraph after the heading, stating that the incorporators adopt the following articles under the [cite the state code number under which you're filing] of [give the state name].

Article I

You insert the name you worked so hard to choose here in Article I. Simply write a sentence like this one:

The name of the corporation is the Paseo Village Workforce Development Initiative, Inc.

Could it be any easier than that?

Article II

Some states require that you affirm that your corporation is *perpetual* (meaning it's intended to exist forever). If your state requires that affirmation, put it in Article II. You can include a statement like this:

This corporation shall exist in perpetuity unless dissolved.

However, chances are good that the state will give you the language to use, if it's needed.

Article III

Article III is a good place to state the organization's purpose. This article is probably the most important because state authorities and the IRS review it to determine whether your organization qualifies as a charitable entity.

Remember that 501(c)(3) organizations must be organized for a charitable, religious, educational, literary, or scientific purpose or another qualifying exempt purpose. (See Chapter 2 for more on various classes of nonprofits.) You've already created your mission statement, right? If so, stating the purpose shouldn't be too difficult. (If you haven't created your statement yet, check out Chapter 4.) Using the Paseo Village Workforce Development Initiative as an example, your purpose may look like this:

This corporation is established to provide workforce-entry soft and hard skills for chronically unemployed individuals residing in Paseo Village. We will work with public agencies and nonprofit organizations in our region to provide 360-degree wraparound services for our participants.

This article also must include a statement of exempt purpose under the IRS code, as in this example:

This corporation is organized and operated exclusively for charitable purposes, within the meaning of Section 501(c)(3) of the Internal Revenue Code or any corresponding section of any future federal tax code.

You must state that no proceeds of the corporation will enrich any individual, except that reasonable compensation may be paid in exchange for services to the corporation. Finally, in this article, you must note that if the corporation is dissolved, any assets remaining will be distributed to another corporation that serves a similar purpose and qualifies as a tax-exempt, charitable organization under the provisions of 501(c)(3) of the Internal Revenue Code. You don't need to identify a particular nonprofit corporation; you just need to affirm that assets will be distributed to one serving a purpose similar to yours.

Article III may be the most critical for getting your nonprofit corporation established and, ultimately, approved for tax exemption by the IRS. If your state or territory doesn't provide good examples of the language required in this article, ask a lawyer about the requirements in your state or territory.

Article IV

All articles of incorporation identify the name and address of an *agent of the corporation,* someone to whom mail can be addressed. This address is considered the address of the corporation until changed. Include the person's name and street address. Post office boxes aren't allowed to be used as addresses.

The agent of the corporation doesn't need to be a director or an incorporator of the corporation. This person can even be your attorney.

Article V

If you have initial directors, put their names and addresses in Article V. Most nonprofits start with three initial directors. If you're incorporating in a state or territory that requires only one director, we still recommend having three. Because nonprofit organizations are formed to provide public benefit, demonstrating that several people are involved as volunteers may strengthen your application to the IRS for tax-exempt status.

Article VI

In Article VI, you list the incorporators' names and addresses. *Incorporator* simply refers to the person who is, or people who are, creating the corporation. Often, the incorporators and the initial directors are one and the same. Again, whether you need one or more depends on your state requirements.

Article VII

If you want your corporation to have members, you define the qualifications for membership in Article VII. You can define classes of membership — voting and nonvoting, for instance. If you don't want members, all you have to say is, "This corporation has no members." Better yet, refer the question to your bylaws, which are easier to amend if you change your mind. If that's what you decide to do, you can use this language:

Membership provisions of this corporation are defined in the bylaws.

REMEMBER

Corporate members aren't the same as the subscribers to a PBS station or the members of a science center or historical society, for example. Members of a corporation have the right to participate in governing the organization.

Article VIII

You may not need an Article VIII in your articles of incorporation. Some forms have a blank space here to add provisions. We don't recommend adding any unless you're sure you know what you're doing. Maybe your group is adamant that all future directors must be elected by 85 percent of the membership. Such a provision probably would ensure that you'd never elect new directors, but who knows? Use this blank space cautiously.

Signed, sealed, and delivered

After you finish writing your articles of incorporation, you must have the incorporator(s) sign them. In some states and territories, you need three incorporators; in others, you need only one. If the articles need to be notarized, the signatures must be added in the presence of a notary public.

Most states and territories charge a fee for filing for incorporation. If your state or territory requires a fee, include a check or money order with the articles and any other required forms, and then mail everything to the appropriate state or territory office. Usually, you mail only the original articles to the state or territory office, but sometimes a state or territory office requires one or more additional copies.

Your next step is to wait. It's hard to say how long the response will take — it depends on the efficiency of the state or territory offices and the volume of incorporation papers it receives. For a surcharge, some states and territories offer an opportunity to expedite processing.

WARNING

Simply creating a nonprofit corporation doesn't make your organization tax-exempt. You also need recognition from the IRS (see the section "Applying for Tax Exemption" later in this chapter) before your nonprofit is a "real" nonprofit. You may need to complete a tax-exempt application in your state or territory, too.

If your articles are in order and your corporate name passes muster (meaning that no other organization in the state or territory has the same name), you receive a certified copy of the articles, stamped with an official seal. Guard this piece of paper as if it were gold. Make copies and put the original away for safekeeping in a fireproof box. You've taken the first step toward starting your nonprofit. Congratulations!

Securing Your Employer Identification Number (EIN)

The first thing to do after you complete your incorporation is to apply to the IRS for an *employer identification number*, or EIN. Even if you don't plan to hire employees anytime soon, you need this number for your application for tax exemption and for all your state, territory, and federal reports. The EIN is similar to a social security number for organizations — it's attached to your nonprofit forever.

Getting an EIN is easy and free. All you have to do is submit IRS Form SS-4. You can either download and print the form from www.irs.gov or complete the online application. As IRS forms go, this one is simple and straightforward and only one page long. If you apply online, we recommend that you download Form SS-4 beforehand to get an idea of the questions you have to answer.

WARNING

Choose only one method to apply for your EIN. Don't mail IRS Form SS-4 and apply online. You may end up with two EINs — a confusing situation for everyone.

REMEMBER

The name of the applicant isn't your name — it's the name of your new organization. As with the incorporation papers, you need to identify an individual as the principal officer and include that person's social security number on the form. Here are some of the other items you need to fill out, line by line:

>> **Line 9:** If your organization is a church or church-controlled organization, select that check box in Section 9a. If it's not, select the Other Nonprofit Organization check box. Specify what sort of nonprofit organization you have — in most cases, Charitable is sufficient. In Section 9b, fill in the state or territory where your organization is incorporated.

>> **Line 10:** Most likely, your reason for applying for an EIN on Line 10 is "started a new business."

>> **Line 11:** On Line 11, the date (month, day, and year) specified on your incorporation papers is the date the business was started.

>> **Line 12:** This line asks for the closing month of your organization's accounting (fiscal) year. Many organizations choose June 30 as the end of the fiscal year. December 31 (the same as the calendar year) is also popular. It's up to you. (See the later section "Dealing with financial information" for more on the fiscal year.)

>> **Lines 13 and 14:** These lines relate to the number of employees you intend to hire and your expected payroll tax liabilities over the coming 12 months. You can enter 0 and No if your organization has no plans to hire staff in the year

ahead. If you do intend to hire people for whom you have to pay payroll taxes, you need to check the IRS withholding tables (www.irs.gov) and estimate the amount of payroll taxes you will owe the IRS.

>> **Line 16:** This line asks you to select the check box that describes your organization's principal activity. You can check the Other option here, but try to be a little more specific when describing your activities in the blank space. You may say *Charitable — Arts,* for example.

The IRS estimates that you'll receive your EIN in four to five weeks if you apply by mail. You receive your EIN immediately if you submit the online application.

Writing Your Organization's Bylaws

Bylaws are the rules by which your organization operates. As with articles of incorporation, different states have different requirements about what must be included in the bylaws, so make sure you contact the appropriate agency in your state or territory to find general guidance about the information you need.

In general, bylaws guide the activities of your organization and the procedures of your board of directors — how many directors, how long they serve, how they're elected, what constitutes a quorum, and so on. Like the articles of incorporation, bylaws are divided into articles. However, because bylaws require more detail, the articles themselves are divided into sections (and subsections, if needed) to address various aspects of the articles.

REMEMBER

You can always change bylaws by following the rules you have set up for your organization in the bylaws.

If you were to review the bylaws of ten different organizations, you'd find variation in the order in which articles are presented. For example, you may find the board of directors specified in Article III or Article V. Bylaws also vary in how specifically they spell out what's required. Some bylaws specify the number and type of standing committees; others give the board president the responsibility of making those specifications. If you don't address a particular question in your bylaws — setting a quorum, for example — most states have a default position in their code that applies to the governing of nonprofit corporations.

TIP

Check out File 5-3 at www.wiley.com/go/nonprofitkitfd6e for a general guide to creating bylaws for your new nonprofit.

Holding Your First Board Meeting

Your organization's first board meeting is more or less a formality, but documenting it is important because it officially kicks off your new nonprofit corporation. If you've named directors in your articles of incorporation, each one should be present at the meeting. You should adopt the bylaws and then elect officers. You may also want to ratify the actions of the incorporator (including adopting the articles and appointing the board), adopt a conflict-of-interest policy, adopt the accounting year, and approve the reimbursement of expenses of anybody who provided the initial monies to incorporate. It's also important to pass a resolution authorizing the board or its designate to open the necessary bank accounts. You need a copy of this resolution to open an account.

Prepare minutes of the meeting and keep them with your articles of incorporation. We say more about keeping records in a later chapter, but now is a good time to start a cloud-based *board book* — a digital folder containing a copy of your articles of incorporation, your bylaws, and the minutes of your first board meeting and every board meeting to follow. If your board meetings will be virtual, save every recording and label it with the date of the meeting — for example, Paseo Village Board Meeting 4-14-22. Also be sure to upload a copy of the letter of determination that acknowledges your organization as tax-exempt when you receive it from the IRS. See the next section for how to apply for tax exemption.

Applying for Tax Exemption

The final step in becoming a tax-exempt charitable organization is to apply for tax exemption from the IRS.

REMEMBER

Keep in mind that *tax-exempt* doesn't mean you're exempt from *all* taxes. You don't have to pay taxes on the organization's income from its charitable activities, and donors who contribute to your 501(c)(3) organization can claim a tax deduction. But if your nonprofit employs staff, it does have to pay payroll taxes like any other employer. And your liability for sales and property taxes depends on your state, territory, and local laws. If your nonprofit has income that's unrelated to its charitable purpose, you're required to pay taxes on that revenue as well.

To apply for tax exemption, you need to request what's known as a *determination letter* or *ruling* — a letter from the IRS stating that it has determined that your organization qualifies as a tax-exempt organization under the applicable sections of the IRS code. You send copies of this letter to foundations, government agencies, and state and territory tax authorities — in short, to anyone to whom you need to prove that your nonprofit organization is indeed tax-exempt.

WHO DOESN'T NEED TO APPLY FOR TAX-EXEMPT STATUS

If your organization is a church, a church auxiliary, or an association of churches, you don't need to apply for tax-exempt status. Also, if your nonprofit had gross receipts of less than $5,000 in any previous year in which you operated, and if you don't expect your revenue to grow beyond this limit, you aren't required to submit an application.

Keep in mind that you still may apply for tax exemption even though you aren't required to do so. Having a determination letter from the IRS acknowledging your tax-exempt status has some benefits. For example, you need to show proof of your exemption to receive a bulk mail permit from the US Postal Service. The determination letter also serves as a public acknowledgment that contributions to your organization are deductible to the donor. If you hope to receive foundation grants, your organization should be recognized as tax-exempt by the IRS as well.

REMEMBER

Be sure to check with your state or territory about what you need to do to register your nonprofit as a tax-exempt organization. Registration and reporting requirements vary from state to state and from territory to territory. Chances are good that you received this information when you contacted your state or territory office to begin your incorporation process; if you didn't, contact the appropriate state or territory government office for more details. You can find contact information on the IRS website at www.irs.gov or by searching the web for the appropriate office in your state or territory.

You request tax-exempt status by submitting IRS Form 1023 (Application for Recognition of Exemption) or IRS Form 1023-EZ to the IRS. You can download the form at www.irs.gov or apply online. Be sure to download the form's instructions at the same time and read the next section, "Tackling Form 1023 online."

Tackling Form 1023 online

As of January 31, 2020, the IRS requires that Form 1023 Application for Recognition of Exemption Under Section 501(c)(3) of the Internal Revenue Code, be completed online and submitted by way of Pay.gov.

You can check out Form 1023 long form at www.irs.gov/pub/irs-pdf/f1023.pdf.

You can opt to fill out the online form on your own or retain the services of an attorney who specializes in nonprofit law to fill out the online form and submit it on behalf of your nonprofit organization.

TIP

Read the instructions carefully at www.irs.gov/instructions/i1023. The instructions for Form 1023 provide various schedules that you may need to fill in and submit if you're applying as a church or school, for example (see the following schedules list for more info). If a schedule isn't required for your type of nonprofit, don't submit a blank one. Toss it into the round file (also known as the trash can).

Here's a list of the schedules and the types of entities they apply to:

Section A: Church organizations

Section B: Schools, colleges, universities

Schedule C: Hospitals, medical research organizations

Schedule D: Section 509(a)(30) supporting organizations, for organizations whose sole purpose is to support one or more public charities

Schedule E: Effective date, reserved for organizations that haven't filed a Form 1023 within 27 months of formation

Schedule F: Low-income housing, which includes handicapped and elderly tenants

Schedule G: Successors to other organizations

Schedule H: Organizations providing scholarships, fellowships, educational loans, or other education grants to individuals and private foundations requesting advance approval of individual grant procedures

TIP

Your organization may be eligible to submit an electronic 1023-EZ application. The good news is that the application is only three pages long. The 1023-EZ is a streamlined version of the regular Form 1023. The filing fee is lower (as of May 2021, the fee is $275 for the 1023-EZ and $600 for the regular 1023). Plus, the IRS processes the EZ forms much faster than the regular form. Processing time for the long form can take six months or longer, while you will typically hear back on an EZ application in two to four weeks. Organizations can file using the 1023-EZ application if

» Gross income has been under $50,000 for the past three years and estimated gross income will be less than $50,000 for the next three years

» Fair market value of assets for the nonprofit is under $250,000

» The nonprofit is formed in the United States and has a US mailing address

Check out IRS Form 1023-EZ at www.irs.gov/pub/irs-pdf/f1023ez.pdf.

Discerning between public charities and private foundations

Public charities and private foundations are both 501(c)(3) organizations (see Chapter 2 for more on these types of organizations), but you need to know the important differences between them before you begin completing the application for tax exemption.

REMEMBER

Private foundations have different reporting requirements from public charities and may be required to pay excise taxes on their investment income. Contributions to private foundations are deductible but are subject to lower deduction limits.

One important factor the IRS determines based on your application is whether your organization is classified as a public charity or a private foundation. Part VIII of the Pay.gov version of Form 1023 addresses this question. Please read the questions and options carefully, and answer or check the ones that fit your newly formed nonprofit organization. If your nonprofit will carry out charitable acts and seek grant funding, check public charity. However, if you are forming a self-serving family type of nonprofit, check private foundation. It's important to note that the tax codes changed in 2020 and now require that a 501(c)(3) private foundation contribute 5% of its gross revenue to eligible 501(c)(3) public charities annually and maintain contribution records.

Establishing public charity status

The IRS applies several measures to determine whether an organization is a public charity. Generally, for a nonprofit to be considered a public charity, it must receive one-third of its revenues from public sources. It's complicated, and we can't cover all the nuances and technicalities here. But, fundamentally, it comes down to how much of your organizational income you receive from the public.

A 501(c)(3) nonprofit organization wanting to be considered a public charity undergoes what's referred to as the *public support test*. To pass this test, the nonprofit needs to demonstrate, over a 5-year average, that one-third of its revenue comes from contributions from the general public, support from government agencies, or grants from organizations that receive their support from the public, such as United Way. So, if your organization's average revenue is $60,000 per year and at least $20,000 a year comes from donations, state grants, and support from United Way, you're home free. Your nonprofit is considered a public charity under code sections 509(a)(1) and 170(b)(1)(A)(vi).

What if your organization doesn't receive a third of its revenue? Fortunately, it may be able to qualify under another test that provides more leeway on the percentage of public support. Under this test, only 10 percent of total revenue needs to come from those public categories. But your organization also must demonstrate that it has an ongoing fundraising program that's reaching out to the public for more donations. Other factors also are considered. If the nonprofit's contributions come in the form of many small gifts rather than a few large ones, it's more likely to be given public charity status. It's even better if your organization's board of directors is broadly representative of the community. And, if the organization makes its facility available to the general public, that's another feather in its cap.

REMEMBER

A 501(c)(3) organization that expects to receive a substantial portion of its revenues from fees related to its exempt purpose (but less than one-third of revenues from investment income) may qualify as a public charity under code section 501(a)(2).

When you reach Part VII of Form 1023 online at Pay.gov, you need to select a check box indicating which public charity classification you seek. Take schools as an example. To apply as a school, you have to submit Schedule B. Your school must provide regular instruction and have a student body and a faculty. In other words, you can't just start an organization and call it a school.

TECHNICAL STUFF

Every IRS rule has an exception or two, and qualifying as a public charity is, well, no exception. Churches, schools, hospitals, public-safety testing organizations, and a few others are automatically considered public charities. If you have an intense interest in this rule, read Chapter 3 of IRS Publication 557, which is available at www.irs.gov/pub/irs-pdf/p557.pdf. If you think your organization falls into one of these categories, select the appropriate check box in Part VII and answer the questions on the appropriate schedule included with Form 1023. But we don't recommend doing so unless you're absolutely certain that you know what you're doing. If you need further advice regarding these categories, we suggest that you consult an attorney.

WARNING

When you start working on Form 1023 online, be sure to review any IRS regulation change notices, which describe new regulations and new instructions. Sometimes, revisions to IRS forms lag behind changes in the regulations. Always be certain you're working with the most recent information.

Describing your activities

In Part IV of IRS Form 1023, you need to enter responses in each text box to describe your charitable activities and how you plan to carry them out. You must provide more detail here than you have in your articles of incorporation or in your mission statement. The IRS wants you to include what you're going to do in order of importance, approximately what percentage of time you'll devote to each activity, and how each activity fulfills your charitable purpose.

REMEMBER

When you fill out this form, chances are good that you haven't started operating yet, so you're simply listing *proposed* activities. If you've created an organizational plan (which we recommend), refer to the plan to make sure you cover all your activities. (Refer to Chapter 8 for help with planning.) If you've been operating your organization, explain what you've been doing and how it relates to your charitable purpose.

A nonprofit that provides cultural opportunities for low-income children may say something like this in Part IV:

> *The charitable purpose of Explore Community Culture is to provide cultural experiences to low-income children residing in the City of Maxwell's public housing complexes. Our nonprofit promotes and delivers its services in the following ways:*
>
> *The primary activity will be to provide tickets, transportation, and supervision for small group field trip experiences to ten cultural institutions located in Merriweather County (Idaho). Parents can attend with their child(ren) and benefit from their first-time cultural experience. Grants will be applied for to support this major portion of our nonprofit organization. (60 percent)*
>
> *Explore Community Culture will maintain a website that provides participation information, parent or caregiver permission forms, and a calendar of annual visitations to cultural institutions in Merriweather County. (20 percent)*
>
> *Screened and trained volunteers will accompany parents/caregivers and their child(ren) on each trip using donated transportation services from our local school district. Trip insurance will be covered by the district. Commercial liability and injury insurance will be covered under the administrative expense line item of our projected annual budget. Corporate donations will also be solicited to pay for the insurance policies needed. (20 percent)*

You're asked more questions about your specific activities in Part IV of Form 1023, including, for example, how and where you intend to raise funds, whether you operate a bingo game or other gaming activities, and the extent of your involvement with foreign countries and organizations. Answering yes to these and other questions in Part IV means that you must attach explanations.

In Part IV, you're also asked whether your organization will attempt to influence legislation. If you answer yes, you're given an opportunity to elect Section 501(h) of the IRS code by filing IRS Form 5768. If you do so, your organization's expenses for allowable lobbying activities are measured by a percentage of your revenue. Chapter 6 has more information about this subject.

Reporting salaries and conflicts of interest

The IRS revises its forms from time to time. In the past few years, Form 1023 has been revised to include more questions about staff salary levels, board member compensation, and business and family relationships of board members and staff. If you pay or plan to pay any staff member or consultant more than $50,000 per year, you need to report this fact. If you compensate or plan to compensate members of your board, you also have to share that information on Form 1023.

WARNING

If you plan to compensate employees, directors, or consultants with *nonfixed payments* — that is, bonuses or revenue-based compensation — be prepared to describe these arrangements in detail.

You're also asked whether the organization has a conflict-of-interest policy and whether compensation has or will be set by comparing salaries of your staff to salaries of similar organizations. Although the IRS claims that these practices aren't required in order to obtain a tax exemption, they are recommended. The instructions for Form 1023 contain a sample conflict-of-interest policy statement. We suggest having your board adopt a policy of this type based on the IRS model that also is consistent with your state's laws.

Part IV is clearly a reaction to increased public and legislative concern about financial abuse and self-dealing in both the nonprofit and business sectors. We say more about the increased scrutiny aimed at the nonprofit sector in Chapter 6. Keep in mind that nonprofits are, in a sense, quasi-public organizations because the government is granting them special status as tax-exempt organizations.

Dealing with financial information

The IRS wants to see financial information. (Surprise, surprise.) New organizations have to estimate their income and expenses for three years — the current year and two years following. Making financial projections sends shivers down the spines of many folks, but it's not that difficult. Ideally, you've made plans for your nonprofit already, and you can take the figures from your organizational plan. If you haven't written a plan, now is a good time to do so. See Chapter 8 for planning information, and Chapter 12 for help in creating a budget.

REMEMBER

When you estimate your income, keep in mind the requirements for qualifying as a public charity. (Check out the earlier section "Establishing public charity status" for details.) Diverse sources of income are important, for qualifying as a public charity and ensuring the stability of your nonprofit.

You also need to choose your annual accounting period, usually referred to as the *fiscal year*. It can be any 12-month period you desire. Most organizations choose as their fiscal year either the calendar year (January 1 through December 31) or the period from July 1 to June 30. Most government agencies operate on a fiscal year from July 1 through June 30, and nonprofits that garner support from government grants and contracts often prefer to operate on the same schedule. Some organizations offering services to schools set the fiscal year to correspond with the academic year. But the choice is yours — you can set your fiscal year from November 1 through October 31, if you want.

Your first accounting period doesn't need to be a full 12 months — in fact, it probably won't be. If you form your organization in September and select a calendar year as the fiscal year, your first accounting period covers only four months, from September through December. If you do decide to begin with a short first year, don't forget to file Form 1023 at the appropriate time to report your activities during that period.

TIP

If you have an accountant, seek advice about the best accounting period for your organization. Remember that your fiscal year determines when future reports are due to the IRS and also when you prepare year-end financial reports for your board of directors. The annual 990 report (see Chapter 6) is due, for example, 4½ months after the close of your fiscal year. So, if your fiscal year is the same as the calendar year, the report is due on May 15. If you always spend early May traveling to the Caribbean, you may want to pick another accounting period.

Collecting the other materials

In addition to the completed tax-exemption application, you need to submit as attachments *conformed* (exact and certified) copies of your articles of incorporation and the certificate of incorporation, if your state provides one. You also need to submit the articles of incorporation and bylaws of your corporation, but remember that bylaws alone don't qualify as an *organizing document,* as do the articles of incorporation.

TECHNICAL STUFF

Every nonprofit applying for tax exemption must have an organizing document. Usually, this document is the articles of incorporation because most nonprofit organizations are incorporated. However, in the United States, associations, trusts, and, in some cases, limited liability companies, also may apply for tax-exempt status. An organizing document for an association may be the articles of association or a constitution; a trust is usually organized by a trust indenture or deed.

Put your organization's name, address, and EIN on each attachment and specify the section of the application that each attachment refers to. [The earlier section "Securing Your Employer Identification Number (EIN)" provides more details on obtaining your organization's number.]

Paying the fee

The fee for filing IRS Form 1023 is $600 for organizations that have had or antic-ipate having revenue of more than $10,000 per year. If your organization has been operating without a tax exemption and has income of $10,000 or less per year, or if you anticipate having revenues of $10,000 or less per year in the future, the fee is set at $275.

Navigating possible contribution barriers until tax-exemption status is approved

After you file your tax-exemption application, your organization is in never-never land for a while. You don't have your exemption yet. Although making an accurate prediction is difficult, the IRS can take between two and six months to act on your application. The process may take longer if the application is queried or rejected because of errors.

During this period, your organization can operate and even solicit contributions, assuming that you've registered with the appropriate state agency. However, you must tell donors that you've applied for a tax exemption and are waiting to hear from the IRS. Assuming that your application is approved, if you submitted Form 1023 and the other required materials to the IRS within 27 months from the time you established the organization, your tax-exempt status is retroactive to the date of incorporation. Another option is to use a fiscal sponsor during this period. (See Chapter 2 for information about using and finding fiscal sponsors.)

If your organization had been operating for a longer period before you submitted Form 1023, the exemption may be retroactive only to the date on which you submitted the application. In this case, you also need to include Schedule E with your application.

TIP

Check with your state or territory officials to find out what steps you need to take to have your tax exemption recognized by your state's or territory's government. If you didn't receive this information when you incorporated your organization, you can find contact information for the appropriate state or territory office by performing a web search.

Chapter **6**

Adhering to Nonprofit Status Requirements

Nonprofits are private organizations, but because they are awarded special tax status and are acting on behalf of the public, they're required to disclose more information than privately held for-profit companies. Nonprofit status is a privilege that requires due diligence in all areas of government expectations. The IRS determines whether your nonprofit is authorized to be a public charity.

One way to think about it is to compare nonprofits to companies that sell shares of stock to the public. These companies must follow the rules and regulations set forth by the Securities and Exchange Commission (SEC) about disclosing financial information. Nonprofits in the United States and its territories must follow the rules of the Internal Revenue Service (IRS) to make financial information available for public scrutiny. In some cases, state, territory, and local governments also have disclosure rules.

Your nonprofit organization can get into trouble with authorities in a few ways. However, keeping your nonprofit status isn't difficult if you follow the rules. This chapter lays out the reporting requirements that you need to follow and some pitfalls to avoid in order to maintain your 501(c)(3) public charity status. (See Chapter 2 for more on 501(c)(3) organizations.)

We don't aim to scare you! Just keep good financial records and stick to your mission, and you'll be fine. (In case you're wondering, the IRS recommends that nonprofit organizations *permanently* keep annual reports to the secretary of state or attorney general, articles of incorporation, board meeting and board committee minutes, board policies and resolutions, and bylaws.)

Check out File 6-1 at www.wiley.com/go/nonprofitkitfd6e for a list of web resources related to the topics we cover in this chapter.

Disclosing What You Need to Disclose

Disclose is a funny word, isn't it? It seems to imply that you're hiding something that must be pried from your clutches. Don't think of it that way. The IRS regulations that lay out the rules for disclosure refer to "the public inspection of information." That's much more genteel. In this section, we briefly cover what you are and aren't expected to disclose to the public.

Note: The information provided in this section is about 501(c)(3) organizations that are considered public charities. If your organization is a private foundation, special disclosure rules apply. Check with the Council on Foundations (www.cof.org) about disclosure requirements.

What you do need to show

What information must be disclosed to the public? (Sorry, we can't help ourselves. We like the word.) It's simple, really. Your three most recent filings of IRS Form 990 and your IRS Form 1023 application for tax exemption and supporting documents — if you filed for your exemption after July 15, 1987 — must all be available to the public.

If you have a question that this chapter doesn't cover, refer to IRS Publication 557, which you can find at www.irs.gov. Publication 557 discusses the rules and procedures for organizations that seek recognition of exemption from federal income tax under section 501(a) of the Internal Revenue Code.

IRS Form 990

Current IRS regulations state that the three most recent Form 990 reports and any schedules and attachments to the reports must be available for public inspection. *Form 990* is the annual report of your annual finances and activities as a nonprofit that you must file with the IRS. The IRS has three versions of Form 990, and the version you file depends on your nonprofit's gross receipts and total assets held. Don't panic! We get into all that in the "Reporting to the IRS" section, later in this chapter.

On Form 990, you need to disclose any compensation paid to board members (although we heavily discourage compensating your nonprofit board members except to reimburse direct expenses). This information is available for public inspection, as are employee salaries and contractor payments of more than $100,000 per year. Also, if you paid any former board member more than $10,000 or any former employee more than $100,000, this information must be reported.

Your Form 990 reports must be available for public inspection at the organization's primary place of business during regular business hours. If you work out of your home or have no primary place of business, you can arrange to hand over the forms at convenient places, like coffee shops and libraries, or mail copies to the person who requested them. You have two weeks to do so. The information also can be requested in writing, and if it is, you have 30 days to respond.

A staff member may be present during the inspection, and copies may be made for the person requesting them. If you make copies on your own copier, you may charge a small fee. (For reference, the IRS charges $50 per copy of a tax return document.) Work with your governing board to decide whether your nonprofit will levy a charge for providing copies of public documents.

IRS Form 1023

If you filed and received your exemption after July 15, 1987, you also must include IRS Form 1023, which is your application for exemption, and all the supporting materials submitted with it in the information you make available for inspection. Although the IRS doesn't say so, we assume that you include your articles of incorporation and your bylaws, if you attached them to your application.

TIP

You need to know the rules and regulations about public inspection of nonprofit materials, but frankly, in the many years we've been working for nonprofits, no one has ever asked to see our forms. This doesn't mean that you won't be asked; however, always practice due diligence and be ready.

REMEMBER

Check your state, territory, and local government requirements to see whether your nonprofit must make other information available under local laws.

What you don't need to show

Until a few years ago, all types of tax-exempt organizations were required to provide names and addresses of donors to the IRS, depending on the level of donation, as part of an annual tax filing. In 2018, the IRS published new regulations regarding donor reporting, and since then organizations exempt from tax under Section 501(a) of the Internal Revenue Code, other than those classified within Section 501(c)(3), are no longer required to report donor names and addresses.

Other items that may remain private include the following:

>> Trade secrets and patents

>> Organization policies

>> National defense material

>> Communications from the IRS about previous unfavorable rulings or technical advice related to rulings

>> Board meeting minutes and contracts

>> Financial audit results

>> Information about the board of directors

If you have questions about a particular item, consult your attorney or tax advisor.

The public disclosure rules offer a nice tool for anyone who gets a bee in their bonnet and wants to harass your organization. So, if you start receiving request after request after request, check with the nearest IRS office. IRS officials have the authority to relieve you of the disclosure responsibilities if they agree that harassment is occurring.

Using the web to satisfy disclosure requirements

You can avoid the hassle of photocopying and mailing your Form 990 by placing the required information on the web. (You need to make available your three most recent 990 returns and your application for exemption.) Be sure that you post an exact copy of the materials, not a summary or a retyped copy. You can scan documents and put them on your website as graphics, but the best way to do it is to save the documents in read-only PDF format using Adobe Acrobat (www.adobe.com). That way your posted documents aren't easily alterable.

Also, Candid now holds copies of IRS Form 990 at https://candid.org/research-and-verify-nonprofits/990-finder. You can add information about your nonprofit to the Candid by GuideStar database. Some states and territories also maintain web databases of Form 990s from nonprofits incorporated in their jurisdictions.

Web access to the materials is handy, but it only relieves you of the responsibility of mailing out copies. If someone arrives at your office and asks to inspect your Form 990s, you still need to be prepared to allow that person the privilege.

Avoiding Excessive Payments and Politicking

Paying excessive compensation and engaging in campaign politics can get a charitable nonprofit organization in trouble. It doesn't happen often, but you need to be aware of the rules.

Determining reasonable pay and benefits

In past years, if the IRS discovered wrongdoing in a nonprofit, it had little recourse but to take away the organization's tax-exempt status. However, when revised tax laws were passed in 1996, the IRS gained the authority to apply "intermediate sanctions" when nonprofits provide excess benefits to certain staff members or other disqualified persons. Board members and their family members — really, anyone who can influence the organization's activities — are disqualified persons.

Excess benefits can include excessive salaries for staff members or a business deal arranged to benefit a disqualified person in which the nonprofit overpays for a service. So, if you sit on a board of directors that decides to rent office space from your uncle at two or three times the going rate, you and your uncle may be in trouble. If you do decide to rent from your uncle, be sure you can document that you're paying a market-rate rent (if not less). Also, you shouldn't participate in the board vote about renting the space.

An excessive benefit for a nonprofit staff member is any sum that's above a "reasonable amount." You're probably thinking, "What's a *reasonable* amount?" and you're right to ask the question. In the case of executive compensation, it's up to the board of directors to find out what a fair salary is for nonprofit managers in your area and for an organization of your size and scope. (See Chapter 11 for tips on determining salaries.)

If the IRS finds that someone in your nonprofit has received an excessive benefit, the financial penalties are severe. The IRS levies a 25 percent tax on the excess amount, and the employee must pay the full excess amount (including interest and the 25 percent tax) back to the organization. If payment isn't received by that time, the tax can increase to a whopping 200 percent. Board members also may be liable for penalties for approving excessive compensation.

These three tips can help you avoid problems with excess benefits:

>> **Avoid self-enrichment and nepotism.** Prevent board members from participating in decisions that may benefit themselves or their family members. And, certainly, don't let the executive director participate in setting their own compensation.

>> **Rely on credible independent information.** You need to know about reasonable costs in business deals and compensation matters.

>> **Provide a written record.** Document the reasons that you make the decisions you make.

REMEMBER

We don't want to frighten you with visions of huge tax bills. We're not saying that you can't pay nonprofit staff well or that you have to undertake a scientific study to determine fair compensation. Use your head, be reasonable, and exercise caution.

Document board decisions by keeping minutes of board meetings. You don't need to keep a verbatim record of board deliberations, but you want your minutes to reflect the discussions you have and the decisions you make. Maintain what's known as a *board book* — a binder that contains copies of your articles of incorporation, IRS letter of determination for tax exemption, bylaws, amendments to bylaws, notices sent to announce board and membership meetings, and a chronological record of your board meeting minutes.

Using caution when getting involved in politics

We aren't saying that you shouldn't get involved in politics, because it's your right to do so. If you want to give your personal support and endorsement to a candidate, by all means do it. But be sure to separate yourself from your nonprofit organization when you do. Nonprofits in the 501(c)(3) category can't support or endorse candidates for political office.

If you want to talk to your legislator about the passage of a bill that benefits your clients, go ahead and make an appointment. But if you find yourself traveling regularly to your state capital or to Washington, DC, step back and consider how much organizational time and money you're spending on the activity. Charitable nonprofits can spend an "insubstantial" amount on direct lobbying activities. If it's 5 percent or less of your organizational budget, you're probably within the limits allowed, according to the people who pay attention to these matters.

REMEMBER

Be more cautious with what's known as *grassroots lobbying,* or attempting to influence the general public to vote in a particular way. If lobbying is important to your overall mission as a 501(c)(3) public benefit nonprofit, you can elect the *h* designation, which requires more financial reporting to the IRS but allows you to spend more money on these activities. To do so, file IRS Form 5768 after you have a look at the regulations in IRS Publication 577.

Why all the fuss? Understanding the increased scrutiny by the IRS

Nonprofit organizations face increasing regulation and public scrutiny in the years to come. Why? Three reasons come to mind:

>> **Disaster relief:** Concern about how nonprofit organizations use contributions that are made for disaster relief efforts

>> **Excessive salaries:** A series of widely reported cases in which some nonprofits, both public charities and private foundations, have paid exceedingly high salaries to executives and trustees and otherwise pushed the limits of ethical behavior

>> **Scandal:** The number and degree of corporate-accounting and insider-trading scandals that have been revealed during the past few years in the for-profit sector

These factors have focused more public and legislative attention on how nonprofit organizations (and for-profit corporations) operate and how their affairs are regulated.

Greater accountability is being asked of nonprofit leaders, both managers and board members, in how money is raised, how conflicts of interest are avoided, and how funds are spent, especially for salaries and expenses. The National Council of Nonprofits has compiled good principles of nonprofit management from several states that provide overall guidance in this area. You can find them at www. councilofnonprofits.org/resources/principles-and-practices.

If you're involved with a start-up nonprofit that's operating on a shoestring, you may be asking yourself why you need to worry about being paid too much. And you're right — you probably don't need to worry. But you should stay informed of changes in reporting requirements. You still need to have good, ethical operating policies in place; maintain good financial records; and document your organizational decisions with board and committee meeting minutes.

If you're already involved with a large or medium-size nonprofit, be aware of the need for independent financial audits and board policies that address excessive compensation, self-dealing, whistleblowers, and conflicts of interest. The IRS provides a sample conflict-of-interest policy in the instructions for filing Form 1023. You can also find a link to examples in File 6-1 at www.wiley.com/go/nonprofitkitfd6e.

TIP

Because the regulatory situation is always changing, and because it varies from state to state, we suggest visiting the websites of Independent Sector (www.independentsector.org) and BoardSource (www.boardsource.org) to keep abreast of the latest developments. If you have an accounting firm performing a review or an audit, those folks should be able to keep you informed about current legislation and verify that you're in compliance.

Reporting to the IRS

The formal name of the report that nonprofit organizations must file annually is Return of Organization Exempt from Income Tax, and the IRS calls it the "annual information return." Everyone else refers to it as "the 990." It *is* IRS Form 990, after all. Depending on a nonprofit's gross receipts and total assets held, a version of this report must go to the IRS each year.

TECHNICAL STUFF

The IRS uses gross receipts to determine which Form 990 your organization is required to file. *Gross receipts* refer to all funds that come into the nonprofit during the tax year before any expenses are subtracted. For example, if you have a special event that brings in $20,000 but you have expenses of $8,000 for a net income of $12,000, your gross receipts for that event are $20,000. This figure is added to grants, fees for services, contributions, and any other income to determine your gross receipts for the year.

No matter which report you file, it must be submitted no later than the 15th day of the fifth month after the end of your annual accounting period — in other words, after the close of your fiscal year. When you filed your application for exemption, you selected your accounting period. If you use the calendar year as your fiscal year, your 990 has to be out the door on May 15.

Tax-exempt organizations seeking an extension will now file a "single" Form 8868 to request an automatic 6-month maximum extension of time to file the annual tax return. Previously, tax-exempt organizations intending to avail themselves of the full statutory extension period would be required to file two consecutive 3-month extensions, provide a valid reason for the extension request, and sign the extension "under penalty of perjury."

The IRS has three versions of Form 990: the 990-N, the 990-EZ, and the long Form 990. The report you file depends on the total gross receipts (and total assets) of your nonprofit organization. We focus on the 990-N and 990-EZ in the next couple of sections, but we do provide some advice for the long Form 990 as well. Most important, if your nonprofit organization is big enough to require filing the long Form 990, we advise that you seek professional help.

Filing Form 990-N

Form 990-N is required for all 501(c)(3) nonprofit organizations (with the exception of churches and church-related organizations) that have annual gross receipts of normally $50,000 or less. This simple form must be filed electronically; in fact, the IRS refers to this form as an e-postcard, so you need a computer, Internet access, and an email address.

The due date for filing this form is the same as for the 990-EZ or the long Form 990: the 15th day of the fifth month after the close of the tax year. However, at present there's no penalty for late filing. You can't file before the end of the tax year.

WARNING

If your organization fails to file the 990-N for three consecutive years, its tax-exempt status is revoked automatically.

To file Form 990-N, go to the IRS website at www.irs.gov/charities-non-profits/annual-electronic-filing-requirement-for-small-exempt-organizations-form-990-n-e-postcard. Follow the link to the e-postcard site. If your organization is new or hasn't filed the 990-N before, you need to register to obtain a login ID before you file the form.

The 990-N asks for the following information:

>> Employer identification number (EIN), also known as a taxpayer identification number (TIN).

>> Tax year (calendar or fiscal filer)

>> Legal name and mailing address

>> Any other names the organization uses

>> Name and address of a principal officer

>> Website address if the organization has one

>> Confirmation that the organization's annual gross receipts are $50,000 or less

>> If applicable, a statement that the organization has terminated or is terminating (going out of business)

Taking it easy with the Form 990-EZ return

If your organization has gross receipts of less than $200,000 and assets of less than $500,000, you can file Form 990-EZ, which is more complex than Form 990-N. The 990-EZ includes a lot of fine print, and the instructions are a good test of the importance of close reading. That said, the instructions are complete, and most terms are well defined. You can make your task easier by seeking help from your accountant or attorney.

REMEMBER

Keep in mind when reading the instructions that the 990-EZ report is used for categories of tax-exempt organizations other than 501(c)(3) public charities. This can be confusing unless you attend closely to the instructions. Because the 990-EZ is used for other types of nonprofits, be sure to select the 501(c)(3) box in Section J.

Fill in the identifying information at the top of the form. Be sure to add your employer identification number (EIN). Also select the correct box to indicate whether you're using a cash or accrual accounting method. If you need help with that question, see Chapter 12.

REMEMBER

Be sure to include a phone number where the IRS and members of the public can contact your organization. Don't forget that the 990 is a public document. So, if you've had an address or name change since you filed your last report, select that box in Section B. If these changes required amendments to your articles of incorporation or if this is the first time your organization has filed the 990-EZ, select the corresponding boxes in Section B. If your tax-exempt application is still pending, indicate that as well in Section B.

If in the past year a single individual has given your 501(c)(3) organization a contribution of cash, a grant, or property that was valued at $5,000 or more, *or* if a gift totaled more than 2 percent of your total grants and contributions, you must file Schedule B with your 990-EZ. If a single person gives you two gifts of $2,500 within the year, you must file the schedule. If you don't have grants or gifts in this range, select the box in Section H to let the IRS know you aren't required to file Schedule B.

REMEMBER

The IRS doesn't require Schedule B to be disclosed to the public. If your organization must file its Form 990 report with its state to satisfy state reporting requirements, check about its disclosure requirements.

Parts I and II

In Part I of Form 990-EZ, you report your financial activities over the past year. Chances are that the two lines that have the highest amount of revenue are line 1 (contributions, gifts, and grants) and line 2 (program service revenue, including government fees and contracts). You may have some income from membership fees for line 3 and income from investments or interest on a savings account for line 4.

Lines 5 through 8 deal with income from sales of materials or assets and income from special events. You're asked to report the costs and expenses associated with the materials sold and any direct expenses associated with fundraising events. In other words, the IRS wants to see a net amount for sales-and-fundraising events. The total you end up with on line 9 is your total revenue for the year.

REMEMBER

If you earn more than $15,000 in gross receipts from fundraising events (reported on Line 6B), you need to complete Schedule G. If any part of these gross receipts came from gaming (6A), such as bingo or pull tabs, you also need to complete Part III of Schedule G.

WARNING

Don't confuse your total revenue with your gross receipts. *Gross receipts* include all the income you receive from sales and special events *before* you subtract expenses. Annual gross receipts (and asset value) determine which Form 990 you submit to the IRS.

Back to Form 990-EZ, report your expenses on lines 10 through 16 in their appropriate categories and total the amount on line 17. Subtract line 17 from line 9 and you have your surplus (or deficit) for the year. This amount goes on line 18. We come back to line 19 in just a minute.

Part II includes lines 22 through 24, which is where you report your assets — cash, savings, or investments as well as property and equipment. (Equipment goes on line 24, other assets. Attach Schedule O with the equipment list.) Total these figures for line 25.

Enter your total liabilities on line 26. They may include accounts payable, outstanding loans, and vacation time owed to employees, for example. Describe these liabilities on Schedule O. Subtract line 26 from line 25 and you have your net assets or fund balance. Put this amount on line 27. If you pay off all your bills and sell all your assets, this amount is what's left over — in theory.

Notice that you need to report assets and liabilities for the beginning of the year and the end of the year. (If this Form 990 report is your first, you provide only end-of-year totals.) Refer to the form you submitted last year for the beginning-of-year figures.

Now go back to line 19 in Part I. Enter your net assets from last year's form on this line. If an adjustment to your net assets was made during the year (usually done by an accountant), enter the figure for this adjustment on line 20 and explain on Schedule O. On line 21, enter the amount of your net assets at the end of the current year.

That's it for reporting your financial activities on Form 990-EZ. It *was* easy, wasn't it?

Parts III and IV

Part III of Form 990-EZ asks you to state your primary exempt purpose. This statement doesn't need to be long, like the one you wrote for your Form 1023 application — a few words will do. You also need to describe your three largest programs, their objectives, program accomplishments, how many people you served, and a total cost for each program. The form has spaces for three separate programs, but if you have only one program, that's fine.

TIP

Part III offers a space to report grants in each program area. This space is for grants made *by* your organization, not grants *to* your organization. You probably didn't make any grants, but if you did, report them here.

Part IV requires a list of your directors, with the board officers identified, and key employees and their addresses. Usually, for smaller nonprofits, the only key employee is the executive director. You also need to state how much time is devoted to each position each week and record any compensation received, including salary, retirement benefits, and expense allowances. If you need more space than what's provided on the form, attach an additional sheet. You don't need to list addresses for any individuals in this section.

Parts V and VI

You're likely able to select No to answer the questions in Part V of the 990-EZ or leave the items blank. But several issues may need your attention:

>> If you've amended your bylaws or articles of incorporation since you filed your last report, select that item and include a copy of the amended document when you send in the form.

>> If you've engaged in any significant activities not reported previously on the 1023 or an earlier Form 990, you should indicate that on line 33 and describe those activities on Schedule O. The same is true if you've discontinued any significant activities.

Line 35 refers to income that may have come to your organization via activities not related to your charitable purpose. This is called *unrelated business income,* and if it totals $1,000 or more, you must report it on Form 990-T. You may be liable for taxes on this income. If you think your nonprofit has income in this category, you're wise to consult an accountant. (For more on unrelated income, check out the nearby sidebar, "How the IRS decides whether income is unrelated.")

>> If your organization loaned or borrowed money during the year from a director, trustee, or key employee — or if it has outstanding loans from the previous year — select Yes on line 38a, fill in the amount on line 38b, and file Schedule L, Part II.

>> In Part VI, lines 46 and 47 ask whether your organization engaged in political campaigns on behalf of a candidate or engaged in lobbying activities. If you can legitimately answer No to these questions, do so and move on. If you have questions about your nonprofit's engagement in these areas, seek advice from an attorney.

WARNING

Campaigning for a candidate under the banner of your nonprofit organization is a serious matter that is grounds for the loss of your tax exemption. An "insubstantial" amount of lobbying is allowed for 501(c)(3) public charities, but this area is filled with shades of gray and shouldn't be taken lightly. Nonprofit organizations can engage in nonpartisan voter registration and public education activities, but to be on the safe side, you should seek professional counsel.

>> List all employees and contractors who were paid more than $100,000 during the last year. Chances are, especially if yours is a start-up organization, and because you're filing the 990-EZ, you can enter *NA* in these sections.

HOW THE IRS DECIDES WHETHER INCOME IS UNRELATED

The IRS definition of *unrelated business income* is based on three questions: Does the income come from a trade or business? Is it regularly carried on? Is it not substantially related to the organization's exempt purpose?

To better understand what these questions mean, consider an extreme example. Youth Leadership Impact, a 501(c)(3) nonprofit with the mission of providing after-school academic tutoring services, recreational opportunities, mentoring, and youth development programming, decides to open a retail school-supply business. It rents a storefront space; purchases shelving, a cash register, and security cameras; hires students as employees; and begins soliciting business. The school-supply business training program does well financially. In fact, in the first year of operation, income exceeds expenses by $10,000. The nonprofit organization uses the money to pay some costs incurred in working with young people in the neighborhood. The problem is that the school-supply business has no relationship to Youth Leadership Impact's charitable purpose. In this case, the organization is required to file Form 990-T and pay appropriate taxes on the $10,000. That's okay, however, because the organization still realizes a profit that can be applied to some of its program costs.

Be sure to have an officer of the organization sign and date the form. Often this officer is the board chair or board treasurer. If you used a paid tax preparer, that person must sign as well.

Schedule A

All 501(c)(3) public charities that submit Form 990-EZ must complete and submit Schedule A (Itemized Deductions) so that the IRS can apply the public support test to determine whether your organization qualifies as a public charity. (Refer to Chapter 5 for a discussion of the public support test.) Although it's a little more complicated and there are other ways to pass the test, in a nutshell, public charities must receive one-third of their support from the public.

During the first five years of a nonprofit's existence, data is collected but the test isn't applied. So even if you're sending in your first 990-EZ, you need to provide the information requested on Schedule A.

In Part I of Schedule A, you're asked to select one box from lines 1 through 11. Most 501(c)(3) organizations that are the subject of this book select either line 7 or line 10. Line 7 applies to organizations that qualify as public charities under section 170(b)(1)(A)(vi); in this case, you also need to complete Part II of Schedule A. Look at the language in Part III to fill in the support schedule for organizations that qualify as public charities under section 509(a)(2). Parts II and III both ask for information about sources of financial support for the organization for the current tax year and the four previous years. If your organization has been in existence for less than this 5-year period, you have to provide information only for the year or years in which your nonprofit has been active. Also, you don't need to compute the percentage of public support in Section C in either part until you've completed your sixth year of operations, although it's a good idea to complete a personal copy of the calculation for the first five years so that you can keep track of how you're doing.

The IRS refers to the appropriate code section for your nonprofit in the letter of determination (tax-exemption letter) it sends you after you file your IRS Form 1023 application for exemption.

Tackling the long Form 990

If your organization has gross receipts of $200,000 or more or assets of $500,000 or greater, you're required to tackle the full Form 990 experience. The 990 emphasizes accountability and transparency in nonprofit organizations, which reflects growing public scrutiny of nonprofits. The first page of the form is a summary of the more-detailed information that follows. You have to describe your mission or "most significant activities" in the first question of Part I. In addition to questions about the number of board members, employees, and volunteers, you must present a summary of the detailed financial information requested in the final pages of the report.

Make no mistake: Completing this report requires more time and effort than the 990-EZ. The long Form 990 spans 12 pages and is accompanied by 16 separate schedules. Although you won't be required to complete all the schedules, you may need to submit some of them, depending on the circumstances of your organization. One section of the 990 is a checklist with questions that must be answered Yes or No. Usually a Yes answer triggers a requirement to complete one of the 16 schedules.

REMEMBER

The IRS estimates that you need 16 hours to learn about Form 990 and nearly 24 hours to complete the form. We think this may be an underestimate. The instruction booklet contains 96 pages of dense reading. Answering the questions and providing the information required on this form should be a team effort. And, if at all possible, we recommend that a member of that team be a qualified accountant. It doesn't hurt to have an attorney on board, either. If you decide to undertake the task of completing the long form without the assistance of professional help, start early and plan to spend lots of time with the instruction manual.

Providing financial information

When you use the long Form 990, you're asked for more-detailed financial information than is needed for the 990-EZ. The IRS wants to know more about where you get your money and where you spend it. Also, all your expenses must be allocated to one of the following categories: grants and similar amounts paid, benefits paid to or for members, salaries, professional fees, occupancy, rent, utilities and maintenance, printing, publications, postage and shipping, and other. You also need to provide a detailed balance sheet. (Chapter 12 includes more information about financial recordkeeping.)

The IRS wants to know which method of accounting you're using and whether you're following certain accounting standards. You're also asked whether your financial statements have been audited or reviewed by an independent accountant. If so, the IRS asks whether your organization has a committee that provides oversight to the preparation of financial statements and audits.

TIP

If it looks like your organization will be required to file the full Form 990 report in the next year or two, start putting in place the accounting system you'll need to collect the appropriate information.

Describing your programs

In the long Form 990, you're asked to describe the program achievements of your three most expensive programs and whether any programs were added or eliminated in the year for which you're making the report. If you did make significant changes in your program offerings, you need to describe them on Schedule O.

The 990 report is a public document and is available for public review, so be sure to take the time to describe your activities and program achievements completely and clearly and without the use of excessive jargon.

Looking at management and governance

REMEMBER

The sections relating to members of the board (the IRS refers to the board as the "governing body"), board policies, and highly compensated and key employees are detailed and require special attention.

For example, you're asked how many board members are independent. An *independent* board member can't be compensated as an officer or employee of the organization or receive more than $10,000 as an independent contractor of the organization. Neither this person nor a member of their family may engage in a business transaction with the organization or with a key employee who would trigger the requirement to submit Schedule L.

Also, although not required by IRS regulations, the 990 asks several questions about board governance. For example, you're asked whether the organization has written policies for the retention and destruction of documents, whether you have a conflict-of-interest policy, and whether you have a whistleblower policy.

Also, the organization must note whether a process exists for setting the compensation of the executive director and other key employees and whether the organization provided board members with a copy of the 990 before its filing. Although not explicitly required, it's good practice to establish these policies and procedures. They'll strengthen and protect your organization.

Getting your Form 990 to the IRS

Your Form 990 report (whether it's the 990-EZ, 990-N, or long Form 990) needs to be submitted on the 15th day of the fifth month after the close of your financial year — unless, of course, you request an extension. If you chose to mail the form, check the most recent version of the instructions to find the address to which the report should be sent. You can file the 990 reports electronically if you want, and some larger nonprofits are required to file electronically. Go to www.irs.gov/efile for instructions on electronic filing. The 990-N can *only* be filed electronically; there are no paper forms for this type of tax return document.

REMEMBER

Large organizations that have assets worth $10 million or more and that submit more than 250 IRS reports in a year must file their 990 returns electronically.

Reporting to Your State, Territory, and Local Governments

You'll almost certainly have reporting requirements for your state, territory, and possibly your local government, especially if you provide services under contract. Sometimes, reporting to the state or territory is as simple as completing a 1-page form, attaching a copy of your 990, and paying a small fee.

WARNING

More and more states, territories, and local governments require registration for fundraising activities. Be sure to check local laws.

Some states and territories require a separate financial form, although we think that most follow the federal form closely. You'll probably receive all the needed reporting information when you ask for the incorporation packet, but if you didn't or you aren't sure, check with your state or territory office that regulates nonprofit corporations. Find the appropriate office in your state or territory by searching the web.

2

Bringing Your A-Game to Nonprofit Management

Get the inside scoop on acknowledging the role of your government board.

See how your board is liable for financial decisions made on behalf of your nonprofit organization and recognize their management oversight duties.

People, whether volunteers or paid employees, are an essential part of every nonprofit organization. Discover how to recruit and manage volunteers and employees.

Grasp your role as the nonprofit's founder and executive director if you're holding dual roles.

Let your mission statement and strategic plan determine your management team members when you're ready to bring staff on board.

Chapter **7**

From the Top: Examining the Nonprofit Management Structure

I f you're the nonprofit founder, you might be thinking: "I am the visionary. I started this nonprofit. I have ownership, and leverage, and I get to tell the board yes or no regarding their decisions. I recruited these members. They're not going to take over my dream of helping this community."

However, as we discuss in Chapter 3, there is no owner of a nonprofit. Instead, a governing board guides and oversees the organization, like an owner might. Understanding the governing board's role in your management structure, processes, and decision-making should be a top priority for nonprofit founders, executive directors, and volunteers alike.

Founders, don't worry — while it may seem like you're turning over the reins to the board of directors, you still can determine your role within the nonprofit organization. You are the founder and you have the vision for moving forward.

In this chapter, we take a closer look at the top-down structure of most nonprofit organizations and explain who wields the most authority and how that impacts the rest of the organization's structure.

REMEMBER

Nonprofit organizations don't belong to any single person or group of founders or governing board. They belong to their stakeholders and the public at-large for the greater good of their mission.

TIP

Check out File 7-1 at www.wiley.com/go/nonprofitkitfd6e for a list of web resources related to the topics we cover in this chapter.

Managing a Nonprofit: A Bird's-Eye View

Exactly what is the management structure for a nonprofit organization? Take a look at Figure 7-1 for an example.

Sample Organizational Chart

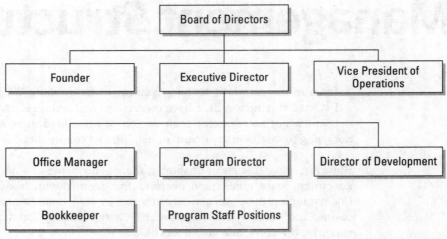

FIGURE 7-1: Organizational chart of a typical larger nonprofit agency.

© John Wiley & Sons, Inc.

Your board of directors is the governing body. They're at the top of your organizational chart. The board has authority over the founder as well as the executive director and advisory board as the nonprofit grows and those positions are added. Though communications are two-way, your board has the final say. The board decides what will be implemented, how much will be spent, and even who will be nominated when the time comes for board elections or expansion.

Appreciating the Governing Board's Role and Responsibilities

As they say, with great power comes great responsibility. Every member of your governing board is responsible for the organization's financial management, operational decision-making process, risk management, and more. In other words, your governing board members are the foundation for a solid and successfully managed nonprofit organization.

Understanding the board's management oversight duties

A nonprofit's board of directors has the legal responsibility to provide oversight and accountability for the organization. The board must ensure that your nonprofit organization is carefully handling the funding entrusted to it. The board must also follow all legal and ethical standards. Recommended governance practices include carrying out the duties behind these three types of responsibilities:

>> **Governance**

- Making policy and strategy decisions.

- Overseeing and monitoring organizational performance.

- Ensuring overall accountability.

>> **Legal**

- Holding at least one annual meeting of the board of directors.

- Creating policies related to disclosing and managing conflicts of interest.

>> **Financial**

- Formalizing the process of setting compensation for the executive director, including approving the compensation package.

- Reviewing IRS Form 990 and ensuring its accuracy before it's filed with the IRS.

- Ensuring that an annual financial audit is conducted.

- Approving financial policies that insure checks and balances with regard to the income and expenses. This includes determining who signs the checks and deposits the money as well as monitoring the income statements on a regular basis. The board can even authorize who can sign grant applications and contracts over a specific amount (typically, the signee is the board president).

A SAD CASE OF NO D&O

Consider, for example, a new nonprofit, without D&O insurance coverage on their board members, that applied for a grant from a major community-based funding source. The nonprofit won a $95,000 grant award to create a rural community outreach program to provide case management, workforce-entry skills, transportation for clients to job interviews, and job placement. When the check arrived, the board treasurer endorsed and deposited the check into the bank. The program had been heavily promoted throughout the rural community. If you don't yet see any red flags in this story, you should! Here are some questions to ask yourself:

- Did the board treasurer have full board approval to accept the grant award on behalf of the nonprofit organization?

- Was there a board resolution to validate the authority to accept the funding? The board must make a resolution to accept grant funds and record it in the board meeting minutes. This establishes a record of funds received.

- Did the board treasurer have approval from the rest of the board's executive committee to deposit the check on their own? The resolution covers the authorization to deposit the funds.

- Did the board treasurer make a copy of the check to add to the next board meeting's agenda? This risk management task creates a record of when the check was dated, which is a signal that the grant-funded program is ready to start its implementation. The copy of the check also provides a clear audit trail for your nonprofit's accountant. A separate accounting record should be created to track expenditures from the grant funding.

Well, here's the rest of the sad story for this rural nonprofit organization. The grant writer who was hired to write the grant application that won a $95,000 award for the nonprofit was also the new program's evaluator. She started to see evidence of improper recordkeeping and forged case management files. As the contracted evaluator, the grant writer started to ask questions about the case management files and why the client documentation was written in the same ink pen color and in the same handwriting when the grant allowed two part-time contracted social workers. Was only one social worker hired? Where were the receipts for transportation vouchers, job interview clothing, invisible computer lab, and training program to help unemployed low-income rural residents? Where? Where? Where?

What do you think happened next? Six months into the 12-month funding cycle, the grant writer felt an ethical duty to speak with the funder and ask them to make an unannounced site visit to the nonprofit's training facility (operating in a large community room of a community-based church). The site visit was unexpected by the program director and pastor of the church (who were both partners in a soon-to-be discovered crime). The outcome of the site visit by the funder resulted in a legal letter demanding 100 percent of the grant award monies ($75,000) back from the nonprofit organization.

A lawsuit was filed as well when the nonprofit did not respond. Oh, did we forget to say that the board had no D&O insurance coverage? When the nonprofit could not come up with the $75,000 from the organization's coffers, the burden shifted to the board of directors. They were clueless, had never heard of D&O insurance, and did not ask the program director or the pastor any questions because they trusted them. And did we mention yet that the board treasurer (the holder of the nonprofit's checkbook) was the program director's wife?

The board of directors became personally liable for repaying the $75,000. Some lost their homes; others had liens put on their homes, preventing them from selling to come up with the monies. Others had their paychecks garnished via small claims court. The court's judgment against the nine board members was harsh but certainly deserved. Why? No candidate for joining a board of directors should be eager to say yes without first asking many questions about protection from financial liability. Fast-forward: The nonprofit has closed. The church board fired the pastor. Sadly, the community lost its trust in everyone associated with the nonprofit.

The buck stops at the board of directors. As such, the board is in a position of liability. If someone is unhappy with your services, if a passerby falls and is injured on the nonprofit's property, or if program staff has overstepped their position with a client, volunteer, or community partner, a lawsuit can even be filed. All eyes will be on the board for taking action, making decisions, and being accountable on behalf of the nonprofit.

Protecting your board from liability

Did you know that fear of personal liability stops many people from joining a board of directors? Some state laws offer protection to people affiliated with public charities. However, this is not the case in every state. So, when you're recruiting board members, ask for their contributions to purchase directors-and-officers (D&O) insurance.

D&O insurance protects the personal assets of nonprofit directors (including board officers) and their spouses in the event that employees personally sue them, vendors, competitors, funders, clients, or other parties for actual or alleged wrongful acts in managing the nonprofit. D&O insurance covers legal fees, settlements, and judgments arising out of lawsuits and wrongful act allegations brought against your nonprofit organization. Costs vary from insurance company to insurance company. Make sure to get several quotes before you settle on a D&O insurance provider.

Redefining the Nonprofit Founder's Role

Every founder needs to determine their role within the nonprofit organization. Probably the most difficult thing to realize is that you won't be the owner of the nonprofit organization. As a tax-exempt nonprofit organization, your nonprofit will be accountable to the people it serves, to its funders, to the attorney general in your state or territory, and to the general public. Naturally, a founder is an important figure in the nonprofit organization that was founded on their vision. Even though founders deserve respect and gratitude, ultimately, there is no such position as founder — however, every founder has a choice to be part of the staff or part of the board.

Suppose that you're most interested in being part of the daily activities in the nonprofit organization. In that case, you could request that the board of directors appoint you as vice president of operations. This means you'd be responsible for overseeing the nonprofit's operations on a day-to-day basis; however, you'd still report directly to the board who would be responsible for giving you strategic direction and assessing your performance.

The chief executive usually serves as an *ex officio* nonvoting member of the board, which provides a shield against conflict of interest and questions about accountability while forming a necessary and constructive partnership with the board.

If you want to ensure that you have a direct say in the nonprofit organization's future, you may want to become a board member and decide to be the first chair. Still, remember that every board member has only one vote — including the chair — and the full board must always speak with one voice to the outside world. However, as the founder, you can form the initial board with members who believe in the organization's mission, share your strategic goals, and devote their time and energy to help you.

Suppose that the nonprofit organization cannot hire staff right away. In that case, you will have a working board where each member has individual fiduciary and governing duties as a board member and individual tasks and responsibilities to carry on the daily affairs. The important issue is remembering which hat each member is wearing at different times to keep accountability intact.

If the governing board decides to create an advisory board, this may be the perfect place to plant yourself as the visionary behind the nonprofit organization. An *advisory board* is a body that provides nonbinding strategic advice to the management of a nonprofit organization. The informal nature of an advisory board gives greater flexibility in structure and management compared to the board of directors.

Adding an Advisory Board

Advisory boards are typically composed of an informal group of accomplished experts and advisors hand-picked by the board of directors. Advisory boards expand the nonprofit organization's capacity, reach, and impact. This list describes the typical types of advisory boards:

>> **Fundraising:** Donors who want a larger role with your nonprofit organization can be asked to join your advisory board.

>> **Programmatic:** Members with your nonprofit's service-area experience can help provide advice on program improvements. Programmatic members can also be asked to serve on an internal stakeholder's evaluation team for grant-funded projects and existing programs that require annual performance evaluations. Advisory board members can spot broken links in program services, incorrect data collection processes, and other red flags that are spotted only when examining the evaluation findings for each program.

If you're the founder, you can always opt to join the advisory board instead of taking a more laborious position such as vice president of operations. However, keep in mind that you're one of many members. Each advisory board member may have differing viewpoints and ideas for how to help the nonprofit organization build its capacity. You're a member, not the leader. Advisory boards have no designated leaders — every member has the same input ability. It takes a consensus of the advisory board members to move a recommendation up to the board of directors for review and possible adoption into a resolution.

The advisory board reports directly to the board of directors. It makes recommendations to the board of directors and takes direction from the board of directors. The advisory board cannot be influenced or swayed by the executive director, program staff, volunteers, or even the nonprofit organization's community partners. Again, the founder may opt to join the advisory board if the board of directors is not a comfortable fit. The advisory board is more relaxed but highly informed in their respective professional fields. Advisory board members come with high levels of education, experience, and expertise, and each member freely offers what they know to help the board of directors on all advisory board assignments. Members work seamlessly, cooperatively, and without subjective motives.

Expanding to Take On an Executive Director

The executive director of a nonprofit organization oversees the heads of each department, such as marketing, human resources, program development, and funding development. After you can start hiring or contracting for staff positions, your most important role is to bring in people from diverse backgrounds. Your hiring or contracting practices must embrace diversity, equity, and inclusion.

Successful executive directors are goal-driven and possess a high degree of motivation and energy. They are *doers*. They have a record of productivity and embracing the importance of the organization's mission.

As executive director, you report to your board of directors, and the chief liaison is the board's chair or president, or CEO. This is the body that hires executive directors, monitors and evaluates their performances, and directs the search for a new executive director if that task becomes necessary. The board's directive becomes your marching order for managing the nonprofit organization.

To be effective in leadership, as the executive director, you must be an excellent communicator and a marathon-like fundraiser, and you must have the vision to put the mission into a long-term view. Your entire staff looks to you for an example of dedication, commitment, and approachability. Your office door should be open unless you're discussing confidential matters. In other words, you must be a hands-on executive director.

Typically, when you see a job posting for a nonprofit executive director, here are some of the typical duties and responsibilities:

>> Collaborate with the board of directors to identify, create, and implement the strategic plan.

>> Identify, recruit, train, and develop a talented team of employees who can lead critical departments and manage subordinates.

>> Develop the organizational culture and promote transparency and collaboration throughout the nonprofit and with community stakeholders.

>> Approve and monitor all fundraising efforts.

>> Represent the nonprofit at community events and with funders in ways that strengthen and oversee the mission and financial stability for future operations, and ultimately, sustainability.

As the executive director, your line of accountability is directly to the board of directors. As your governing board, they approve, monitor, and guide your duties and responsibilities to the nonprofit organization. Often you are directed by the board to downsize staff because the board is carrying out their fiduciary role to keep the nonprofit in operation. The board may see red flags in the monthly and annual expenditures that must be addressed. Reducing staff size is typically the first step in stopping the bleed of expenses that may eventually be more than the revenues coming into the nonprofit. As much as you may want to defend not laying off key staff members, the board's decision must be followed swiftly and with explanations to staff about what is happening and why such difficult decisions must be made.

REMEMBER

You must respect your line of accountability to the board of directors. When the board directs you to do something that you may not agree with, keep in mind that *they* are responsible for the governance of the nonprofit organization. Every action that occurs in the day-to-day operation of the nonprofit comes under the jurisdiction and scrutiny of the board of directors. Their volunteer (unpaid) role is selfless. The board's focus should always be on the nonprofit's mission, vision, and legacy in the community.

Chapter **8**

Strategic Planning: Embracing the Ongoing Process

The word *planning* can be intimidating. It brings up images of daylong meetings in stuffy conference rooms with consultants wielding dry erase markers. Of course, not all planning takes that sort of effort. People make plans all the time, from organizing vacations to deciding how to complete all their errands on a Saturday afternoon.

Strategic planning is a group project that calls for research, brainstorming, discussion, and, in the end, agreement on a goal and the strategies and tactics needed to reach that goal. Simply put, *strategic planning* is deciding where to go and how to get there. The planning process helps ensure that your stakeholders are headed in the same direction.

In this chapter, we cover planning for nonprofits in all its forms, from organizational planning to work planning to program planning to facility planning. Plan to join us!

TIP

Check out File 8-1 at www.wiley.com/go/nonprofitkitfd6e for a list of web resources related to the topics we cover in this chapter.

Understanding the Importance of Planning

No nonprofit organization has unlimited funds. Even the largest, wealthiest nonprofit needs to decide how to allocate its resources effectively. Planning helps you make decisions about how to align your organization's mission with its resources by answering questions such as these: "Is now the best time to invest in a new program?" "Is our safe house program still filling a community need?" "Is our resilience training center convenient to the people we're trying to serve?"

A nonprofit organization undertakes planning for a few reasons, as listed here:

>> To build a structure that guides its activities in pursuit of its mission

>> To allocate organizational resources in the most effective ways

>> To create a framework against which the organization's performance can be evaluated

>> To adapt to changes in the external environment

>> To reach agreement among board, staff, and community stakeholders on desirable goals for the organization and well-considered ways to meet those goals

Think of a plan as a blueprint or scheme describing what needs to be done to accomplish an end. In an ideal world, if your organization completes every step of its plan, you achieve your goals. However, not all plans are written as recipes that — if followed closely — will serve up a perfect meal. Scenario plans, for example, help an organization think through alternatives it may choose among; other planning approaches invite organizations to assess and revisit their strategies frequently.

REMEMBER

The *act* of planning has value apart from the document that's ultimately created. That's because, in theory, the strategic planning group comes to a shared understanding of your nonprofit organization's mission, and the decision-making process ensures that everyone understands what needs to be done and agrees that it's worth doing.

Making Your Organization's Strategic Plan

Strategic planning is what people usually think about when they consider planning — and previously a strategic plan covered a period from three to five years of nonprofit operations; however, today, in this changing and often volatile global economy, we advise creating a short-term strategic plan. Let's focus on one year (your founding year). The strategic plan is the guiding document where you set goals for the organization and describe the objectives that must be accomplished to achieve those goals. The plan also includes action steps, timelines for achieving the objectives in order to achieve your goals by the end of the plan year, and designations for who will carry out each action step.

Soon after your board of directors approves your mission statement and vision statement (see Chapter 4), use those statements to begin drafting your strategic plan. Follow these steps for successful planning:

1. **Hear from stakeholders.**

2. **Research and make decisions about goals and the strategies to meet them.**

3. **Draft the plan.**

4. **Submit the final draft to the full board for discussion and adoption.**

5. **Act on the plan.**

6. **Routinely evaluate your progress.**

REMEMBER

Planning is an ongoing activity. Planning for the purposes of refining objectives, creating a budget, and developing fundraising programs goes on all the time. This means that the strategic plan needs to be revisited routinely (we recommend monthly) to determine your progress in meeting the plan's goals, objectives, and overall organizational performance. In the last quarter of your current year's strategic plan, determine goals that weren't met and why, and then start working on the strategic plan for the upcoming year.

Getting ready

Make no mistake: An all-out strategic planning effort requires considerable time, energy, and commitment from everyone involved. Some nonprofits spend a year or more developing a strategic plan.

Don't jump into the strategic planning process without understanding that it will add to your workload and complicate your life for a while. Keep in mind that you can't plan by yourself. If you're the executive director of a nonprofit organization who thinks that a full-bore planning effort is needed but the board of directors doesn't agree, don't try to start the process on your own. Take a couple of steps backward and begin the work of persuading board members that planning is worth the effort.

WARNING

Don't start the strategic planning process if your nonprofit is in crisis mode. It's tempting, for example, to launch a strategic planning effort if you just lost a major source of funding. But you have more immediate concerns to deal with in that situation. Delay strategic planning until you see a period of smooth sailing.

If you have the support, and if foreclosure isn't hanging over your agency's head, the best way to get started is to form a *strategic planning committee.* This small group of board members, staff, and one or two outside people can take on the role of guiding the strategic planning process and, in the beginning, pull together the questions, facts, and observations that you need in order to make your strategic planning decisions.

Working with your nonprofit's mission and vision statements

Reviewing the organization's mission and vision statements is one of the first tasks facing a new nonprofit that's developing a plan. (Chapter 4 covers mission and vision statements.) Ask yourself these questions:

>> Is the problem the nonprofit set out to solve still a problem?

>> Do the organization's current programs and activities address the mission in a meaningful way?

>> Is the mission statement clear yet flexible enough to allow the organization to grow and adapt?

>> Does the vision statement still reflect where we want to be as an organization five years down the road?

REMEMBER

Keep your mission statement in mind throughout the strategic planning process. At every turn, ask yourself: "If we do this, will we be true to our mission?"

Hearing from all your stakeholders

Unless you have a very small organization, you probably can't include every single person in the planning process. You do need to include all stakeholder groups, however. A *stakeholder* is someone who has a reason for wanting the organization to succeed. Paid employees and members of the board certainly qualify. But these two groups, who are the most closely connected to the nonprofit, are by no means the only people who have a stake in the organization's success.

DESIGN THINKING

Design thinking is an approach to solving creative problems from the design field. Its application to business settings is widely associated with the Institute of Design at Stanford. The key to design thinking is clearly defining a problem, considering present and future conditions, and identifying a number of solutions — always with the end user of a product or service in mind. In design thinking, you experiment with those solutions, intending to fail fast until the best result emerges.

Some nonprofit organizations and foundations are applying the principles of design thinking to their planning work. It resembles traditional strategic planning in that it begins with an analysis of present conditions, but it's different in that it assumes that organizations can't think through the best solutions via discussion: Testing prototypes and learning from failure are the keys to charting a future course. The d.school offers a virtual 90-minute crash course in design thinking on its website, and we've included a link in File 8-1 at www.wiley.com/go/nonprofitkitfd6e.

In our view, you also should include a representative from each of the following groups in planning:

>> Users of services

>> Community leaders

>> Donors

>> Volunteers

TIP

Check out File 8-2 at www.wiley.com/go/nonprofitkitfd6e for a sample strategic planning retreat agenda. It gives some guidance in organizing your own planning retreat.

REMEMBER

One purpose of strategic planning is to bring together stakeholders in pursuit of a common goal. People work harder to achieve the goals when they're asked to help set the goals.

WARNING

Guard against bias. Sometimes people get so close to the situation they're evaluating that they can't see the true picture with an objective eye. Include outside people who gain no personal benefit from the outcome.

Also, don't assume that all your stakeholders know what they're talking about in every instance. For example, if someone says that receiving a grant to pay the costs of a program start-up is a piece of cake, check with potential funders before you agree that it's an easy task.

Yes, honesty can create conflict. Be prepared for it. Set some rules for attending strategic planning meetings. Make sure that all participants have a chance to state their cases. Arguments can be productive if they exchange ideas about what is best for the organization and don't disintegrate into shouting matches.

Surveying the external situation

Early in the strategic planning process, you need to collect information about external (outside) factors that influence your nonprofit's operation. Someone, or a subcommittee of the strategic planning committee, should find the answers to the following questions and distribute them to everyone on the committee before the formal planning meetings begin:

>> What are the demographic and other trends in our area and in our organization? Will these trends have an impact on the number of people or animals who may need or use our services in the future?

>> What are the trends in the professional arena in which our nonprofit operates? Are new methods being developed? Are we complying with current laws regulating our field? Does the future show a shortage of professionally trained staff? Is technology changing the way people acquire knowledge or services?

>> Are other nonprofits providing similar services in the community? If so, how are our services different? Should we be working together? How are we distinctive?

>> How stable are the funding sources on which we depend? What about changes in government funding? Changes in our earned revenue? Can we find new potential sources of funding?

The decisions you make are only as good as the information on which you base them. Therefore, it's important to find the best and most up-to-date data available that may have an impact on your organization and its programs, and it's important not to overlook unfavorable trends.

You may want to collect information from the general public or the constituents served by your nonprofit. We also recommend conferring with major donors, foundation representatives, and other nonprofits or government agencies that work closely with you. Surveys, interviews, and focus groups are ways to gather input from the public. Before you undertake any of these techniques, however, spend some time thinking about what you want to learn. Write a list of questions for which you want answers.

PLANNING FOR UNCERTAINTY

No matter how well you plan, circumstances can, and probably will, change. So, of course, creating a strategic plan requires that you make assumptions about the future; sometimes these assumptions turn out to be wrong. Maybe, for example, a dependable funding source drops out of the picture; maybe a major industry in your city closes its doors; or maybe new government regulations affect your programs. Unexpected events within your nonprofit or in your community can dump cold water on your carefully designed plans.

But this doesn't mean that your nonprofit should abandon planning. Fundamentally, planning is about making decisions that are based on the best available information and the most careful thought you can muster. If conditions change or a new opportunity arises, the analytical muscles that your organization has developed through that thoughtful decision-making should prepare it to respond quickly and appropriately to apply new strategies. Remember that all plans are living, breathing documents and can be adjusted as conditions change.

TIP

If possible, consult with someone experienced in preparing surveys or interview protocols, because the phrasing of questions and the way you distribute your surveys affect the answers you get. Look for expertise in this area from consulting firms that work with nonprofits, at local colleges and universities, or from marketing or market research firms.

REMEMBER

Bad information leads to bad decisions. Or, put another way, garbage in, garbage out. When gathering background information to guide planning decisions, take the time to seek out the most accurate, up-to-date facts available.

Looking at the internal situation

In addition to surveying the environment in which the organization operates, you need to expend some effort assessing the organization itself. Consider the following factors when doing an internal analysis:

>> What are the organization's major accomplishments? What are its milestones?

>> Whom does it serve and what does it offer them? If we're a new nonprofit organization, whom will we serve and what can we offer them with limited start-up funding?

>> Is the board of directors fully engaged with the organization? Should any weaknesses on the board be filled? Is the board engaged in aggressive fundraising?

>> What are the staff's capabilities? Does the organization have enough staff — and the right staff that is sufficiently trained and licensed? If we can't hire staff yet, how can our volunteers help us in delivering services?

>> Do our governing documents — such as our articles of incorporation — allow for our current and planned activities?

>> Is the organization's office and program space in the right location and of the right size? If we're working out of a personal residence until we can afford to lease office space, how can we appear to be more established? Can we use a personal mailbox address for correspondence? How do we explain this to potential funders?

>> Does the organization have adequate technology? Are its technology systems integrated with one another? Do employees and/or volunteers need additional training in using technological tools? Are equipment needs anticipated?

>> Has the organization operated within its budget? Is financial reporting adequate? Are appropriate financial controls in place? If we're not ready yet because we don't have a large budget, how can we put these controls in place?

>> What does the organization's program cost and how does it pay for it? If we're a new nonprofit, how can we identify funding for our programs? Can we charge a fee for services? How will the community react if we charge a fee for our services?

>> Does the organization have a variety of funding sources? Are those funding sources stable? If we're a new nonprofit, where do we start with introducing ourselves to potential funders and donors? What is the board of director's role in securing early funding and contributions?

Calling in the SWOT team

One common way to analyze the information you've collected is to perform a *SWOT* analysis, which is the acronym for *s*trengths, *w*eaknesses, *o*pportunities, and *t*hreats. A SWOT analysis is usually done in a facilitated meeting in which the participants have agreed-on ground rules. If you prefer, stakeholders can complete their individual versions of the analysis and then come together to discuss the results as a group.

SCENARIOS FOR THE FUTURE

Scenario planning is an approach that involves imagining several futures in which your organization may find itself and then using those imagined futures to determine the strategies that your nonprofit needs in order to thrive in the years to come. The practitioners of scenario planning don't pretend that they're prophets or seers, but this planning method provides a framework for thoughtful conversations among the leaders of the nonprofits, corporations, and government agencies that engage in it.

Scenario planning pushes you to define the most pressing issue facing your organization. For example, if your organization works to provide equal access to information technology for everyone, you may want to ask which aspect limits some people's access now — whether it's equipment, service costs, training, or available Internet access — and which conditions are changing that might solve or exacerbate the problem. After you've figured out the question you want to address — often the most difficult thing to do — you need to collect as much information as possible about trends that may impact access to technology. That may include future cost projections for computers; projected family-income figures; trends affecting libraries, adult education, and after-school programs that have provided free access to technology; business trends in the technology industry; and efforts by local governments to provide wireless access to their communities, to name only a few.

Then you can begin thinking about how the future may play out by creating several descriptions — some would say *stories* — of possible future conditions. After you arrive at this point, you begin to talk about the roles your organization might play in each of those stories that would enable it to fulfill its mission.

TIP

We recommend using a professional meeting facilitator. A facilitator brings experience and a neutral viewpoint to the proceedings and can be effective in helping a group arrive at a consensus about organizational goals — even goals that may be unpopular with some staff or board members.

Be honest when looking at your organization's strengths and weaknesses. It's tempting, for example, to put the best face on the activities of the board of directors. They're volunteers, after all. How much time do they *really* have to give to the organization? But if you avoid identifying important deficiencies because you don't want to hurt someone's feelings, your planning efforts will be handicapped by bad information.

For example, the results of a SWOT analysis for an organization providing counseling services to unemployed adults may look something like this:

Strengths

>> The program staff is highly qualified and committed.

>> Clients give program services a high-quality rating.

>> The organization has an accumulated budget surplus equal to approximately five months of operating expenses.

>> Program costs are funded largely by local government grants.

Weaknesses

>> The cost per client is higher than in similar programs.

>> Contributed income from individuals is low.

>> The programs aren't well known to the general public.

>> The organization has no community partnerships with other nonprofit organizations, government agencies, or large-scale corporations.

Opportunities

>> The closure and shrinking of nearby industries indicate that more members of the client base will be working as part-time independent contractors without employee benefits.

>> The organization's marketing campaign has attracted additional visitors to its website.

>> The organization has modest cash reserves to invest in growth.

>> No one in the organization has discussed how the board of directors can help start an endowment fund for the organization.

Threats

>> Local government (the primary funding source) has announced plans to open its own job training and placement programs in three years.

>> Over the past five years, program costs have increased at a rate of 3 percent per year.

As this example shows, one or more items often can be listed as both strengths and weaknesses. Here, the fact that the nonprofit organization is largely funded by the government is a strength, but it's also a weakness because it creates a situation in which the organization relies on a single source of funding.

A review of this SWOT analysis reveals a nonprofit organization that has been successful in providing quality services and getting those services funded by government contracts. It has been financially prudent and developed modest cash reserves. However, the working conditions are changing for its clients, and the program's future may be in jeopardy if it continues to rely heavily on government resources. A major new competitor is entering its field.

This nonprofit organization has limited time and resources to diversify revenues. If its government funding is cut completely, it may have to close, spending its cash reserve on connecting its clients to other services, meeting with its donors to thank them, telling stories of its clients' successes on its website, providing modest severance packages to loyal employees, and taking necessary accounting and legal steps to close.

In the meantime, because its clients need new entrepreneurial and planning skills to manage their changed employment status, it has the opportunity to develop distinctive programs responding to current needs. It also has opportunities to develop an individual donor campaign led by the board of directors; meet with other nonprofits, local colleges, and business leaders about sharing counseling and training services; and seek coverage of its programs in the local media.

REMEMBER

A SWOT analysis can be a powerful guide to developing a plan because it looks at both your nonprofit organization's inner workings and external environment. As your committee moves on to the next planning step, where you decide together on goals and strategies for coming years, it can refer to the SWOT analysis as a reminder to celebrate and further develop strengths, tackle weaknesses, and prepare for change.

TIP

Check out File 8-3 at www.wiley.com/go/nonprofitkitfd6e for an example of how you can map your organization's strengths, weaknesses, opportunities, and threats to determine your overall SWOT.

MAPPING THE MATRIX

One approach to planning that may work well as a tool to guide your nonprofit organization is the creation of a *matrix map*. The matrix map encourages nonprofits to take a hard look at their dual bottom line (measuring fiscal performance and positive social impact) — at how well the goods and services they provide address their mission *and* at each of those services' costs and earning potential. To create a matrix map, you and your planning committee follow these four steps:

- Identify each of your lines of business or activities.

- Assess how well each of those activities addresses your mission.

- Analyze how well each of those activities covers its costs, by either charging fees and admissions or attracting grants and contributions.

- Create a chart or matrix that illustrates how programs compare to one another according to value in addressing your mission and contribution to the organization's financial stability.

The result of this process — easily understood illustrations comparing an organization's programs — can help a planning committee choose among options. Check out File 8-4 at www.wiley.com/go/nonprofitkitfd6e for a sample matrix map.

Putting the plan in writing

After the research, analysis, and discussion, it's time to determine future directions and put the results into a final plan. Ideally, the plans of your nonprofit organization become apparent after sifting through and discussing the material that's assembled. If the strategic planning group can't reach a consensus, it may want to test its ideas on the board of directors or a few trusted peers to help it come to an agreement.

TIP

It can be easy to come up with a long laundry list of goals and then skim lightly over the strategies you'll use to achieve them — we recommend limiting your goals to a half dozen or fewer and paying full attention to the related strategies.

Ensuring that your goals make sense

Organizational goals need to be specific; measurable when they're attached to time-bound objectives; and attainable within one year. The easy way to get started with writing your goals is to start them with verbs. By using verbs to write your strategic planning goals, you're indicating that action will occur to enable the goals to be achieved within each year's strategic plan.

Here are some examples of well-written strategic planning goals:

>> Provide the Village of Hempstead's families in need of funding to adopt a child with the needed resources to enable their family to become complete.

>> Empower homeless women in San Diego County to change their lives via our new social services street outreach and safe-shelter program.

>> Educate high school students enrolled in the Biloxi school district about the importance of diversity, equity, and inclusion in the school setting, future workplaces, higher education, and life.

>> Create a farm-based shelter-and-adoption program for the lower desert's feral cats.

Itemizing the parts that form your strategic plan

When you reach a consensus about your organization's goals, assemble a written strategic plan. The components of the plan should include the following items, in the order shown:

>> An executive summary

>> A statement of the organizational mission and vision

>> A description of the strategic planning process

>> Organizational goals

>> Strategies to achieve those goals (measurable objectives and implementation plans for programs and services)

>> Appendixes that contain summaries of the background material used to determine the strategic plan, including a list of the people who participated in creating the strategic plan

Assign the task of drafting the document to your best writer. When the draft is finished, the strategic planning committee should review it to ensure that everything in the plan is stated clearly. Submit the final draft to the full board for discussion and adoption.

WARNING

A common failing of strategic planning documents is the use of jargon and vague language. A strategic plan that uses such wording and lacks clarity is a poor guide and does nothing to increase your credibility with your constituents or your funders. You don't want readers to finish reading it and ask, "What is it that they're going to do?"

TIP

Check out File 8-5 at www.wiley.com/go/nonprofitkitfd6e to see an example of how a strategic plan may be presented.

Adjusting your strategic plan when necessary

Although having a strategic plan is important, flexibility in its implementation is just as important. Things change. Reviewing your strategic plan is an ongoing activity — preferably monthly but at least quarterly, your board, executive director, and program staff should revisit it to check on the progress you've made and identify whether assumptions and predictions were correct. You may find that you need to employ new strategies to achieve your carefully developed goals.

Putting Plans into Action

Unfortunately, too many well-crafted strategic plans end up in a drawer or on a bookshelf. Participants may have expended great effort to create the document, and board and staff may have formed close bonds during the strategic planning process. But if the decisions made during that board/staff retreat at the charming lakeside inn aren't translated into tasks, what's the point — other than camaraderie?

REMEMBER

No matter what sort of strategic plan you create — organizational, fundraising, marketing, program, or facility-related — you need to break the larger, all-encompassing strategies into a sequence of steps that enables you to chart your progress over time. The following sections help you do that.

Defining and setting goals, objectives, strategies, and outcomes

Getting lost in all the terminology of strategic planning is easy. Here are brief definitions of four common terms — goals, objectives, strategies, and outcomes — using a simple example of traveling from Chicago to New York to attend a professional conference:

>> *Goals* are your organization's aspirations. Goals can be set at the organizational level, the program or department level, or the individual employee level. Using a road trip as an analogy, a goal is to arrive in New York, having left from Chicago.

>> *Objectives* are smaller steps that one must accomplish to reach a goal, and they're always stated in a way that can be measured. So, on a trip from Chicago to New York, an objective may be to drive 325 miles on the first day. When you pull into the motel parking lot, you can check the odometer to see whether you've achieved your objective.

>> *Strategies* are approaches or ways to achieve goals. Usually, more than one option exists. You can travel to New York by several methods: plane, train, automobile, bicycle, or on foot. After considering the costs, your schedule, and your hiking ability, you decide to travel by car.

>> *Outcomes* describe the results of reaching a goal. In this example, you reach the goal — New York — and learn useful information at your conference. Outcomes are written in past tense.

To see how all four terms come into play, look at the example of a development plan in Table 8-1. Reading from top to bottom, you have the whole plan, from organizational goal to outcome.

TABLE 8-1 **Organizational Goal to Outcome**

What We Call It	Example
Organizational goal	Diversify income.
Strategic goal	Develop a reliable annual campaign.
Objective 1	By the end of Year 1, retain 80% or more of current annual fund donors.
Objective 2	By the end of Year 1, increase new prospects by 100% (the baseline is zero), by way of board and advisory committee contacts.
Objective 3 Strategy	By the end of the first quarter in Year 1, increase the number of new prospects responding to the January fundraising campaign by 10% or more. Increase individual contributed income.
Outcome	Increase organizational finances from new funders who have committed to contributing to the next three annual fundraising campaigns.

REMEMBER

Don't get bogged down in terms. How you label the different steps in your plan is less important than clarifying what you need to accomplish and the steps you'll take to succeed.

Creating a work plan

You can see in Table 8-1 that the objectives are measurable results. Achieving each objective in the table requires several steps. Here's where *work plans* (also referred to as action plans) come into play. Work plans break tasks into small steps so that they can be easily managed.

Work plans — the nuts-and-bolts of strategic planning — contain strategies for achieving specific objectives, identify deadlines for completion, and note who's responsible for completing the task. A work plan answers the following questions for each objective:

>> What is the end result?

>> How long will it take to do the job?

>> Who will be responsible for doing the job?

>> What resources are needed?

A typical work plan may look like Table 8-2.

TABLE 8-2   **Sample Work Plan: Create an Appeal Letter**

Objective	By When	By Whom	Resources Needed	Date Completed
Attend workshop on fundraising letters	February 28	Allen	Find workshop via the Foundation Center	February 26
Draft letter and seek feedback	March 15	Allen and board committee	Committee meeting for feedback	March 15
Revise and copyedit letter	March 20	Ashley and Gina	Experienced editor	March 25

Work plans require that a job be broken down into smaller tasks. In Table 8-2, for example, the three objectives can be split into even smaller tasks.

WARNING

Be aware that you can take the creation of a work plan to the point of absurdity. Don't make work plans so detailed and specific that writing the plan takes more time than doing the work that the plan specifies.

Planning for Programs

Program planning is such an important part of nonprofit work that we think it needs its own section. Nearly all nonprofit organizations provide a service of one sort or another. The organization provides services by way of programs. A small nonprofit may have only one. Larger nonprofits may have dozens. No matter how many programs you have, you may be thinking of adding a new one or changing the ones you have. We walk you through the process in the following sections.

Working as a team

When you're developing programs for the first time, it's important to create a team that includes the executive director, program staff, volunteers, and community partner representatives. Your team members will all have insight on how to plan successful programs. Each team member brings a different viewpoint to the program planning process, so it's important to listen and capture their input.

TO EXPLAIN YOUR PROGRAM, TAKE A TIP FROM THE BUSINESS SECTOR

If you were starting a new business and looking for investors, one of the first things you'd do is create a business plan. Nonprofits are wise to follow this model when developing a new program. A business model is useful in explaining the program and can form the basics of grant proposals when you seek funding.

Business plans should include the following information:

- An executive summary that covers the main points of the plan
- An explanation of the need for the program and who will use it

  (This information is comparable to the market analysis in a for-profit business plan.)

- A description of the program and your strategies for implementing it
- Why your organization is best poised to implement the program
- Résumés and background information about the people who will provide and manage the program services
- Three-year projections of income and expenses for the project, including an organizational budget for the current year

As with strategic planning, program planning should be done as a group exercise. It doesn't have to be as extensive as the strategic planning process, but you gain more acceptance of the new program and guard against omitting important details when you work with others to develop new programs.

The best and most productive way to facilitate a program planning team session is to guide the discussion using the Theory of Change Program Planning Worksheet.

Think ahead with all planning efforts about how you are going to evaluate the program and the data you will be collecting.

TIP

Check out File 8-6 at www.wiley.com/go/nonprofitkitfd6e to see an example of a Theory of Change Program Planning Worksheet.

A *theory of change* is a description of why a particular way of working will be effective, showing how change happens in the short, medium, and long terms to achieve the intended results. A theory of change can be developed at the beginning of the program planning process or to describe an existing program (so that you can evaluate it). It's particularly helpful if you're planning or evaluating a complex program, but it can also be used for almost every decision-making process.

The Global Partnership for Sustainable Development Data created a useful theory-of-change document. Check out File 8-7 at www.wiley.com/go/nonprofitkitfd6e to view this example.

Most theories of change also include *outputs* (the quantifiable results the program will produce) — for example, ten partnerships established and supported or five in-kind contributions from new partners. You're projecting the results or outcome of your program implementation's impact.

Assessing needs

A *needs assessment* is an important part of program planning. If you're thinking of starting a new program, for example, a needs assessment to determine whether the program is necessary should be the first step you take.

A needs assessment is more or less a research project. You don't necessarily need to hold to the strict requirements of scientific inquiry, but just as you do when collecting information to help guide strategic planning, you should do everything possible to ensure that the information is accurate and free of bias.

Determining the questions to be answered

Your needs assessment should evaluate the answers to the following questions:

>> **Are other organizations providing the same service?** Obviously, you don't want to duplicate services if another organization is already doing the job. If you believe that your competition isn't doing a good job, that's another question. Jump to the second point.

>> **How many people might use the service?** Making a good estimate of the number of people the new program will serve is important. Doing so helps you justify establishing the program and helps you plan for staff needs.

>> **Can and will people pay for the service?** If so, how much? How many of the people you hope to serve will need discounted tuition or scholarships, for example?

>> **Do we need to meet any special requirements for providing the program?** Does the program need to be near good public transportation? Is parking important? Will people come to the neighborhood where you're providing the services? Will the program require you to register your services, obtain licenses, or obtain operating permits?

>> **What are the trends?** Will the number of people using the service increase or decrease in the future? Is the population in your community increasing, decreasing, or staying the same?

Researching the best solutions

Just as when you collect information for strategic planning, your goal in program planning is to find the most accurate, unbiased data available. Don't depend on only one source. Here are some ways to get the information you need:

>> **Talk to colleagues in your community.** Ideally, you have relationships with the people and organizations that provide similar services. Ask their opinions about your ideas for new programming.

>> **Look at census data.** The best sources for population information are the numbers collected by way of a census (www.census.gov). Some municipal and regional planning groups also publish population-growth projections. These projections are estimates, but census data doesn't represent an absolutely accurate count of the people in your community, either. Gather all the numbers you can get.

>> **Visit a funding information network or the Candid website.** By looking at funding trends, you can piece together a picture of which services are available and who is supporting them. You can find a funding information network library near you at `https://candid.org/find-us` or subscribe to its services online at the Foundation Directory Online by Candid. In addition to guiding you to potential funding sources, this website's *Philanthropy News Digest* (PND by Candid) shares research and articles produced by foundations.

>> **Get information from current or potential users of the service by distributing questionnaires and hosting focus groups.** The questions you ask determine, in large part, the answers you receive. If possible, find someone who has experience in preparing survey questions to guide you.

>> **Look at similar programs in other communities.** Although you can't always depend on the experience of others fitting exactly with your particular situation, examining what others have done is always wise.

TIP

Check out File 8-8 at `www.wiley.com/go/nonprofitkitfd6e` for a sample needs-assessment questionnaire.

REMEMBER

Some people say they don't want to share an idea with others because they're afraid someone may steal it. Although you can't rule out the chances of this happening, we believe that it's a rare occurrence. In almost all cases, being open about your plans is a good idea.

Brainstorming the resources needed to implement new programs

Just because a new program is needed doesn't necessarily mean that your organization should be the one to start it. You need to take other factors into account. Work with the program planning team and invite your board treasurer or financial director or accountant to join in the program planning session. Look at *all* aspects of what it takes to fund, implement, evaluate, and continue a new program after the first round of start-up funding.

Consider the factors in the following sections when assessing your ability to start a new program.

Estimating the cost of programs

A new program almost always adds expenses to your organizational budget. If we were to contemplate it long enough, we could think of an example in which increased program costs aren't a factor, but we don't have all year.

To be sure that you don't get yourself into a financial hole, carefully project the extra costs you'll have from additional staff and increased space, equipment, and insurance. After you have solid expense projections, you have to project where you'll find the added revenue needed to pay these costs.

Evaluating organizational and staff capability

Does your nonprofit organization have the knowledge and expertise to provide the program services? This question may not be a concern if the proposed program is merely an extension of what you've been doing. If your organization is branching out into new areas, however, be sure that you or someone else in the organization has the credentials to provide a quality program.

Also pay attention to hidden staff costs. For example, consider whether your current program director will have sufficient time to provide adequate supervision for the new program. Will you need to hire a new staff person or consultant to implement the program? Is this a one-time cost or a recurring cost to continue the program? Will this person require a computer, cellphone, insurance, or office space?

Remembering special requirements

Check whether you need additional licensing, accreditation, or permits to provide the program. This is especially important for human-services programs. For example, if you've been working with teenagers and want to expand to elementary and preschool children, find out whether your program space must meet additional building-code requirements in order to serve a younger client group.

Fitting it into the mission

From time to time, we're all tempted by the idea of doing something new. Gee, wouldn't it be nice if we could sell goldfish in the front lobby? But you have to ask yourself what selling goldfish has to do with your organization's mission. If you go too far afield, you can detract from the hard work of addressing your organizational purpose. Also, if you go beyond what is permitted by your purpose statement in your articles and bylaws, you may be acting unlawfully beyond your organization's authority and perhaps outside of its tax-exempt status.

Thinking long term

An idea that looks good today may not look good next year or the year after. Don't forget that costs rise year after year. Your staff appreciates occasional raises. Try to imagine where the program will be five and ten years into the future.

Funding sources may be available to launch a new program or expand services. But it's wise to have a plan for sustaining the program after it's launched, by identifying funding sources for its ongoing support after the initial funding source is gone.

Facility Planning: Finding a Place to Do Your Work

If your organization is grappling with a move to a new (or its first) office building, you're facing important decisions. And guess what? You need to write a plan!

This effort is likely to have three phases:

>> Planning for your needs

>> Identifying possible locations

>> Analyzing the feasibility of the locations you find

How much space and of what kind?

Before you go out to seek a location, make a list of your organization's specific needs. If you've ever shopped for an apartment or a house, you know that some features are critically important and some are desired but not essential. Breaking down your space needs by function and then including a list of general requirements helps. Consider current programs as well as programs you're planning to introduce in the near future.

TIP

For help with anticipating and specifying all your organization's facility needs, check out File 8-9 and File 8-10 at www.wiley.com/go/nonprofitkitfd6e.

Location, location, location

Many nonprofit organizations have learned the hard way that having a beautiful new facility doesn't necessarily mean that their students, patients, or audiences will go there. First and foremost, you must think about what would be the right location for your programs and clients. We suggest that an organization conduct a simple marketing test of a location it's considering. This "test" may take the form of a written survey, interviews, or an open house/walk-through at the proposed site followed by a discussion with current constituents. Also, talk to nearby residents, merchants, and the local police, and spend time observing the site at different times of day. Finally, check the zoning for the desired location and make certain that your proposed use for it is permitted.

Organizations often move to larger facilities when they want their programs to grow, and they discover the hard way that offering more seats, classes, or therapy sessions doesn't necessarily mean that they'll be used. Do you have clear evidence of growing demand for your services and that your organization's current physical space is inhibiting its growth? When you conduct your marketing test, you need to discern whether more people will visit your new location: Reach out to both potential clients and your current followers.

The ideal location may change over time as neighborhoods change. Even if your organization has been based in one place for a long time, before signing a new lease, explore whether its location is still meeting its needs.

Owning, leasing, or taking a free ride

Stability, convenience, and cost — in addition to location — are key factors to consider when selecting your organization's home. In this section, we discuss the implications of ownership and leasing, or of accepting donated space.

REMEMBER

In considering your real estate choices, also consider the context. Is the real estate market changing? Are interest rates rising or falling? How well are tenants' rights protected by law? Is the building that you want to lease likely to be sold?

The pros and cons of owning

Because of the tax benefits of private homeownership, many people assume that owning a building is best for a nonprofit organization. Although a nonprofit's building can be a valuable asset, remember that a nonprofit is already exempt from paying most business taxes, so any interest it may pay on a mortgage or building loan isn't a deductible expense — it's just an expense.

Here are two possible advantages of building ownership:

>> **Ownership stabilizes costs.** If your organization is based in a real estate market where prices are rising, purchasing a building may help to prevent steep rent increases or an untimely eviction.

>> **Ownership improves the public image of your organization.** Organizations owning their own buildings appear in the public eye to be stable institutions. This perception may help them raise money.

Major disadvantages of building ownership for nonprofits can be that it increases the staff's workload and requires a continuing investment. If the organization buys a building that's larger than its needs, it may become a landlord to others and must be prepared to advertise the property, negotiate leases, and manage maintenance and repairs. Whether or not it has tenants, it becomes fully responsible for the building's care. Rental income it collects can be an unrelated business taxable income. Check with a tax attorney for advice before entering into this type of arrangement.

WARNING

If your nonprofit organization buys its own building, be sure to set aside a cash reserve for building maintenance. Otherwise, if a boiler explodes or the roof leaks, you may have to suspend operations for an extended period to fix the problem.

Considering renting

When you rent a home for your nonprofit organization, you're taking on costs that you need to cover month after month. Often these costs increase from year to year. Rent may not be the only such expense. Here are a few questions you should answer fully before signing a lease:

>> What costs are covered? Is your nonprofit responsible for all or some of the utilities?

>> How long is the lease, and does it include options for you to renew it at a similar rate?

>> If property or other taxes increase while you're a tenant, do you pay for the increase or does the landlord?

>> Which repairs are the landlord's responsibilities and which ones are yours?

>> Who's responsible for routine building maintenance?

>> What will the landlord permit you to change about the building?

Deciding whether to accept a freebie when it's offered

Taking a free ride through the donation of space sounds wonderful, doesn't it? Indeed, it lowers your operating costs and enables you to use more of your resources for programs. But you must be willing to look a gift horse in the mouth.

A free building is worthwhile only if it's in the right location, is the right size, and offers the right amenities. Doing effective work is difficult in an inappropriate space. Ask yourself this: If the building weren't free, would you have chosen it for your nonprofit?

Making a move

Organizations with what seem to be straightforward plans for moving into new facilities often overlook the true costs of making such a move. Some spaces may need to be altered to suit your organization's needs. Even when you fit right into your new offices, you encounter one-time charges such as signs, cleaning deposits, phone and Internet hookups, and fees or deposits for starting up your utilities. Don't forget marketing costs to let the public know you have moved.

REMEMBER

The most important *things* for you to move are your constituents. You want to make a thoughtful, sustained effort to invite them into your new facility.

Deciding to take on a capital project

What if no existing building suits your organization's needs? You may be in for a major effort to substantially renovate a space or construct a new building. If you're one of these brave and hardy types, you want to read this part of the chapter along with Chapter 19, which addresses in greater detail how to plan and raise money for building projects.

Even a small organization with the right board and campaign leadership can manage a successful capital campaign if its expectations are reasonable. So can organizations whose projects are happening at the right place and at the right time — such as those organizations based in community redevelopment areas or low-interest bank loans for community development.

To determine whether your organization can manage a capital campaign, you need to plan — no surprise, right? Your facility plan should ask hard questions, including these:

>> What will the project cost?

>> Are your board members in a position to contribute to a capital campaign above and beyond their usual annual gifts to your organization?

>> Do public or foundation resources in your region support capital projects? Are they likely contributors?

>> Do you have staff knowledge and time to contribute to this effort?

Having examined these preliminary questions, organizations that are considering capital campaigns often complete a planning step called a *feasibility study* — research most often led by a consultant who interviews people who support the organization and other generous donors in their communities whose grants and gifts are essential to its success. As with other types of planning, you're gathering information from key stakeholders, but you're focusing your attention on those who may become contributors. From these interviews, the consultant estimates how much the organization is likely to raise with a capital campaign. Find out more about this practice in Chapter 19.

Chapter **9**

Evaluating Your Work: Are You Meeting Your Goals?

How do you know whether your nonprofit organization is meeting its goals? How do you know whether your approach is valid, your staff is qualified, and your clients benefit from what you do? When your nonprofit's resources are scarce, you may want to put all of them into providing direct benefits to the people you serve. But, wait. When resources are scarce, they must be used in the best possible way. That's why you have to set aside some of the organization's time, money, and attention for evaluation.

Most organizations gather information during the normal course of doing their work. A good evaluation can be one in which you collect information in a consistent, systematic way and ask the right questions so that you learn from its patterns and particulars. This chapter outlines what goes into a meaningful evaluation and explains how to interpret the results and implement any necessary changes.

TIP

Check out File 9-1 at www.wiley.com/go/nonprofitkitfd6e for a list of web resources related to the topics we cover in this chapter.

REMEMBER

We use the word *evaluation* as a general term in this chapter to mean any act of reflecting on the quality and success of your nonprofit's work. Some professionals differentiate between an assessment and an evaluation, however. An *assessment* is the ongoing use of measures or tools (such as exams or surveys) to indicate progress being made, and an *evaluation* is a systematic, rigorous comparison of one's results to defined expectations or standards or another program. Check out File 9-2 at www.wiley.com/go/nonprofitkitfd6e for more definitions of evaluation terms.

Knowing the Importance of Evaluation

Unlike for-profit businesses, nonprofits can't evaluate their performance solely by showing a profit at the end of the year or by increasing the value of their stock. Indeed, they may generate a budget surplus to invest in their future work, but that isn't their primary purpose. Some people say that nonprofits have to achieve a *double* bottom line, one in which their finances are healthy and their activities are meeting their goals — or what a friend of ours calls "an appropriate balance of mission and resources." That's where evaluation comes in: It can measure how successful you've been at focusing on your purpose and achieving your challenging goals and objectives.

Evaluating your work goes hand in hand with every aspect of leading and managing your organization. An evaluation can

>> Tell you whether your planning strategies are working and whether you need to adjust them

>> Guide you in hiring the right staff for the work to be done and in making good use of volunteers' time and energies

>> Help you draft your annual budget by pointing out where resources are most needed

>> Convey the information you need to market your work to the constituents you want to serve

>> Strengthen your fundraising by arming you with information for reports on your work to foundations and donors

>> Alert you if a program is having the effect that you want to achieve with your clients.

In short, to know where you're going, you need to know where you've been. Evaluation can tell you whether you're on the right road or need to recalibrate your route.

Working Through the Evaluation Process

You've probably been part of an evaluation before, whether a personal perfor-mance evaluation or a program evaluation, but maybe you've never been in charge of the entire process. Not to fear: This section provides an outline of the process, gives you some pointers about what to evaluate, and helps you select who will perform the evaluation.

Evaluations have three main components:

>> **Set up an evaluation.** This step involves determining the type of evaluation you need to perform, asking the right questions, assigning someone the responsibility to gather and analyze the information you need in order to answer those questions, and deciding where and how you'll find that information.

>> **Conduct the evaluation.** During this step, you gather the information you need consistently and measure what you're learning in an honest (and perhaps even self-critical) way. You may find that you need to devise tools to gather that information — such as surveys of constituents, focus groups, formal observations, or one-on-one interviews. Pre- and post-tests are an easy way to ascertain if learning or other desired outcomes have taken place.

>> **Interpret the data.** In almost all cases, your understanding is deeper (and your findings more valid) if you compare the information you compile to something else. That "something else" may be results for the people you serve before they participated in your program. It may be results for people who didn't participate in any comparable program (a placebo). Or, it may be results for people who participated in a different kind of program. We address this stage in the section "Analyzing Results and Putting Them to Work," at the end of this chapter.

Selecting the right kind of evaluation

Evaluations come in many varieties. The type you choose depends on whether a program is brand-new or has been refined, how much is known about what works in the field in which you're operating, whether you want to prove that your approach is a model that can influence others, and how much money you have to invest in evaluation.

Your organization may consider these two basic types of evaluation:

- » **Formative:** You analyze the progress of your nonprofit's work while your work is in process.

- » **Summative:** You reach the end of a phase or a project and reflect on its accomplishments.

Now that you can drop these terms easily into conversations, let us introduce three other kinds of evaluation you want to know:

- » **Process:** Did the project do what it was supposed to do and on schedule? Did you acquire an office, hire three key staff, promote programs, or sign up participants? Very good. In your process evaluation, tell your readers about the steps you took — the story of your program activities.

- » **Goal-based:** In a goal-based evaluation, you measure what took place and compare it to the original intentions. Did the project reach its goals? For example, your goal may be to "establish a tuberculosis awareness program in the southeastern quadrant of the city that reaches 500 individuals during its first year." Determining whether a program was established is simple; figuring out how many people the program reached is a little more difficult. This answer depends, of course, on the method the project is using to reach people. In other words, you must define what you mean by *reach* before you start measuring the program's results.

- » **Impact or outcomes evaluation:** In an impact evaluation, you ask whether you met your objectives and outcomes. Did the project achieve the desired results and make a meaningful difference? Although it requires time and attention, this type of evaluation is relatively straightforward. For example, if you oversee a tuberculosis awareness program, a desired outcome may be increased numbers of people being tested for TB and, if they have contracted it, taking their medication consistently to improve their health and reduce the likelihood they will infect others. Evaluating such an outcome requires an in-depth study of the population in that section of the city to determine whether they acted on the knowledge they gained and — if they were infected — continued to follow a strict regimen for taking their medication. Public health department data about rates of tuberculosis infections can be tracked yearly for the neighborhoods served.

One of the hardest and most important things to ascertain in an outcomes evaluation is whether your organization has set the most meaningful objectives and outcomes.

SHAPING AN OUTCOMES EVALUATION

As an example of shaping an outcomes evaluation, let's say your organization provides shelter to people who have no home. You may have identified the following aspirations:

- **Measurable Objective 1:** By the end of the funding cycle, increase temporary housing availability by 25 percent for chronically homeless adolescent males.

- **Measurable Objective 2:** By the end of the funding cycle, increase by 40 percent the number of clients completing self-assessment competencies to identify barriers to their finding and maintaining secure housing.

- **Measurable Objective 3:** By the end of the first quarter, increase by 10 percent the number of people per month who enroll with local and federal subsidized housing programs.

- **Outcome 1:** An increased number of chronically homeless adolescent males have taken advantage of nightly shelter beds, counseling, and connections to subsidy programs to secure long-term, affordable housing.

Suppose this were your organization and your evaluation to devise. In that case, you could measure whether you met the first three objectives by keeping intake records for people staying at your organization and taking advantage of its counseling and referral services. It would be harder to measure the outcome, but possible if you had good working relationships with the local and federal housing program staff or if part of your organization's work involved sending out caseworkers to check on former clients to see how they're doing, which would have a major impact on your program budget.

If you want to consider whether you've established the right objectives and outcomes or whether there may be a better way to serve your constituents, you can

- **Survey your constituents** to find out how they lost their housing and ask what they think they most need to maintain a stable place to live.

- **Talk to colleagues** (perhaps partners at the local and federal programs with which you're working) about gaps in services available to people who lack stable housing.

- **Invest in research into your region's job and housing markets,** and investigate the types of leases or mortgages that were common to people who lost their apartments or homes. You may find that your best goal is to address some of the root causes of your constituents' situations.

Planning for evaluation

Before you jump into launching a new organization or program, we strongly recommend that you decide how you'll evaluate it. That way, from the beginning, you can set up methods for collecting information, identify who will be responsible, and budget for the costs. By establishing an evaluation plan at a program's inception, you can collect initial information about the people or places you plan to serve. Hence, you have baseline data to which you can compare your results.

A logic model provides a visual outline of your program or project's resources, goals, and intended outcomes. Your logic model can guide you in understanding what you need to know about your nonprofit's work and its results. We provide a sample logic model in File 9-3 at www.wiley.com/go/nonprofitkitfd6e.

REMEMBER

You want to gather baseline information about the people you serve. Trying to backtrack later to re-create such information is profoundly difficult.

As you set up your evaluation, first identify the purpose and audience. Are you trying a risky new approach to offering a program? Do you need to fulfill the requirements of a government contract? Are you expected by a foundation to share your results with peer organizations doing similar work? Should your evaluation follow standard practices or protocols in your field? Are you hoping to publish your results to be read by a general audience? Or, do you just want to share what you learn with your board and staff to make program adjustments and strengthen your work?

Before you design detailed surveys and interview plans, ask yourself what information your nonprofit already has at hand. It may include attendance records, referrals from other nonprofits, unique visitors to your website, instructors' progress reports, numbers of trees planted, and many other data points that can illustrate your program's progress and reputation.

REMEMBER

As you're evaluating your work, be sure to share and discuss what you discover with your board and staff. Strong nonprofit organizations remain self-critical, learn from their work, and press themselves to do better.

Does your evaluation need to be completed on a particular timeline? Whether that timeline is short or long can affect whether you undertake a simpler or more elaborate evaluation plan.

Also critical are the resources you have at hand to invest in your evaluation. Resources may include money to pay for consultants, invest in focus groups, or purchase data sets. The term also includes staff and volunteer time. We've heard estimates that an organization's taking on a rigorous evaluation will require 15 percent of the executive director's time. We can't swear that it's an accurate estimate, but it's a valuable reminder that staff oversight and leadership are needed even if you hire experts to manage the work.

The WK Kellogg Foundation offers a primer on evaluation for its grantees. We provide links to it in File 9-1 at www.wiley.com/go/nonprofitkitfd6e.

Crafting valuable questions

The most important (and often the hardest) step to take in evaluating your non-profit organization's work is to ask the right questions. What do you need to know to understand whether you've been successful?

If your organization has written a long-range plan, an obvious place to begin is by looking at the measurable objectives defined in that plan and asking how you will know whether you've met them. You may want to push yourself harder and ask whether you met your outcomes, which describe the longer-term, significant change you intend to achieve.

Here are some other topics nonprofits often ask about when evaluating their work:

>> **Cost-benefit:** What does it cost per person to provide the service? Is that more or less than an industry standard? If you have multiple programs, does the one being studied cost more or less per person than others?

>> **Sustainability:** Have you been able to raise the funds needed to continue the program? Have you been able to retain qualified staff?

>> **Staff and board reflection:** What are you learning from your work? What have you done well, and what has surprised you?

>> **Participation:** Are you attracting the people you intended to serve?

>> **Client satisfaction:** What do your constituents say about the program? Do they refer others to it? Do they believe their suggestions and criticisms are taken seriously?

>> **Volunteer engagement:** Are you attracting and retaining volunteers? How do they rate their satisfaction with their participation? Do they refer others to your volunteer opportunities?

>> **Best practices:** If you work in a field in which studies have identified the traits of effective programs, does your program have those traits?

>> **Context:** Has the context in which you offer your services changed? How has that affected the people you serve? Have their needs changed?

>> **Critical feedback:** What do experts (theater critics, researchers, and so on) have to say about your work and how it compares to the work of others?

>> **Model program:** Do others recognize you for the quality of the program? Are you called upon to share your approach and advise others?

TIP

Don't be afraid to ask yourself, "What needs to happen for our nonprofit to no longer be needed?" Maybe it's that streams and creeks are running free, a healthy marsh system is in place, and your town's low-lying areas are no longer flooding. This answer may seem far away from what you can achieve in three or five years. Still, it's valuable to ask the question and remind yourself that your nonprofit wasn't created to operate forever but rather to work toward achieving a meaningful outcome.

Choosing evaluators: Inside or outside?

One key decision you must make about your program evaluation is who will be responsible for conducting it. The work may involve gathering information from several staff members and clients, and after that, information is compiled, analyzing what it means. You need one or more people to

>> Design the evaluation plan and clarify the questions to be asked

>> Create the evaluation tools (surveys and interview protocols, for example), if needed

>> Collect the information to be analyzed (or train others to collect it)

>> Organize and analyze the findings and write a report

If you're undertaking a simple process evaluation, a well-organized and fair-minded staff member can be put in charge. Who else can better understand the purpose of the organization and the nuances of what it's trying to do than someone directly involved in the work? To institute some checks and balances in the process, one person may be responsible for compiling the information. Then a team of staff or board members may discuss its interpretation before a report is written.

"Inside" evaluation offers several advantages. It's usually less costly than hiring an outsider, and the insider doesn't need to be briefed on the work of the nonprofit. On the other hand, the selected person may not be trained in the evaluation process, and some staff members may resent having their work judged by a fellow staff member. Also, those steeped in the day-to-day work of a nonprofit may find it difficult to step back and cast a critical eye over it. Their closeness to the work may bias the findings. Clients and staff may be more forthcoming with an outside person or one they don't know.

REMEMBER

A person who works inside your organization may do a good job of reporting whether programs meet their goals. It can be harder for that person to recommend other approaches that may be more effective.

If you're undertaking a more-complex evaluation, you may want to hire a professional evaluator who knows your field and writes well. In hiring such a person, you gain the advantages of their expertise in research methods, knowledge of the work of comparable organizations, and lack of bias in interpreting the information collected. An assessment made by an independent evaluator may be taken more seriously by your funders and peers. Of course, we can't claim that anyone who is paid a fee by your nonprofit to work for you is 100 percent unbiased: That person may hope to be hired again in the future.

What if you have a modest budget and still want good consulting practices to be worked into your evaluation? Three approaches we've used in the past have been to

» Contact local colleges and universities to see whether a graduate student or faculty member is interested in evaluating your work for academic credit, a dissertation, or a publication.

» Hire an evaluation firm to design your tools and protocols, train your staff to implement them, and then write an independent analysis of your findings after your staff has compiled them. Your staff will do the more time-consuming part of the project, but the professional adds design expertise and an outside perspective.

» Compile information to be evaluated internally, share it with an evaluator, and hire that person to analyze and write about the findings.

Conducting Your Evaluation

After you have thought through the planning steps, refined the questions to be asked, chosen your tools for measuring results, and put the right person in charge of your evaluation, doing the work to study your program or nonprofit is relatively easy. You'll want to decide on a time frame (either a single discrete period or a defined number of days or hours per month) for conducting your study and stick to it. If someone on your staff is responsible for the evaluation, be careful that the individual isn't pulled away by other tasks.

If you're using a survey, an exam, or a checklist for making observations, make sure it's designed by someone who knows how to word and structure such a tool. (We write more about surveys in Chapter 13.) How that tool is used is just as important as its design: If several staff members or volunteers are helping collect data, be sure to brief them as a group before they begin so that everyone is recording the information in the same manner. Of course, you should check for and insist on accuracy and thoroughness. Data is meaningless if it's gathered inconsistently.

Analyzing Results and Putting Them to Work

Imagine that you've collected and organized the information to tell you what you want to know about your organization. It's at hand in lists and charts and graphs. Now you know whether your programs are outstanding and whether your work enhances your clients' lives.

Wait! Not so fast. Just as you must decide on the right questions to investigate as you set out on your evaluation, you need to ask questions about the data you've compiled. Having data and descriptive information isn't the same thing as having knowledge and understanding. Now you must interpret the information and decide how to apply it.

TIP

Evaluation software can help you organize and review your findings. The website Idealware reviews nonprofit program evaluation software. You can find a link in File 9-1 at www.wiley.com/go/nonprofitkitfd6e.

Interpreting results

Although it may seem unscientific, we suggest that you ask yourself what your hunches are before you look closely at the information compiled. Be honest with yourself: What do you think the findings will show, and what do you wish they would show?

Often a moment of insight comes when the pattern revealed in the data isn't what you expected to find. As you identify any such surprises, you can probe more deeply to ask why and how those results didn't meet expectations.

After you've read the data against your assumptions, it's time to look at it anew as though you had no expectations. What general picture does it present? What stands out? Is the information consistent over the year, or does it vary — perhaps according to the season, age of participants, or changes in your staff?

We recommend that you include others in this exercise — ask a few key staff and board members and maybe even a few of your constituents. What do they see? What is surprising to them? Of course, if you hired an evaluation consultant, let that person's experience guide you at this phase.

REMEMBER

Although you don't want to confuse people with ambivalent or anything-goes interpretations, seeking more than one point of view can be valuable. Bring a balanced perspective to the findings: Don't embrace all the praise and discount all the criticism (or vice versa). You can learn from both.

ASKING MORE OF THE DATA

Any finding, whether it's positive or negative, is worth probing more deeply. Let's take the case of an education policy and advocacy group as an example. The group invested in a communications manager and an improved website and data systems to expand its reach. When it wanted parents and other community members to know about legislation under review in the state senate or assembly, it sent alerts by email and social media posts.

Because the group was using the web and social media as its programmatic tools, it made sense for the group to look at its online analytics, many of which looked good:

- Its email list was growing steadily, and the click-through rate to its website was higher than the industry average.

- The number of unique visitors to its website grew from month to month, and, on average, visitors read three pages when they went there.

- The number of people who "liked" the group on Facebook grew steadily, and many of them shared its posts with others.

- A small but gradually expanding number of people followed its tweets.

These are good signs of a growing online presence, but it's still worth asking whether the people who like the group on Facebook also take action and contact their representatives or talk to their school boards about the subjects raised. Social media friends and followers are good, but do they include people with influence in local or state government or education policy?

As is true in many cases, the depth and quality of involvement of people in this organization were more important to its success than the total number of passive fans.

Using your evaluation to strengthen your work

You've looked at your evaluation findings with trusted colleagues; you've turned them inside out and upside down to see them from every angle. Now it's time to interpret them, to tell their story. Likely what you've discovered is not all positive and not all negative. Perhaps you've noticed that some services are rated more highly than others, and some short-term objectives have been met, but others remain elusive. It's time to step back from your organization and programs, and acknowledge any disappointing results, and set short-term and long-term goals to improve upon them.

A program may be flawed in its design, in how it's executed, or in who is leading it; and its effectiveness can be smothered by external circumstances that are beyond its control — a shift in the economy or demographics, a change in public policy, or even a natural disaster, like the COVID-19 pandemic, can derail it.

Some changes will be obvious and easy to make. Maybe a different program schedule would be more convenient for working parents, or better training for volunteers would make them feel more involved and successful. When your findings suggest no easy responses, turn to ideas from others — best practices in your field, model programs, or scholarly research. Don't forget to ask the clients you serve.

Evaluation findings also should be shared with your board, which is ultimately responsible for your nonprofit's fulfilling its mission and purpose. It may decide that some programs aren't a good investment of the nonprofit's hard-won resources and recommend cutting them.

Telling the truth

If your evaluation results are disappointing, face them honestly and share what you've discovered. You may share them discreetly with your board or with the funders who know you well, but doctoring your data or analyzing the findings in a disingenuous way can hurt your organization's reputation and that of your evaluation consultant if you hired one. And all that time and effort you put into your evaluation is lost if you allow it to sit on a shelf collecting dust.

Sharing the evaluation results with your stakeholders

Every person at the program planning meeting represents your stakeholder's group. The term *stakeholder* refers to any individual or group interested in your nonprofit organization. Stakeholders include people directly involved, such as board members, people you serve, donors, community partners, or foundations that give you grants (past, current, and future). This group is entitled to see the outcome of the grant-funded program's planning, implementation, and evaluation processes. When you share how well your program did (qualitatively and quantitatively), you engage in *dissemination,* which means to spread something, especially information, widely. As a transparent public tax-exempt charity, you need to determine how you want to share your evaluation findings.

These days, the public deeply values transparency. Unless your evaluation report contains confidential information, we recommend that you create an executive summary of your findings and publish them as a brochure or PDF available from your website or shared in a meeting with your stakeholders.

TIP

You may find that a poor evaluation lowers staff morale, but if those staff members are invited to participate in creative problem-solving, improving customer service, and other goal-setting activities, working with the evaluation can contribute to building their teamwork and resolve.

Ultimately, you must embrace and attempt to understand the evaluation findings. Many people start nonprofits based on their ideals, and many of them work long hours with limited resources to achieve quite ambitious results. Achieving those results depends on collecting good information and interpreting that information with integrity and resolve.

At the end of the day, the purpose of your evaluation is to benefit your nonprofit organization and the stakeholders it serves.

IN THIS CHAPTER

» Recognizing what motivates volunteers

» Setting up your volunteer program

» Recruiting volunteers

» Making sure a volunteer is right for your nonprofit

» Helping volunteers do their work

» Showing your appreciation and thanks

Chapter 10

You Can Count on Me! Working with Volunteers

Millions of potential volunteers are just waiting for the right nonprofit organization to invite them to volunteer. Just about every nonprofit charitable organization uses volunteers in some capacity. For example, in most cases, board members serve without compensation. And, for many nonprofit organizations in the United States, volunteers do all the work, from planting the trees to paying the bills. Even if your organization employs paid staff, volunteers still provide valuable services. Organizations depend on volunteers to staff telephone hotlines, lead scout troops, tutor students, coach youth sports teams, serve hot meals, organize fundraising events, and stuff envelopes. If you're going to manage a nonprofit organization, you need to know how to work with volunteers.

Of course, you may be sitting alone in your office and asking, "Where are these millions of volunteers?" This chapter offers suggestions to help you determine what kind of volunteers you need, how to find them, and how to keep them happy after they arrive.

TIP

Check out File 10-1 at www.wiley.com/go/nonprofitkitfd6e for a list of web resources related to the topics we cover in this chapter.

Knowing Why People Volunteer

The classic stereotype of a volunteer is someone who has lots of time to spare and is looking for something to do. Although this perception may have been true in the past, when many women stayed out of the workforce and gave their free time to charity, that stereotype no longer fits; however, even today women still represent the largest majority of volunteers. It's still true that more women volunteer than men, but people between the ages of 35 and 54 are the likeliest to volunteer. This is the age range when both men and women are likely balancing careers with raising families, not to mention taking care of aging parents, going to the gym, and keeping up with email and social media.

Why is it that people, even very busy ones, volunteer their time? We think it's because they've recognized the benefits of volunteering time to a favorite organization and because nonprofit organizations have become smarter about asking them.

REMEMBER

Understanding why people volunteer makes it easier for you to find volunteers, organize their work, and recognize their contributions. However, not everyone is motivated by the same factors. People volunteer for a variety of reasons, including their desire to

» **Help the community and others.** Helping others usually comes to mind first when people think of the reasons that people volunteer. But as you see when you read deeper into this list, volunteers' motives aren't always this simple.

What appeals to retired volunteers? Being able to give back to their communities on their own terms and when they're available and healthy enough to volunteer.

» **Express their values.** Believing in an organization's mission is an important motivator for volunteers. A person who believes it's important for all children to have access to a quality education is more likely to volunteer at a local school or tutoring program.

» **Increase self-esteem.** Volunteering makes people feel better about themselves. Giving a few hours a week, or even a month, to an organization creates good feelings.

>> **Help out their friends.** Friends are often the first people we turn to when we need help. Volunteering is also a helpful way to get together with friends regularly.

>> **Make new friends.** Volunteering is usually a social activity. People often use this opportunity to meet interesting people who share their interests and values.

>> **Try out a job.** People considering a job in the nonprofit sector often discover that volunteering is a good way to take a peek at what happens on the inside.

>> **Polish their résumés.** Adding volunteer experience to a résumé shows a commitment to helping others or to working in a particular field.

TIP

What appeals to young volunteers? Being able to earn community-service credit hours for their high school or college community-service requirements.

>> **Develop new skills.** A volunteer job often gives people an opportunity to learn how to do something they didn't already know how to do.

>> **Enjoy something they love.** Many volunteer jobs come with intrinsic benefits for their participants. Ushers at the symphony get to hear the music. Gardeners removing invasive plants from a native plant preserve get to spend a day in a beautiful natural setting.

Keep this list in mind and you'll realize that you don't have to focus your recruitment efforts exclusively on retired people or others who have a lot of leisure time. If you provide an environment in which volunteers can bring their friends, meet others who share their interests, and learn new skills, you can attract even the busiest people to volunteer work. Remember that you have no reason to be apologetic about asking for help: Volunteering benefits the people who step forward to assist you.

Designing a Volunteer Program

Most start-up organizations depend on volunteers because money to pay staff is unavailable. But the lack of resources isn't the only thing that drives a nonprofit to operate with an all-volunteer staff. Some nonprofits make a deliberate decision to operate solely with volunteers to contain their costs and to achieve results with a collective effort among people who care deeply enough to contribute their time and energy.

Many nonprofit organizations struggle to engage volunteers who reflect the racial and ethnic diversity of the communities they serve. Creating a more inclusive volunteer program will send a message to your funders (we represent the entire community), your board members (we are practicing diversity, equality, and inclusion organization-wide), and to potentially interested volunteers (we want everyone to consider volunteering for our organization).

» **Shift your language.** You're not selling used cars — you're tapping into the core of humanity's existence by asking people to contribute their time to help other people or animals. Your goal is to touch their hearts and minds when asking someone to give up their time to help others. When you're seeking volunteers to care for rescue animals, for example, talk about the animals you've had throughout your life. Strike a chord of familiarity, soften their hearts, open the way for a conversation about your organization, its mission, and why it needs dedicated volunteers to help it reach full capacity in delivering services to others.

» **Build relationships.** When someone finally agrees to volunteer with your nonprofit organization, *acknowledge their contributions.* Ask about their health. Make small talk to build a friendship relationship versus a formal boss/volunteer relationship. Take the time to get to know your volunteers — each and every one of them. Remember their names and know what they like to do when it comes to volunteer assignments.

» **Understand socioeconomic differences.** You must understand what motivates every volunteer and how you can personalize your relationship with that person. Even an effort as small as using a volunteer's first name versus Mr. or Mrs. Smith makes a difference. Take the time to listen to volunteers when they have recommendations for improvement or are concerned about your location or the type of people you serve. Be grateful that they're giving their time to your organization.

» **Be observant.** What does the volunteer who is homeless like to do? What are the undiscovered skills you see in their attempts to carry out their volunteer work? Maybe someone is bilingual and can help with translating for a client who doesn't speak English. Or the volunteer might have insight into the behavior of another homeless person that is critical for you to know in order to understand irregular behaviors, such as always being late, eating everyone else's leftovers in the kitchen, or standing by the heater during winter.

» **Strive for inclusive representation.** If all the people who are homeless stand around in the backyard to eat their lunch while everyone else eats in the volunteer lunchroom or board meeting room, you aren't practicing inclusiveness. How can that hurt your organization? It can damage its reputation, goodwill, and mission in the community you serve.

Considering a volunteer coordinator

Although volunteers don't expect to be paid every two weeks, that doesn't mean they come without costs. Recruiting, training, managing, retaining, and thanking volunteers require effort from someone in the organization. We recommend assigning someone the job of *volunteer coordinator*, a person responsible for overseeing or performing the following duties:

>> **Recruiting:** Volunteers don't grow on trees. Depending on how many volunteers you need and the turnover rate of current volunteers, recruiting may be a continuous process.

>> **Training:** Volunteers don't come to work knowing everything they need to know. They can do any job for which they're qualified, but don't expect them to know the ropes until they're told what to do and how to do it.

>> **Scheduling:** Volunteers need a schedule. Scheduling is even more important if your organization uses volunteers to staff an office or manage other tasks that require regular hours.

>> **Appreciating:** Volunteers need to know that their work is valuable to the organization. This item is the last on our list, but it may be the most important. You don't have to pass out plaques, but we do recommend heartfelt acknowledgment. Saying thank you and regularly acknowledging the impact made by volunteers is essential to retaining your volunteers.

TIP

If your organization depends heavily on, or is staffed exclusively by, volunteers, consider recruiting your volunteer coordinator from among board members or more experienced volunteers. You can create committees to take responsibility for many jobs, but some detail-oriented tasks — such as scheduling or bill-paying — are better managed by a single responsible person.

Determining your need for volunteers

Look around your nonprofit organization and decide how many volunteers you need and what functions they can perform. We recommend creating (or helping your volunteer coordinator create) a schedule of tasks to be completed — planning what needs to be done and how many people it will take to do the work. Table 10-1 lists the kinds of volunteer assignments you may jot down. By having such a list and prioritizing the tasks, you know what to do when an unexpected volunteer walks in the door.

TABLE 10-1 Sample Volunteer Task List

Task	Number of People	Time
Data entry — donor list	1 person	3 hours per week
Social media posting and monitoring	2 people	5 hours per month
Answering the telephone	8 people	36 hours per week
Childcare	2 people	3 hours on Saturdays
Filing	1 person	2 hours per week

WARNING

You can have too many volunteers — almost nothing is worse than asking people to help and then finding that you have nothing for them to do. You may want to have both your chart of immediate tasks (such as shown in Table 10-1) and a few back burner projects — such as sorting team uniforms by size or taking inventory in the supply cabinet — in case you end up with more people than you need on a given day.

In the beginning, you may have to experiment before you know exactly how many volunteers you need for a particular job. For example, you may eventually discover that a 2,000-piece mailing takes about five hours for four people to complete. You also may find that preparing the soil and planting 200 seedlings takes two volunteers a full day.

TIP

Don't overlook one of your largest resources for volunteers. Many corporations want their employees to have volunteer days where a group of their employees go out and volunteer together. This can often lead to the company donating to your nonprofit organization as a result of their employee community engagement policies and perks.

Writing volunteer job descriptions

Volunteers perform better if they know what they're supposed to do. Preparing job descriptions for volunteer positions also helps you supervise better and know what skills you're looking for in volunteers. (Take a look at Chapter 11 for detailed information on writing a job description.)

Volunteer job descriptions should be even more complete than paid-employee job descriptions. If you can break jobs into small tasks, all the better, because volunteers often share the same job. For example, a different person may answer the office telephone each day of the week. In that case, to bring consistency to the job, you should store by the telephone a job description that includes a list of telephone procedures, staff extensions, frequently used telephone numbers, and other important information.

Also, part of your job descriptions should include what background checks your organization will conduct, and that all references listed by the volunteers will be checked.

TIP

Check out Files 10-2 and 10-3 at `www.wiley.com/go/nonprofitkitfd6e` for sample volunteer job descriptions.

Organizing volunteers

Many nonprofits invite their volunteers to join a committee. Committees enable volunteers to step forward, offer their best skills, and learn how to do new things. An advantage of forming committees is that it reinforces the social benefits of volunteering. As committee members get to know one another and figure out how to manage their tasks successfully, you or your volunteer coordinator can step back and let them take full responsibility. Using this approach, you find out if the person is reliable, will show up on time, follow through on tasks, and has a good disposition.

Here's a fictitious example that gives you an idea of how to organize committees: The Healthy Diet Project provides telephone referral and information sources for people seeking help with weight loss. It was started by three people who had lost weight and decided to help others do the same. A ten-member board of directors provides governance for the Healthy Diet Project and assumes key volunteer roles in the organization. The nonprofit has five committees, each of which is chaired by a board member but made up of individuals who provide volunteer services:

>> **Telephone committee:** The Senior Health and Wellness Program provides most of its services via telephone. The office receives about 100 calls each day from people seeking information about weight loss and referrals to health clinics and counselors. The telephones are answered 12 hours a day, from 9 A.M. to 9 P.M., Monday through Friday. Two volunteers share responsibility for the phones in three-hour shifts. The nonprofit needs 40 volunteers each week to answer phones and provide information. The Senior Health and Wellness Program also needs backup volunteers in case someone is ill or can't make their shift for any reason.

>> **Program committee:** This committee researches programs to which callers can be referred, maintains the database containing referral information, and provides training to telephone volunteers. Committee members include one physician, two registered nurses, two dieticians, and one physiotherapist who provide professional oversight.

>> **Publicity committee:** The Senior Health and Wellness Program uses several methods to tell the public that its services are available. The publicity committee prepares and sends news releases and creates and distributes public service announcements to radio stations. In addition, the committee operates a speakers' bureau of people who have benefited from the program's services. The committee has also developed a website, a Twitter feed connected to any news that's posted on the website, and a Facebook page; each of these outlets offers basic information about weight loss and invites readers to sign up for a monthly email newsletter. The website maintains links to recommended programs in cities across the United States and Canada.

>> **Fundraising committee:** The Senior Health and Wellness Program raises funds in several different ways, including annual senior-oriented walkathons, email appeal letters sent to people who have joined its contact list by way of its website, and gifts from businesses promoting a healthy lifestyle. Committee members plan and coordinate the fundraising events, write and transmit the appeal letters, and make personal calls on the business sponsors. They also call on all volunteers to make personal gifts, identify possible donors, and provide lists of contacts.

>> **Administration committee:** The Senior Health and Wellness Program receives individual donations from people who use its services, grants from foundations, and limited support from the regional area agency on aging in the city in which it's based. The fundraising and community outreach committees are responsible for maintaining the organization's financial books, writing thank-you letters to donors, and maintaining a database of past donors.

REMEMBER

You may discover other tasks that can be assigned to additional volunteer committees. The kinds of jobs that need to be done vary, depending on the type of service your organization provides. The point to remember is that volunteer work needs to be organized (and supervised) in much the same way as paid work.

In an all-volunteer organization, the responsibility for ensuring that the work is done in a timely and effective manner resides with the board of directors. The board must be committed to finding new volunteers and supervising their work. And board members must be ready to step in to do a job if no volunteers can be found.

REMEMBER

Board members who also serve as program volunteers must remember to keep their roles as board members (governance and fiduciary) separate from their roles as program volunteers. In the latter case, the volunteers are operating like staff, not board members. Yes, there's a difference. See Chapter 3 for information about understanding and defining board members' roles.

Hunting for Volunteers

Most organizations are always on the lookout for volunteers. After all, volunteers move away, grow tired, lose interest, or take new jobs with new hours. If your organization depends on volunteers, you probably need to maintain an ongoing recruitment process. This section shows you how.

Getting the word out

To cast a wide net, you need to use more than one method to find volunteers — and you don't want to spend much money on those methods. After all, you're looking for free help. Persistence matters: Good volunteer recruitment is like a healthy habit that you want to repeat. Here are a few of the most common and most successful methods for recruiting volunteers:

>> **Placing announcements in the media:** Newspapers and radio and television stations sometimes publish or air short public service announcements for nonprofit organizations. (Head to Chapter 13 for more information about writing and distributing news releases.)

>> **Posting fliers:** Grocery stores, churches, coffee shops, college campuses, laundromats, schools, and civic buildings often have bulletin boards where you can post announcements. For best results, place them thoughtfully. For instance, put your call for foster homes for kittens at the pet food store and your community garden poster at the plant nursery.

>> **Taking advantage of word of mouth:** Encourage your current volunteers to recruit others. Have a bring-a-friend day with time for socializing. Ask volunteers to post your posters in their places of business, and don't forget to invite your own friends and associates.

>> **Contacting schools and churches:** Both of these institutions look for ways for students and members to become involved in community service. *Service learning* — by which students learn about a topic by volunteering in their communities — is a growing practice. In fact, many high schools and colleges maintain centers for community relations and student volunteering.

REMEMBER

Reach out to the young people in your area. By doing so, you benefit from their skills and ideas, and you also contribute to training the next generation of volunteers!

>> **Relying on clubs and fraternal groups:** Many professional and social clubs include serving the community in their missions. From Kiwanis International and local Elks Lodges to the Junior League, chamber of commerce, and

campus-based sororities and fraternities, clubs and membership groups can be excellent volunteer resources.

>> **Approaching corporations and businesses:** In some communities, businesses look for community involvement opportunities for their employees. If a company has a community relations, community affairs, or corporate giving department, it's likely to be a good place to begin asking about employee volunteers.

>> **Going online:** Finding volunteers may be as easy as booting up your computer. Besides posting volunteer listings on your organization's website, you also can post on other sites. Several organizations maintain databases where your organization can list its volunteer needs. Prospective volunteers can search the databases by zip code and the type of volunteer work available. Check out the following sites:

- *VolunteerMatch* (`www.volunteermatch.org`) invites nonprofits to set up accounts identifying the kinds of volunteers they need.

- *Points of Light* (`www.pointsoflight.org`) manages several projects linking volunteer centers to one another. Its HandsOn Network links volunteers at 250 centers in 30 countries to meaningful projects. It also operates networks for youth volunteers, alums of AmeriCorps who want to continue volunteering, and corporate volunteers.

- *Idealist* (`www.idealist.org`) and Craigslist (`www.craigslist.org`) are other widely used tools for finding volunteers.

- *United Way* (`www.unitedway.org`) may have a volunteer tutoring or mentoring program in your area.

- *Youth Service America* (`www.ysa.org`) helps you involve young volunteers in your work. It organizes an annual global youth-service day and other opportunities for volunteers between the ages of 5 and 25.

Nonprofit organizations also recruit volunteers from their pages on social networking sites, such as Facebook, Twitter, and LinkedIn. To get your name out there, create a page for your organization. These platforms work particularly well when you describe specific activities that your contacts can do to assist your nonprofit, and when people who know your organization well post photographs and news for their friends to read. Their networks extend your nonprofit's reach. Chapter 13 provides more information about using social media to make friends and influence people.

REMEMBER

Opportunities to do things with friends motivate many people to volunteer.

Looking for volunteers at other organizations

No, we don't suggest that you steal volunteers from other nonprofits, but some organizations do exist to provide volunteer help. Many communities have volunteer centers that participate in a national network of organizations that recruit and place volunteers in nonprofits.

Similarly, the Corporation for National and Community Service (www.nationalservice.gov) was established by Congress in 1993 to operate AmeriCorps, Senior Corps, the Social Innovation Fund, and the Volunteer Generation Fund. This agency is charged with encouraging national service via volunteering and helping nonprofits and public agencies make the best use of this resource. The corporation awards grants that help organizations strengthen their community by the use of volunteers.

REMEMBER

If your organization wants to take advantage of a program offered by the Corporation for National and Community Service, you may need to apply for a federal or state grant, which usually requires sound accounting procedures and extensive reporting of program activities. Turn to Chapters 17 and 18 for information about government grants.

Finding volunteers with special skills

If you're looking for volunteers with special training or experience, spend some time thinking about where you can find them. Limit your recruitment efforts to places where you're most likely to identify the people with the talents you need.

Suppose that your organization is seeking someone with accounting experience to help maintain your books. Local accounting firms, corporate offices, and professional accounting societies may be good recruiting grounds for someone who can assist with bookkeeping. If your organization needs help with a legal matter, some bar associations link nonprofits to attorneys who are willing to volunteer. Most importantly, don't forget about the Service Corps of Retired Executives (SCORE). Here is their website: https://www.score.org.

TIP

Sometimes your nonprofit competition won't mind sharing contacts who are loyal to a particular kind of volunteer activity. In our city, for example, several organizations host film festivals once each year, and volunteers who love to see the films volunteer to sell tickets, greet the media, and manage other tasks, migrating from one festival to the next. Rather than detract from their contributions to one organization, their "migrant" style of volunteering makes these volunteers more knowledgeable and strengthens their skills. When recruiting for short-term volunteer assignments, don't be afraid to ask your "competition" if you can invite some of their great bird watchers, marathon runners, brownie bakers, or scarecrow makers.

Hiring interns

Interns are specialized volunteers who come to you as part of an education or training program. In most cases, a student intern's goal is to develop practical, hands-on work experience.

Sometimes internship programs require your organization to pay a fee or provide the intern with a modest stipend. If you pay a stipend, be aware that you may be creating an employer-employee relationship that is subject to federal, state, and local laws, including minimum wage requirements, employment taxes, and other obligations. If you're working with an established internship program in your community, these potential liabilities are likely covered. If you're recruiting interns on your own, refer to fact sheet 71, Internship Programs Under the Fair Labor Standards Act, available from the Department of Labor website (www.dol.gov/whd/regs/compliance/whdfs71.htm). You may also want to consider adding interns to your liability insurance policy. (Refer to the later section "Insuring your volunteers" for more details.)

As with employees and volunteers, you should provide the intern with clear expectations about duties, attendance, and other aspects of the job. If you decide to go this route, be ready to spend time supervising and evaluating the intern's job performance. Don't forget that the intern's experience is part of their grade.

Interviewing and Screening Volunteers

Require potential volunteers to fill out job applications just as though they were applying for paid work. Ask for references and check them. Review résumés and conduct formal interviews. (See Chapter 11 for information about job interviews.) Avoid paranoia, but don't discount your gut feelings, either.

If you're using volunteers in professional roles, such as accounting, check their qualifications just as you would check the qualifications of an applicant for a paid position. This process may offend potential volunteers, but it's far better to make sure that the person can do the job, even if they're doing it for free.

If you're placing volunteers in sensitive jobs, such as working with children or providing peer counseling, screen your applicants carefully. Criminal background screening, including a fingerprint check, is sometimes required by law, by licensing requirements, or by your insurance carrier. Some states and counties also require a test for tuberculosis. Check with local authorities about the requirements in your area.

TIP

Check out File 10-4 at www.wiley.com/go/nonprofitkitfd6e for a volunteer intake form.

REMEMBER

We realize that screening can be a delicate issue. You're walking a tightrope between the right to privacy and the right of the organization to be sure that no harm befalls its clients. The failure to undertake a background check potentially can result in liability problems for the individual who "hires" the volunteer. Some potential volunteers may be offended by background checks. Explain that the procedures aren't directed at them personally but are in place to ensure that clients are protected. Also, treat all volunteer applicants the same. In other words, don't pass up screening someone just because they're a personal friend.

A CHEAT SHEET FOR THE FAQs

Be prepared to answer questions when people call to volunteer. If you're already using volunteers to answer the telephone, prepare a list of common questions and answers and place that list near the telephone. Here are some sample FAQs that the Senior Health and Wellness Program, a fictional nonprofit discussed in the earlier section "Organizing volunteers," may need:

- **What are the hours I would be needed?** We answer the phones five days a week, from 9 in the morning until 9 at night. We ask people to work a three-hour shift once a week.

- **How will I know what to say?** All volunteers receive one day of training. Training is offered once a month, and almost always on Saturdays.

- **What kind of advice can I give?** Our volunteers can't give medical advice or advice on specific diets. Volunteers refer callers to existing services and professionals. We ask volunteers to be positive and to offer general support to all callers.

- **How do I know where to refer people?** We have an extensive database of weight-loss-related counseling services, physical therapists, and senior exercise programs at local community centers. It's a simple matter of looking through our computer database to find the appropriate phone numbers.

- **What if I get sick and can't cover my shift?** We have volunteers on standby to cover unexpected absences. If you aren't able to volunteer on a regular, weekly basis, you may consider being a backup volunteer.

- **Are we asked to do any other work?** Sometimes we ask volunteers to help with mailings between phone calls.

- **Will you pay my auto (or public transportation) expenses?** We're sorry, but our budget doesn't cover reimbursing volunteers for expenses. Some expenses may be deductible on your income tax, however. You should check with your tax specialist.

- **Can I deduct the value of my time from my income taxes?** No, the IRS doesn't allow tax deductions for volunteer time.

These questions and answers also can be printed in a brochure and mailed to potential volunteers who request more information. Be sure to include background information about your organization in the mailing.

Managing Your Volunteers

Just like managing paid employees, working with volunteers requires attention to management tasks. Volunteers need training and orientation as well as clear, written lists of responsibilities and expectations. Basic expectations for volunteers are easily outlined in a *volunteer agreement form.* You also want to maintain records of the time and tasks volunteers contribute to your organization and consider whether to include volunteers in your insurance coverage.

TIP

Check out File 10-5 at `www.wiley.com/go/nonprofitkitfd6e` for a sample volunteer agreement form.

Providing adequate training

The degree and extent of volunteer training depends on the type of job you're asking them to do. Volunteers who answer telephones, for example, may need more training than those who stuff envelopes for the publicity committee. To successfully answer phones, these volunteers need to know background information about the program or service, information about the types of services available, proper telephone etiquette, and emergency procedures, among other details.

TIP

If you need to provide a full day's training or training over a longer period, we suggest consulting with a professional trainer to either provide the training or help you design the curriculum. Although you may be concerned about investing too much of volunteers' valuable time in training, remember that key motivations for volunteering include meeting people and enjoying time with friends. Trainings can be great opportunities to introduce volunteers to one another and build camaraderie among them. It's a good idea to schedule refresher training sessions for ongoing volunteers, too.

In addition to offering on-site training, give volunteers written materials that restate the information covered in the training. Include with these materials attendance requirements, details about whom to contact in case of illness, and other necessary information that volunteers may need to know when carrying out their tasks.

Larger organizations that use many volunteers sometimes publish a *volunteer handbook.* This type of handbook doesn't need to be an elaborately printed document — it can be several typed pages stapled together, a simple loose-leaf notebook, or a PDF posted on the organization's website. The more information you provide, the better your volunteers can perform.

Keeping good records

Keep records of your volunteers and how much time they spend doing work for your organization. Potential donors and funders may be impressed by the number of volunteers and the time they donate to your nonprofit organization. Or you may be asked to provide a reference for a volunteer who's working to develop job skills or providing a service in an organized volunteer program. You also may need to dismiss a volunteer who's unreliable, and having clear, written records of hours and tasks can justify that difficult act.

If you use professional volunteers to perform tasks that you'd otherwise have to pay for, you can include the value of the volunteer time as an in-kind contribution on your financial statement. Chapter 12 explains more about financial statements.

Insuring your volunteers

Typically, nonprofit organizations carry liability and property insurance. Almost all states require that workers compensation insurance be in place to cover on-the-job injuries to employees (but not necessarily to volunteers). Beyond this basic insurance, coverage depends on the type of services provided and the degree of risk involved.

Keep in mind that volunteers usually aren't liable for their actions as long as they work within the scope of the volunteer activity to which they've been assigned, perform as any reasonable person would perform, and avoid engaging in criminal activity. Unfortunately, people these days have become more eager to file lawsuits. If someone sues you or one of your volunteers, you have to legally defend the case even if it's without merit. One advantage of having liability insurance is that your insurance carrier takes on the responsibility of defending the suit.

Workers compensation may or may not be available to volunteers in your state. If you can include volunteers under your state law, consider doing so, because a workers comp claim usually precludes the volunteer from filing a suit for damages against your organization. Plus, you want a volunteer who suffers an injury to be covered.

Insuring volunteers is a subject of debate in the nonprofit sector. Some people take the position that insurance agents and brokers try to persuade you to insure anything and everything. Others believe that liability insurance and, in some cases, workers compensation insurance should be provided. As is the case with all insurance questions, evaluate your risks and decide whether the cost of insuring against risks is a good investment. For example, if you fail to provide protection to a volunteer who is seriously injured, the reputation and future success of your organization can be harmed. This process is called *risk management.* To find information about risk management for nonprofit organizations, contact the Nonprofit Risk Management Center (www.nonprofitrisk.org).

Saying farewell to bad volunteers

If you work with lots of volunteers, especially volunteers who perform complex and sensitive jobs, you may discover one or more volunteers who lack the skills or personalities to perform at an acceptable level. We hope you never face this situation, but if you do — for example, maybe someone is giving out inaccurate information or acting rudely — do *not* ignore the situation.

Discussing the problem behavior with the volunteer is the first step. Treat this meeting as if you're counseling a paid employee whose job performance is below par. Written job descriptions, written standards for performance, and records of volunteer time and contributed tasks are important when discussing problem behavior.

WARNING

Exercise caution when meeting with a volunteer about their unacceptable behavior, especially if you have no clearly written performance guidelines. Volunteers who are released have been known to sue nonprofit agencies. If you have concerns about this possibility, consult an attorney before you do anything. Also, ask another member of your paid staff to sit in on your meeting with volunteers when you're disciplining them or letting them go. Witnesses are critical when you get sued. The he-says-she-says rationale doesn't stand up in a court of law. Witnesses are gold. You can also record the meeting as well as document the reasons for dismissal in the volunteer's personnel file.

REMEMBER

Talking to someone, volunteer or not, about poor work is never pleasant. However, if someone working for your organization is being disruptive, giving out inaccurate information, or otherwise causing potential harm to your program or the people you serve, you have a responsibility to correct the problem. Plus, the other volunteers probably know that this volunteer isn't pulling their weight and will appreciate that poor performance is not acceptable.

Showing Appreciation for Your Volunteers

Volunteers give their time and, in many cases, expertise to help your organization succeed. It's only right that you thank them and thank them often. Thank them in the hallway after they've completed their work for the day, and also formally recognize their contributions. Here are some standard ways of recognizing volunteers:

TIP

>> **Annual recognition event:** This kind of event is the most formal (and probably the most expensive) way of thanking volunteers. Some organizations have a sit-down dinner or wine-and-cheese reception once a year to say thanks and give awards to volunteers who've made extraordinary contributions.

>> **Gifts:** Although tokens of appreciation may be much deserved, we recommend caution when giving gifts to volunteers. Don't spend lots of money buying presents, because you can bet that some volunteers will ask why you're spending scarce nonprofit money on something that isn't necessary. Getting a local business to donate gift certificates or other items is a better way to go.

>> **Admission to performances or events:** If your organization presents plays, musical performances, lectures, or readings, consider offering free admission to some events.

>> **Public acknowledgment:** You can identify your volunteers in your newsletter or on your website. An alternative is an annual newspaper ad that lists the names of your volunteers.

>> **Thank-you letters:** Don't underestimate the power of a simple thank-you note. Unless you have hundreds of volunteers, make sure you write the notes by hand. Most people appreciate a handwritten note more than a form letter or email. Try to let volunteers know how their work has made a difference.

In addition to thank-you letters and recognition events, you can increase volunteer satisfaction (and retention) by treating volunteers well on a day-to-day basis. Here are some easy tips to keep volunteer satisfaction high:

>> **Don't make volunteers work in isolation if you can avoid it.** Many volunteers give their time because they enjoy socializing with others.

>> **Vary the job to avoid boredom.** You may need help cleaning the storeroom or hand-addressing 1,000 envelopes, but try to assign jobs that offer more mental stimulation as well.

>> **Pay attention to the work done by your volunteers.** Your interest in what they're doing adds value to their work and recognizes that many of them are volunteering to develop new skills.

>> **Help volunteers understand your nonprofit's work.** If they've been answering the telephones in the front office, give them a behind-the-scenes tour or a chance to observe or participate in other activities of the organization.

>> **Bring in pizza or cookies once in a while as an impromptu thank-you.** Food can provide a great break from a monotonous job or a celebration of a major task's completion.

>> **Talk to your volunteers.** Get to know them as friends of your organization who are committed to its work.

IN THIS CHAPTER

» **Preparing your organization for paid employees**

» **Taking care of the groundwork**

» **Interviewing and hiring potential staff**

» **Getting a new hire started**

» **Handling the day-to-day management**

» **Working with contracted consultants**

Chapter **11**

Working with Paid Staff and Contractors

Some nonprofits have paid staff from the beginning. For example, nonprofits that start out with grant funding to operate a program may have paid staff. Other nonprofits may start more slowly, with the board of directors and other volunteers initially doing all the work and hiring paid employees later. And many nonprofits never have any paid staff. These organizations may use consultants or rely on volunteers.

No rules exist about when a nonprofit organization should start employing paid staff. The organization must determine whether it has enough work to justify employees and whether it has the resources to pay salaries and associated expenses. Hiring your first employee should be cause for celebration. It means that your nonprofit has reached a milestone in its development. But it also means that the organization (and the board of directors) will have more responsibilities to raise funds and ensure that proper personnel policies are put in place and followed. This chapter covers the details.

Check out File 11-1 at www.wiley.com/go/nonprofitkitfd6e for a list of web resources related to the topics we cover in this chapter.

TIP

Determining Your Staffing Needs

Knowing when to take the leap from being an all-volunteer group to being a boss or a paid employee isn't easy, and it's not a leap to take without looking at where you're about to land. Hiring employees creates responsibilities for the board, not the least of which is making the payroll every two weeks or every month. You also need to pay payroll taxes and provide a workplace, equipment, and — don't forget — guidance and supervision. Expect to take on more bookkeeping duties and more complex financial reports because you need to keep track of payroll records, vacation time, and sick days — and choose which holidays your organization will observe. (The last one should be a snap, right?)

To ease into the transition, a nonprofit may begin by hiring an independent contractor to handle a specific task, such as bookkeeping or grant-writing, and then go from there. (We discuss working with independent contractors and consultants later in this chapter.)

A variety of situations, such as these examples, may signal that it's time to hire your first employee:

REMEMBER

>> **A staff that's pushed to the limit:** Volunteers are growing tired, and the work isn't getting done as well or as quickly as it should.

>> **Increased demand for services:** Your organization's services have increased to the point that someone needs to focus consistently on administrative details.

>> **Increased resources:** Resources have increased to the point that you can now pay a regular salary.

>> **The need for specialized skills:** The organization is starting a new activity that requires someone with a specific professional license or degree, and no volunteer is appropriately qualified.

>> **Increased responsibility after receipt of a grant:** The nonprofit receives a major grant that provides more resources *and* requires significant record-keeping and program management.

Hiring salaried employees should be a long-term commitment. For this reason, you need to have sufficient cash flow to ensure regular payment of salaries, benefits, and payroll taxes.

TIP

A crisis can sometimes take place when a volunteer-run organization hires its first staff member. Knowing that they're now paying someone to be responsible, board members may decide to "sit on their hands" and let others do the work. The hiring of your first staff member is a good time to honor board and volunteer contributions to the organization (to maintain motivation) and to invest in a board retreat or training event that reminds everyone of the work ahead and the board's important role in it.

WARNING

When you add paid employees to your organization, you assume legal responsibilities that begin with the recruitment process. We recommend that you consult *Human Resources Kit For Dummies,* 3rd Edition, by Max Messmer (Wiley), to be sure you cover all the bases.

Getting Your Nonprofit Ready for Paid Employees

Before you write a job description or place an ad online, you need to invest time in some upfront prep work, readying your nonprofit organization to take on paid employees. This preparation, which we cover in the following sections, includes writing personnel policies, setting up payroll systems, and choosing benefits.

Developing your personnel policies

Personnel policies and procedures outline how an organization relates to its employees. These policies are essential for both supervisors and employees because they provide guidelines for what's expected in the workplace and on the job. The guidelines lay out expectations for employees, ensure that all employees receive equal treatment, and provide the steps necessary for disciplinary action when needed (see the later section "Following the reprimand-and-dismissal process" for more info about disciplinary action).

Many start-up and small organizations that have only one or two full-time employees give personnel policies a low priority. We suggest, however, that you begin early to formalize your rules by spelling them out in an employee handbook. Doing so doesn't take *that* much time, and it can save you headaches down the road.

WARNING

You must follow federal and state, and (sometimes) local labor laws when establishing personnel policies. The US Department of Labor website (www.dol.gov) contains the latest information on federal laws. If you're uncertain about whether you can require certain behavior or work hours from your employees, consult an attorney.

When forming policies, begin with the easy stuff: Decide on your organization's office hours, holidays, vacation policy, sick pay, and other basic necessities.

Determining work time and off time

Most organizations follow the lead of others when setting holiday and vacation policies: Although you find a lot of variation, many nonprofits in the United States grant two weeks' vacation per year to new employees. Employees typically receive more vacation time after a longer period of service, such as three weeks after three years, and four weeks after five to eight years. The most common sick leave policy is ten days per year. While you're at it, you want to give some thought to bereavement and maternity/paternity-leave policies.

Paid vacation time is a benefit to both employees and employers. Employees return from vacation rested and ready to give their best efforts to the organization. For this reason, you should encourage people to take vacations during the year in which they earn the vacation. Most organizations and businesses don't allow employees to accrue vacation time beyond a certain amount. This policy ensures that employees use vacations for the purpose for which they're intended. Such a policy also limits the need to make large cash payments for unused vacation time when employees resign or are terminated.

When it comes to choosing on which holidays your organization will close, follow the US federal holiday schedule — banks and government offices are closed for business because many of these holidays fall on weekdays. Also, because many of these holidays fall on Monday, some of them will result in your staff and volunteers having a three-day weekend. Check the US Office of Personnel Management at www.opm.gov/policy-data-oversight/pay-leave/federal-holidays/#url= Overview for the dates of federal holidays by year.

January: New Year's Day, Martin Luther King Jr. Day

February: Washington's Birthday

May: Memorial Day

July: Independence Day

September: Labor Day

October: Columbus Day

November: Veterans Day, Thanksgiving Day

December: Christmas Day

REMEMBER

If you ask your employees to work on a federal holiday, you will undoubtedly have to pay them overtime in compliance with federal wage and labor laws.

TIP

Consider reviewing the personnel policies of other nonprofit organizations in your area. A few telephone calls to other executive directors may help answer questions that arise as you refine your policies. Community Resource Exchange has sample personnel policies in its Sample Personnel Manual section at `www.crenyc.org/resources/tools-publications`.

Covering other important items

In addition to vacations and holidays, which are discussed in the earlier section, you should add statements that cover the following basic areas in your personnel policies:

>> The ability of the board of directors to change the policies

>> Nondiscrimination in employment, usually presented as a policy established by the board of directors — especially important if your organization is seeking government grants or contracts — and other policies established by the board

>> Procedures to encourage and protect employees and volunteers if they report wrongdoing — a whistleblower policy, in other words

   The National Council of Nonprofits provides guidance in this area at `www.councilofnonprofits.org`.

>> Policies regarding parental leave and long-term disability

>> Hiring procedures and the probationary period (described in the section "Evaluating your new hire's progress," later in this chapter)

>> A statement of the employment termination policy, including a grievance procedure

Many organizations also include a statement of the organization's mission and values and a brief outline of its history.

Exploring payroll setup options

When an organization begins employing workers, it first must establish a payroll system. The organization needs to decide how often to distribute paychecks, for example. Some states specify how frequently employees must be paid. Check with your state's department of labor about possible rules governing payment frequency. If your state doesn't specify payment periods, you can disburse paychecks on any schedule you choose — weekly, biweekly, semimonthly, or monthly. In our experience, semimonthly is the most common schedule for payment.

REMEMBER

Biweekly means every two weeks and results in 26 paychecks per year; *semimonthly* means twice a month and results in 24 paychecks per year.

TIP

Although in-house staff can handle payroll, contracting with a payroll service is a better option. Most banks either provide payroll services or can recommend a service. Payroll services are inexpensive — they're almost always cheaper than assigning a staff person the job of handling payroll. They make the proper withholding deductions based on income level, number of dependents, and state laws; make tax deposits; and maintain a record of vacation and sick leave. Usually when you contract with such a service, it requires that you keep enough funds on deposit with the company to cover two or three months of salaries and benefits.

WARNING

If you decide to handle your own payroll, be sure to make tax deposits on time. Failure to pay federal and state payroll taxes can get your organization in serious trouble and can even result in personal liability for board members. Check the Internal Revenue Service (IRS) website (www.irs.gov) for the latest information.

Here's a list of typical types of deductions, although state tax laws vary:

>> Federal income tax

>> Social Security and Medicare (must be matched by the organization)

>> State income tax

>> State unemployment and disability insurance

Providing benefits and perquisites

Health insurance is a benefit that your organization may or may not be able to provide to its paid employees. The cost of health insurance decreases based on the size of the group to which you belong. If your organization has only a single employee, purchasing health insurance may be costly unless you can join a larger group. Check with your state association for nonprofit organizations to see whether it has a health insurance program that covers your employees. The Council of Nonprofits (www.councilofnonprofits.org) has information and links to other helpful websites, including your state's nonprofit associations.

After your nonprofit organization is thriving, you may want to consider offering more benefits, such as retirement plans and long-term disability insurance.

Preparing to Hire

After you write your personnel policies, put your payroll system in place, and choose your benefits, you're finished with the groundwork needed to hire one employee or a hundred employees. You're probably just hiring one person for now. To set off on that path, you need to clearly describe what the job entails, set salary levels, and announce the position. This section walks you through those important steps.

Composing a job description

One of the first things you should do when looking to hire a paid employee is to write a job description for the position you want to fill. Completing this exercise helps you clarify the skills needed for the job and guides you in selecting among applicants. The final description serves as a job blueprint for the new employee.

A job description usually includes

>> A short paragraph describing the job and the work environment

>> A list of duties and responsibilities

>> A list of skills and abilities needed for the job

>> Experience and education required

>> Special qualifications required or desired

TIP

We include several standard job descriptions at www.wiley.com/go/nonprofitkitfd6e. See File 11-2 for an executive director job description, File 11-3 for a development director job description, and File 11-4 for an office administrator job description.

When writing a job description, keep in mind that work in nonprofit organizations can be split into these three broad areas:

>> **Services:** Services are the reason the organization exists in the first place. They may, for example, develop protected open space on a coastal bluff, provide home visits and hot meals to seniors, or organize after-school activities for children. This list is almost unlimited.

>> **Administrative functions:** These functions include bookkeeping and accounting, office management, property or building management, marketing, website design, clerical services, benefits administration, and contract management. You can add to this list as needed.

>> **Fundraising:** This area falls under various names, including *resource development* and *advancement*. Depending on the size of your organization, one person may be in charge of all aspects of raising money, or different people may specialize in writing grants to foundations and government agencies, creating sponsorships with corporations, or raising money from individual donors.

The larger these areas (or departments) are, the greater the specialization within them. But when you're looking to hire your first staff member, that first person may have job responsibilities in more than one area, and perhaps even in all three areas. It may seem to be too much to describe in a single document, but that complexity and the high level of responsibility this person will have make it particularly important to create a job description that's crystal clear.

Considering necessary qualifications

Some nonprofit jobs require various levels of formal education and special training. If you're hiring someone to provide counseling services, for example, that employee probably needs to meet certain education and licensing requirements to provide the services legally. If you're hiring someone to work with children, the applicant may need to pass various background checks or drug testing, depending on the laws of your state.

TIP

Professional and business associations can provide helpful information about job qualifications. In addition to any degrees and certifications, you may want to specify that applicants have a certain amount of experience doing the work you'll ask them to do. However, if you do so, be prepared to pay a higher salary to fill the position.

WARNING

You can't, of course, require that an applicant be of a particular ethnic background, race, age, creed, gender, or sexual orientation. You can't deny employment to someone who is expecting a child. Neither can you refuse employment to a person with a disability as long as that person can perform the job with reasonable accommodations.

Establishing nonprofit salary levels

Deciding on a fair salary for your employees isn't easy. Compensation levels in nonprofits range from hardly anything to six-figure salaries at large-budget organizations. (Keep in mind, however, that large nonprofits represent only a small percentage of active nonprofits.) We guide you through the process in the next two sections.

Considering factors that affect salary

Although exceptions always exist, the following factors may determine salary levels:

>> **Geographic location:** Salary levels differ from place to place because of the cost of living. If your nonprofit is in a major metropolitan area, expect to pay more to attract qualified staff than if you're located in a rural area.

>> **Experience and education:** Someone with ten years of experience can command higher compensation than someone just beginning a career. Education levels also affect salary, as does having specialized knowledge or skills.

>> **Job duties and responsibilities:** Employees who direct programs and supervise others typically earn more than employees who have fewer responsibilities.

>> **Nonprofit type:** Compensation levels vary from one nonprofit to the next. Organizations providing health services, for example, typically have higher salary levels than arts organizations.

>> **Union membership:** Labor unions set standards for salaries and benefits in many fields, from musicians to nurses and educators.

>> **Organizational culture:** This category, which is more difficult to define, is connected to the organization's traditions and values. For instance, nonprofits with boards of directors filled with business and corporate members often offer higher salary levels than organizations with boards that have no corporate perspective.

Scoping out salaries of comparable positions

A salary survey, which you can conduct by phone or mail, is a good way to assess the current salary levels in your area and for your nonprofit type. Telephone surveys probably should be done from board president to board president because most people are reluctant to reveal their own salaries. Mail surveys can be constructed so that respondents remain anonymous.

The simplest method of finding salaries of comparable positions is to look at other job listings. Not all ads give a salary level, but those ads that do can give you a general idea of what others are paying for similar work.

Some nonprofit management organizations conduct annual or biannual surveys of salary levels in the areas in which they work. More often than not, access to the surveys requires payment, but it's probably a good investment because these surveys tend to be the most complete and up to date. A good place to inquire about salary surveys is at your state association of nonprofits (see the National Council of Nonprofits website at www.councilofnonprofits.org). Idealist Careers also has links to nonprofit salary survey information at www.idealistcareers.org/salary-surveys. Local community foundations also may be a good resource of salary data in your geographic area and for the budget size of your organization.

TIP

Using a search firm can be helpful in hiring, especially if the position requires a national search. Be prepared to pay a hefty fee, however. Fees are often based on a percentage of the first year's salary.

Announcing the position

After you decide on the qualifications and skills needed for the job you want to fill, advertise its availability. Here's a list of places to publicize your job opening:

>> **Professional journals:** If you're hiring for a professional position, professional journals are the place to advertise the job. Search the web to track down the addresses of appropriate trade-specific journals.

>> **Websites:** The web has become a valuable marketplace for job seekers. Many websites charge a fee for posting a job opening. Work for Good (www.workforgood.org) and Idealist Careers (www.idealistcareers.org) are popular sites. Also consider craigslist (www.craigslist.org/about/sites#US), Monster (www.monster.com), CareerBuilder (www.careerbuilder.com), and LinkedIn (www.linkedin.com).

>> **Word of mouth:** Spread the word to other nonprofits — especially those in your field — places of worship, and anywhere else people congregate. Place a job description on your website and announce it on your Facebook page and Twitter feed. Don't forget to email the announcement to colleagues.

Making the Hire

When it comes time to make the big decision, sifting through résumés, conducting interviews, and deciding on an employee can be a daunting task. Sometimes, the right choice jumps out at you; at other times, you have to choose between two or three (or two dozen!) candidates who have equal qualifications. That's when making up your mind becomes difficult.

Looking at résumés

Résumés and cover letters give you the first opportunity to evaluate candidates for a position. Respond quickly with a postcard or an email to tell applicants that you have received their materials. If possible, give a date by which they can expect to hear from you again. Doing so reduces the number of phone calls asking whether you've received the résumé and when you plan to make a decision. It's also the polite thing to do.

REMEMBER

Résumés come in various formats, and we offer no strong opinion about which one is best. Regardless of how the résumé is organized and whether it's on paper or online, here are the questions we ask ourselves when reviewing a résumé:

>> **Is it free of typographical errors and misspellings?** A typo may be excused if everything else appears to be in order, but more than a couple of errors implies that the candidate may be careless on the job.

>> **Is the information laid out in a logical, easy-to-follow manner?** The relative clarity of the résumé can give you insight into the applicant's communication skills.

>> **Does the applicant have the proper job experience, education, and licenses, if needed?** We like to give a little slack on experience because sometimes highly motivated and effective employees are people who have to grow into the job. Also, nonprofit organizations often receive résumés from people who are changing careers. They may not have the exact experience you're looking for, but the knowledge they gained in their previous jobs might easily transfer to the position you're trying to fill.

>> **How often has the applicant changed jobs?** You can never be guaranteed that an employee will stay as long as you want, but you have to ask yourself, "If I hire this person, will they pack up and move on even before finishing job training?" At the same time, don't automatically let higher-than-average job-switching turn you off to an excellent candidate. Maybe the person has an explanation. Ask.

Cover letters can also be good clues to an individual's future job performance. For one thing, you get an idea of the applicant's writing abilities, and you may even gain some insight into their personality. Some job announcements state that a cover letter should accompany the résumé, and some even go so far as to ask the applicant to respond to questions such as, "Why are you well suited to this job?" or "What do you think are the major issues facing so-and-so?" It's up to you to decide whether asking a list of questions enables you to more easily compare applicants to one another.

TIP

If good writing skills are required for a job you're posting, ask applicants to include writing samples with their cover letters and résumés.

You'll probably reject at least half the résumés out of hand. We never cease to be amazed by how many people apply for jobs for which they lack even the minimal qualifications. We realize that searching for a job is difficult and frustrating, but we also wonder whether applicants read our Position Available ads as closely as they should.

Separate your résumés into two groups — one for rejected applications and one for applications that need closer scrutiny. Send the rejected candidates a letter or an email thanking them for their interest. From the other pile, decide how many candidates you want to interview. Reviewing the résumés with a couple of other board members to bring several perspectives to the choice is often helpful. One technique is to select the top three applicants for interviews. Reserve the other applicants for backup interviews if the first three are unsuitable or if they've already accepted other jobs.

Interviewing candidates

After you've chosen the top three to eight résumés, invite the applicants in for an interview. Interviewing job candidates is a formidable task. Big companies have human resources departments with trained interviewers who spend their days asking questions of prospective employees. We're neither human resources specialists nor trained interviewers, but here are some tricks we've learned over the years:

» **Prepared lists of three or four standard questions that you ask all applicants enable you to compare answers across applicants.** The interview shouldn't be so formal that it makes both the candidate and you uncomfortable, but standardizing it to some degree is beneficial. Here's a short list of typical questions:

- Why are you interested in this position?
- What do you see as your strengths? As your weaknesses?
- How would you use your previous work experience in this job?
- What are your long-term goals?

» **Team interviews with three or more people can give interviewers good insight into how the applicant will perform in board and community meetings.** You can test communication and teamwork skills between candidates and existing staff and volunteers. Also, different people notice different aspects of each applicant's responses or behaviors.

TIP

Avoid making the candidate face a large group, which might make any reasonable person unnecessarily nervous.

» **If an employee isn't your first hire and the job to be filled is for a director or supervisor position, have each finalist meet at least some of the staff they'll supervise.** Giving staff members a chance to meet their potential new boss is courteous, and their impressions are helpful in making the final selection.

WARNING

You can't ask applicants personal questions about their age, religious practices, medical history, marital status, sexual orientation, or racial background. You can't ask about arrests or felony convictions without proof of the necessity to ask. Nor can you ask whether someone has children or about any physical or mental conditions that are unrelated to performing the job. Workforce has a useful article about interview questions at www.workforce.com/news/interview-questions-legal-or-illegal-2.

Taking notes during the interview is acceptable, and you may also find that preparing a checklist on which you can rate the applicant in different areas is a helpful exercise. If you do, try to rate applicants discreetly. A job interview is stressful enough without letting the applicant know that you rated them a 3 on a scale of 1 to 10.

Digging deeper with references

Letters of recommendation can be helpful starting points in evaluating candidates, but we assume that no one would include a negative recommendation in an application packet. Therefore, we do think it's necessary to check references by telephone or even in a personal meeting, if possible.

But sometimes, even talking to references provides little useful information. A job applicant wants to put their best face forward, so naturally they choose people with favorable opinions as references. Also, employment laws are such that speaking to a former employer often yields little more than a confirmation that your applicant was employed between certain dates.

If you do have the opportunity to have an exploratory conversation with the candidate's former employer, pay close attention to what the person is *not* saying, and attend to the description of the candidate's abilities. For example, if you need someone who is attentive to financial details but the former employer talks only about the applicant's friendliness and phone manner, you may not have found the right person for your position. Some typical questions ask what duties the applicant handled in previous jobs, what their strengths and weaknesses were on the job, whether they had a positive attitude toward work, and whether the reference would rehire the candidate.

If the applicant is working for another organization, don't contact the current employer. You don't want to breach the person's confidentiality.

TIP

Check out File 11-5 at `www.wiley.com/go/nonprofitkitfd6e` for a sample reference-checking form.

You can conduct formal background checks of education credentials, criminal history, and other information as long as you receive the applicant's permission. In addition, a sex offender check should be completed on any person that you might hire. If you feel that this type of research is necessary, we suggest hiring a reputable company that specializes in this sort of work. However, you can conduct informal Internet searches about the applicant.

REMEMBER

The lengths to which you go to collect information about an applicant depend on the magnitude of the position. If you're hiring someone to lead a large and complex organization, you likely want to dig deeper into a candidate's background than if you're hiring a data entry clerk. But for any position, you want to know as much as possible about an individual's previous job performance before making an offer.

Making your decision

We can't tell you how to make the final decision about whom to hire. You have to weigh qualifications, experience, poise, and desire. These decisions can be difficult, and, frankly, you may not be certain that you've made the right choice until the new employee performs on the job. If possible, gather more than one opinion.

If qualifications and experience are equal, intangible factors come more into play. Will the candidate fit well into the organizational culture? Will the candidate's style of work fit with the organization's management style? Do the applicant's professional goals fit with the organization's goals? If this employee is your first, is the candidate a self-starter type, or do they need active supervision to do a good job?

WARNING

Document your reasons for making a personnel decision: Base those reasons primarily on the candidate's performance in previous jobs and experience that's relevant to your position. Be cautious when making a personnel decision based on intangible factors. A candidate who's charming may be a treat to have around the office, but that doesn't always mean the person will do the job well.

Onboarding a New Hire

Much hard work is behind you after you've made a hiring decision. But keep in mind that any employee's first days and months are challenging, and you want to give careful attention to helping your new staff member make a good start.

Confirming employment terms in writing

After a new employee accepts a position orally, we recommend that you send a letter to cement the details in writing. Enclose a copy of the personnel policies (see the section "Developing your personnel policies," earlier in this chapter) and place a signature line near the lower right corner of the letter so that the new hire can acknowledge receipt of the letter and the personnel policies. Ask the employee to return a copy of the signed letter to you, and keep the letter in the employee's personnel file.

The letter should specify the employee's starting date, job title, and salary as well as other information that you agreed to in the pre-hire discussions held between the organization and the employee. For example, you may include a brief statement about the employee's responsibilities and agreed-on work schedule.

TIP

Check out File 11-6 at www.wiley.com/go/nonprofitkitfd6e for a sample hire letter.

Getting your new hire started on the job

REMEMBER

In the United States, one of the first things a new employee must do is complete a W-4 form (for income tax withholding) and an I-9 form (to show proof of the employee's legal right to work in the country). These forms are required by law and are available on the IRS website (www.irs.gov).

After all the necessary paperwork is out of the way, you need to spend some time acclimating your new hire to the working environment. New employees don't begin producing at top form on the first day of work. Absorbing the details of the organization and discovering the ins and outs of new job duties take time. This fact is particularly true when the person hired is the organization's first employee and has no model to follow.

Whether you're a board member for an organization that's hired its first employee or the director of an organization bringing someone new onto the staff, here are some ways to ease an employee's transition to a new job:

>> **Provide good working conditions.** You may think that a reminder to purchase the basic furniture and tools someone needs to perform their work is too basic, but we've heard about new employees who faced not even having a desk on their first day.

>> **Show the new person around.** Provide a tour of the office and programs and introduce the new hire to volunteers and board members. Review office emergency procedures on day one. Oh yeah, and don't forget to show the new employee where the restroom is!

>> **Give the employee information about the organization.** Make available the organization's files and records, including any policies and guidelines that affect the employee's duties and the performance of their work. Reading board minutes, newsletters, solicitation letters, donor records, and grant proposals will steep the person in the organization's work.

>> **Answer questions.** Encourage new employees to ask questions, and provide the answers as soon as possible. Particularly if the person is the organization's one-and-only employee, board members should check in regularly, making themselves available as resources. Being a one-person staff can be lonely and overwhelming.

>> **Offer special training.** A new employee may need special training — for example, about a software program or laws and regulations specific to your nonprofit — to perform the job. Sometimes you may have to send the employee to a workshop; at other times, they can be trained by a board member, a volunteer, or another staff member.

Evaluating your new hire's progress

REMEMBER

Conduct a performance evaluation within the first six months of employment. The evaluation should be written (and added to the employee's personnel file) and discussed in a meeting with the employee. Rating employees on a number scale on various aspects of the job was once the common format. Today, a narrative evaluation that addresses performance in achieving previously agreed-on goals and objectives is much more helpful.

TIP

Many employees are happier in their jobs if they have ongoing opportunities to learn about new areas and develop new skills. An annual employee review is an excellent opportunity to review professional development goals with the employee. It's also a good time to review ways — via workshops, training, or trying on new roles — that the person may continue to grow in the job.

Looking to the future: Creating a professional development plan

You should establish professional development goals for new employees as soon as they come on board to work for your nonprofit organization. Even if you're not budgeted for employee travel to trainings, workshops, and employment-related conferences, everything you need for training is offered virtually, on the Internet. Many professional development courses online are free or low-cost. Investing in a new employee's future is critical to their employment retention in your nonprofit organization.

When you're thinking about the types of professional development needed, consider looking at your strategic plan's goals. How will those goals be achieved if new staff aren't trained in the goal's areas of implementation? For example, if one of your strategic plan goals is to create a community lending library for children at the level of elementary school, you might have your new employee take an online course in offering appropriate reading materials for young children or starting a lending library. Or, if you've just hired a grant management assistant who needs to be trained in all aspects of using a spreadsheet and grant management software, get that person started on their professional development track on day one on the job.

Look at other online training options that will enable your new employee to complete at least one type of training every month. Have the employee report back to you to describe what they learned and how they will apply it in the workplace. Encourage self-directed learning as well. Some of the following websites offer free or low-cost professional development training:

>> **Shaw Academy:** A low-cost, online Microsoft Excel training course (`www.shawacademy.com/courses/business/online-excel-course/`)

>> **Intuit QuickBooks:** Free online QuickBooks accounting product training (`https://quickbooks.intuit.com/accountants/training-certification/`)

>> **Nonprofit Ready:** Free online grant-writing classes (`www.nonprofitready.org/grant-writing-classes"www.nonprofitready.org/grant-writing-classes`)

>> **Allison:** Free online human resources course (`https://alison.com/courses/human-resources`)

>> **Grants Learning Center:** Free online federal grant management training (`www.grants.gov/learn-grants.html`)

>> **Nonprofit Learning Lab:** Free online fundraising, grants, volunteer management, and marketing training (`www.nonprofitlearninglab.org/webinars`)

Managing Employees

Much of this chapter focuses on small organizations that are hiring their first staff members. In these organizations, the board oversees the staff member, and someone taking on the coordinator role — either board or staff — oversees the volunteers.

What if your organization has grown more complex? Everyone needs a boss. In nonprofit organizations, the board assumes that role for the executive director, who in turn provides supervision to other employees, either directly or by way of a management team. The common way to visualize these relationships is in an *organizational chart,* a schematic drawing showing the hierarchical management relationships in an organization.

A chart such as the one shown in Chapter 7 (refer to Figure 7-1) may be overkill for your nonprofit, especially if you're the only employee, but for larger organizations, charts help delineate management responsibilities and clarify who reports to whom.

Recognizing what a manager or supervisor does

This list describes the various aspects of responsibility in managing employees:

>> **Planning:** Planning occurs at all levels, beginning with the board of directors, which carries out organization planning, and ending with the custodian, who plans how best to complete cleaning and maintenance tasks. Managers should work closely with the employees they're supervising to develop department and individual goals.

>> **Leading and motivating:** You may want to add *inspiring* to this category. Good management grows out of respect and cooperation. Be sure that staff members are familiar with the organization's goals and that they know how their work helps foster those goals.

>> **Gathering tools and resources:** Don't ask someone to dig a hole without giving them a spade. In other words, you can't expect employees to do a good job if they don't have the means to do it. Time, equipment, proper training, and access to information are necessary.

>> **Problem-solving:** This is one of the most important aspects of good management. You can bet that problems will arise as you manage your organization and employees. Be understanding and creative in solving these problems. Ask for help in the form of ideas and suggestions from the employees you supervise.

>> **Evaluating:** Employees should receive formal evaluations once each year. Effective evaluation begins with goal setting, and you want to help subordinates set clear goals and objectives.

Clarifying the lines of communication

We can't say enough about the importance of good communication. If your nonprofit has only a staff member or two, your job is easier than if you need to communicate with several dozen employees. Either way, good communication is essential. You also must clarify the lines of communication. In other words, staff below the level of executive director shouldn't be able to communicate directly with the board of directors.

REMEMBER

One person, and one person only, is the direct communicator with the board: the executive director.

Of course, confidentiality is important in certain matters. For example, if the organization is contemplating a major change, such as a merger with another organization, certain information needs to be withheld from the staff by the executive director and the board. On the other hand, letting rumors circulate about changes that may affect staff can create worse problems than being forthcoming about the details of a potential change. Give people as much information as you can, and be sure they have a chance to tell you how they feel. However, in sharing critical information, be sure to get the board's approval first.

REMEMBER

Communication is a two-way street. A good manager or supervisor keeps an open ear and devises ways to ensure that all employees have a way to voice complaints, offer suggestions, and participate in setting goals and objectives.

Holding regular staff meetings

Too many meetings can be a waste of time, but having regularly scheduled staff meetings is a good way to transmit information to employees, give them an opportunity to offer input and feedback, and keep everyone working toward the same goal. Tend to these tasks when arranging staff meetings:

>> **Schedule regularly occurring meetings in a standard time slot.** Hold meetings no more often than once a week and no less often than once a month, depending on the needs of the organization.

>> **Provide an agenda for every meeting.** Nothing is worse than attending a meeting that has no purpose and no direction.

>> **Keep to a schedule.** Unless you have big issues to talk about, one hour is usually long enough to cover everything you need to discuss.

>> **Provide time on the agenda for feedback.** Be sure that everyone has a chance to speak.

Writing emails to staff

Use emails to introduce new policies and other important information so that you eliminate misunderstandings. By putting the information in writing, you can clearly explain the situation. If the policy is controversial, distribute the email shortly before a scheduled staff meeting so that employees have an opportunity to respond.

Some larger organizations create staff e-newsletters that cover organizational programs and achievements. People work better if they receive recognition for their work. Stories about client successes, gains made by the organization, and announcements about staff comings-and-goings help instill feelings of accomplishment and organizational loyalty.

For very large organizations, a dedicated website or intranet that's accessible only to employees can transmit information and offer staff the opportunity to provide feedback and communicate with one another.

Chatting around the water cooler

Although formal written communication is important, nonprofit leaders also need to communicate informally by being accessible to staff in the hallways and around the water cooler. Some people communicate concerns better in an informal setting than in a staff meeting. Managers or supervisors who sit behind closed doors all the time often have a difficult time relating with their staff. However, don't force the camaraderie. Let it develop naturally.

Following the reprimand-and-dismissal process

It's important to have personnel policies in place that specify the steps for reprimanding an employee as well as ending employment when necessary. Be sure to follow them to the letter.

Firing should never be the first step when an employee is falling short of your employment expectations. If someone you've hired is doing less than a stellar job, follow these general steps:

1. **Identify and document the issues**

2. **Coach the employee to rectify the issue.**

3. **Create a performance improvement plan — that is, lay out in writing the steps for the person's improvement.**

REMEMBER

Many people deserve an opportunity to improve. Speak candidly and firmly with the employee about the level of improvement or change in behavior you expect. Set written goals for an improved performance, and specify a date for a follow-up consultation.

4. **Terminate the employee if they show no significant improvement after the improvement plan.**

5. **Conduct an exit interview.**

Even in a tiny nonprofit organization, the key to not being sued is to document, document, and then document even more. Always have a board member sit in on an exit interview. Let the employee have their say and vent their frustration. In today's world of people who make a living from filing and winning lawsuits, a witness is needed for all dismissals.

6. **Respect the employee's privacy.**

   Don't share your complaints with others; discuss the matter only with the board chair.

7. **Encourage the employee to leave as soon as the termination meeting ends, watch as they collect their personal items, and then walk them to the exit.**

   You have to make this effort because a single disgruntled former employee can damage your organization's records and documents in a few days, hours, or even minutes.

Check out this excellent article from Entrepreneur.com for additional guidance on how to discipline and fire employees: www.entrepreneur.com/article/79928.

Wrongful discharge lawsuits are common and can be *expensive*. As a precaution, you may want to investigate the possibility of employment liability coverage. If you need to terminate an employee and are unsure how to proceed, consult with a human resources specialist, your insurance carrier, or an attorney. The upfront investment may save you much time, expense, and trouble later.

Sometimes, organizations have to let employees go because they no longer have sufficient money to pay the employees' salaries. If you're a boss in this situation, try out these suggestions:

» **Give the employee as much warning as possible about the date of termination.** Don't keep it quiet while pulling out all the stops to raise money to save the position. Surprising employees with the bad news is inconsiderate.

» **Try to plan ahead and provide some severance pay to help out while the employee seeks a new job.** Although you may want to keep the person on the job until the last possible minute, good employees deserve good treatment. If someone leaves your agency with good feelings, you're in a better position to hire them back later.

» **Offer to serve as a reference or write letters of recommendation.** If the money isn't coming in and you can't find a way to keep the employee on, this gesture is one of the best things you can do.

Working with Independent Contractors

Maybe your organization isn't quite ready to take the leap into the employment waters. However, if you have work that needs to be done that volunteers can't do, working with an *independent contractor* may be a way to accomplish some organizational goals.

According to employment and tax laws in the United States, you can hire people in two ways: as salaried employees or as independent contractors. Rarely do you say to yourself, "I need an independent contractor to design my web page" or "I need an independent contractor to write more grants for us." More commonly used terms are *consultant* and *freelancer*. For example, a small organization may contract with an accountant or a bookkeeper to maintain financial records and prepare financial reports.

Independent contractors aren't just a resource for small organizations: Large-scale, well-heeled nonprofits also use them. A good organizational consultant, hired as an independent contractor, can bring a fresh perspective to assessing an organization's work, a depth and breadth of experience that the organization hasn't yet developed, and focused attention to a project — say, the writing of a new strategic plan — that staff can't give while managing day-to-day operations.

Differentiating an independent contractor from an employee

Technical differences between employees and independent contractors are reflected in how you hire, pay, and manage them. Independent contractors are almost always paid a flat fee or hourly rate for their work — ideally, on a schedule that's set out in a contract that specifies the work to be done and the fee. Although you don't have to withhold federal and state payroll taxes, you need to file IRS Form 1099, which records the amount paid over a full year (usually, a calendar year) and the contractor's social security number or their business's federal tax ID number (EIN).

REMEMBER

Proceed with caution because a thin line often exists between an independent contractor and an employee. Just because someone works a limited number of hours each week doesn't mean that the person should be considered an independent contractor. The IRS doesn't look kindly on trying to pass off employees as independent contractors. Here's a short list of factors that differentiate an independent contractor from an employee:

>> **Independent contractors are just that — independent.** Although setting time parameters for the job is fine, contractors typically are free to set their own schedules and work with little direction from the organization. They typically provide their own offices and equipment.

>> **Duties should be written into a contract, and the contractor should provide invoices for services provided.** The contract should be limited to a specific period, and no vacation time or sick leave should be provided.

>> **If you have to provide extensive training for the contractor to do the job, chances increase that the contractor may be considered an employee.** In hiring an independent contractor, you're supposed to be engaging someone with specific expertise.

>> **A contractor who is working only for your organization and is putting in many hours each week may be considered an employee.** If you hire a contractor with the idea that the relationship will continue indefinitely rather than for a specific project or period, or if that contractor provides services that are a key part of your regular business activity, such as executive director, the IRS believes that you likely have the right to direct and control that worker's activities. To the IRS, this association looks like an employer-employee relationship.

WARNING

If you think you may be pushing the envelope on the question of contractor vs. employee, consult an attorney or a tax specialist who can give you proper advice. Authorities are increasingly scrutinizing the distinction between regular employees and independent contractors. The IRS may require employers who pay individuals as contractors, when they're really employees, to pay back payroll taxes and penalties. Board members and responsible managers can be held personally liable for these taxes.

The IRS has defined *common-law rules* for determining whether someone is an employee or an independent contractor. Check IRS Publication 15A, *Employer's Supplemental Tax Guide,* for a definition of these rules. The publication is available on the IRS website at www.irs.gov.

TIP

If you want to hire someone for a short-term assignment or a limited number of hours and the work is taking place in your offices, using your equipment, and requiring your regular supervision, consider using a temporary employment agency. The agency handles the employee's benefits, including employment taxes, and reassigns them if they're a poor fit for the job. Although using a temp agency may cost more than hiring the person directly, the agency can help you find someone who's qualified.

Establishing the roles for independent contractors

Independent contractors can help you with just about any aspect of your organization, from managing personnel matters to hooking up a computer network. But nonprofits most commonly bring them in to help with

>> **Fundraising:** Fundraising consultants help with grant-writing, planning for fundraising, special events, direct mail, and major gift-and-capital campaigns, among other methods of raising funds.

>> **Organizational development:** Organizational development consultants may guide your board and staff through a planning process or help you develop the tools needed to evaluate your organization's work, to name just two examples.

>> **Marketing and public relations:** Consultants can help you spread the word about your organization's good work by handling a public relations campaign directed at the media, developing your website, creating compelling brochures and newsletters, creating short promotional films, and many other strategies.

>> **Evaluation and assessment:** Evaluators can take an in-depth look at an organization's programs, bringing specialized skills to that assessment and the value of an unbiased point of view.

Have a clear idea of what you want to accomplish before you seek help. Sometimes you don't know exactly what you're aiming to accomplish, but you should still try to articulate as clearly as possible what your aim is in hiring a consultant before you go looking for one.

Finding a consultant: Ask around

We have no single best way to find consultants. You can certainly search the web for nonprofit consultants who work in your area, but we think one of the better ways is to make a few calls to other nearby nonprofits or funding agencies. You may also be able to find a consultant by inquiring at a nonprofit support organization.

TIP

We prefer consultants who have more than one way of doing things. Not all nonprofits are alike, and what works for one may not work for another. Also, as your project evolves, you may find that you need a different kind of help than you originally imagined. Believe us: Changes happen all the time. Ask the consultant whether they're willing to consider revisiting the project goals along the way and adjusting the approach if the need arises.

Some consultants work as sole practitioners; others work in consulting companies. Working with a company or consulting group may give you access to more varied expertise. On the other hand, consultants working alone tend to have lower overhead expenses, so their fees may (and we stress *may*) be lower.

Interviewing consultants

Interviewing a consultant is similar to interviewing a regular job applicant. You want to review the résumé carefully to see whether the candidate's experience and expertise match your needs. Don't be intimidated just because the person sitting across the table from you has more experience than you do. That person is working for you. Ask any questions that you feel are necessary so that you can be sure you've chosen the right person.

Interview more than one person before you make your decision. As with interviewing for staff positions, having more than one person present at the interview is important because it lets you see how the prospective consultant interacts with a small group and gives you multiple perspectives on the consultant.

TIP

You may have the opportunity to use a volunteer consultant supplied by a program that provides free or low-cost assistance to nonprofits — interview these individuals just as you would paid consultants. Remember that you'll invest time in working with this person, so you need to be certain that they're right for your organization.

Ask interviewees to describe their method or approach to the problem or project that you're seeking to solve or complete. You shouldn't expect them to give you a full-blown plan in the interview, but you should expect a good picture of the initial steps they'll take. Also, if your project culminates in a written report, ask the applicant for writing samples.

Developing and executing the contract

You need to have a signed contract with every consultant with whom you work. These points should be clearly stated in the contract:

>> **The scope of work and expected results:** You can include more or less detail here, depending on the type of project. If you're hiring the consultant to facilitate a one-day retreat for your board of directors, be sure that the contract includes the preparation time needed. Also, will the consultant be writing a report after the retreat? Try to touch on as many details as possible. The more specific, the better. Sometimes, if the scope of work is detailed, that detail is included as an attachment to the main part of the contract.

>> **Fees, of course:** Some consultants charge an hourly rate plus expenses; others charge a flat rate that may or may not include expenses per project. The contract should state that you must approve expenses over a certain amount. Or you can write into the agreement that expenses are limited to a certain sum each month. Consultant fees vary, just like salaries, from one geographic area to another and depend on the type of work to be done and the consultant's experience.

WARNING

Don't pay fundraising consultants a percentage of money raised. Although some consultants, grant-writers, and, in particular, telemarketers work under this arrangement, percentage payment isn't considered good practice by most fundraisers and nonprofit managers. See the Association of Fundraising Professionals' code of ethics (www.afpnet.org) for more information about this issue.

>> **The schedule of when you'll pay the fees:** Some consultants who work on an hourly basis may send you an invoice at the end of the month. Consultants working on a flat-fee basis may require advance payment on a portion of the fee. This is fine. It's protection for the consultant, who probably has as many cash flow issues as you do. Don't make the final payment before the project is completed, however. Be sure to ask the consultant for an estimate of out-of-pocket expenses and the plan for billing you for such costs.

>> **Special contingencies:** What if the consultant gets sick? What if your organization faces an unforeseen crisis and you have no time to work with the consultant? What if you've chosen the wrong consultant? You should include a mutually agreed-on way to end the contract before the project is completed. A 30-day cancellation notice is common.

>> **A timetable for completing the work:** You and the consultant need to negotiate the timetable. Have you ever had remodeling work done on your house? You know that contractors can get distracted by other work, right? That's why having a schedule is vital.

>> **The organization's role in the project:** If the consultant needs access to background materials, records, volunteers, board members, or staff, you must provide this access in a timely manner so that the consultant can complete the job on schedule.

>> **Required insurance:** What if your consultant injures someone in the course of working on your project? If the person is uninsured, the liability can become your organization's responsibility. Just to be on the safe side, many consultant contracts include standard language about the consultant's responsibility to carry liability insurance and pay workers compensation insurance and other legally required benefits if the consulting company has employees who will be working on your project.

>> **Ownership of the finished product:** This point doesn't apply to every consulting project, but if yours focuses on developing a study or report, specify in the contract whether your organization or the consultant has (or both have) the rights to distribute, quote, and otherwise make use of the results. Often, the organization has the right to publish and produce the report if it properly credits the author and if the consultant owns the copyright and has permission to make use of lessons learned in articles or future studies. Sometimes, you agree to seek approval from one another before using the work.

TIP

We think that having the consultant prepare the contract is a good idea. It's the final chance to make sure the person understands what you want done. You may suggest changes when you see the first draft.

IN THIS CHAPTER

» **Drawing up a budget for an organization**

» **Constructing additional budgets for specific projects and programs**

» **Using your budget to make decisions**

» **Forecasting revenue and expenses**

» **Understanding financial statements**

» **Adopting good financial practices**

Chapter **12**

Money Matters: Preparing Budgets and Financial Reports

Nonprofit organizations are expected to spend wisely and honor the trust placed in them by their donors and other stakeholders. As a result, they need to be especially skilled at budgeting and operating an organization within its means.

Creating budgets is a critical part of program planning, grant-writing, evaluation, and organizational sustainability. Maintaining a financially stable organization is one of management's most important tasks. To achieve that stability, a nonprofit needs to keep clear records and base its decisions on accurate financial information. Asking the right questions about financial reports is one of the board's key responsibilities.

The best things in life used to be free. Though volunteers can accomplish a lot, the true reality check happens when no money equals no program and no payroll.

TIP

Check out File 12-1 at www.dummies.com/go/nonprofitkitfd6e for a list of web resources related to the topics covered in this chapter.

Making a Budget = Having a Plan

Making a budget is yet another form of organizational planning (the topic of Chapter 8). Often, the budget is completed hand in hand with other types of planning. A *budget* estimates how you intend to gather and disburse money on behalf of your organization's mission. In the course of a year, the cost of utilities or cable Internet may rise, and the cost of transportation and technology upgrades may fall. You're not expected to employ extrasensory perception in making a budget — just to be reasonable, thoughtful, and attentive to organizational costs.

If your organization doesn't spend more than it takes in, and if it holds on to a little emergency money at the bank, why does it need a budget? Writing and agreeing on a budget is an important process for your staff and board because it sets priorities. It's a discipline that keeps your organization on solid ground.

Beginning with zero

In many businesses, the annual budget is made by looking at what happened in the preceding year and adjusting numbers up or down, based on the work that lies ahead. When you're starting a new budget, however, you have no preceding year's results to consider. In that case, you start with zero and carefully consider each number you use to build your plan. Zero is a hard place to start, but it's where every new nonprofit organization begins.

A budget has two key sections: income and expenses. (See Figure 12-1 for typical line items.) Because dreaming up expenses that exceed your organization's means is easy, we suggest that you begin with income, making conservative estimates for what you may earn and what you may attract in contributions. As you work on the contributed income estimates, you also may want to look at Chapter 14, which discusses developing a fundraising plan.

Examining income

The income statement is commonly separated into two general categories:

>> **Earned, or revenue:** Contract, sales including e-commerce, or fee income, for example

>> **Contributed, or support:** Grants and contributions, for example

Anatomy of a basic budget

INCOME

Earned Income

        Government contracts

        Product sales

        Memberships

        Interest from investments

            Subtotal

Contributed Income

        Government grants

        Foundation grants

        Corporate contributions

        Individual gifts

        Special events (net income)

            Subtotal

            TOTAL Income

EXPENSES

Personnel Expenses

        Salaries

        Benefits @ _% of salaries

        Independent contractors

            Subtotal

Nonpersonnel Expenses

        Rent

        Utilities & Telephone

        Insurance

        Office supplies

        Program materials

        Local travel

        Printing

            Subtotal

            TOTAL Expenses

            Balance (the difference between Total Income and Total Expenses)

© John Wiley & Sons, Inc.

FIGURE 12-1: A sample budget, showing how line items usually are named.

Ask yourself these common questions as you begin developing the income section of your budget:

>> Will you offer services or products for which you'll charge money? How many services, and how often? How many people are likely to use them? How much can you reasonably charge? How soon will you be ready to offer them?

>> Can you sell memberships to people and give them premiums or discounts in exchange for paying those fees?

>> Are the founders and board of your organization able to contribute some start-up funds? Are they willing to ask their friends and associates to contribute?

>> Is your organization well positioned to receive a grant or grants?

>> Are you capable of sponsoring a fundraising event?

>> Can you provide visibility to a business sponsor in exchange for a contribution?

Evaluating expenses

In anticipating expenses, start with anything concerning the payment of people. That list may include these elements:

>> **Salaries for employees, both full time and part time:** On your budget, list each position by title and identify the full-time salary and the percentage of full time that person is working for you.

>> **Benefits for salaried employees:** You need to pay, at minimum, approximately 15.3 percent of salaries to cover federally required benefits, such as social security, Medicare, and unemployment tax contributions. Some states also require disability and workers compensation insurance, and local jurisdictions may require paid sick leave. Many organizations provide paid leave to employees for vacations, illnesses, and jury duty. Your organization also may provide health and dental insurance or a retirement plan for its employees. If so, you should compute those costs as percentages of the total salaries and include them in your budget as benefits. Benefits are listed immediately after salary expenses.

TIP

When setting up employee benefits, check on both federal and state requirements. The US Department of Labor website, www.dol.gov, is a good guide to federally required employee benefits.

WARNING

Employee benefits may cost more than you think. According to the Bureau of Labor Statistics in March 2021, benefits — across all employment sectors — represented 31.3 percent of total compensation to employees.

>> **Fees for services to consultants or service agencies:** You may hire a publicist, a grant-writer, an evaluator, or another type of consultant to handle important tasks. Such consultants are responsible for paying their own tax and insurance costs. Show fees paid to consultants after salaries and benefits in your budget. Check out Chapter 11 for information about working with consultants (also referred to as independent contractors).

At this point, compute a subtotal for all your personnel costs.

Next, identify all nonpersonnel expenses, beginning with ongoing operating costs that allow your organization to do its work. These expenses may include these elements:

>> Rent

>> Utilities

>> Telephone and Internet

>> Office supplies

>> Printing

>> Insurance

New organizations often have special start-up costs for the first year, including nonprofit registration and filing fees. For example, you may need to purchase desks and chairs, computers, signs, shelving, and office cubicles, and you may need to pay for training for new staff members, first and last month's rent, telephone and Internet hookup costs, and a photocopier or postage machine lease. Finally, you may have costs associated with the specific nature of the work of your organization. These expenses range widely but can include diagnostics tests, carpentry tools, classroom supplies, and printed materials.

As much as possible, keep notes in your budget files about the estimates you made while drafting a budget. Keeping a worksheet helps you remember your assumptions and follow the budget.

TIP

We present three different organization budgets at www.wiley.com/go/ nonprofitkitfd6e —Files 12-2, 12-3, and 12-4.

TIP

Defining a good budget

In a good budget, the income and expenses are equal to one another, which is what the term *balanced* budget means. Although balance is a good state to achieve, we recommend that you work to produce modest surpluses each year so that you can cover any unexpected costs. Many organizations slowly develop a *cash reserve,* or money put aside in case unexpected expenses arise. Organizations that need to use their cash reserves take care to replace them as soon as possible. Often, their boards set policies for how large a reserve they aspire to set aside and how quickly expended reserve funds must be replenished. A common rule of thumb is that organizations should create cash reserves equal to at least three months of their operating costs.

TIP

In File 12-5 at www.wiley.com/go/nonprofitkitfd6e, you can find "Monthly Information Every Nonprofit Needs to Know."

As a general rule, your budget looks healthy when you show multiple sources of income. Why? Wouldn't it be easier to keep track of one or two major grants and contracts? Or a single annual special fundraising event?

This rule is based on the adage "Don't put all your eggs in one basket." What if a power outage strikes on the night of your gala? What if one of your major grant or contract sources changes its guidelines? Your programs can be jeopardized.

Finally, a good budget is realistic and is based on an honest assessment of the resources a nonprofit can earn and raise. In leading a nonprofit, be forward-thinking and optimistic about producing high-quality, meaningful work, but also bring a sober brand of that optimism to creating financial plans.

TIP

The Wallace Foundation created a section of its website at www.strongnonprofits.org, featuring resources to help nonprofits improve their financial management. We've provided a link in File 12-1 at www.wiley.com/go/nonprofitkitfd6e.

Budgeting based on your history

As the first year passes and your organization develops programs, it also develops a financial track record. After you have a financial history, anticipating the future can be easier. You need to analyze every assumption you make, but at least you have a baseline of revenues and expenses from the first year.

Here are some questions to consider when drafting budgets in future years:

>> What are your earned income trends? Are they likely to continue or change? Do you face any new competition or opportunities?

>> How many of your current year's grants or contracts may be renewed, and at what levels?

>> How healthy is the current financial environment? Will it affect your previous donors' abilities to give?

>> How likely are you to increase individual giving or special-events revenues in the coming year?

>> What's the duration of all employees' employment periods? Anticipate the timing of possible annual raises and the need for additional staffing.

>> Do you offer benefits that kick in after an employee has worked with you for three months or six months or five years? If so, don't forget to include these increased costs.

>> When does your lease obligate you to pay for rent increases or taxes?

>> Have rate increases been scheduled for utilities, postage, or other services?

>> Does your organization need new technology — perhaps additional or upgraded hardware, website development, or software?

Understanding and isolating general administrative and fundraising costs

Some of your organization's expenses are defined as general administrative or fundraising costs and aren't considered program expenses. The expense of having an audit, for example, is allocated to general administrative costs, and mailing costs for your end-of-the-year fundraising letter are identified as fundraising. IRS Form 990, which nonprofits file annually, asks organizations to present their expenses in a format that shows which annual costs are for general administration and which are for fundraising. (See Chapter 6 for more about preparing Form 990.)

Accounting for in-kind contributions

Some nonprofit organizations benefit from donated goods and services rather than, or in addition to, contributed and earned cash. Suppose that a local business provides office space for your organization so that you don't have to pay rent, 50 volunteers contribute labor to your organization each week, and a major advertising firm sponsors a free marketing campaign to promote your work. These gifts of goods and services are called *in-kind contributions.*

How can you show these valuable resources in your organization's budget? First, we encourage you to make the effort. If you don't show these contributions, your budget doesn't truly represent the scope of your organization, and you're underplaying how much the community values its work. On the other hand, mixing the in-kind materials and services with the cash can make following and managing your budget confusing.

What's the solution? We prefer creating in-kind subheadings within the budget or summarizing all the in-kind contributions at the end of the cash budget in a separate section.

REMEMBER

If you choose to include in-kind items with the cash in your budget, don't forget that when you receive an in-kind good or service, it's a source of income, and when you make use of it, it's an expense. Often nonprofits fail to show the expenditure of an in-kind contribution, and it can make their budget appear to have more available cash than it really has.

Keep records of volunteer time if you're going to include it in your budgets or financial reports. Generally *accepted accounting principles* or GAAP, which is a framework outlining standards and rules for accounting, say you should show the value of volunteers' time in your financial statements if they improved a financial asset of the organization (for example, if volunteers rebuilt a greenhouse owned by a nonprofit botanical society) or if the organization needed a task to be performed that required a special skill, the volunteer had that skill, and the nonprofit would have paid for that help if it had not been volunteered (for example, if an attorney reviewed the nonprofit's lease *pro bono*).

TIP

Annually, Independent Sector computes a standard average value for volunteers' labor, both nationally and by state. (In 2021, the national average was $28.54 per hour.) Check out File 12-1 at www.wiley.com/go/nonprofitkitfd6e, where you can find a link to these tables on the Independent Sector website.

Creating Budgets for Programs or Departments

If your organization focuses on a single service, you can skip ahead to read about projecting cash flow. If you manage several programs or departments, each of these programs has a budget that must fit within the overall organizational budget.

REMEMBER

It is important to include program staff, the finance director or accountant, and the board of director's finance committee in the budget planning process when the budgets are being prepared for individual departments or programs. All of these stakeholders should be onboard and engaged in developing the individual budgets, monitoring expenditures, and knowing the bottom line (funds remaining) your entire fiscal year.

Suppose that when your nonprofit organization begins, you offer only one program — an after-school center that provides tutoring and homework assistance for low-income children. The program really clicks, and more and more children begin showing up after school — some because they need tutors, but others because their parents are at work and the kids need a safe place to go. To serve these new participants, you add art classes and a sports program.

So now, instead of one program, you have three. Each has its own budgetary needs. A program coordinator trains and recruits the tutors and purchases books, notebooks, and school supplies. The art program requires an artist's time, supplies, space for art making, and access to a kiln. To offer a sports program, your agency rents the nearby gym, hires four coaches, employs a volunteer coordinator to recruit parents and other assistant coaches, and purchases equipment. The specific costs of a program — books, art supplies, coaches — are its *direct* costs.

But each of the three programs also depends on materials and services provided by the people who work on behalf of the entire organization, such as the full-time executive director of your agency, the part-time development director, and the bookkeeper.

Each of the three after-school programs also uses the organization's offices, utilities, telephones, and printed materials. The costs that the various programs share — such as the executive director's salary, bookkeeping services, rent, and telephone bills — are *indirect* costs. You can think of these shared costs as the glue that holds the nonprofit together.

REMEMBER

When you prepare a program or department budget, you should include both direct costs and indirect costs.

Direct costs are pretty straightforward. For example, you know what you have to pay your tutors per hour, and you know how many hours they work. But indirect costs can be sticky, and we don't say that because they're the organizational glue. They're sticky to deal with because determining how to divide them accurately among your organization's activities is difficult. Many grant makers are reluctant to pay true indirect costs associated with programs, and, if your organization depends heavily on grants, that reluctance can put you in the awkward financial position of being able to pay for a famous basketball coach but not to turn on the lights in the gym.

TIP

With every new decade, foundations and government organizations are recognizing the short-sightedness of under-supporting nonprofits' overhead (or indirect) costs. For example, a group of foundations commissioned researchers at Rand Corporation to write the report "Indirect Costs: A Guide for Foundations and Nonprofit Organizations," which recognizes their importance. You can find a link to it in File 12-1 at www.wiley.com/go/nonprofitkitfd6e. Nearly a decade ago, the federal Office of Management and Budget (OMB) published new guidance that clarified that a nonprofit's indirect costs were legitimate expenses and should be reimbursed. Further, the Real Cost Project and Nonprofit Overhead Cost Project (see links in File 12-1 at www.wiley.com/go/nonprofitkitfd6e) illustrate the conversation among nonprofits and foundations to recognize that supporting indirect costs is critical to nonprofits' health and abilities to deliver effective programs.

If your organization is relatively small, with just a few programs, you may be able to keep accurate records for how staff members spend their time, how many square feet in a building a program uses, and even how many office supplies each staff member checks out of the supply cabinet. Based on those records, you can fairly estimate your indirect costs.

As your organization grows in complexity and number of programs, you may compute indirect costs by using a formula you derive based on your direct costs. We outline sample formulas and steps to derive them in Table 12-1.

TABLE 12-1   **Computing Direct Cost Percentages for an After-School Center**

First, add all direct costs:		Program	Direct Costs of Each Program
Tutoring and homework assistance	$46,000		
Arts and crafts	$60,000		
Athletics	$164,000		
Total direct costs:	$270,000		
Then compute the percentage of total direct costs that each program represents:			
Tutoring and homework assistance	$46,000 ÷ $270,000 = 17%		
Arts and crafts	$60,000 ÷ $270,000 = 22%		
Athletics	$164,000 ÷ $270,000 = 61%		

In many cases, you can reasonably assume that the indirect costs of a program correlate to its direct costs, or that a program that's more expensive requires more oversight of staff and more use of office space. In the case of the after-school center, all the indirect costs — which include a salary for the part-time director, a contracted bookkeeper, rent, utilities, telephones, and printing — total $130,500.

Using this figure, we can put together the direct and indirect costs into a true financial picture of each program by multiplying the $130,500 in indirect costs according to the percentages we computed for direct costs in Table 12-1. We outline the proposed allocation in Table 12-2.

TABLE 12-2

Allocating Indirect Costs for an After-School Center

Program	Formula	Indirect Cost Amount
Tutoring and homework assistance	$130,500 × 17%	$22,185
Arts and crafts	$130,500 × 22%	$28,710
Athletics	$130,500 × 61%	$79,605

Sometimes organizations write a project budget by identifying all the direct costs in detail and then showing the indirect costs as one lump sum at the bottom of the list of expenses. But some funding sources balk at paying for indirect costs when they're presented this way. The funders want to know what actual expenses contribute to those indirect costs. We recommend that you show the specific indirect costs item-by-item rather than lump them all together (unless some of those items are quite small). For the tutoring program, for example, you would show 17 percent of the executive director's salary, 17 percent of the bookkeeper's fees, and so on.

TIP

File 12-6 at www.wiley.com/go/nonprofitkitfd6e shows the tutoring program budget with the indirect costs specified alongside the direct costs.

There's one exception to how you calculate and claim indirect costs when your organization is applying for a federal grant (see Chapters 17 and 18 for guidance on grant researching and writing): The US OMB created an easy track for non-profit organizations applying for federal grant funding. Rather than wait months to negotiate an indirect cost rate with a federal agency, nonprofit grant applicants can use the *de minimis* rate of 10 percent. This is 10 percent of the grant that can be used for indirect costs. Indirect costs are 10 percent of your project's actual budget request amount. For example, if your project budget request is $100,000, your indirect cost rate will be $10,000. When your grant is funded, you would receive $110,000.

The new guidance means that nonprofits should be able to focus more on their missions and should be under less pressure to raise additional funds to subsidize federal grant awards. Though you're not ready to apply for any federal grants yet as a new nonprofit, in a few years when you are ready, do not confuse your internal operating budget's indirect costs with the language of federal grant-making agencies in their grant application budget instructions. You are limited to claiming the 10 percent *de minimis* rate with the feds.

Working Frequently with Your Budget

Your budget isn't capable of getting up and walking out of the room, but it needs to be an active document. If you simply create it once a year to stash in a file folder and submit with grant proposals, it doesn't do you much good. A good budget is reviewed often. A good budget guides and predicts.

REMEMBER

Numbers in budgets are meant to be compared. One critically important comparison looks at actual income and expenses alongside the original projections you made in your budget. Most organizations create a spreadsheet that includes columns for these elements:

>> Annual budget

>> Year-to-date income and expenses

>> Current month's budget (½ of the annual budget)

>> Current month's income and expenses

Pay close attention to where you're exceeding the budget and where you're falling short. Use your progress as a guide to adjust fundraising or expenditures. Keep a close eye on the organization's cash flow projections.

TIP

At www.wiley.com/go/nonprofitkitfd6e, in Files 12-7 and 12-8, you can see two examples of tracking actual income and expenses in comparison to budgeted income and expenses. To take a critical, long view of your financial progress, use the Five-Year Financial Trend Line in File 12-9.

Here are several other useful exercises to help you ensure that your budget is "living and breathing" (up to date and being monitored closely.)

>> Involve your staff (paid and volunteer) in the early stages of drafting the coming year's budget. If you can't afford all their dreams, involve them in setting priorities.

>> Three months before the beginning of the new fiscal year, meet with a small committee of board members to review and refine a budget draft. Present the draft with options and recommendations to the entire board for discussion and formal approval.

>> If your organization's situation changes significantly, prepare and adopt a formal budget revision. Budget revisions are time consuming, but don't try to proceed with a budget that doesn't reflect the size and scope of your organization. You don't want to try to find your way through Maine with a map of Utah.

» Provide budget copies monthly or quarterly to your entire board or board finance committee. Encourage the board treasurer to summarize the organization's financial situation and invite questions and discussion at each meeting. One important board action is reviewing the financial report at each meeting.

» Keep notes in your budget file about changes you recommend for years ahead. For example, as you hire additional staff or eliminate staff positions, your salaries line item will fluctuate. As you project these changes, your budget may change in the future.

Because revenues aren't earned, grants aren't received, and expenses aren't incurred in equal amounts every month throughout the year, we recommend that you also project your cash flow (see the following section).

Projecting Cash Flow

A *cash flow projection* is a subdocument of the budget that estimates not only how much money you'll receive and spend over the course of a year but also *when* you'll receive and spend it. This projection breaks down the budget into increments of time. Some organizations create quarterly (three-month) projections, some monthly, some weekly. Our personal preference is to plan the cash flow monthly.

Although grant-making organizations and major donors are likely to want to see the budget (and may want to see the version that compares projections to actual amounts), your cash flow projection generally is a document for you, your board, and possibly a loan source.

If you think of a budget as the spine of an organization — supporting all its limbs — the cash flow statement is its heart and lungs. A good cash flow statement is in constant motion, anticipating and following your every move. Based on the careful way you developed the budget, you may know that you're likely to have enough revenue to cover the organization's expenses in the coming year. The cash flow helps you figure out whether you'll have that money at hand when you need it.

Constructing your cash flow projection

To set up a cash flow projection, begin with a copy of your budget and add details to the names of all the various categories. For instance, under Foundation Grants, write down the names of every foundation from which you now receive money and of any from which you anticipate receiving a grant. Add the same kinds of details for the expense categories. For example, under Utilities, add separate lines for each bill you receive, such as water, electricity, gas, and sewer service.

We recommend that you project forward by going backward. Sounds contradictory, doesn't it? Create columns for the most recently completed three months of your year. Review your records. Put any income received into the appropriate periods, and write down all your expenses in the right categories and time periods. If you've forgotten any categories, you have a chance to add them. Having these actual figures for the recent past helps you see patterns of income and expenses.

Now, begin projecting: Go back to each line item and write down the estimated amount that's due during each monthly period. Begin with the easy items — like the rent that's a constant amount due on a certain day or the employer's share of federal payroll taxes. Then look at the consistent bills that vary over time. If your utility bills are high during winter months because your agency is using the furnace more, don't forget to project that increase. If you manage a community vegetable garden during the summer that increases water usage, project for that increase as well.

As you get into the flow of making predictions, you can easily become too optimistic about your anticipated income. If you've applied for a grant that you're just not sure about, don't put it into your cash flow projection. If your annual fundraising event raises between $25,000 and $32,000 each year, project $25,000 in income. The reason? You'll have no problem knowing what to do when you have more money than anticipated, but you may have a problem making up a shortfall! Your cash flow projection is supposed to warn you if you're about to fall short.

You're almost finished at this point. As a next step, look back at your financial records to see how much money you had at the beginning of the first month of your cash flow projection. Place this figure in a Balance Forward row as the first income item for the first month period. Add it to all the income for that month and subtract that month's expenses. The difference gives you the next Balance Forward amount that belongs at the top row for the next column of income for the *next* monthly period. And keep going. The balance for each month is steadily carried over to the top.

Table 12-3 shows a highly simplified sample of a cash flow projection.

See File 12-10 at www.wiley.com/go/nonprofitkitfd6e for a detailed sample cash flow projection, and check out File 12-11 for a blank form you can use to begin your own cash flow statement.

TABLE 12-3 **Simple Cash Flow Projection**

Income	1/1–1/31	2/1–2/28	3/1–3/31
Balance forward	$21,603	$9,845	$43,445
Government contract		$65,000	
Williams grant	$15,000		
Power company contribution			$2,500
Board giving	$4,000	$750	
Total income and balance forward	$40,603	$75,595	$45,945
Expenses	1/1–1/31	2/1–2/28	3/1–3/31
Payroll	$22,197	$22,197	$22,197
Health benefits	$2,111	$2,111	$2,111
Payroll taxes	$2,775	$2,775	$2,775
Rent	$2,500	$2,500	$2,500
Electric company	$675	$675	$580
Telephone	$435	$450	$475
Office supplies	$65	$120	$120
Travel and transportation		$1,322	$8,700
Total expenses	$30,758	$32,150	$39,458
Balance:	$9,845	$43,445	$6,487

Deciding what to do if you don't have enough

You probably won't have more income than expenses in every single month throughout the year. During some periods you get ahead, and at other times you fall behind. Your goal is to sustain a generally positive balance over the course of time and be able to cover your most critical bills — payroll, taxes, rent, insurance, and utilities — in a timely manner.

REMEMBER

Some government agencies and foundations pay grants as reimbursements for expenses after you've incurred them. You may need to prepare your cash flow plan accordingly while waiting to be reimbursed.

We want to promise that you'll always have enough resources to sustain your organization's good work. But certain periods will be lean. Then what? First, your cash flow projection should help you anticipate when you may fall short. It enables you to plan ahead and solicit board members who haven't yet made gifts in the current year, send letters to past donors, cut costs, or delay purchases.

We also recommend being proactive about contacting your creditors. If you think you can't pay a bill on time, call and ask for an extension or explain that you're forced to make a partial payment now with the balance coming in a few weeks. Your ability to do business depends on your earning and sustaining other people's trust. If you can't have perfect credit, being honest and forthright is the next best thing. It's hard to do, but important.

WARNING

Don't hide behind your bills, thinking that if you say nothing, nobody will notice. If you're facing a period of debt, tell your board. Also, call anyone to whom you owe money and explain the situation and your timeline for paying your bills. Among other things, your honesty helps them with *their* cash flow. And when your expenses are exceeding your income, always try to cover your federal, state, and local tax obligations because fees and interest on unpaid taxes add up quickly. If covering those obligations is impossible, don't forget to call those agencies. Setting up a payment plan, both over the phone and in writing, can prevent your assets (or a board member's) from being frozen.

Borrowing to make ends meet

Before you go this route, you are bound to report the status of your finances to the governing board. Regardless of how bad the financial outlook may seem to you, reporting them to your board of directors is essential. Remember transparency and the board's fiduciary responsibility role. Prepare, present, and listen to their directives.

Another route to managing cash shortfalls is to borrow the money you need to cover your bills. Your cash flow statement can help you plan the size and duration of the loan you need. Here are some of your options if you need to borrow money:

>> **Ask a board member for a loan.** If the board member can help, you can probably secure the loan quickly, but borrowing from a board member is appropriate to do only if you act in accordance with your organization's conflict-of-interest policies and applicable law, and if the board member can provide the loan at market rates or below market rates. Make sure to sign a promissory note with the lender and record the board's formal approval of accepting the loan in its meeting minutes.

>> **Ask local foundations whether they know of a loan fund for nonprofit organizations.** Some associations of grant makers and government agencies offer loans at low interest to their grantees facing cash flow problems. Such a program is likely to be more sympathetic to your needs than a commercial lending institution may be.

>> **Apply for a small-business loan at your bank.** If your organization has no credit history, securing a bank loan can be challenging. However, foundations sometimes make this process easier by guaranteeing these bank loans for nonprofits.

>> **Check to see whether you qualify for a line of credit from your bank.** A *line of credit* allows you to borrow up to a certain sum for a specified period. When the organization repays the borrowed amount, often it can't borrow from its line of credit again for a designated period. Your organization may want to apply for a line of credit even if it doesn't expect immediate cash flow problems. Doing so can provide a safety net for emergencies.

>> **As a last resort, borrow the money from an organizational credit card.** Do this only if you're positive that you can repay the loan quickly and cover the interest.

REMEMBER

Borrowing money requires time and preparation and usually costs your nonprofit in the form of interest payments. However, borrowing is better than damaging your nonprofit's reputation or incurring severe penalties and interest charges — particularly on tax obligations.

Putting money away to make a nonprofit strong

Over the past several years, nonprofits, foundations, and consultants have talked and published articles about the importance of nonprofit *capitalization*. The idea is simple: If a nonprofit has savings, it can respond to urgent needs and take advantage of opportunities. Just as a family is better positioned to manage a flooded basement or invest in a small business if it has set aside some money, nonprofits should set goals for saving working capital.

Any business — including a nonprofit — needs money to operate, and it also needs money to grow, to test ideas, and to change its programs or structure. Working capital is that grow-and-test money that makes a nonprofit adaptable and also that allows it to invest in long-term needs, such as gradually replacing aging equipment.

Many grants and government contracts limit how you can spend project money, so if you want to develop working capital, we recommend turning to individual donors or setting aside a small portion of your earned revenue each month. We also recommend setting tangible goals for this effort — perhaps the cost of replacing essential equipment or operating for four months with no new income while you set up programs and write grants.

Keeping Your Books Organized and Up to Date

After you've created a budget, you need to set up a system for keeping consistent, organized records of your financial information. You may choose to do your book-keeping by hand or with accounting software. If you're interested in bookkeeping by hand, *Nonprofit Bookkeeping & Accounting For Dummies*, by Sharon Farris (Wiley), can guide you. If you prefer to have a computer do the math for you, we name some software options later in this section.

Accounting, like the world of nonprofits, has some specific ways of doing things. In the next section, we explain the two fundamental accounting approaches.

Differentiating the various accounting systems

You'll encounter two standard systems for compiling and presenting information about your organization's financial history: cash and accrual. Here are some ways they differ:

>> **A cash system closely resembles the way most people keep their checkbooks.** You enter income into the books when you receive and deposit a check or cash. You enter expenses when you pay a bill. Many find a cash system to be a comfortable approach because it's straightforward. When your books show a positive balance, you have money in hand or in the bank.

>> **An accrual system recognizes income when it's promised and expenses when they're obligated.** Suppose you receive a grant award letter from a foundation promising your organization $60,000 over a two-year period. This grant will be paid in four checks of $15,000 each. In an accrual system, you enter the entire $60,000 as income in your books when that money is promised — when you receive the grant award letter. On the expense side, you enter your bills into your books when you incur them — which may be before you pay them.

WARNING

Each of these approaches has possible disadvantages:

>> In cash books, your organization may owe money in unpaid bills, but those debts aren't apparent because they aren't on your books until they're paid.

>> In cash books, your organization may have been awarded a large grant but may look poor because you haven't received the check.

>> In cash books, it's more difficult to tell whether you owe payroll taxes.

>> In accrual books, you may have been promised a large contribution but not yet received it. You may have no cash in hand, but your books look as if you have surplus income.

Keeping books by an accrual system is standard accounting practice for nonprofits and is recommended by the Financial Accounting Standards Board, so this section of the book assumes that you use an accrual system. To be honest, however, small organizations can often squeak by with a cash system on a daily basis and then transfer funds to an accrual presentation once each quarter or at the end of their fiscal year.

Considering accounting software or an accountant

If you decide to use software to keep your books, you can purchase types that are designed specifically for nonprofits, which have some different needs and use a few different terms than for-profit businesses. We recommend that you choose one of these products meant for nonprofits, though accountants differ on whether it's necessary. Some accounting software packages that many small nonprofits use include QuickBooks or QuickBooks Online by Intuit, Sage 50cloud, and Fund E-Z.

If more than four or five people at your organization will be using the accounting software, if your budget exceeds $1 million, or if you need to track many programs, you'll likely want to invest in more-complex accounting software. Two options are Abila MIP Accounting and The Financial Edge, by Blackbaud.

Also important, if your nonprofit has multiple full-time staff members, it needs systems to manage payroll and track time and attendance. Intuit's Online Payroll and Paychoice (PAI Services), a cloud-based service that integrates well with QuickBooks, is popular among small organizations. Larger nonprofits may prefer Automatic Data Processing (ADP), Sage 50cloud Payroll, or Paychex.

TIP

The online journal Idealware (`idealware.org`) is an excellent source of articles, blogs, webinars, and forums about technology for nonprofits. We include a link to it at `www.wiley.com/go/nonprofitkitfd6e` in File 12-1.

REMEMBER

When creating your start-up budget, include accounting software — the cost of purchasing the package or online service, of setting it up, and of being trained to use it. As your organization grows and you need more sophisticated software, the setup time will be greater.

You also have the option, if budgeted, to work with a CPA or an accountant. Often, having that personal touch with someone to speak to or to sit down with you and your board to explain the financial aspects makes clear All Things Financial.

Reviewing the Numbers: Financial Statements and Audits

Budgets and cash flow statements predict your organization's financial future. But you also need to review each year's annual income and expenses in a financial statement. When your nonprofit organization is small and lean, your staff or bookkeeper can prepare its financial statements. As it grows and becomes more complex, you'll likely hire an outside accountant to prepare and audit its financial statements.

Preparing financial statements

If a budget is a document about the future, a financial statement tells the story of your organization's past. Nonprofit organizations retain and review their financial records throughout the year, and they prepare a financial statement at least once a year, at the end of the fiscal year. (See Chapter 5 for more information on a fiscal year; and see File 12-12 at `www.wiley.com/go/nonprofitkitfd6e` for tips for reading financial statements.) Many organizations also prepare monthly or quarterly in-progress versions of their annual financial statements.

Although good nonprofit accounting software can organize your financial information for you, preparing and interpreting financial statements is a special area of expertise that goes beyond the scope of this book. Many nonprofits seek outside professional help for this essential task. If hiring such assistance is beyond your organization's means, we recommend that you become acquainted with *Nonprofit Bookkeeping & Accounting For Dummies,* by Sharon Farris, and *Accounting For Dummies,* 6th Edition, by John A. Tracy, CPA (Wiley). If you do choose to prepare your own financial statements, you may want to hire an accountant at year's end to review them for accuracy.

The information in your annual financial statement resembles (but may not be identical to) the 990-EZ or 990 financial report that your organization is required to submit annually to the IRS. (You can find more information about the differences between these types of 990s and filling one out in Chapter 6.) You'll also include your financial statement in your board orientation packets and with requests for funding. Some organizations publish it in an annual report.

Seeing the value of an audit

At year's end, your organization may be required to or may choose to have its books audited by a certified public accountant (CPA) or firm. This service involves a formal study of the organization's policies and systems for managing its finances, a review of its financial statements, and commentary about the accuracy of those statements.

TIP

If you hire a CPA to conduct your audit or financial review, make sure the person has knowledge about or expertise in nonprofit organizations. Nonprofits use some accounting terms and bookkeeping methods that differ from for-profit businesses.

The accountant may issue an *unqualified opinion,* meaning that the statements appear to be accurate. In "auditor talk," the accountant didn't find a *material misstatement* — false or missing information. If the auditors have recommendations to make about how money is managed or how finances are recorded and reported, they may issue a *management letter* to the board about how the organization can improve its practices. These letters can contain a wide array of recommendations. For example, the auditors may tell the board that the organization didn't consistently collect original receipts before writing checks to reimburse staff; that staff travel costs increased dramatically without that increase being approved by the board (and recorded in board minutes); or that the organization's employees are owed so many vacation hours that the organization's work could be jeopardized if everyone were to take their deserved holiday.

Although some nonprofit organizations look on a management letter as a scolding, its point is to help organizations safeguard their financial health by strengthening their policies and recordkeeping.

A representative of the auditing firm should present, formally and in person, any insights from the audit to the nonprofit board or audit committee. Often a draft version of the audit is first shared with the audit committee, providing it with an opportunity to respond before a final version is formally accepted by the board.

Following this presentation and discussion — which may lead to a revision of the audit draft — the board should vote to formally accept the audit. If the audit or management letter contain recommendations for improving financial procedures or other matters, the nonprofit board should discuss them with the executive director and write a brief, formal letter acknowledging the points made and how the organization will respond.

TIP

The National Council of Nonprofits provides a helpful online Nonprofit Audit Guide, and we've included a link in File 12-1 at www.wiley.com/go/nonprofitkitfd6e. You'll also find there the article "Get the Most Value from Your Audit," from the online journal *Blue Avocado*.

Knowing whether you need an audit

When do you need to conduct an audit? Use the following guidelines to help you determine the answer:

>> **Many states require nonprofits that receive revenues over a specified amount to conduct audits.** This varies by state. Check with the office that regulates nonprofits in your state (usually, the attorney general's office) to see whether it has specific audit guidelines.

>> **Nonprofits that directly spend $750,000 or more in federal funds in a fiscal year are required to conduct an OMB A-133 audit — commonly called a Single Audit.** It has a fancy name because it's based on the OMB Circular A-133, and it takes a particularly close look at how government funds are tracked within the organization and whether the organization complies with federal laws and regulations.

>> **Some other kinds of government programs also require audits of specific grants or contracts.** Other funders may also require audited statements from applicants.

Even if it isn't required, your board may decide that it's a good idea to have an outside CPA examine the books. Doing so provides reassurance that a financial system is healthy and the organization is working with accurate financial information.

REMEMBER

If your organization is required to have an audit, some states require your board to form an audit committee and have rules about its composition. For example, in California, the board president, board treasurer, and paid staff members may *not* serve on this committee. The committee selects the audit firm, reviews a draft of the audit and any recommendations from the auditors, and, if necessary, investigates any practices that should be changed.

Although your organization can learn a great deal from an audit, the practice isn't appropriate or necessary for every nonprofit. The process is expensive and time consuming. A less-expensive option is having a CPA firm provide a formalized compilation or financial review of annual statements. Smaller nonprofits often take this route to cut down on costs but still provide some level of comfort and assurance to funders that the organization has the appropriate level of financial controls in place and that their financial statements are likely accurate.

WARNING

Many nonprofits wonder whether they should seek *pro bono* audits from accounting firms or ask a board member's firm to audit their books. Although we're big fans of contributed services, a *pro bono* audit is a bad idea, and asking a board member for assistance is a very bad idea. An audit should be prepared independently of the organization's staff and board. It loses its value as the voice of unbiased, outside validation when provided as a gift.

Reading Your Financial Statements

Audited or not, prepared by you or by a bookkeeper or an accountant, your organization needs to produce financial statements, and it's critically important for you and your board members to understand how to interpret them. So in this section, we show you everything you need to know, including how to identify the two parts of a statement and how to arm yourself with the right information.

Getting to know the parts of a standard financial statement

Nonprofit financial statements include two important substatements:

>> **The *statement of financial position* (also called a *balance sheet*) provides an overview of how much an organization is worth.** It outlines how much money is available in bank accounts and other investments; the value of property, furniture, and equipment; immediate bills; and other debts and liabilities. The basic formula at the heart of this statement is Assets – Liabilities = Equity.

>> **The *statement of activities* outlines "Support and Revenue" and "Expenses and Other Losses," which tell you how much money the organization received in the past year, its sources for that income, and how it spent that income.** The basic formula at the heart of this statement is

Revenues – Expenses = Net Income. Statements of activities divide an organization's income and expenses into these three categories:

- *Unrestricted funds* were available to spend in the fiscal year covered by the statement.

- *Temporarily restricted funds* were promised or awarded in the year covered by the statement, but they were given to the organization for it to spend in the future or for a specific task that isn't yet complete.

- *Permanently restricted funds* were given to the organization for permanent investments — such as endowments. Earnings on such money may be used toward the organization's costs (your board will set a policy about how much of these earnings may be used, subject to applicable state laws), but the amounts donated as permanently restricted gifts shouldn't be spent on current activities.

The statement of activities also contains a statement of *functional expenses,* which details expenses spent on programs and those expenses that were exclusively for general and administrative costs and for fundraising costs.

WARNING

Many staff and board members are drawn to nonprofit organizations because they're knowledgeable about the services they provide, but their eyes glaze over when they're faced with financial statements. This lack of interest in finances is understandable but can be dangerous: The board and staff are stewards of the organization's resources, and the board accepts the responsibility of providing fiscal oversight. If your board lacks members with financial expertise, your board orientation could include training on reviewing and understanding nonprofit financial statements. BoardSource and other nonprofit service organizations also can help board members understand what they're reviewing and what questions they should ask to ensure financial integrity.

TIP

We include a sample of an audited financial statement at `www.wiley.com/go/ nonprofitkitfd6e` in File 12-13 and some tips for reading an audit in File 12-14 that you can use to become familiar with which terms are used and how the information is organized.

Asking the right financial questions

At your fiscal year's end, when you've completed the financial statement, we suggest reviewing the following points, either as a board or within the board's finance committee. You can ask different questions about the statement of position (or balance sheet) and the statement of activities. The answers arm you with a clear understanding of your organization's financial health.

Looking at the statement of position, compare some of the numbers, asking these questions:

>> **Do the cash and cash equivalents exceed the accounts payable?** If so, the organization has enough cash in the bank to pay its immediate bills to vendors.

>> **Are accounts payable increasing over time?** You'll see fluctuations in amounts owed from month to month and from year to year, but if accounts payable are steadily rising, the nonprofit's bills are getting ahead of its capability to pay them.

>> **Do the total current assets exceed the current liabilities?** If they do, the organization has enough money readily at hand to cover all its immediate obligations, such as bills and taxes, employee benefits, and loan payments.

>> **How much of the assets are made up of property, equipment, or other durable goods the organization owns, and what is the nature of those assets?** Some organizations appear to be financially healthy because their total assets are high, but they may have trouble covering immediate expenses if all those assets are items that are hard to sell.

>> **Does the current liabilities section show a high amount of payroll taxes payable?** If so, the organization may be delinquent in paying its taxes.

>> **In the liabilities section, do you see an item for a refundable advance or deferred revenue?** If you see this item, it means money paying for a service was given to the organization before the organization provided that service. Make sure the organization has sufficient assets — preferably cash — to provide the services it has promised.

>> **Has the revenue-to-date ratio changed?** To see whether income is coming into your organization in a steady and reliable way, divide the current year's revenue by the prior year's revenue at the same point. If your revenue is steady over time, the ratio figure you'll compute is close to 1. If the ratio is less than 1, money is coming into your nonprofit at a slower rate.

>> **Are you using temporarily restricted funds for other purposes?** *Temporarily restricted net assets* consist of money from foundations, donors, or customers for which the organization must still perform some kind of service. For example, if your nonprofit receives a foundation grant to produce a particular play and subscribers buy advanced tickets to that play, the money you receive from those sources is considered temporarily restricted until you produce the play. What if you need money immediately to pay the rent?

Sometimes organizations borrow from their temporarily restricted funds for such a purpose. If you do so, the temporarily restricted funds should be restored as quickly as possible. Otherwise, you won't have the money you need to produce the play. To see if temporarily restricted net assets have been spent, divide cash plus accounts receivable by temporarily restricted net assets. The ratio should total 1 or higher.

>> **Has the organization borrowed money?** If so, the amount appears in the liabilities section as a loan or line of credit. Compare its total unrestricted net assets to the total amount borrowed. If the numbers are similar, the organization may have cash at hand, but all of it must be repaid to a lender. This is not necessarily bad if the situation is temporary: Organizations may need to manage their cash flow with judicious borrowing.

The financial statement will be dated, and the answers to the questions you have just asked should give you a good picture of the health of your organization over its entire history leading up to that date. Now it's time to look at the statement of activities, which illustrates what happened in the past year. Two simple questions summarize that story. Look to the bottom of the page to see:

>> **Is the change in net assets a negative or positive number?** If it's negative, the organization lost money in the previous year. If the loss is a high number, ask why it took place. If it's a modest amount, ask whether it's part of a downward trend or something that rarely occurs.

>> **Is the number shown for total net assets a positive number?** If so, the organization is in a positive financial position (even if it lost money in the past year). That's good news!

REMEMBER

In accrual accounting, if an organization receives a multiyear grant, the entire amount of that grant is shown as revenue in the first year. If that grant is a major part of the nonprofit's annual revenues, it may create a high positive net balance in the grant's first year that is followed by apparent losses in year two and year three. You may want to footnote this situation in presenting your finances to your board or funders. If your books are audited, you can ask the CPA firm to include a footnote about it in the audit.

Managing Financial Systems

Even in a small organization, you want to establish careful practices about how you handle money and financial documents. If you have a one-person office, creating all the following controls may be impossible, but you should try to implement as many of them as possible:

>> **Store records safely.** Store checkbooks, savings passbooks, blank checks, financial records, and cash in a locked, secure place. If you're banking online, use secure passwords — multiword or nonconsecutive letters with numbers and symbols. Don't write your passwords down and don't allow your computer to remember them.

>> **Back up financial records.** Regularly back up financial records that you keep on computers, and store a copy offsite in a safe location.

>> **Balance responsibility among members.** Assign to different people the functions of writing checks, signing checks, and reconciling bank statements. If you can arrange for three different people to perform these tasks, that's great. If not, maybe a board member can double-check the bank statements. Look for accuracy and for anything that looks fishy, such as payments to vendors you don't recognize. Embezzlement is rare but possible, and taking these steps is a way to detect it. Trust us: We've discovered such a case!

>> **Require two signatures on checks or bank transfers over a specified amount.** We can't give you a standard amount for this practice: It depends on what qualifies as an unusually high transaction for your nonprofit. You can adopt this requirement as an internal policy and enforce it as a way of ensuring board oversight of large transactions. Although your bank probably monitors large or unusual transactions and may contact your organization if it notices unusual activity on your account, these days few banks accept responsibility for enforcing a two-signature policy on customers' checks.

>> **Retain all banking documents.** Retain in organized files, subject to a document retention/destruction policy, all paperwork that backs up your banking documents. These documents may include personnel time sheets, box office or other records for tickets sold, receipts, and invoices. You may scan and retain them as electronic documents, if you want. If you do so, we highly recommend backing up the files and carefully protecting passwords.

>> **Keep good purchase records.** Keep an itemized list of any furniture or equipment you purchase or receive as donations (including computers), noting the date they were purchased or received and their value.

Blue Avocado (www.blueavocado.org) published a helpful article, "Treasurers of All-Volunteer Organizations: Eight Key Responsibilities," and we include a link to it at www.wiley.com/go/nonprofitkitfd6e in File 12-1.

Chapter 13

Marketing and Branding

You may think that marketing has no place in the nonprofit sector. After all, if an organization's work isn't driven by the dollar, and if its focus is on meeting a community need, why does it need to hawk its services? If your motivation is to do good, isn't it aggressive to broadcast your purpose and presence in the nonprofit community?

But wait. *Marketing* — the process of connecting consumers to services and products — is just as critical to the success of nonprofit organizations as it is to for-profit businesses. Both nonprofit and for-profit businesses depend on getting the word out about their existence, and the message from both is the same: "Here we are, and here's what we can do for you. Come and check us out. Use our services." For nonprofit organizations, that message adds, "And please help us in our work by making a contribution."

You can go far if you have the "goods" — good planning, good stories, good services, good networking, and good luck. And, of course, persistence.

TIP Check out File 13-1 at www.wiley.com/go/nonprofitkitfd6e for a list of web resources related to the topics we cover in this chapter.

Taking Care of the Basics

Before you begin tackling client surveys and media releases, you need to spend a little time making sure you have a few basic communication tools in place. These tools help you tell your clients, audiences, donors, and the general public who you are and what you do.

In this section, we provide some tips for the most basic communication tools that every nonprofit — large or small, new or old — should have.

TIP

Before we go much further, we want to introduce you to a few websites that can help you understand and use technology for nonprofit communications and management. Reviewing these sites will help you determine what you need, TechSoup (`www.techsoup.org`) provides free and discounted software packages to qualified nonprofit organizations. The online community Nonprofit Technology Network (`www.nten.org`) helps nonprofits use technology tools to their best advantage. Another great website to peruse is Salsa (`https://www.salsalabs.com/blog/nonprofit-software-selection`), which guides you in selecting the right software solution for your nonprofit.

Designing a logo and letterhead

Your organization's letterhead should include its name, address, phone number, fax number, and email and website addresses. Many organizations also list their board members on the letterhead. Doing so is an excellent way to highlight the board members' affiliations with your organization, but if your board is rapidly changing and growing, you may be reprinting the letterhead every few weeks. You may also want to include a tagline that briefly identifies what your organization does, like "Feeding the hungry in Evansville." Often the tagline is a phrase drawn from your mission statement and also appears on the home page of your website.

A *logo* is a graphical image that represents the mission of an organization. Many people remember pictures more vividly than words, so they may remember your logo more easily than they remember your organization's name. Don't resort to using standard computer font symbols or clip art when designing your logo. If you need to be frugal, ask around your community to see whether anyone knows a graphic artist or a printer with a good eye who can help you create an eye-catching and original design. If you can't locate anyone, we recommend a simple solution: Choose an attractive typeface in which to present your name. You can get fancier later.

Or you can look into using one of the following helpful websites to create your logo:

>> **99designs** (https://99designs.com/): Write up a bit about your organization's mission and what you're looking for and 99designs will post your information for designers all around the country to submit ideas. There is also a great article on color trends on this website (https://99designs.co.uk/blog/trends/color-trends/)

>> **Canva** (www.canva.com/): Canva is a graphics design platform used to create social media graphics, presentations, posters, documents, and other types of visual content. You can create your logo and use it in a letterhead template provided for you.

Whether it's complex or simple, as you're creating your logo, produce several drafts, spend time looking at those drafts, and show them to others, asking for feedback. You don't want to grow weary of seeing your logo or hear that someone is confusing it with the logo of another group in your community.

Preparing an organization overview or brochure

An *organization overview* is a one-page description of your organization's mission and programs. You can enclose it with news releases, grant proposals, and fundraising letters. Place copies in the lobby or reception area for visitors to read. Feature it prominently on your website.

As you grow, your organization may want to get a little fancier and produce a brochure with photographs or graphics. This can be either a paper document or a page on your website. An effective brochure clearly conveys the essence of your organization. Make it inviting and readable. Visual elements help to make a more attractive document and often enable you to tell your story in fewer words.

Maintain consistent colors and design elements among any printed materials and your website. You're creating a face and a voice for your organization, so try not to send out mixed messages.

Creating a website

Having a web presence is as important as having an article about your nonprofit organization on the front page of a metropolitan city's newspaper — maybe more important. People looking for your nonprofit should be able to find you on their computers and smart devices. A basic website isn't difficult to create: You convey the key message of your agency on the home page and then provide a few additional pages where people can find out more about your organization's leaders and programs. Including photographs of your organization's work in action can make it more appealing to visitors. Most important, let visitors know how they can learn more about you, become involved with you, and do more with you. Don't forget to add a Donate Now link where website visitors can click on and contribute to your nonprofit organization. (See Chapter 15 for more information on raising funds from individual donors.)

Here are a few key features we highly recommend:

>> **Get Involved page or menu of pages:** Let readers know what they can do to help your cause. Involvement invitations can range from removing debris from handicapped-accessible hiking trails to shooting and uploading photos of the playground your nonprofit is building to sharing information with potential donors about the organization's work.

>> **Contact page with phone numbers and email addresses:** A contact page not only suggests that you're available to provide more information but also supplies a means by which your organization can begin gathering email addresses for further communications about events, programs, and fundraising.

>> **Map and transportation instructions:** If your organization provides services at a physical location, provide a map and transportation instructions (parking and bus routes, for example) to help people find it.

  If you're collecting information from donors, volunteers, or others who come to your website, it's a good practice to develop and make available a privacy policy and an unsubscribe option on your website that connects them to a newsletter or other emailings.

>> **Icons for all your social media networks:** It's an easy way for your website visitors to follow your organization. (At the end of this chapter, we cover how to use social media to promote your organization.) You can also add the icons to the signature in your email and ask your staff to follow your lead.

In good time, you can add bells and whistles to your website: a gallery of photographs or short videos, articles about your field, a blog or discussion board, and much more. But keep in mind that as you add features to your website, you're also increasing the number and types of components that need to be maintained. If you need to learn about designing and building a website, have a look at *Web Design All-in-One For Dummies,* 2nd Edition, by Sue Jenkins, and *Building Websites All-in-One For Dummies,* 3rd Edition, by David Karlins and Doug Sahlin (Wiley).

In File 13-1 at www.wiley.com/go/nonprofitkitfd6e, we provide a link to the top 200 nonprofit websites of 2020, analyzed for their various qualities and strengths. Take a look for inspiration, and also search for the top nonprofit websites of previous or subsequent years.

If you're looking for assistance with creating a website, you may find free or low-cost help at a local college or university. Often students majoring in graphical arts, design, educational technology, and technical writing are required to complete internships or capstone projects as part of their degree programs. You may find a talented, eager designer by contacting the department or by reaching out to the campus's community-service learning program. Another option is to search online for a graphic artist at Volunteer Match (www.volunteermatch.org). If you do use such a volunteer, make sure that person leaves behind clear information about how you can continue to refresh the site in the future.

An unattended website leaves a bad impression. Broken links and out-of-date information tell the reader that your organization is paying no attention to communicating with its stakeholders. If you have a website, assign someone in your organization the task of checking it and updating it regularly. If the budget allows, consider hiring a web design firm or web-savvy individual to create and maintain the site.

Producing annual reports and newsletters

Begin producing an annual report after your first year of operation. You can publish it as a letter, a website feature, or even a booklet. Usually, the annual report features the financial statement for the year, along with an overview of recent accomplishments. It may also include introductory letters from the board president and executive director of your organization. An annual report conveys the image of an accomplished organization that's transparent in its communications. The messages such reports convey build trust among people seeking organizations' services or considering making contributions.

A newsletter offers background stories and information about your organization. You can publish a newsletter as a feature page or slide show on your website, as a PDF document linked to your website, as a printed or photocopied document, or in email. Issuing a newsletter is a great way to stay in touch with your organization's stakeholders. It can take them behind the scenes of your organization. You can use an electronic newsletter to profile members of your staff or board or your stakeholders; alert followers to upcoming events; summarize research; and announce news about your organization's work. Electronic newsletters can be sent via email, saving your nonprofit postage and trips to the post office.

Taking care of your service population — your most important marketing tool

If your stakeholders (audiences, patients, clients, volunteers, and board members) aren't treated well, you can make major investments in advertising and public relations but still struggle to find new customers and retain old ones. Small adjustments in your service delivery model(s) can make a big difference to your nonprofit organization's image.

REMEMBER

If your nonprofit is likely to receive calls from people requiring counseling or emergency assistance, *make sure* that everyone answering the phone is thoroughly trained in how to calm a caller and provide an expedited referral.

MAKING CUSTOMER SERVICE A DAILY HABIT

The trick to providing exemplary customer service is to work at it in little ways all the time. Every staff member and volunteer needs to be aware of the importance of customer service. We offer five key areas to address if you want to improve (or maintain) your service levels:

- **On the telephone:** Spell out to all staff and volunteers how to answer the phone politely and otherwise use it to maximum effect. Provide a cheat sheet with lists of extensions, instructions on how to forward calls, and any other useful information. Simple additions to a greeting, like "May I help you?" or telling the caller the receptionist's name can set a friendly, professional tone.

  Make a rule for yourself to return all calls within 24 hours or, if that's not possible, within one week. Let callers know, via voicemail greeting, when they can expect to hear from you. If you're selecting a voicemail system, make sure it's user-friendly for callers. We prefer a small number of transfers within the system and options for modifying standard recorded announcements with more personal and pertinent messages.

- **At the door:** Someone needs to (cheerfully) answer the door. If you're in a small office with no receptionist and the interruptions are frequent, you can rotate this task among staff members or volunteers. If visitors must use a buzzer or pass through a security system, try to balance the coldness of that experience with a friendly intercom greeting and pleasant foyer.

- **Before and after a sale or donation:** If you have tickets to sell, make them easy to buy. Accepting only cash is far too restrictive. The banker managing your business account can help prepare you to accept credit card orders. Also, consider selling tickets over the web — a number of web services assist small businesses and non-profits with web sales and online donations. If a customer isn't satisfied with your service, invite the customer to give feedback — and listen carefully. Offer a partial or complete refund. Doing so wins loyalty.

- **With a note:** Keep some nice-looking stationery and a rough draft of a standard message handy so that writing thank-you notes is easy. Handwritten notes are more personal and often make a stronger impression than formal, typed letters or email messages. However, expressing your appreciation in a timely way is more important than the form of that appreciation. Use email if you can get to it more quickly. Write a thank-you note for a contribution within a few days of receiving it.

  If your organization receives donations — like a 9-passenger van or a semitrailer full of donated canned foods — have an acknowledgment email ready that confirms the item's receipt and states when the person submitting it can expect to hear from you.

- **In the details:** An old saying suggests that the devil is in the details, but that's also where you find the heart and soul of hospitality and service. Store notes in a database about the interests, connections, and preferences of board members, donors, volunteers, and other stakeholders. Find out the names of board and committee members' significant others and be prepared to greet them personally at events and on the phone or video calls.

Discovering Who You Are: First Steps to Marketing

You've put the basic tools in place and your programs are up and running, but you sense that something is wrong. You know that you're addressing a need and that your agency is highly regarded. Why aren't your programs full? How can you engage more people in the important work you do?

If a marketing program is what you need (and we believe it is), the first step is understanding your current situation — what you do, whom you serve, who admires your work, and who is willing to support it. When you know the answers to these questions, you can begin to build marketing strategies that highlight your organization's strengths and are tailored to all your key audiences — the people who walk through your doors every day to receive your services, your board members and staff, your donors and volunteers, and the community at large (all stakeholders).

Recognizing the current market

If you want to improve the way you reach the public, you first need to know how your current marketing works. Who are your potential clients and stakeholders? How did they find out about your organization? Why do they make use of your programs? The following sections help you answer these kinds of questions.

Surveying stakeholders to gain important info

You may never discover who learns about your organization in the newspaper or sees your sign every day on the bus, but some people — those with whom you directly communicate — can be identified. Start by defining your core group — the most important — and work outward from there.

Suppose that your organization is a senior home–care agency that provides in-home care for the elderly in your community. Home–care services include managing medication, monitoring vital signs and communicating irregular readings to the client's doctor, cooking nutritious meals, and helping with mobility issues. These are the current stakeholders, working from the core to the outer boundaries:

>> The board and staff (and their friends and relations)

>> Contracted staff and volunteers

>> Home-health caretaker association

>> Visiting nurses

>> Hospice

>> Nursing homes

>> Assisted living facilities needing supplemental staffing (fee for service agreement)

>> Area agencies on aging (regional office for subcontracting opportunities)

>> Subscribers to your quarterly e-newsletter

>> People visiting your organization's website

Drawing up this list of interested people is easy enough. But for marketing purposes, you need to know as much as possible about the characteristics, backgrounds, and interests of each group. Here are some things you can do to collect this sort of information:

Create a database of your supporters by gathering names and addresses from every possible source within your organization. Sources might be checks from donors, subscription forms from online newsletter subscribers, sign-up sheets from volunteers, or email messages sent to the Contact Us address on your website. Enter these names and addresses into a database that can sort them by last name, type of contact, or date of entry; if you're planning to send traditional mail to them, sort them by zip code. Articles at Salsa (www.salsalabs.com/blog/nonprofit-software-selection) can help you choose a database software program.

TIP

>> **Review the zip codes appearing most frequently on your list.** If you're in the United States, you can visit the US Census Bureau website (www.census.gov) to find demographic information about residents in those zip code areas.

>> **Ask the three libraries whether they collect demographic data when visitors apply for library cards.** Then ask whether they can share that information with you. Some public agencies offer information about their stakeholders on their websites.

>> **Ask a few standard questions of schools or other groups when they call to sign up for a tour.** Don't engage in a lengthy interview, but find out how they heard about your program, why they want to visit it, and whether they have other needs you may be able to address. You can gather similar information when collecting registrations online.

>> **Insert brief, clearly worded, and inviting surveys in the programs at your public events.** At the beginning and end of an event, make a public pitch explaining why people should respond to the surveys. Make pencils or pens available. Create incentives for completing the form, such as a free museum membership for a person whose survey is drawn at random. Make it easy for visitors to your website to subscribe to announcements or services, and send a brief survey to them by email. The higher the response rate, the more accurate and useful the survey information.

TIP

Your surveying may be *quantitative* (measuring the degree to which people do something or believe something) or *qualitative* (delving deeper into understanding their beliefs and behaviors). Generally, quantitative surveys are distributed and collected — either as paper documents or online — and qualitative surveys are presented by an interviewer in a guided conversation.

REMEMBER

There's an art and a science to writing an effective survey: The way questions are worded can influence the answers you receive, and you want to receive clear, candid responses. If you want help developing a survey, check with local colleges and universities for faculty members or graduate students who understand survey techniques and who may be willing to give you some guidance. You can also find survey subscription services and sample surveys on the web that give you ideas about wording questions. One such service is SurveyMonkey, which also is a host website for Zoomerang (`www.surveymonkey.com`.)

TIP

In Files 13-2 and 13-3 at `www.wiley.com/go/nonprofitkitfd6e`, you can find two sample surveys that may suggest wording for survey questions.

Organizing and interpreting the responses

After you have survey results, you can compile the responses by hand or use a spreadsheet program such as Microsoft Excel or Google Spreadsheet to tally responses. Of course, if you've used an online surveying service, it compiles the responses for you.

If survey responders identify themselves and you want to keep track of information and opinions they share to inform your fundraising or volunteer-recruitment staff, incorporate their information into the database you're developing of your supporters. Check Salsa (`www.salsalabs.com/blog/nonprofit-software-selection`) for recent reviews of constituent relationship management (CRM) software options. Such programs allow you to record every point of connection you may have with an individual, from workshop attendance to dance contestant to donor. If you don't want to go that route, Microsoft Access and FileMaker Pro are commonly used tools that can be adapted to your needs.

You may discover that you serve several distinct groups of people among your target service population. For example, low-income senior citizens may need your services but are hesitant to ask — however, you can think about talking to local gerontologists. They may be able to refer their elderly or frail patients to your home-healthcare services. Other senior citizens who are fit but may live alone and need some help from time to time may have younger family members who are unaware of your services but would refer you to their parents or grandparents, aunts or uncles, or other relatives who can benefit from your in-home health-and-wellness services.

With this valuable information, you may be able to recognize ways to reach more people who resemble the ones you're already serving. The more challenging task is to reach and entice new groups of people.

TIP

Do people you don't know gather at your organization's community programs? Sponsor free drawings in which contestants compete for prizes by filling out forms with their names, email addresses, and phone numbers. Think about giving away exercise bands or laminated cards with the food pyramid showing their suggested daily intake of each of the food groups.

DESIGNING A USEFUL SURVEY

Developing a picture of your current stakeholders is critically important to creating a marketing plan, and a good survey can serve as your camera. If you're going to the effort to conduct a survey, it needs to have a purpose, and it must be clear and direct. Here are some general guidelines to keep in mind:

- If your survey is long, fewer people will complete it.

- If you offer (the always popular) multiple choice questions, be sure to have one or two open-ended questions as well so that people have a chance to speak their minds.

- Be careful not to ask *leading questions* — questions that suggest the answers you hope to hear.

- Explore different kinds of information by asking how convenient and appealing your events and services are and by asking patrons what other kinds of programs they would enjoy.

- Ask current stakeholders how they found out about you. The answers tell you which forms of your current marketing efforts are effective and begin to suggest how you can best further spread the word about your programs.

TIP

A benefit of designing a survey online is that you can make it engaging by using the techniques of branching or piping. In such a survey, someone's answer to one question alters the next question that's asked. For example, if you were to say that you prefer ice cream over pie for dessert, you would next be asked whether you prefer chocolate, vanilla, or spumoni.

If you discover that your target audience likes services but is afraid to let a stranger into their residences, emphasize in your marketing effort that your team members are screened and bonded and carry company smartphones with location trackers on them when assigned to a client. If you find that your potential clients are very low-income, you can have a Medicare/Medicaid advocate on your staff to help them find ways to pay for your services.

One of your most difficult marketing tasks is analyzing the very basis of what you do and how you do it. You may feel that your community is where you're likely to find high populations of senior citizens, but the surveys may point out that these specific seniors who are clustering together in 55-and-over communities are highly active and not in need of your services. Consider visiting their clubhouses when exercise classes are taking place (obtain permission first from the property manager or recreation director). Leave pamphlets, and then stick around to ask whether anyone has a relative in need of home-healthcare services. If you feel like an undertaker waiting around for the next body to show up, shake off those thoughts. You can do this!

Soliciting detailed feedback from focus groups

Surveys are useful for providing you with general information. You read them looking for an overview of what most people think and feel. Focus groups are another common tool for gathering information from constituents. Because they're based in conversations, they often give you more specific, nuanced responses. Perhaps you want to know what small-business leaders think of your agency; a focus group of businesspeople can help you uncover their attitudes and needs.

When producing a focus group, remember to limit the number of questions asked to fewer than ten (five or six is ideal). Provide healthy refreshments to create a convivial environment. The conversation will likely be more candid if it's led by an elderly volunteer facilitator, not someone clearly identified with your organization. Seek permission from participants to record their discussions.

Defining whom you want to reach and how

Armed with information about the people who already know about your nonprofit, you're now ready to extend your reach by defining target groups you want to serve and discovering how best to reach them. In general, begin with your current constituents and work to expand within their demographic group or to others who are similar to them.

WARNING

As you shift your attention to reaching new groups, be cautious: You may alienate and lose current followers. The more different demographically your new target groups are from the people you now serve, the more difficult and expensive your marketing task may become.

HOW MARKET RESEARCH CAN OPEN YOUR EYES

A small nonprofit alcoholism treatment center for women was started in San Francisco in the late 1970s in response to studies that found multiple programs to help alcoholic men but few focused specifically on women. No local service of this type focused on helping Spanish-speaking or immigrant women.

The program's mission was to provide comprehensive counseling and alcohol treatment services to low-income women, particularly those originally from Mexico or Central America. Four years into the nonprofit's history, its programs were full and effective, and it had won prestigious contracts from the city. The center had even launched a capital campaign to create a permanent home. It appeared to be very successful. With one exception. The women being served were mostly middle class and white. A few were African American. None came from the neighborhood where the program was based.

The board realized that the center needed to change its image and marketing strategy. From interviews with women from the center's target population, the board and staff realized that the stigma associated with alcoholism was particularly strong among Mexican and Central American families, and women from these cultural groups were struggling with alcoholism in private.

The center began a multifaceted campaign to change this situation, beginning with cultural sensitivity training for counselors. When the center hired new staff, an aggressive effort was made to find Latinas to fill positions. The group published all brochures and other informational materials in Spanish and held news conferences for the Spanish-language press. The center hired a Latina outreach counselor to meet with community groups, churches, and schools and to develop connections and a system of referrals to the agency.

Within two years, more than one-third of the women served were low-income women from Mexico and Central America. The marketing aimed at this community was well worth the investment. Fulfilling the organization's mission depended on it.

Here's another example: When you run a local history archive and have audiences of low-income students, middle-income mothers of toddlers, and affluent docents (tour guides) and volunteers, logical new target audiences may include

>> Family members and classmates of the students using the libraries

>> Mothers and toddlers from a wider geographical area surrounding the libraries

>> Docents and volunteers who assist other local cultural institutions

>> Friends and acquaintances of the docents

Your marketing plan should then be tailored to reach these groups. To succeed, you may need to change both how you present your work and how you spread the message about that work. Consider some of the ideas in this list to reach the following groups:

>> **The students' classmates and friends:**

- Contact local history teachers and work with them to link their lessons to archival materials in your collection. Invite them to bring their classes to see your exhibits and archival collections.

- Offer student internships and then use your interns as docents for the school tours.

- Invite the students who now use the library space to help in planning, researching, and presenting an exhibit. Honor them for their involvement at the exhibit's opening, and provide them with invitations for their friends and acquaintances.

>> **More mothers and toddlers:**

- Advertise or place articles about your organization's work in local newsletters for parents of young children.

- Post fliers about your organization's work at parks, playgrounds, local stores that sell goods for small children, and other cultural institutions with children's events.

- Provide childcare at lectures and weekend programs.

» **Docents and volunteers who also help other organizations:**

- Advertise or place articles in your local volunteer center's newsletter.

- Contact local parent-teacher organizations and offer their members special tours or presentations.

- Co-host an event with another local cultural organization, and combine your email lists to extend invitations. Invite guests to sign up for your newsletter or announcements to keep in touch with them in the future.

» **Friends and acquaintances of your current docents:**

- Hold a volunteer recognition party and provide each of your volunteers with ten or more invitations for friends and acquaintances.

REMEMBER

The cost of implementing new programs and spreading the word about them can add up quickly. Consider what resources you have available (including your time) before committing to big changes in your organization.

MARKETING ON A SHOESTRING

Effective marketing doesn't have to be expensive. It can be based on multiple grassroots efforts that are small in scale and specifically targeted. *Guerrilla marketing* is the term for marketing that's cheap, creative, and effective. Jay Conrad Levinson's website (www. gmarketing.com) is a good place to find out more about low-cost marketing.

The guerrilla approach may use sandwich boards with provocative messages, cards passed out to people waiting in ticket lines, or enticing online offers. In a famous guerrilla marketing example from the business world, an Internet start-up company offered families $5,000 to name a child after one of its products. The point of guerrilla marketing is to get customers talking about your organization and its products in order to develop powerful word-of-mouth advertising.

Another low-cost tip is to apply to Google AdWords for support from its nonprofit component. Qualified organizations can apply for up to $10,000 a month in keyword advertising. We haven't used this feature, but you may want to check it out at www.google.com/grants. The program isn't available for government entities, schools, or hospitals.

Reaching Your Audience via Mass Media

What if you want to reach all the people, all the time? We're sorry, but you can't. You can, however, extend your reach beyond the contacts known by your friends and family, by approaching mass media — print and electronic newspapers and magazines, local radio and television stations, and the web. Although some nonprofits pay for advertising to spread the word, most organizations rely on free publicity from the media.

Planning for effective publicity

Before contacting the media, first decide which story you want to tell and whom you want to reach with that story. What's distinctive and important about your organization's work? Why is it newsworthy? Be honest: Analyze your idea as though you're a news editor who has to choose among many stories from various sources. How does yours stand up to the competition?

THE ART OF SHAPING A NEWS STORY

A few years ago we were involved as grant makers in supporting the creation of a mural on the exterior of a community center next to a small urban park. One of San Francisco's best-regarded mural artists led the project and spent a great deal of time talking about images to use in the mural with the park's neighbors and people who used the building. People kept mentioning a young couple who had been killed in the park in a random, accidental shooting several years earlier. Although it wasn't the original subject idea, the artist included the couple's portraits in the painting, surrounded by images representing peace and renewal.

The story of the mural's unveiling was presented to the media as a public memorial event for the neighbors and families of the young couple. Front-page, color images of the piece appeared in both the morning and evening editions of the newspaper the next day, and five television stations covered the event that evening. An acclaimed artist completing another mural wouldn't have been a story, but a neighborhood mourning two lost teenagers was hot news.

We hope your nonprofit never needs to tell a tragic story, but we give this example to show that not all good work is news. Tragedy is news. Drama is news. Breakthroughs are news. Surprises are news. Stories that connect to current trends are news.

Ask yourself about your proposed story's relevance: Will it affect the lives of its readers? Is it timely? Does it contain conflict, intrigue, or prominent people? We uncovered some good advice from the American Land Rights Association about writing news releases, and you can find a link to the article in File 13-1 at www. wiley.com/go/nonprofitkitfd6e.

TIP

Reporters often have more story ideas than they have time to cover them. You can increase your chances of coverage if you write (or record or film) a basic document and vary it to address the different media interests that you appeal to, making use of your multiple story angles.

Developing a media list

A *media list* is a compilation of names, addresses, email addresses, and phone numbers of contacts at local (or national) print and electronic newspapers and magazines, local radio and television stations, and the web.

The media list is a valuable tool that you refine and expand over time. Some metropolitan areas have press clubs and service organizations from which you can buy membership lists, providing a basis for your list. The databases at Cision (us. cision.com), a comprehensive online media service, encompass contacts across traditional and social media platforms. Cision also offers educational programs and tools for communicating with government contacts. A full membership to Cision can be expensive, but the cost of a one-time search is reasonable.

WARNING

Journalism is a rapidly changing field, with frequent layoffs and employee turnover, so it's important to update your media list often.

TIP

For all the nuances of media-list development and management, we recommend that you take a look at *Public Relations For Dummies*, by Eric Yaverbaum, Ilise Benun, Bob Bly, and Richard Kirshenbaum (Wiley). The general objective is to build two working lists — one that you use with practically every news release you send out and the other for specific opportunities for publicity. The latter group may include examples like these:

>> **Social and entertainment editors** to whom you send news of your annual benefit gala

>> **Social and business editors** to whom you announce new members and officers of your board

>> **Opinion page editors** for letters to the editor

>> **Sunday magazine supplement editors** for in-depth profiles of leaders in your field of work

>> **Features columnists** for amusing anecdotes or unusual news

>> **Writers of blogs** on topics related to your work

Understanding how the media works

Different media outlets require different amounts of lead time. In an ideal situation, you begin your efforts to reach the media four months — or even longer — in advance of that hoped-for coverage. The first two months are spent creating news releases and public service announcements (PSAs) and shooting photographs. Always check with the publication beforehand to find out how much lead time is necessary.

TIP

Many organizations create on their website a media section where they post news releases, background information, and high-resolution images with captions and photo credit information. This tool enables your media contact to expand on the information you send and download preferred photos for publication.

After you've completed the initial legwork over the first couple of months, you start distributing the materials:

>> Most monthly magazines need to receive news releases and photographs at least two — preferably three — months in advance of publication (even earlier if they're published quarterly or bimonthly).

>> At the same time as you're emailing the release to magazines, send advance notice to your most important daily and weekly outlets.

>> Send PSAs — see the later section "Putting together public service announcements (PSAs)" — two to three months before the time when you hope they'll be used. Although most stations have set aside time for broadcasting nonprofits' announcements, they need time to rotate through the many announcement materials they receive.

>> News releases to daily and weekly papers should be sent four to six weeks in advance of the event you want covered. You may also send follow-up releases approximately ten days before the event. You should certainly make follow-up phone calls.

>> Releases inviting members of the media to attend a news conference or witness a special event or announcement can be sent three to ten days in advance of the event. If a news outlet is reluctant to cover your announcement, invite a reporter to visit your program and see your good works firsthand.

TIP

Take rejection graciously if your media contact declines to use your story. You need to be able to go back to these people in the future. If you receive a rejection, ask the reporter for honest feedback about the kinds of stories that would better fit their needs.

Submitting materials to your media contacts

Each section of a newspaper and each part of a TV or radio program is made up of materials from multiple sources that are competing for time and space. You improve the odds of receiving attention in the media by providing clear, accurate, and provocative materials in time for consideration and possible use by reporters and broadcasters.

We recommend the following steps when you submit material to the media:

1. **Even if you've purchased a reputable media directory, call to confirm the most appropriate contact person for your story at the media outlet.**

   Whether it's a newspaper, a radio station, a TV station, or an online outlet, ask about the format that each one wants you to use in your submission.

   Most media outlets want your news release, photographs, and recorded materials to be sent via email. Paste the news release into the body of the email so that the recipient doesn't have to mess with an attachment.

2. **Submit clear and accurate written materials and labeled, good-quality photographs.**

   The media generally want photographs to be in the form of high-resolution JPEGs, which work well in print.

3. **Call to see whether your materials have been received.**

   Take this opportunity to ask whether more information, further interview contacts, a different format, or additional photography are needed.

4. **If requested, submit additional information immediately and call to confirm its receipt and clarity.**

5. **If you don't receive a clear response (either "Yes, we'll cover it" or "Sorry, I don't see the story here") to your initial release, call again in a few days.**

6. **If a member of the media covers an event you've announced, provide a media packet (generally, by providing a link to an electronic file).**

   A media packet commonly contains a news release, fact sheet, background information, and photographs. It briefs the reporter about your event and makes it easy for someone to check facts when writing a story. If a reporter is covering your event, introduce yourself and be available to answer questions or introduce the reporter to key spokespeople. Don't be a pest, though: Let reporters find their own stories.

   You can help the reporter write a better story by recruiting ahead of time stakeholders who have benefitted from your program and are willing to be interviewed.

7. **If your situation changes and the news release is no longer accurate, immediately call in the change and, if necessary, revise and resubmit your original release.**

When making calls and sending emails to members of the media, recognize that they're busy and often working to meet deadlines. If you ask brief, clear questions that they can respond to quickly, you'll find it easy to engage them. For example, "How many photographs would you like?" is easier to answer than "What do you want a picture of?"

At www.wiley.com/go/nonprofitkitfd6e, you can find a sample news release (see File 13-4), media alert (see File 13-5), calendar release (see File 13-6), photo caption (see File 13-7), and photo permission form (see File 13-8).

Getting your event into community event calendars

Getting your organization's events listed in newspaper calendars and broadcast on TV and radio can be critically important to attracting a crowd. Readers, viewers, and listeners use these calendars to help them decide how to spend their time on, say, a Thursday night. If your event is listed clearly and accurately, you're in the running.

Larger newspapers and many other media outlets assign the preparation of calendar sections to specific editors — when you put together your media contacts list, make sure you identify the calendar editors. And, to improve your access to this important source of publicity, contact the calendar specialists in advance and ask for instructions on formatting their preferred calendar listings and for how far in advance of the event to submit your information. Sometimes publications provide these explicit instructions — or the specific form you need to complete — on their websites.

Putting together public service announcements (PSAs)

Many radio and television stations allot a portion of their airtime to broadcasting *public service announcements (PSAs)* on behalf of nonprofit causes. Although these stations rarely give away their best viewing and listening hours to this free service, sometimes they tack on PSAs to the end of a newscast or special program during prime time. But even an announcement played during the morning's wee hours can reach many people.

PSAs are brief. Most are 15, 30, or 60 seconds long. You may submit them as written text to be read by the stations' announcers, or you may submit them recorded or filmed on a CD or DVD or as an emailed podcast for direct broadcast. Many stations are more willing to use PSAs that are already recorded or filmed, but this isn't universally true. If you submit a prerecorded PSA, also send a print version of the text. Some stations string together several announcements in a general public announcement broadcast, and it's easier for them to work from text.

If you choose to submit a prerecorded PSA, make sure it's of broadcast quality with excellent sound and/or images. If you're the narrator, spit out your gum! If you mumble or if the images are blurry, stations can't use the material. Using the voice of a celebrity — even a local luminary — for a prerecorded PSA can be particularly effective.

REMEMBER

The challenge to writing PSAs is to clearly convey a lot of information in a few words. Write your message and test it against the clock. If you're rushing to finish it in time, it's probably too long. Ask someone else to read it back to you, and time that person. You don't want to be the only one who can finish it in 15 seconds.

TIP

File 13-9 at www.wiley.com/go/nonprofitkitfd6e is a sample PSA addressed to a media outlet.

Using Social Media for Fun and Profit

How many people do you know without a Facebook account? Probably not many. Facebook, Instagram, LinkedIn, Twitter, and other platforms have penetrated multiple generations and cultures and enabled everyone to view photos of the children of their cousins and the pets of their friends and acquaintances. It doesn't matter if you think social media platforms are a positive step forward or the first step on a slippery slope toward the total destruction of personal privacy — social media is here, and it's not going away.

You shouldn't be surprised to hear that nonprofit organizations are working to turn Facebook and other social media applications to their advantage. After all, what could be better than the opportunity to communicate easily with clients, volunteers, and donors — and to recruit more of the same? You can let people know what you're doing without the hit-and-miss efforts of trying to place articles in mass media publications.

In this section, we give you an overview of the most popular social media tools and some tips for getting the most out of the time you spend on Facebook, LinkedIn, Twitter, and other sites that may become popular in the future.

Developing a social media policy

If you have staff and volunteers posting on your organization's social media platforms, you're wise to establish guidelines for what information is and isn't appropriate to reveal to the public and to use a tone that builds a positive image of your nonprofit.

In your social media policy, address these points:

REMEMBER

>> **Be professional.** Blog posts, status updates, and tweets determine your organization's online face. Review all posts before posting. The spell checker is your friend.

Keep your personal social media play separate from your organization activities.

>> **Post regularly.** Update regularly to keep your content fresh. We recommend creating a calendar and assigning responsibility for updates so that your information is routinely refreshed.

>> **Know what's appropriate to post.** Announcements, awards, milestones, and general news about the day-to-day activities of your organization are all worthy of posting. Never circulate rumors, gossip, bad news, or the like on social media. Here are some other tips about posting:

- **Ask questions.** Engage your audience in conversation.

- **Respond to comments as soon as you can.** Don't be defensive about negative comments.

- **Photos and videos typically draw more comments and likes than text postings.** You can add images to your website, or, if you have more images than your website can hold, open a Flickr account for still photos and upload videos to YouTube or Vimeo. Let people know when you've added new material by posting links on your social media pages.

- **Secure permission to post the names and photos of people who work at your organization or of clients who receive services.** If you find good photographs on the Internet that you want to use, be conscientious about requesting permission to use them. Providing a photo credit isn't sufficient — you need permission (from the photographer and the subject) to use the images.

» **Respect copyrighted material.** Ask permission to repost (if you can't just post a link) and give proper credit.

» **Prepare to respond to comments, and develop policies for responding to social media comments.** Engaging with the public is the essence of social media, and many of the responses you receive will be positive ones, but you also need to be prepared for criticism or even offensive feedback.

» **Use good judgment.** Don't post anything you wouldn't want your mother to see or that you wouldn't want to read on the front page of your local newspaper.

In addition to questions of taste and tone, be sure that employees and volunteers understand that no 501(c)(3) nonprofit organization can take a stand on political campaigns for public office. And although you can't ban your staff and volunteers from using their own social media accounts for personal activities, remind them that their friends probably know where they work and that a tasteless or vulgar post can reflect badly on the organization.

TIP

We provide links in File 13-1 at `www.wiley.com/go/nonprofitkitfd6e` to information to help you develop your social media policy.

Planning your social media posts

Because social media can swallow up a lot of time, especially if you're distracted by cute cat videos, you should develop a plan before jumping into promoting your nonprofit via social media channels. Knowing the outcomes you want to achieve on social media helps you post or tweet information that is useful to both your organization and your followers.

Here is a list of questions to answer:

» What is the primary goal? Do you want to make more people aware of your services? Do you want to recruit volunteers? Do you want to raise money? Do you want to drive people to your website?

>> How will you achieve that goal? After you determine the goal, set an objective. For example, you may decide to recruit ten new volunteers over the next three months.

>> Whom will you target? If your nonprofit is a community theater, for instance, you can look for people who enjoy the dramatic arts, as either audience members or performers.

>> How much time can you spend implementing your plans? Can you spend an hour each day? Three hours a week? Do you have volunteers who can help?

We don't think it's necessary to create a formal plan document, but the more specific you can be about your goals and objectives, the more successful you're likely to be. We suggest *Social Media Marketing For Dummies*, by Phyllis Khare (Wiley), for good information about using social media marketing.

TIP

Track visitors' activity on your website and social media networks so that you can see how you're doing and make adjustments as necessary. Google Analytics (www.google.com/analytics) can help you do this. As you use these analytics and observe which features and posts attract the most attention on your social media pages, you can shape future content and campaigns to reach maximum numbers. Also keep an eye on qualitative information, such as whether influential people follow you on Twitter, whether your contacts share and retweet your material, and whether the comments you attract are thoughtful and well-informed.

Choosing your social media platforms

We doubt that anyone has been successful in developing a complete list of all social media applications, because so many now exist and new ones are being launched almost daily. However, in the following sections, we list three that you cannot afford to ignore.

Facebook

For a company that was founded in 2004, it's amazing that Facebook can be called the granddaddy of social networking. If you do nothing else, you should create a Facebook Page and begin collecting fans and likes. The company claims nearly 3 billion users worldwide. And although it's unlikely that you'll generate interest from more than a tiny percentage of all users, it's the best place to carve out the niche for your nonprofit.

Facebook provides advice, including a resource guide and examples of how nonprofits are using the platform to advance their work. Visit www.facebook.com/nonprofits to find good ideas that you can adapt for your nonprofit's page.

Keep your organization's page separate from your personal account. Facebook provides a tutorial (https://socialimpact.facebook.com/learning-support/getting-started/create-a-page-for-your-nonprofit/) to guide you in setting up a page for your nonprofit. In addition, *Facebook For Dummies*, by Carolyn Abram and Amy Karasavas (Wiley), is a step-by-step useful resource.

TIP

Facebook used to manage a Causes feature that can now be found on a discrete platform: www.causes.com. Causes.com guides its users to organize boycotts, raise money, and build volunteer involvement.

Twitter

In the first quarter of 2021, Twitter had 262 million users, less than Facebook's 2.9 billion, according to web reports at the time of this writing, but Twitter can be a powerful driver for traffic to your website and your Facebook Page. Tweets are limited to 280 characters (it was 140 characters when it was launched), so don't plan to publish any essays on Twitter. On the other hand, it's perfect for writing a snappy headline and adding a link to the essay or blog post on your website.

TIP

You build Twitter followers more quickly if your tweets have an authentic voice that sounds like a person who wants to have a conversation with followers — not someone who's reading a news release or shouting slogans.

Retweeting Twitter posts that you want your followers to see is an effective way to participate in the Twitter community. Remember that posting photos can be a fine way to promote a program or an event. You can find a guide for nonprofit use of Twitter at www.twitter4good.com. Also check out *Twitter For Dummies*, by Laura Fitton, Anum Hussain, and Brittany Leaning (Wiley).

LinkedIn

LinkedIn is frequented by business folks and professionals, and who could be better to network with, especially when you're looking for potential board members or corporate connections? Create a company profile page for your organization. Remember that this is a professional network, so, you know, keep it professional. *LinkedIn For Dummies*, by Joel Elad (Wiley), provides in-depth information about the ins and outs of LinkedIn.

We can tell you from experience that posting your nonprofit organization's wish list on LinkedIn can result in monetary contributions as well as product donations. Before you do this, make sure you have requested connections from foundation and corporate executives (directors, board members, CEOs, and finance directors) as well as foundation grant-making program officers. Search, write an introductory message, and click Connect. Of course, not everyone will accept your request to connect, but you need only a few to start the donations rolling in to your nonprofit organization.

LinkedIn groups can be a good way to exchange information with people who share your interests. If you're feeling adventurous, you can open your own group for your board members and volunteers. While you're at it, encourage those board members and volunteers to identify in their profiles their participation in your nonprofit. Declaring their affiliations with your organization can be a subtle but effective way to introduce their professional associates to your work.

Protecting your online reputation

Not all the information that people find about you online is generated by your organization. A number of online services rank and rate nonprofit organizations against such criteria as financial health, use of resources, transparency, and constituent feedback. Just as none of us can control gossip, you have no power to change the data these services use or their ways of interpreting that data. However, you can provide them with information, remain vigilant so that you're aware of any critiques, and be proactive if your nonprofit is criticized.

TIP

One step in protecting your online reputation is regularly searching for the name of your nonprofit online. This practice can guide you to any weaknesses (or strengths) in your reputation and also alert you to someone fraudulently using the name of your organization to raise money. Such scams are rare, but they do take place — particularly during disasters or other emergencies.

Here's a list of major sites that review nonprofits so that you can provide them with up-to-date information:

>> The **Better Business Bureau's Wise Giving Alliance** (www.give.org) rates more than 1,000 national nonprofits. Local BBBs also review nonprofits — approximately 10,000 of them. They use a range of standards to grade nonprofits. You can strengthen your rating by building your board of directors and making sure it meets more than three times a year, paying attention to the balance between your management costs and program expenses, being honest and transparent in fundraising materials, and providing options for donors who want their names to remain private. You can also gain a seal as a BBB Accredited Charity, for which you'll have to pay a fee on a sliding scale from $1,000 to $15,000 per year.

>> **Charity Navigator** (www.charitynavigator.com) analyzes the finances, apparent effectiveness, and accountability and transparency of approximately 6,000 of the largest US charities with revenues of more than $1 million, and assigns ratings from 0 to 4 stars. If you're a new, emerging nonprofit, you're

unlikely to be included on this charity rating site, but it might be helpful to understand how nonprofits are assessed so that you can plan for the future.

By studying a few sample profiles of nonprofits on the Charity Navigator website, you can discern how it analyzes nonprofits. Apart from the long-term hard work of growing your organization and containing overhead costs, your nonprofit can improve its rating by creating and following conflict-of-interest and whistleblower policies and publishing a donor privacy policy on your website.

>> **GuideStar by Candid** (`www.guidestar.org`) offers an array of nonprofit information and is particularly valuable for posting three years of nonprofits' most recent Form 990s. You can strengthen your presence on GuideStar by writing the profile of your organization and verifying that your most recent forms are posted. The IRS provides Form 990 directly to GuideStar by Candid, and occasionally sees a delay.

COLLECTING DONATIONS BY CROWDFUNDING

Crowdfunding (also called crowdsourcing) is a form of online fundraising that can benefit from the social networks you've developed. Kickstarter (`www.kickstarter.com`) and Indiegogo (`www.indiegogo.com`) are two of the best-known crowdfunding sites.

Kickstarter, which is all about projects, isn't specifically designed for nonprofits. You can't use Kickstarter to raise funds to support the ongoing costs of your nonprofit, for example. But if your work involves making a film or producing a play, Kickstarter may be the place to go. Fundly (`fundly.com`) lets you raise funds for a cause, as long as your organization is recognized as a 501(c)(3) public charity. Fundly is just for nonprofits and works well with Facebook. So, if your organization has a lot of Facebook friends and you're eager to try out crowdfunding, Fundly may be a useful fundraising tool. For more details about these innovative funding initiatives, check out *Crowdsourcing For Dummies*, by David Alan Grier, and *Kickstarter For Dummies,* by Aimee Cebulski (Wiley).

Using crowdfunding platforms involves some costs, so research carefully before you commit your organization to any one of them. Also, don't expect the contributions to flow into your organization's bank account without doing lots of work to publicize the campaign to your friends and followers. If you need a review of the principles of raising money from individuals, look at Chapter 15.

3
Raising Funds Successfully

Know where your money is coming from, by writing a detailed fundraising plan and creating a fundraising budget.

Check out the many ways you can ask individuals to donate money to your organization. Many small donations can add up over time.

Go big and plan a special event that will draw in the dollars. The event may take a lot of work, but the payoff can make it worthwhile.

Nonprofits often receive grants as a source of income. Find out where to look for grants and how to apply for them.

Capital campaigns provide large amounts of funding for specific purposes — often property or buildings. Figure out how to establish a realistic plan and launch a campaign.

Chapter **14**

Creating a Fundraising Plan

I f an organization is going to provide a public service, it needs money. Plain and simple. It may be run by volunteers and need just a little money, or it may need lots of money to pay for employees, office space, and formal research. If it's a brand-spanking-new start-up organization, it needs money, or what's called *seed funding.*

Any nonprofit — whatever its purpose — grows out of someone's idea or passion (maybe yours!) to make the world better. Raising money is inviting others to share in your belief and passion.

Successful fundraising also is based on a plan, and a good plan recognizes an organization's likeliest sources of funding. After all, different kinds of causes appeal to different people or institutions. You'll find exceptions, but for most organizations, a good fundraising plan assumes the nonprofit will ask a variety of sources for support. No organization should put all its eggs in one basket and imagine that its entire omelet will come from a single generous plump chicken.

In this chapter, we show you how to create a plan for gathering your funding eggs from a number of nests. For those of you whose organizations are new, we offer some ideas for where to begin.

Check out File 14-1 at www.wiley.com/go/nonprofitkitfd6e for a list of web resources related to the topics we cover in this chapter.

Recognizing Who Can Raise Funds

Federal tax codes designate more than a dozen different kinds of nonprofit organizations (which we discuss in Chapter 2). This book focuses on those that are authorized under section 501(c)(3) of those tax codes and that qualify as public charities. Such nonprofits are exempt from paying certain kinds of taxes, and their donors can take tax deductions for making contributions to them (unless they are foreign 501(c)(3) organizations or among those whose purpose is testing for public safety). (We discuss grant-making foundations in Chapter 17.) The Internal Revenue Service (IRS) makes it easier for them to award their grants only to 501(c)(3) public charities. And if they want to award a grant to a for-profit entity or individual, they have to complete more steps to satisfy the IRS. Many individual donors and foundations are motivated, in part, by that tax law. Therefore, this chapter and the fundraising chapters that follow are written about 501(c)(3) nonprofit organizations with public-charity status.

Churches, if they operate solely for religious and educational purposes, and very small organizations (if their annual gross receipts are less than $5,000) that are performing a public service can receive contributions that are tax-deductible to their donors even though they may not have applied for and received 501(c)(3) status from the IRS.

Forty-nine states and the District of Columbia require charities to file registration forms before engaging in fundraising solicitations. Each state defines its registration requirements differently. For example, some allow universities, hospitals, or churches not to register. You can see which states require such registrations at the website of the Council for Nonprofits (www.councilofnonprofits.org/tools-resources/charitable-solicitation-registration). If your state requires charities to register, make sure you do so before you start soliciting funds. After all, not filing the forms can cause your organization to lose permission to operate in your state or even, in rare cases, lead its officers and board members to be charged penalties. If you hire a fundraising consultant, both that consultant and your organization may need to file. If your organization raises money from games of chance (such as a raffle or casino night), you likely need to register for permission to do that as well.

Naming Possible Funding Sources

Before plunging ahead, we need to introduce some of the terms we use in this chapter to describe the different kinds of contributions an organization may seek. Here's what you need to know:

» **Grants:** *Grants* are formal contributions made to an organization by foundations, corporations, or government agencies, often to help the nonprofit address defined goals. Some grants, called *project* or *program grants,* are for trying out new ideas or enhancing existing programs. Others, called *general operating grants,* support the overall work of an organization.

» **Corporate contributions:** Some corporations create their own foundations (that award grants), and some award contributions directly from their business coffers by way of corporate giving programs — often managed from their public affairs, community relations, or marketing departments. Many corporations give *in-kind* gifts — contributions of goods and services — rather than or in addition to cash contributions.

» **Individual contributions:** Gifts to organizations from private individuals represent the largest portion of private money given to nonprofit organizations (69 percent in 2019). Individual donors can support specific activities or the nonprofit's general costs. You might seek these contributions by postal mail or email, phone call, or face-to-face visit; via your website or social media; or at special events. This list describes some common types of individual contributions:

  • *Annual gifts:* A contribution written once a year to a charity is called, appropriately, an *annual gift.* The consistency of such gifts makes them of great value to the recipient.

  • *Major gifts:* As suggested in the name, a *major gift* is a large amount of money. For some organizations a major gift may be $1,000, and for others it may be $500,000.

  • *Memberships:* Similar to an annual gift in some ways, a *membership* is a contribution made once a year. The difference is that you often make a membership gift in exchange for a benefit or service from the nonprofit, such as discounted admission to programs. Some nonprofits are structured so that members play a role in their governance, but that's a different, more formal relationship than calling a contributor a member because they paid to join. (See Chapter 5 for details on having members in your organization.)

According to IRS regulations, a donor who receives a free gift in exchange for a contribution to your nonprofit organization cannot file a tax deduction for the value of that gift if it exceeds more than 2 percent of the contribution. The donor can deduct only the portion of the contribution that exceeds the fair market value of any items received. If that donor's contribution is more than $75, your nonprofit is required to provide a written disclosure of the value of the gift to the donor. In your thank-you note, you can write, "The estimated value of goods or services provided in return for your donation is $ (fill in the appropriate value)." The nonprofit also should acknowledge in writing to a donor any gift of $250 or more. Acknowledge contributions within seven to ten days with a personal, handwritten thank-you note. Thank-you notes sent by email convey the message that you're too busy to show personal appreciation. Donors will find another nonprofit organization to support financially over the smallest infractions of how you recognized their contributions.

- *Planned giving/bequests:* These gifts are contributions that donors make to nonprofit organizations in their wills or other legal documents specifying what happens to their money and property either during their lifetimes or after they die. Generally, the donor works with a trust officer at a bank or a law firm to design the planned giving. Large nonprofits often employ staff members who specialize in providing donors with technical assistance in this area.

- *Crowdfunding:* Nonprofits may seek donations from individuals by setting up special online campaigns known as *crowdfunding*. The nonprofits contract with web services providing technology platforms that help them spread the word, collect the funds, and acknowledge the donors. Usually these campaigns focus on a service or product that the nonprofit wants to produce within a limited time frame for a specific amount of money. Crowdfunding also may be used to attract investors to for-profit businesses.

- *Special events:* From marathons to chicken dinners to online auctions, fundraising events generate income that supports organizations. Contributors can deduct from their taxes the portion of any event ticket that's above and beyond the cost of the meal or other goods received at the event. Individuals, corporations, and small businesses are the likeliest supporters of special events. We talk more about special events in Chapter 16.

Weighing Your Fundraising Capacity

Different approaches to raising funds work best for different kinds of organizations. When you make a fundraising plan, you have to be both ambitious about your goals and realistic about what's likely to work for you. As you try to figure out how much money you can glean from each possible funding source, answer the following questions:

>> **How far do your services reach?** Do a lot of people understand, care about, and benefit from your organization's cause? Do you focus on a small geographic area or work at a national or international scale? The answers to these questions tell you whether your nonprofit should be casting its net close to home or all over the country or world.

>> **Are you one of a kind?** If you're unique, you may have a more difficult time explaining to potential donors who you are and what you do. But you may have an advantage when you appeal to foundations that like model programs and new approaches to solving community problems.

>> **How urgent is your cause?** When a pandemic occurs or hurricanes flood a community, if your nonprofit is on the scene providing emergency shelter and food, you'll find that social media tools can be particularly effective in raising money from people who understand the importance of responding quickly.

>> **Does your cause elicit strong feelings?** Even if it doesn't appeal to large numbers of people, a hot topic with a few passionate believers can still attract major gifts. However, organizations that focus on potentially controversial topics — such as family planning or eliminating the death penalty — may find that corporations and businesses are uncomfortable with having their names associated with the cause.

>> **How well regarded are your leaders?** Most people feel better about supporting an organization when they believe in its leaders — whether they're famous research scientists or well-liked next-door neighbors. People give money to people they trust, so your organization's leaders (both staff and board) are critically important to its fundraising.

>> **How well known is your organization?** Just as any commercial company with a well-known brand name has an easier time selling its products, a nonprofit with a widely recognized name often has an easier time attracting contributions from individuals. On the other hand, an agency with a low profile that's recognized by experts for doing good work may be more successful with foundations.

>> **Whom do you know?** Your nonprofit's contacts are important to its ability to raise money, especially when seeking funds from individuals. Knowing somebody who may write a big check is great, but knowing a lot of people who may write small checks is just as beneficial. Crowdfunding is a good tool for securing multiple, smaller contributions.

>> **What can you provide to a donor?** Many donors appreciate when they benefit from their gifts to you, so look at what your nonprofit can provide. Maybe your organization can offer contributors the best seats in a concert hall, print their names in the programs, and introduce them to the lion keeper. Organizations that are easily able to give tangible items and special recognition to donors may be particularly successful with membership drives or corporate campaigns.

>> **Do you have fundraising expertise?** Do staff members, board members, or volunteers have experience with raising money? If not, can your organization afford to hire expert help?

>> **Can you cover the needed fundraising costs?** Special events and *direct mail* (fundraising letters sent to large numbers of people) are expensive forms of fundraising. Grant-writing takes time, but its cost is affordable if you have trained and/or experienced board members, staff, or volunteers who can help. We say more about fundraising costs in the later section "Plotting fundraising costs."

>> **How does this year's fundraising climate compare to last year's?** Apart from the value and importance of your wonderful organization, donors give money according to their capabilities, and those capabilities change with the times. Corporate mergers, natural disasters, and economic downturns all affect how much money your organization can raise.

Drafting a Fundraising Plan

Setting out to raise funds is a lot easier when you have a guide to follow. After you analyze your nonprofit's fundraising potential, we recommend that you follow these guidelines to create a fundraising plan for your organization:

>> **Set preliminary goals.** Ask yourself how much you need to raise to cover your organization's costs in the year ahead. Naming a clear and reasonable financial goal is the first step in your planning.

>> **Ask whom you know.** Brainstorm lists of contacts — both the ones you and your board have now and the ones you want to have in the future. As you gather names, ask yourself the best way to approach those contacts — whether it's by formal proposal or a game of golf.

>> **Research.** The research phase asks who might contribute *and* how much they might give. Using donor lists from other organizations, the Internet, and advice from others, find out as much as you can about potential sources. Continually build lists of prospects and then refine and edit them as you go.

>> **Estimate costs.** List the tools you need for fundraising — perhaps a simple fact sheet, a Donate button on your website, or a bowl of pancake batter to fuel a breakfast at the firehouse. Research the costs of those tools and the fees for consultants if you use them, and then estimate the staff time devoted to fundraising. Also remember to invest in a good recordkeeping system.

>> **Get real.** Draft a schedule of what needs to be done, and when. Assign staff members, board members, or volunteers to different tasks and — this is important — agree to a system of checking in with one another to make sure you're all completing assignments. (We address this step in the later section "Moving to an Action Plan.")

TIP

In budgeting for fundraising, you will, of course, want to include the cost of registering to raise money in your state, if required. If you're thinking of fundraising in a wider region or nationally, look into the costs of those registrations in other states. This strategy can help you determine how broadly you want to focus your fundraising.

The following sections outline these steps in greater detail.

Setting a preliminary monetary goal

A first step in your fundraising plan is to look at your estimated expenses for the year ahead. Spending this money should allow you to do the work your nonprofit has laid out in its organizational plan, as described in Chapter 8. For help connecting expenses to activities, see Chapter 12.

Have you ever daydreamed about winning a lottery and how you would spend that megahaul of cash? In that frame of mind, you might daydream a fundraising goal that depends on your nonprofit's receiving a seven-figure gift from a billionaire or the nation's largest foundation. That's great fun to imagine, but do you even know that billionaire or what that foundation supports? Your fundraising goal should be aspirational yet realistic.

Look at the competition and the amount of funds your organization has raised in the past. Set goals that allow you to cover your essential costs but that also seem reasonable based on the experience of your staff and board. This step grows easier over time as your organization develops a track record and solid donor relationships.

Asking whom you and your board members know

If your organization is brand-new, brainstorm with your founding board members the names of people and organizations they know who may support your cause. If your organization has been around for a while, begin by listing its previous contributors. Annotate the list by identifying which supporters are likely to contribute again. Then stretch your thinking to consider new prospects — people who know your work or who support other causes that are related to yours. You may even ask a few loyal donors to contribute to this brainstorming exercise.

After you begin this effort of generating names and ideas, you start to notice prospects all around you. A good fundraiser is ever vigilant, collecting names from news stories, athletic event programs, public television credits, donor display walls in buildings, and related organizations' websites and annual reports.

REMEMBER

This kind of brainstorming is best for identifying possible individual donors, but don't restrict your thinking at this stage. Go ahead and name all the prospects you've observed and thought of, including

>> The foundations and government programs that fund other organizations like yours

>> The corporations where your board members or volunteers work or those that make products that relate to your nonprofit's work

>> The business associations or clubs that raise money for good causes

>> The churches and places of worship in your neighborhood that offer community support and volunteers

Researching and refining your prospect list

Professional fundraisers will tell you that the three keys to raising money are research, research, and research. To see what they mean, consider this scenario: You know that your next-door neighbors belong to an upscale golf club. When you see them outside, they wave and say, "We're heading off to the club today." You're likely wondering how they can afford to belong to a high-end country club when you both live in a moderate-income community and drive vehicles more than a decade old. First, never judge a book by its cover! Never assume that a neighbor isn't a potential prospect for seeking contributions for your nonprofit organization. After all, potential prospects don't always spend their entire income on grandiose houses, new cars, or designer clothes. They may have one thing they love to do and they make time to do it, like belong to a county club. However, many people are also living below their means so that they can practice altruism. But you may also look harder at your neighbors' other interests or where they work. For example, their employer may sponsor local events (such as the annual charity fundraiser for community nonprofits) or match its employees' charitable contributions. A little research can go a long way!

Professional list brokers and services can provide data about potential donors, but you don't need to follow that expensive, formal route. Local digital news media, the Internet, social media, and informal conversations can tell you a great deal about your neighbors' affiliations and interests. You just need to pay attention and keep notes about what you learn.

After you've brainstormed a list of individual donor prospects, review the list of names with board members, volunteers, and trusted associates. Mark which of your prospects seem to be highly likely, somewhat likely, or unlikely to donate to your efforts, based on what their interest appears to be in your organization's purpose, whether someone you know can contact them personally, and how much they've given to other nonprofits.

Researching institutional sources

If you want to raise money from foundations and government agencies, you'll likely begin by using the directories, databases, and websites specifically geared toward helping grant applicants. However, if your brainstorming session uncovers institutions as prospects, be sure to check out their websites or printed annual reports for information on their current guidelines and giving priorities. You can find details about institutions that don't have their own websites by subscribing to Candid's online directory at https://candid.org/find-funding. Search for federal government agencies and programs at the Grants.gov website (www.grants.gov). See Chapter 17 for more information about conducting foundation research.

As you conduct your research, you're likely to uncover other prospects that you didn't think of when brainstorming, and you may also eliminate many that you discover are inappropriate.

Estimating how much your prospects will give

Identifying names of possible donors is just the beginning of the puzzle. You also need to estimate the amounts your prospective donors may give. For this estimate, you have to continue your research. For example, you may find clues by tracking down the approximate amounts of their contributions to other organizations that publish their donor lists.

For your foundation prospects, you can look up sample grants awarded to similar projects in the Search Grants section of *The Foundation Directory* online (find it at `https://candid.org/find-funding`). (If you lack access to a library that subscribes to this directory, you may want to purchase your own subscription.) You can also find grant lists for foundations by downloading their IRS Form 990 tax reports from the Candid Learning (`https://candid.org`) or GuideStar by Candid (`www.guidestar.org`) websites. We recommend using "990s" as research tools for studying small and midsize foundations: PDFs of 990s for large-budget foundations can be enormous and unwieldy.

Estimating how much money you may receive requires research into each type of donor. You also want to set overall goals — perhaps attracting a certain number of new donors, sustaining many of the contributors your organization has had in the past, and persuading certain previous donors to increase their gifts.

Plotting fundraising costs

As you probably already know, raising money costs money. No organization receives every grant or gift it seeks. So, before you put your fundraising plan into action, you need to make sure that your organization can afford its potential fundraising costs and that the possible returns outweigh those costs.

Fundraising costs should be a modest part of an organization's budget, but that said, they're real costs, and organizations shouldn't feel that they have to hide them. The costs are higher when the organization is starting up or launching a major new fundraising effort. These costs likely will decline after a few years — although in 2019 Nonprofit Tech for Good's research (`www.nptechforgood.com/2019/07/21/82-fundraising-and-social-media-stats-for-nonprofits`) showed the following information about donors:

>> The average online gift in 2018 was $96.40.

>> 8.5 percent of overall fundraising in 2018 came from online giving.

>> The typical return donor made a second donation around 349 days after the initial donation. However, 19 percent of donors return within the first 90 days.

If your new nonprofit is looking to raise funds from 100 donors in the year of operation, using the average donor amount just mentioned, you would need to round up, on average, 1,000 donors. Now let's return to reality: Not every donor gives the average gift amount. Some donors give less, and others give more. So, to be safe, your fundraising plan should reach out to at least 2,000 potential donors — which can be expensive. According to an article in GuideStar by Candid, the average nonprofit spends as much as $400 a month plus online donation fees (yes, online!). It's the cheapest way to solicit for funds. Think about the cost of printing an appeal letter, purchasing envelopes, postage, and the time (and effort) it would take to get that letter out of your door and into the hands of potential donors. The old way of fundraising isn't necessarily the cheapest way.

REMEMBER

Raising money by way of special events, mass mailings, and telemarketing are expensive fundraising methods. However, all of the above may be worthwhile if they bring visibility, new donors, or unrestricted support to your organization. You and your board of directors will have to decide which route to take when it comes to carrying out your fundraising plan. Read more in the following section about the factors that go into making these decisions.

Considering the time and money you'll invest in fundraising

Here's a quick look at the costs — in terms of both time and money — of the fundraising activities your organization may consider using:

>> **Grants and contracts:** Most of the costs of securing grants and contracts are labor costs for planning and writing the grant proposal. Sometimes you need to travel to meet in person with the agency awarding the money, so don't forget to budget that, too.

WARNING

Pay attention to each grant maker's requirements for reporting the results of a project and make sure you can afford to complete the report. Some grants require the collection and analysis of extensive data. Some require audited financial statements.

>> **Corporate sponsors:** Businesses and corporations may require visible recognition for their contributions to nonprofit organizations. Such support is often called a *sponsorship,* and the nonprofit and corporation agree up front to the type of acknowledgment they expect — whether it's a corporate logo printed on volunteers' T-shirts or a 6-foot banner announcing a company's support of a children's playground. Costs of printing T-shirts, banners, and other promotions generally are incurred by the nonprofit organizations.

>> **Individual contributions:** Costs related to securing individual contributions include salaried staff members' time spent compiling lists of possible donors and the tools used for making successful donation requests. Common tools are solicitation letters and emails, brochures, and printed reply envelopes. Adding capacity to your website so that it can accept online contributions is another important investment. Don't forget the cost of registering to fundraise in the states where you're targeting donors.

Often when you think of solicitation letters, you probably think of *direct mail* — hundreds of thousands of letters sent to purchased lists of potential donors. Although direct mail can be quite a successful form of fundraising for some causes — medical emergencies, animal rescue, or civil rights, just to name a few — it's also *expensive.* A new, emerging nonprofit can make good use of letter-writing by preparing a small mailing of appeal letters addressed to people who already know its work well, asking its board members and volunteers to make personal appeals to people they know, or by using email rather than snail mail.

Some organizations hire companies to handle telephone solicitation campaigns. Be cautious if you take this step: Some of these companies charge a high percentage of the money raised in exchange for providing this service. Others are reputable and valued by the nonprofits they serve.

>> **Special events:** Special events can be a helpful way to introduce new people to your organization, but producing such events can be one of the more expensive ways to raise funds. Spending 50 percent or 60 percent of the income from an event to pay for costs is common. After all, printing, advertising, food, and entertainment all cost money. Also, special events are labor intensive, so make sure you have an experienced volunteer group or detail-oriented staff to work on special events if you go this route.

>> **Planned giving:** If your nonprofit isn't familiar with tax laws regarding wills and estates, it may need to employ or hire on contract a planned giving expert (or attract one as a board member). Bringing this person onboard can be expensive in the short term, but doing so can yield important long-term support for your agency.

Planned giving works best for organizations that have been around for a long time and that show good prospects for continuing. Universities, museums, and churches come to mind. Small, new groups have a difficult time attracting bequests.

Keeping good donor records

Before your nonprofit starts to raise money, you need to set up a system for keeping timely records on all its donors. This system can be a Microsoft Excel spreadsheet or a specialized electronic database for donor development or constituent relationship management (CRM). For foundation grants, be sure to note deadlines for applying for grants and submitting final reports. While you're at it, you'll want to develop your organization's policies for protecting the privacy of your donors' information. You can find guidance about this topic at the Association of Fundraising Professionals' website. We've included a link to its code of ethics in File 14-1 at www.wiley.com/go/nonprofitkitfd6e, and we encourage you to search the association's site for additional information about donor privacy protection.

TIP

For individual donors, a good records system can help you keep information up to date about when and how you've contacted them, who in the organization knows them, how and why they gave their gifts, and whether you promised any special recognition or invitations when they contributed. Because nonprofits hope to talk to or keep in touch with their donors over time, recording their spouses' and children's names, their interests, their business affiliations, and any other pertinent personal information also is worthwhile.

If you decide to use an electronic database system to manage your donor records, you can choose a program that focuses specifically on fundraising, or choose one that keeps track of every connection you have with anyone and everyone, including clients, ticket buyers, professional peers, donors, and volunteers. The software that tracks every kind of connection often is called a customer relationship management (CRM) system.

WARNING

Specialized CRM software can increase your efficiency in recordkeeping, but when buying a system, consider the staff skills and the time you can devote to managing the program as well as your budget. Also check on setup charges and the availability of technical backup support. For example, open source software — which is made available for free use by anyone — is readily available for you to download and use, but it may not come with consistent technical support if you run into problems.

You can find reviews and articles at `www.idealware.org` to help you choose among different kinds of donor, member, and CRM systems. To help you start your search, here's a quick look at three CRM system options:

>> **CivicCRM** (`https://civicrm.org/`) is available license-free to nonprofits. Although it's an excellent tool, you likely need someone with technology skills to set it up for you.

>> **Salesforce** (`www.salesforce.org/nonprofit`) provides nonprofits with as many as ten free subscriptions, as a part of its Power of Us program. Many nonprofits take advantage of the free subscription but then purchase apps or modifications to shape it to their needs.

>> **SugarCRM** (`www.sugarcrm.com`) offers a free, open source community edition of its software along with editions that require reasonable monthly subscriptions.

Some nonprofits choose to prioritize a system that focuses exclusively on keeping track of donors and potential donors. A few options are described in this list:

>> **DonorPerfect** (www.donorperfect.com) focuses on donors but has some support for members, volunteers, and other contacts. It offers an online version for a reasonable monthly fee.

>> **DonorSnap** (www.donorsnap.com) is a good, reasonably priced option that offers technical and setup assistance. If you're using the QuickBooks system for bookkeeping, it integrates easily with it.

>> **eTapestry** (www.etapestry.com), available from Blackbaud, offers a free trial for trying out its system. You can subscribe at different levels and prices based on your estimated number of donor records. (The basic service accommodates up to 1,000 records.)

>> **GiftWorks** (www.frontstream.com) is a reasonably priced software option with a reputation for being easy to use.

TIP

After you choose the system that's right for your organization, check out whether you want to join TechSoup (www.techsoup.org). TechSoup members can purchase donated or discounted software for their nonprofits. You may find what you want at a reasonable price.

Initially, when you urgently need grants and gifts to start up your organization, keeping good records may seem to be a time-wasting activity, but in the long run, thorough records allow you to raise more money. You can start with a simple approach and upgrade it over time, but every time you shift to a new system, be prepared to invest time in the change.

The point of investing in a donor management system is to save and develop the best information you can about the people who are connected to your organization. That information will do you no good if you aren't using it to actively build relationships with those entries in your database. Motivating the donors you already have is much less costly that recruiting new ones. Make sure you're spreading the word about your organization and its fundraising messages across a range of platforms, such as Facebook, Instagram, Twitter, YouTube, blogs, radio, and print media. When thinking about calculating these costs, consider the time you'll invest. If you're more than a one-person band, build responsibility for building connections into everyone's job description.

Moving to an Action Plan

A good fundraising plan includes the practical details that move it from being a list of goals, contacts, and costs to being a road map for your fundraising destination. The following steps help you incorporate these practical details:

1. **Assign tasks, gather tools, and make a calendar.**

   For each of the revenue areas in your plan (government, foundations, corporations, and/or individuals), indicate who's going to work on raising the money, how many prospective sources you need, and which tools you need to meet your goals (such as fundraising letters, photographs, web newsletters, social media campaigns, membership cards, or an online donation system). Then outline a general time frame for how long your fundraising efforts will take and research specific deadlines for government, foundation, and corporate grants.

   Include in your calendar a schedule for staff, board, and volunteers to check in with one another on progress made toward completing assigned tasks.

2. **Link your cost estimates to each fundraising goal.**

   You've already estimated costs of the time and tools you need in order to raise funds (see the earlier section "Plotting fundraising costs"). Now you need to create a fundraising cash flow outline that shows when you need upfront money and when you can expect to secure income from your efforts. Keep in mind that some foundations have a rather lengthy period from letter of intent to grant funding, sometimes as long as 12 months. Individual donors may have only one time of year (just before the end of the year, for example) when they make charitable contributions.

3. **Gather the fruits of your labor into one document — *that* is your funding plan!**

   The finished plan likely consists of these elements:

   - Sources sought and fundraising goals (for example: foundation grants, $50,000; and special event revenues, $7,500)

   - Prospects identified (both current and prospective contributors), along with amounts you expect them to give

   - Number of prospects you need to achieve your goals in each category

   - List of who's responsible for making particular contacts or contributing other services to raising the funds

   - Estimated costs of pursuing the contributions in each category

   - Timeline and cash flow projection

TIP Many agencies create an optimum fundraising plan as well as a bare-bones fundraising plan — one based on their hopes and one based on what they must secure to survive. During the course of the year, they rebalance and adjust their plans.

TIP Check out the two sample fundraising plans (see File 14-2 and File 14-3) and two sample fundraising budgets (see File 14-4 and File 14-5) at www.wiley.com/go/nonprofitkitfd6e. One set is for a small school music organization, and the other is for a slightly larger neighborhood park improvement organization.

Planting the Seeds for a New Nonprofit

One tried-and-true rule of fundraising is that people give money to people they know. They also give money to causes they care about. However, making a contribution is an expression of trust. That means the likeliest contributors to a new nonprofit organization are people and agencies who know and admire its founders and their work.

Hitting up family and friends before asking others

We know of a few people who have launched their organizations with the help of major grants from a government agency or a large, national foundation, but many more of them start close to home with gifts from their families and friends. In most instances, the new nonprofit founder invests a substantial amount of money in the vision. Board members contribute as well as their founding board members and the people who know them. They then build out from that inner circle of relationships, gradually creating networks of associations to include local businesses, and business associates who often not only contribute initially but also become annual contributors.

We asked some people who founded organizations how and when they received their first contributions. One invited 20 people to her house and, after delivering a convincing pitch and consuming some good wine, persuaded most of them to write checks. Another started a youth mentoring program from his dorm room when he was a college student. He talked the college financial aid staff into helping him identify paid work-study opportunities so he had the funds to begin his project, and then he charged his volunteer mentors modest membership fees to cover basic costs. Another noticed a city department's neglect of small city parks after budget cutbacks and, by knocking on local politicians' doors, secured a city grant to involve volunteers in park clean-up days. Yet another rounded up all family members on a video call and asked for their help in starting a new nonprofit that would be named in memory of a recently deceased family member. Yes, we know: That's *tugging* the heart strings to open the purse strings.

REMEMBER

Many organizations start up with contributions from individuals, in part because individuals often make up their minds more quickly than businesses or foundations.

Raising funds with special events

Although special events are one of the more expensive ways of raising money, you probably can see real advantages to including them in the fundraising plan for a new organization. Events create a way to inform dozens or hundreds of people about your organization at the same time. The best part is that those people then begin to spread the word about your good work. Events don't have to be elaborate — a gathering of a dozen people can be a good start. Read more about special events in Chapter 16.

Getting to know community foundations

When approaching foundations, you may believe that you're at a disadvantage because your project has no track record. On the contrary, some foundations specifically like to support start-up projects and organizations. If your agency is new, when you're using *The Foundation Directory*, check the Types of Support listings to see whether the foundation you're looking at awards *seed funding* — that is, support for new activities. If the foundation makes grants in your field of interest and geographical area, it may be a good prospect for helping you launch your organization. Find out more information about conducting foundation research in Chapter 17.

Assessing your capabilities to apply for government grants

WARNING

Government grants (described in Chapter 17) and contracts may provide significant underpinnings for a new effort, but they come with three distinct disadvantages for new nonprofit organizations:

>> **They generally take longer to secure.** The review-and-approval process may be slow, and many government agencies have only a single annual deadline.

>> **They often require grantees to comply with rules and regulations regarding permits, board policies, hiring practices, audits, and financial reporting.** Although their rules may be good rules, when you're just starting out, your organization may still be working out its systems and policies.

>> **They sometimes require their funded organizations to spend money upfront and then submit invoices in order to be reimbursed for an agreed-on amount of money.** If you have few sources of income, you may have no funds available for this upfront spending.

Chapter **15**

Raising Funds from Individual Donors

Everyone has had some experience with asking for money. Maybe you sold cookies for a scout troop when you were a child. Maybe you asked neighbors to sponsor you in a summer read-a-thon for the school library. Maybe you once had to call mom and dad when you were stranded at a bus station in Poughkeepsie and couldn't make it home in time for their 25th wedding anniversary.

These moments can be awkward, but asking for money for yourself and asking for money for an organization you believe in are quite different. Organizational fund-raising can feel good because it helps you do something important for a cause you care deeply about. The hard part is finding the right words to say, the means of conveying those words, and the audience who is receptive to those words and who will donate to your nonprofit organization.

Responding to the right cause, the right message, and the right person, individual donors give to many kinds of organizations. In fact, they represent the largest portion of private contributions in the United States. According to Balancing Everything, in 2020 about 80 percent of all donations in the United States came from individuals. This chapter shows you how to sharpen your own fundraising ideas and persuade individual donors to give to your organization.

REMEMBER

Often when people think of raising large amounts of money for organizations, they think of securing major grants from foundations or sponsorships from corporations. But we recommend that your nonprofit also include individual giving as a part of its fundraising plans. In total, individuals give more to nonprofits than do foundations or corporations, and most individuals allow you to use the funds contributed for whatever your greatest needs may be. That kind of flexibility adds considerable value to a contribution — even if it's just $50.

TIP

Check out File 15-1 at www.wiley.com/go/nonprofitkitfd6e for a list of web resources related to the topics we cover in this chapter.

Understanding Why People Give

The key rule of fundraising is, "If you don't ask, you won't get." Taking the step of asking is critical, but so is knowing *how* to ask. According to marketing experts who study motivations for doing just about everything, people contribute to nonprofit organizations because they want to

- >> Feel generous
- >> Change the world
- >> Exhibit compassion
- >> Have a sense of belonging to a group
- >> Feel a sense of well-being or of safety
- >> Be recognized

By understanding these underlying donor motivations, you can phrase your request in the most effective way. Appeals to new donors often ask them to "join" or "become part of" a movement or cause in order to touch on the desire for belonging. Appeals also call on donors' compassion and idealism, and they commonly link the needs of particular constituents served by a nonprofit to the well-being and security of an entire community. That's making the most of asking.

REMEMBER

When you find yourself hesitating to ask someone for a contribution, keep in mind that you're not begging — you're offering an opportunity to be part of something worthwhile. Giving your organization a gift can make the donor feel good.

REGISTERING TO SOLICIT DONATIONS

All states, including the District of Columbia, and certain local jurisdictions require organizations that solicit charitable contributions to file registration forms before soliciting. This registration is meant to protect the public from solicitors touting illegitimate causes. The regulations differ from state to state. Typically, the rules don't apply unless the nonprofit raises more than $250 a year (which we hope you will!). Check with your state's attorney general's office to be sure your nonprofit is in compliance with all laws. Also check local laws when raising money by way of what's known as *charitable gaming* (bingo, raffles, and pull tabs, for example). Laws regulating these activities often differ from county to county and from city to city.

What if you're raising money online? Guidelines adopted in 2001 by the National Association of State Charity Officials (NASCO) state that any nonprofit that uses fundraising tools to target donors in a specific state must register in that state. This registration requirement extends to any organization that receives contributions from a state via its website on a repeated and ongoing basis — whether or not it's specifically targeting donors in that state. Plus, Form 990 for nonprofits asks organizations where they are registered to fundraise. If you're seeking donations nationally, consider all relevant states, and remember to renew your registrations annually.

Stating Your Case

A *case statement* is a tool that nonprofits often use when asking for a contribution. It's a short, compelling argument for supporting the nonprofit that can be presented as a one-page information sheet, a section of your website, or a glossy folder filled with fact sheets, photographs, budgets, or charts. It should be professional, factual, and short enough that readers will read it all the way through.

REMEMBER

A good case statement can be used in many ways in fundraising:

>> **In-person:** After talking about the agency with a potential donor, you might leave behind a copy of your case statement for consideration.

>> **By phone:** If you need to phone a potential donor, you keep the case statement close at hand as a reminder of the key points to make about the agency.

>> **By mail, email, or blog:** If you mail or email a fundraising letter, or write a blog about your nonprofit, you can borrow wording from the case statement to write that item or include a link to or copy of the case statement with the appeal.

Instructions for writing a case statement resemble a recipe for stew or soup: A few basic ingredients make any version of this dish delicious, and the cook can spice it up with whatever other quality ingredients are at hand. Follow these steps:

1. **Make notes about the following subjects. Be selective — allot no more than 100 words to any of these items:**

   - The mission statement and vision statement of the organization

   - The history of the organization (from founding to current)

   - The services it offers (include your location[s] and maps)

   - Data illustrating the organization's key accomplishments

   - Affidavits, reviews, or quotes from enthusiasts who have benefited from the organization's work

   - The organization's future plans

2. **Toss in no more than 50 words on each of these topics:**

   - The organization's philosophy or approach to providing service

   - The pressing and validated (data sources) needs that the organization works to address

   - The quantitative ways the organization measures or recognizes its success

3. **Stir in whatever else you have on hand, including**

   - Compelling photographs of the organization's work

   - Quotes and testimonials from clients, partners, donors, and others

   - Tables or maps illustrating growth — for example, the increasing numbers of clients the organization serves or the expanding geographical area it serves

   - An overview of the organization's budget and finances, particularly if the budget is balanced and the finances are healthy

   - Anything else that shines a light on the agency, such as publications completed or awards received

4. **State the giving opportunities your nonprofit offers.**

   The giving options must be clear and uncomplicated. Donors want to understand how their contributions can make a difference. Sometimes giving opportunities are linked to the cost of providing services, such as the cost of

   - Providing a 24-hour respite for terminally ill children so that their parents and caregivers can take a break

- Upgrading a community recreation center

- Rescuing and rehabilitating abandoned canines

- Planting an acre of edible crops for elderly homeless people

Sometimes opportunities are linked to premiums or gifts the donor receives in return — for example:

- For a gift of up to $50, the donor receives a daily calendar planner as a token of thanks.

- For a gift of several hundred dollars, the donor's name appears on a brass plate on a wish list tree displayed in the lobby.

- For a gift of $1,000, the donor receives a table for ten at the annual appreciation dinner meeting for donors (note that the community also purchases tables for $1,000).

- For a gift of several thousand dollars, the donor's name is etched on a tile in the memory garden of a nursing home.

- For a gift of $5 million, the new addition to your facility gives naming rights to the first donor to ante up with this large donation.

REMEMBER

For a contribution of $250 or more, acknowledge the gift in writing and specify the date of the contribution and the amount. If you give this donor something of value in exchange for the contribution, you should mention the value of that premium in your acknowledgment letter (because donors must deduct the fair market value of gifts if they itemize their contributions to your organization in their tax filings). Check out File 15-2 and File 15-3 at www.wiley.com/go/nonprofitkitfd6e for examples of acknowledgment letters.

TIP

When writing the case statement, you don't need to follow the exact order in which we list the elements. Lead with the strongest points and leave out the less compelling items. Choose a strong writer to draft the piece and then test it on others — both within and outside your agency — to see whether it tells a clear, impressive story.

When the case statement is written, produce it for distribution and make sure to match its look to your nonprofit and its intended audience. If your nonprofit is a modest, grassroots organization, the case statement should be simple and direct in its presentation. If it's an environmental organization, you may want to distribute the case statement online instead of using paper. If it's an internationally known opera company, the case statement should look dramatic and elegant.

RECOGNIZING YOUR DONORS

Before acknowledging a donor in print, on a donor wall, or in another public manner, always ask the person for permission and ask how they want to be listed.

When choosing how to recognize donors, consider the cost of the recognition, the nature of the activity supported, and the way the donor recognition advances (or doesn't suit) your organization's purpose and mission. A simple, printed list of names is dignified and inexpensive. Although donor gifts cost money, having your organization's name printed on T-shirts or tote bags that donors wear or carry throughout the community may be an effective way to promote your work. However, if you spend too much on gifts, you can annoy donors or leave them wondering how much you need their contribution.

Creating an Elevator Speech

Sometimes you encounter magical, unplanned moments when you have a potential large donor at the meeting table or in church or at the golf course. You can't just blurt out that you'll be sure to send along the case statement. In this case, you have to become an on-the-spot public speaking parliamentarian and give your best elevator speech. Why is it called an elevator speech? Because it was named to position your mind in an elevator with a philanthropist who knows nothing about your nonprofit organization and you have (maybe) all of three minutes to pitch your nonprofit organization in what's famously named an elevator speech. How fast can you talk? What can you see to make the ask? Will the elevator ride end before you speak your most important information?

Here's an example of an elevator speech (time yourself when you read this aloud — it should be three minutes or less):

> Hi, I'm Mary Jones, the executive director of G.A.S.K.I.N.S. Charities, a faith-based nonprofit organization located ten minutes away from your corporate headquarters. I am honored to share an elevator with you this afternoon. We are holding our capital campaign this year. The monies raised will help us secure a storefront building in Wapato that will serve as our outreach center. Although we're faith-based, we serve everyone — from food box distributions to nearby community members to emergency supplies for people who have been evicted and hotel vouchers for ten-night stays while our case management teams work to secure permanent housing. I imagine that you're asked often for donations. Anything you can do to help us secure our new handicapped-accessible building will help tremendously. Can we set a follow-up meeting so that you can learn more about our work with the community?

At this time, Mary is handing the other elevator passenger (a CEO of the largest insurance provider in the Midwest) her business card. She is smiling yet humble.

TIP

An elevator speech can happen anywhere, anytime. You have to be ready and avoid freezing up from the fear of talking to a notable stranger. Your *ask* could happen at church, a grocery store, the doctor's office, a public meeting, a fundraising event, on a bus or subway or commuter train, or in an elevator. Write your elevator speech's most important points down. Practice and memorize them. Watch yourself in a mirror while speaking. How does your face look? Are you smiling or tense? Are you pronouncing your words clearly or rambling a bit too fast? Are you more worried about time than content?

We practice the elevator speech that we wrote for Mary, and it's less than one minute — just enough time for the person we're speaking with to listen and comprehend — and not to be annoyed by talking too long. Keep in mind that you're not selling cleaning solution door-to-door — you're delivering a fast pitch that can result in six-figure donations. You can do this!

Identifying Possible Donors

The doorbell rings, and you open the door to greet an adorable child you've never met. The child is selling fruit baskets to raise funds to buy band instruments at school. You played in a band when you were young, so you place an order for a fruit basket, secure the specifics on when and how it will be delivered, and then wish the little junior fundraiser great success.

A few minutes later, the doorbell rings again, and you open the door to greet a second adorable child. You know this child because he lives next-door. You remember when his mother brought him home as a newborn and when you watched him ride his first bicycle down the sidewalk. He's selling the same fruit baskets to benefit the soccer team at his school: They need equipment and uniforms. You buy *five* fruit baskets with plans to donate this bounty of produce to the local homeless shelter.

Rich or poor, most of us are influenced in our charitable giving by how well we know the people, either directly or indirectly, who are doing the asking. Mapping the personal connections of each member of your organization is a key first step in identifying possible donors.

Drawing circles of connections

Figure 15-1 represents a common brainstorming exercise that nonprofit organizations use to identify possible individual donors. This exercise is most effective if both staff and board members participate. Follow these steps:

1. **Identify the people who are closest to the organization — those within the inner circle.**

This inner circle includes staff and board members and active volunteers or clients who frequently use the organization's services.

2. **Identify those people who have the second-closest relationship to the organization.**

This second circle may include family, close friends, and coworkers of those people in the inner circle, former staff and board members, neighbors of the organization and its inner circle, volunteers, and clients who sometimes use its services.

3. **Take one more step backward and identify the people who make up the third circle.**

These folks may include grandparents or cousins of those people in the inner circle, old friends whom they haven't seen recently, friends of former staff and board members, and former or infrequent users of the organization's services.

4. **Identify the friends, relatives, and other associates of those who make up circles 2 and 3.**

5. **Search for your cause-related friends and associates.**

Look for people who may not know anyone involved in your organization but who demonstrate an interest in the subject and the purpose it represents (as indicated by their memberships, their magazine subscriptions, or their contributions to similar organizations). Follow the local media and watch for people who have a connection to your cause because of their personal experiences. For example, maybe their child was born with the congenital disease your nonprofit is studying, or maybe they come from a forested part of the state and care about the preservation of old-growth trees.

You can continue enlarging your circle of connections, but with every step you take from the center to the outside, the bond between the organization and the potential donors weakens. As that occurs, the cost of raising money from the people who inhabit those circles increases. Eventually the cost of securing gifts from an outer circle becomes higher than the likely amount of income to be gained, and it's time to stop.

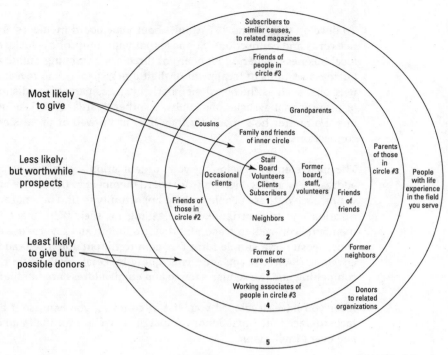

Most likely
to give

Less likely
but worthwhile
prospects

Least likely
to give but
possible donors

FIGURE 15-1:
Drawing circles of
connections helps
you identify
possible
individual donors.

Subscribers to
similar causes,
to related magazines

Friends of
people in
circle #3

Grandparents

Cousins

Family and friends
of inner circle

Staff
Board
Volunteers
Clients
Subscribers
1

Former
board,
staff,
volunteers

Occasional
clients

Parents
of those
in
circle #3

People
with life
experience
in the field
you serve

Friends
of
those in
circle #2

Friends
of friends

Neighbors

2

Former
neighbors

Former or
rare clients

3

Working associates of
people in circle #3

4

Donors
to related
organizations

5

© John Wiley & Sons, Inc.

REMEMBER

How do you know when it's time to stop and back up? Most organizations try to keep the cost of their overall fundraising at or lower than 20 percent of their budgets. However, when you're starting out, particularly with some kinds of fundraising strategies, such as mailings or special events (see Chapter 16), your percentages may be higher in the first few years. These approaches generally begin to bring in significant contributions as you deepen your relationships with your donors and they renew their gifts. If you're still just breaking even on a fundraising activity in year three, it's time to back up and refocus your approach.

Getting a list of potential donors from your board of directors

Every year, or before you start work on a special event or a letter-writing campaign, ask each of your organization's board members to provide the names of ten or more people they know. This exercise is useful for developing a solicitation list.

TIP

Most people can sit down and list ten friends and associates off the top of their heads. However, when you ask your board members to produce a list in that way, they're unlikely to exhaust all their connections and relationships. If you hand the board members starter lists of people they may know and then ask them to edit and add to that list, you're likely to get many more names.

To develop this starter list, think about your board members and their probable networks and connections. Suppose that your nonprofit is lucky enough to have a local business leader on its board of directors. Searching online and scouring the business sections of local print or digital newspapers can reveal a variety of connections, such as the board member's business partners and suppliers; members of professional associations, clubs, or other boards; and close neighbors. Everyone, no matter how modestly they live, has a web of professional and personal connections.

The next step in developing your organization's network of connections is to address personalized letters from board members to the people on their lists, providing each of those people with an opportunity to find out more about your organization and to contribute. When asking for their help, make it easy for board members' contacts to respond: Provide a link to an easy-to-use donation page on your website or a simple form for them to fill out and a self-addressed, stamped envelope (SASE). If you send your query by email, make sure the subject line is compelling and the sender's name and email address are familiar to the recipient.

After you have developed your list of contacts, you can use it as the basis for a face-to-face individual donor campaign, as well as for mail and email campaigns and event invitations.

Growing a Major Gift

Face-to-face visits are the best way to secure larger contributions, what fundraising professionals call *major gifts* (see Chapter 14 for more information on major gifts). Rarely does someone now knock on a door, deliver a short speech, and depart with a check for a large amount. Generally, several contacts must take place before a major donor is ready to make a commitment. In this process, often called *cultivation*, the comparison of planting the idea, tending the relationship, and harvesting the result when it's fully grown is an apt one. It takes time. In this section, we break down the key steps and tips for growing a major gift.

TIP

Before you talk yourself into making a phone call or sending a letter rather than sitting down to talk to a donor face-to-face, remember that it's more difficult for donors to say no to someone sitting in front of them.

Deciding who should do the asking

If possible, the board member or staff person who knows the potential donor should make the visit. If that isn't possible, the visiting team should be made up of two people who are peers of that person — perhaps a board member who's a local business leader and the executive director. Be careful not to overwhelm a potential donor with a large group. Two or three people are plenty.

Preparing to make your request

It's time to ask someone for money: Take a deep breath. In preparing for this moment, you need to remember that you're not asking for something for yourself — you're inviting the potential donor to belong, to be a part of something worthwhile. When planning how to describe the reason for the gift, step back for a moment and remember why volunteering for the organization is important to you. How did you become involved? What lives have you seen changed with the organization's work? Move forward with confidence, armed with your personal story and your case statement, which will remind you of the key points you want to mention.

Breaking the ice

Open the conversation with easy material. What did you find out about this person while conducting research, and how do you know each other? Maybe your kids attend the same school or you're both soccer fans. Try to use a low-key topic to open the conversation rather than force a heavy sales pitch on your target. The key is to create rapport.

REMEMBER

A brief round of small talk can ease the conversation's start, but don't waste a potential donor's time. Let them know how you became involved in the organization, and then briefly give an overview of its attributes and the current situation. Team members should take up different pieces of the conversation, remembering to let the potential donor talk, too, and paying close attention to the signals they send. Keeping the meeting comfortable for the prospect is critical.

Adopting the right attitude

When soliciting gifts, be firm and positive but not pushy. Pay attention to how the potential donor is acting or responding and step back if you discover they aren't feeling well or their business has taken a difficult turn. Also allow periods of silence: Don't rush to fill in every conversational pause — let the contact have time to reflect and respond.

Just as you can see signs of when *not* to press the case, you also may notice signs of readiness when the discussion is going well. The potential donor may express interest in observing a program at the nonprofit. The person may display pride in their familiarity with the field in which the nonprofit is working. Be a good listener as well as a good presenting salesperson.

TIP

Asking someone to contribute to an organization is easier when you've already made a gift yourself. Even if you can't make a large contribution, you'll feel more confident about asking others if you've already contributed — and the potential donor will find you more credible.

Timing the request: An inexact science

Many people don't believe in asking for a specific contribution at the first meeting. They believe in setting the stage — letting a prospective donor know that a campaign or a special program is coming up and that the organization will seek their help in the future. At a second visit, they encourage this person to see a program in action or meet other board members at an informal gathering. The goal is to build a relationship, inviting the potential donor to feel as though they want to belong with the people leading your agency.

For certain major gift campaigns, fundraisers use a feasibility study. In such a study, someone from outside the organization interviews board members and potential major donors, seeking their impressions of the organization and forming an idea of the size of the contribution they might make. This process helps the organization to set realistic goals *and* warns the "research subjects" that the agency plans to come knocking at their doors.

REMEMBER

As with any cultivation, the timing of the harvest is critical. When the time is right, it's like recognizing a piece of fruit that's ready to be picked. Make a date for a follow-up visit. Plan a setting where the conversation can be congenial but focused. Don't rush (a common failing), but don't leave without asking. If the answer is disappointing, ask for feedback on your visit and try to figure out which aspects of your case the potential donor finds most (and least) compelling. Maybe the donor wants a naming opportunity that you didn't present, or maybe they feel loyalty to a similar organization. Or maybe the timing isn't right because the donor has just promised a major gift to another cause, but in a future year would consider making a sizable gift. Sometimes prospective donors reconsider at a later time, so always seek permission to stay in touch.

Treading lightly when making the ask

Before asking a potential donor for a contribution at one of your follow-up meetings, find out everything you can about the person's gifts to similar causes. (To do so, you can scour donor lists and ask board members who know this person.) This information helps you ask for an appropriate amount.

Many people believe that you should ask for an amount that's somewhat higher than what you expect to receive, because making a request for a generous gift is flattering to the donor. However, you don't want to ask for so much money that the potential donor feels that whatever they give will be a disappointment. Donors commonly say, "I can't do that amount, but I'll consider half that amount, if it would be a help." (Add your own zeroes.)

REMEMBER

In most cases, when the donor suggests a level, you don't want to haggle — you can become annoying and cause the person to back out of contributing. You *might* gently push for a higher amount by using the personal-connections angle, however: "We were hoping you might become one of our $50,000 donors, along with Jeff Stone and Merilee Iverson, but whatever you can provide would be a big help."

Expressing gratitude for the gift

One of the most important parts of your major gift campaign is thanking contributors. Do it within a day after any in-person visit is made, a pledge is made, or a gift is received. We recommend an immediate phone call or email and a handwritten note. If you acknowledge a donor thoughtfully and graciously, and follow up that thank-you note with newsletters, web posts, or other information about the organization's accomplishments, you're strengthening your relationship with that contributor and making the person feel as though they're part of your organization. That's good manners and smart fundraising. Even if your in-person visit is unsuccessful, send a short note to thank the prospect for their time.

Raising Funds by Mail

Direct mail, the practice of soliciting donations by way of large-scale mailings, grows out of a sophisticated and fascinating area of fundraising. Your organization may be too small to make investing in a direct-mail campaign worthwhile, but you can use valuable tips from the big guys and develop small-scale letter-writing and emailing efforts that yield good results.

Taking the direct-mail route

If you want to try large-scale direct-mail fundraising, we strongly recommend that you hire a direct-mail consultant or firm to handle the campaign. Direct-mail fundraising can be an expensive investment, and you want the best, most up-to-date professional advice available.

Successful direct mail depends on the following factors:

>> A cause that's meaningful to many thousands of people across your state or the country

>> A compelling, well-presented letter that makes its reader believe that your nonprofit can make a difference

>> A well-chosen mailing list, usually purchased from a list broker

(Opt-in email lists also may be purchased from these brokers.)

>> If you're using regular mail, nonprofit bulk rate postage, which saves you a significant amount over commercial mailing rates

>> Easy, clear ways your letter readers can respond to the request by using a return envelope, response card, or website Donate button

>> Testing your letter and list at a modest scale before sending the letter to hundreds of thousands of names

>> A mailing schedule by which you solicit donors several times each year

TIP

When you write a fundraising letter, many potential donors will read your letter's P.S. content before they read the body of the letter, so include compelling information there, such as a testimonial from a client or information about a matching gift.

TIP

To secure a nonprofit bulk mail permit, you must apply to the United States Postal Service, completing PS Form 3624. Check out File 15-1 at www.wiley.com/go/nonprofitkitfd6e for a link.

Successfully raising money by way of the postal mail system depends on gradual development of a loyal cadre of donors who respond by mail. Fewer than 1 percent of the people you initially mail to may send contributions, but after they give, you add them to your *donor list* — and, according to research from Fundraising123, an average of 30 percent of those donors will make a second contribution.

Building loyalty among donors has become more challenging than in the past. It's just as important to apply the principles of cultivation and relationship-building with donors reached by postal mail or email as it is with those you meet face-to-face. This situation might mean sharing personalized news announcements from your charter school's principal, sending invitations to special events or online webinars, or even passing around links to YouTube recordings of newborn baby seals.

Donors who make repeat contributions are likely to stick with your organization for several years, making three or four (or more!) contributions in that time, and they may increase the size of their contributions. Adding to this value, you'll uncover prospects for major gifts and planned giving (contributions from bequests) among these donors. (Find out more about major gifts and planned giving in Chapters 14 and 21.)

WARNING

Before your donor list develops into a significant and loyal resource, a direct-mail campaign on your organization's behalf may only break even on the cost of the initial letter-writing campaign. You may even lose money. That's why direct mail may not be appropriate for a small or start-up organization. You need to be able to cover significant upfront costs and not expect a strong return on that investment for several years.

Inspiring volunteers to steer a letter-writing campaign

Given the risks and costs of direct mail, we recommend that you borrow some of its techniques and work on a more affordable scale, using your organization's volunteers to help with a letter-writing campaign. When you enlist the help of your small-but-mighty contacts list in combination with the writing skills of your volunteers, the letters will be done and out the door in no time. The key to success is targeting donors to whom the staff, board, and volunteers are already connected in some fashion and then personalizing their letters.

REMEMBER

A fundraising letter isn't just a letter — it also consists of a mailing envelope, a reply envelope and card, and sometimes a brochure, a copy of a newspaper clipping, or a photograph. All these pieces should relate to one another and convey a clear, compelling message.

The outer envelope should be inviting to open. For instance, did you use a first-class stamp? Did you handwrite the address and add a special message? Is the envelope a different color and size than standard envelopes to draw attention to its importance? The letter itself should supply enough information that readers feel involved in the cause. Most of the letter should be dedicated to describing the problem that the organization is trying to solve. After that, the letter should discuss how the situation can be turned around for the better and the organization's specific method or program for doing so. Make the tone personal by using the personal terms *I* and *you*. Close the letter with a vision for how things will look if the plan succeeds. Keep paragraphs short and emphasize key points with underlined or bolded text.

Always make it easy for a donor to respond, by offering return envelopes and clear information about how to give via your website. Always include your mailing address, website, email address, and phone number on the letter, in case a donor misplaces the envelope or other materials included in the mailing.

TIP

Your nonprofit can secure a permit from the post office to offer postage-paid return envelopes. Although it's more expensive per delivery than first-class stamps, your nonprofit ends up paying only for the envelopes that are sent back (and we hope that those envelopes contain donations).

TIP

Check out File 15-4 at www.wiley.com/go/nonprofitkitfd6e for an example of a solicitation letter sent to individual donors.

Try out the letter first on your organization's internal lists of board contacts, clients, and donors. Then continually build your potential donor list by making it a habit to collect names, addresses, and emails at events you present and at meetings and conferences you attend.

Just as important as collecting names for your list is taking care of those names. You want to develop a good system for recording information about any donors in order to thank them, keep in touch with them, and ask for their support again in the future. You'll find that database programs to manage your donor information come in various degrees of complexity and prices (see Chapter 17). Choose the one that's best for your needs.

TREATING DONORS WELL FOR GREAT RESULTS

Good fundraisers recognize the importance of treating donors well. In fact, the Association of Fundraising Professionals has even developed a thoughtful Donor Bill of Rights that offers standards to follow (www.afpnet.org/Ethics/Enforcement Detail.cfm?ItemNumber=3359) as well as an E-Donor Bill of Rights (https://afpglobal.org/donor-bill-rights).

Good treatment of donors includes allowing them to tell you when they don't want their addresses shared with other organizations. You can include a check box on the reply card where they can indicate their preference for preventing their information from being traded or sold. If you send email solicitations, be sure to include a safe unsubscribe option for donors who want to be removed from the mailing list.

Raising Money the "E" Way (Easily and Electronically)

Just as your website and electronic-communications system are tools for serving your constituents and marketing your work, they are tools for raising money. Although giving in response to traditional mail has been declining, online giving is growing at a faster pace than overall giving. Blackbaud, which manages donor data for more than 8,800 varied US charities, reports in "50 Fascinating Philanthropy Stats" (www.blackbaud.com/files/50-fascinating-philanthropy-stats/giving-breakdown.html) that its clients saw overall giving increase 1.0 percent in 2019, but online giving increased at the higher rate of 6.8 percent. Although this growth in online giving suggests that it should be part of your fundraising plans, it still represents a modest portion (about 7 percent) of overall fundraising. We don't recommend letting it be your only fundraising approach: It's a good tool when it's used in combination with other methods.

Given that more and more of us make online purchases and read electronic media, why is online giving downright *tepid?* Part of the answer lies in who is giving online: Donors tend to be younger people who make smaller gifts. The 2020 report by Nonprofit Source (https://nonprofitssource.com/online-giving-statistics/online-fundraising/) notes that the average monthly online gift is $128.) Part of the answer is the importance of relationships: Many people find the Internet to be relatively impersonal and are unlikely to make a major contribution online.

Online fundraising has worked quite well in certain contexts — especially disaster and emergency relief campaigns, for which donors want to respond quickly. People also respond well to online fundraising by organizations they know well, such as their college alumni associations.

Building and maintaining relationships by using email and related tools

We cannot emphasize enough that fundraising is about building relationships with people. It's in a nonprofit's best interest to keep donors informed about what the organization is doing. It can't hurt to get to know the people who give money to your nonprofit, and the Internet can be of help with both tasks.

The most frequently used feature of the Internet is email. It's easy to use, and it's cheap and fast. Many nonprofit organizations produce monthly (or more frequent) online newsletters about their work. Distributing these bulletins to donors is a helpful way to keep them informed about how their contributions are making a difference.

If you're sending bulk emails, you may want to use an email marketing service that can help you build a list, set up your message in an attractive format, and make your message more likely to be received (and not land in a spam folder). Some of these businesses allow nonprofits to send a certain number of messages without charge.

As a first step, obtain an organization email account and address that enables people to contact you (and enables you to begin building an online mailing list).

Your organizational emails, website, or other social media should connect and point to one another so that no matter how someone comes across your nonprofit online, they will find several options for staying in touch.

When using email to raise funds, you want to compel readers to click through to your website, where they can read more about your organization and find out how to contribute. Remember to mention your online donation option in every piece of mail and email you send, and place the Donate button in the same place on each page of your website.

Related online tools you want to have at hand include

>> **A website:** Your site should feature clear, timely information, calls to action that encourage readers to get involved, a Contact Us option linked to your email address, and an easy-to-use click-through Donate button that enables website visitors to make contributions online. If you have a wish list of equipment and supplies that people can donate, place a link to that list in a prominent location (perhaps accompanied by a link to your online wish list registry at a website like Amazon (www.amazon.com), where donors can make quick purchases that are delivered straight to your organization's door. You can read more about creating a website in Chapter 13.

>> **A brief electronic newsletter:** This e-newsletter should feature an intriguing subject line and be highly readable. Imagine your typical reader: *If* they open it, they'll scroll through it quickly. You should write a compelling sentence or two about each topic, inviting the reader to click through to your organization's website and read more about it (noticing the Donate button while there).

>> **An organization blog:** A blog is a useful tool for inviting comments and feedback. Tools for creating a blog are available for free at a number of websites.

>> **Social networking accounts:** Social marketing options include Facebook, LinkedIn, Google Groups, Twitter, Pinterest, Instagram, and many others. These social networking tools remind people of your organization and urge them to take action on your behalf. Some of them provide features specifically for sharing information about organizations (such as Facebook Pages) or can be used as avenues for raising money. One example is to add a Facebook-compatible app — such as GoGetFunding (www.gogetfunding.com) or FundRazr (www.fundrazr.com) — to your nonprofit's Facebook profile.

TIP

At www.wiley.com/go/nonprofitkitfd6e, File 15-5 and File 15-6 provide sample newsletters, and File 15-7 shows how a nonprofit uses email correspondence to develop a relationship with a potential donor. File 15-8 offers tips on how to solicit donations from your website and social media outlets.

Building your email address lists

When corresponding with people who contact you via email or your website, consider them prospective donors. If you're emailing a new correspondent, ask whether the person wants to be added to your mailing list. Make this invitation a habit, and respect those who decline. Others will accept, and slowly and steadily you'll build your list.

Even though you can find robust email services that are free to use, many nonprofits choose to pay for commercial email services. Typically, they provide templates that will make your email messages look better. You receive less spam, less phishing, and more reliable delivery of your email. Though we always recommend checking product reviews and talking to others, a few frequently used email services are Constant Contact (www.constantcontact.com), Google Apps for Nonprofits (www.google.com/nonprofits/products), MailChimp (www.mailchimp.com), and Vertical Response (www.verticalresponse.com).

REMEMBER

Email address lists, like mailing address lists, can be purchased, traded, or borrowed. A nonprofit may be willing to lend or trade its list with another nonprofit that has a similar mission. When using a borrowed list, you must respect the privacy of the people listed. Don't pass along the list to others without permission, and always offer an unsubscribe option. The list normally is for one-time only use.

Using your website as a cultivation tool

A website can never replicate a face-to-face encounter with another person, but if you design your site to grab and hold a visitor's attention, you can succeed at attracting donors. Strategies may include the ones listed here:

>> Short profiles of clients, donors, volunteers, and staff members

>> Strong visual features — graphical design elements, photographs, and short videos

>> Short films or slide shows of the organization's activities

   One marine mammal rescue organization featured a story about a stranded sea lion's rehabilitation.

>> PDF files containing studies your nonprofit has conducted or curricula it has developed and links to information and resources about the field in which it works

>> Specific fundraising campaigns, such as Be a Hero, with a monthly gift to a search-and-rescue organization or Adopt an Acre, where you sponsor an acre of restored prairie grasslands

>> Opportunities to volunteer

>> Invitations to readers to provide contact information — and promises of specific, enticing rewards if they do so

>> Blogs and chat rooms on subjects related to your work

>> A clear and easy-to-use donation feature for making contributions and information about how donations will be used to make a difference

TIP

When incorporating photos and graphical material in your fundraising materials, be sure to secure permission and give appropriate credit to the photographer or artist.

The longer a website keeps visitors involved, the likelier it is to build their trust and interest.

Most websites have a Contact Us page. Make sure this option is user friendly and that someone on your staff is responsible for replying to queries quickly and courteously. Include opportunities for readers of the website to sign up for your electronic newsletter or other information and to leave an email address and/or telephone number.

TIP

You may build the most amazing website on the planet, but if readers aren't finding it, it's not fulfilling its role for your organization. One critical question is how to attract the notice of search engines. Some agencies sit back and wait for a web spider to find their page; some submit their page to search engines one by one, which can be time consuming; and some hire a service to submit their information to the leading search engines. See *SEO For Dummies*, 7th Edition, by Peter Kent, for information on getting your site noticed by search engines.

Setting up an online donation portal

If you have good technology support and a website that includes a system for securely collecting money, you can insert your own Donate Now button. However, many nonprofits find it easier to contract with a "donate now" service.

Choosing from the number of available options can be daunting. When choosing one, think about the giving experience from the point of view of your nonprofit and from the perspective of the donor.

From the perspective of your nonprofit, look carefully at how and for what an agency charges fees. Most online contribution services charge a setup fee, a monthly fee, and a per-contribution fee. Sometimes you can avoid the monthly fee, but when you do, you often pay a higher fee for each contribution you receive. Some less-expensive nonprofit technology services charge lower fees but send you your contributions in a lump sum, so you receive only the money, not the donor records. On the other hand, some services charge for keeping the donor records or for allowing you to upload them to your computers. You should also check on ease of use, and number of types of credit cards accepted. Some services allow you to add boxes on the donor form where contributors can select premium gifts or choose to receive a newsletter.

Also consider the experience of making the donation from the point of view of your donors. With some services, such as PayPal and Network for Good's basic DonateNow, a donor who clicks the Donate Now button on your website can immediately tell that they're making a gift by way of a different website. Check to see whether the service you're using allows you to modify the look of that donation form so that it matches the look and feel of your website and graphics. This strategy can reassure nervous donors that they're in the right place.

We recommend checking Double the Donation's website (https://doublethe donation.com/tips/payment-processing-tools-for-nonprofits/) for helpful information about choosing online donation and credit card processing tools.

REMEMBER

If you hire a marketing service to develop and maintain your organization's website, consider the breadth of the services you're purchasing. Will the agency design your website for you? Will it thank your donors? Will it integrate data about customers who pay to attend your workshops with information about those who contribute money? Will it manage a donor database for your online contributions? And is it a 501(c)(3) nonprofit organization or a for-profit entity? (If it's a nonprofit, it may be registered to raise funds in all states requiring such registrations, and this can save your organization significant fees.)

Finding financial support from a crowd

Another method of raising money online, *crowdfunding* or *crowdsourcing,* involves seeking donations from people whom you reach via your email records or social media. Potential donors may learn only about your project, or they may be directed to a page that features a dozen or more projects to choose among — one of which is yours.

Crowdfunding services provide individuals and enterprises with tools to conduct focused, time-sensitive campaigns to raise money. Someone seeking contributions must name a specific amount to be raised and a specific project to be launched or completed. Some crowdfunding services (such as Kickstarter) are *all-or-nothing* — fundraisers receive none of the pledged gifts until they meet their goals. Although this strategy can seem to be a drawback, it also can motivate donors to give larger gifts or make additional contributions after their initial investments. Crowdfunding isn't exclusively for nonprofit organizations, but some platforms that include nonprofits among their clients are Fundly (www.fundly.com), Indiegogo (www.indiegogo.com), Kickstarter (for creative projects; www.kickstarter.com), and Kiva (for interest-free microloans; www.kiva.org).

Distributing your fundraising via volunteers

Technology provides novel ways for your organization's supporters to help raise money. In *distributed fundraising,* sometimes called *peer-to-peer fundraising,* an individual supporter creates an online donation account for your organization, and through that account speaks directly to friends and family about your organization's work, urging them to contribute or volunteer. Often they do this in concert with a campaign you're promoting directly. This is a good task to ask your board members or tech-savvy volunteers to do for you.

A peer-to-peer fundraiser can add a widget or badge that can be added to a website, blog, or social media page. They then distribute the page through their networks (for example, to blog subscribers). Your volunteer fundraiser often uses an existing service to set up the page and collect contributions. Some of these services are Network for Good, Change.org, Changing the Present, FirstGiving, and

Causes.com. Your volunteer will want to pay attention to the comparable setup fees and percentages of contributions collected by these services.

WARNING

Though involving your known supporters and volunteers to help raise money for your nonprofit is a useful idea, you face a risk in distributed fundraising if an individual who isn't authorized or known by the nonprofit raises funds in the name of the organization. If this situation arises, contact the donor and the fundraising platform to stop the unauthorized solicitations.

Soliciting text message donations

Many charities now accept donations made via mobile phone text messages. Text message contributions have been particularly strong for natural disasters and other emergencies. Over a decade ago, the American Red Cross raised some $12 million via its text-to-give campaign for Haitian earthquake relief. Mobile phone services waived texting fees for donors. Charitable giving via text message platforms continues to grow steadily.

To set up this service, your nonprofit organization registers with a donations processor that, in turn, works with cellphone providers to add an agreed-on contribution size to the user's cellphone bill.

A typical texted donation is modest in size, though a nonprofit may secure a new donor who is motivated by being able to take action immediately and by the relative ease of remembering a code word and phone number rather than a long website or street address. A text-to-give campaign works best when your nonprofit has an active social media network or highly visible public event (such as a benefit concert) by which it can spread the word.

WARNING

Nonprofits should be aware of certain disadvantages. The biggest one is that it's difficult to form a relationship with a texting donor. Your nonprofit and the donor are working through a processing service such as mGive (www.mgive.com), and your organization won't gain access to the donor's information. This list describes other disadvantages:

>> **Upfront costs:** Leasing a short vanity code (one you choose) from the Short Code Registry can cost $1,000 a month or $500 for a randomly selected code. Furthermore, mobile vendors charge a one-time setup fee of $3,000 to $10,000 for a unique (vanity) short code and $1,500 for a shared short code.

>> **Small contributions:** Nonprofits are legally permitted to ask only for modest gifts of $5 to $10 when soliciting via text message, and cellphone carriers may limit the number of gifts donors can make monthly.

- » **Fees charged:** The processing service charges a modest fee for each donation.
- » **Delays:** Contributions appear on the nonprofit's phone statements and are released after the phone bill is paid. It may take up to 90 days for the donor's gift to reach the nonprofit.

An alternative to texted donations is the use of QR codes, which are two-dimensional barcodes that appear on numerous products. Nonprofits can feature their QR codes on newsletters, solicitation letters, T-shirts, and invitations. Donors scan these codes with their mobile devices to connect with the nonprofits' websites and make contributions.

WARNING

With the growing use of mobile devices, QR codes would seem to be a helpful means for engaging with donors, but not all devices come equipped with QR code readers, and potential users of the codes may first have to download apps on their mobile devices. They also may grow frustrated if the downloads are slow or are hard to navigate.

Telemarketing: Dialing for Dollars

In the mid-1980s, direct mail was a wildly successful means of fundraising for many organizations. By the late 1980s, it had declined. Households were receiving too much direct mail, making recipients less inclined to read it, and the costs of printing and postage rose. That's when the dinner hour began to be interrupted by incessant telemarketing calls.

Now, with many people using Caller ID on their phones, and with cellphone numbers being difficult to collect for calling purposes, it's harder to succeed with telemarketing. Yet the phone is a powerful tool for connecting with others, and it's not yet time to abandon it in fundraising.

Here are some benefits of telemarketing:

- » **It's hard to ignore.** A human voice engages you in a conversation, and you must respond. It's not like a paper letter that you can toss into the recycling bin without the author noticing.
- » **It's affordable.** If you use trained volunteers to make the calls, you can manage a campaign for a reasonable cost.

>> **It's scalable.** As with direct mail, you can use some of the elements that shape a large-scale, professional telemarketing project for a modest campaign.

The disadvantages? Donors grow annoyed and may stop contributing if called too frequently. Plus, if you have no volunteers to make the calls, some commercial telemarketing firms take a high percentage (as high as 75 percent!) of any funds raised, discouraging donors who want to see fundraising costs remain low.

WARNING

Citizen complaints about intrusive telemarketing have led to the creation of the National Do Not Call Registry, which makes it illegal for businesses to make tele-marketing calls to people who register. In 2008, Congress passed legislation to make enrollment on the registry permanent. At present, nonprofit charitable organizations are exempt from these rules. However, if an individual asks to have their name removed from a nonprofit's call list, a third-party fundraiser must comply. Check the status of these regulations before embarking on a telemarket-ing campaign. Public policy articles on the Association of Fundraising Profession-als website (`www.afpnet.org`) are good places to check, as is the National Do Not Call Registry website (`www.donotcall.gov/faq/faqbusiness.aspx#ExemptOrg`).

The key steps to running a telemarketing campaign are writing a script, training volunteers, organizing follow-up calls, and — of course — thanking, cultivating, and upgrading donors over time. We explain everything you need to know in the following sections.

Perfecting a script

Every call should open with a clear, direct, personal greeting: "Hello, Mr. I'm-Getting-the-Person's-Name-Right, I'm Ms. Call-a-Lot, and I wanted to talk to you about the work of the Scenic Overlook Preservation Fund Committee." Let your listener know right away that you're soliciting a contribution and calling on behalf of a particular nonprofit.

Having connected with the call recipient, the caller then tries to link that person's interests and behavior to the reason for the call:

>> If the person is a past donor, begin with a hearty thank-you.

>> If the person has been involved in a related cause or effort, mention how important that work is.

>> If the person lives near the scenic overlook, mention how beautiful it is and the community's concern for the fragile surrounding environment.

You may notice a tricky moment in the call when you want the potential donor to relax and listen so that you can tell your story and not be interrupted. To increase the caller's chances of keeping call recipients on the line, the script should be

>> Engaging and information-packed (to hold the listener's attention)

>> Upbeat about the possibility of improvement or change

>> Deeply concerned about the current situation

>> Explicit about the time frame in which the situation needs to change

>> Specific about the amount of money the caller hopes the listener can contribute

TIP

Check out File 15-9 at www.wiley.com/go/nonprofitkitfd6e for a set of telemarketing do's and don'ts and a sample telemarketing script.

Training your board and volunteers as callers

Telemarketing can be an excellent board or volunteer group effort. Early evening (6 P.M. to 8:30 P.M.) on weeknights is generally considered the best time to call, but — as you've probably noticed — telemarketers now frequently call during the day and on weekends as well.

Gather your volunteer team an hour before beginning. Feed them a good meal and give them a pep talk. Building camaraderie among the callers can relax anyone who's nervous. Setting a group goal for the evening and mapping it on a big chart can build morale.

Inform callers that they must deliver the message in a crisp, clear, and friendly voice. They shouldn't rush, but neither should they leave holes in the conversation that the call recipient can close before the caller can ask for a contribution. They should ask for a specific contribution and confirm the amount. They also should tell potential donors that they're volunteers; this may make call recipients more likely to pay attention.

Provide callers with information about each household they're calling, including a recommended gift request. You base the request on the potential donor's past contributions to your organization and others. Sometimes you're just guessing. That's okay, as long as your callers are good listeners and deftly adjust the amount they're requesting in response to what they hear. If, after a gift is pledged, you feel that you asked for too little money, don't despair. You can ask the donor to upgrade the gift the next time.

Collecting the pledges

If a pledge is made, the caller should thank the donor and try to get the person to either provide credit card information over the phone so that the gift can be charged immediately or promise to return the contribution within a certain time. Ask the caller to confirm the spelling of the donor's name and address before saying goodbye.

REMEMBER

At the end of the evening, everyone present should write brief, personalized thank-you notes. For contacts who promised gifts but didn't charge them over the phone, send the thank-you notes with pledge forms (indicating the specific amount of the promised contribution) and return envelopes.

Every telemarketing campaign suffers from a percentage of unrealized promises, and callers want to keep that percentage as low as possible. You may ask a small number of your volunteers to reconvene for a short follow-up calling session a month after the initial campaign to jar loose any contributions that haven't yet been received.

Chapter **16**

Planning Onsite and Virtual Special Events

From glamorous dances under the stars to community garden foodfests at sunset to pancake breakfasts at the local firehouse, social gatherings are part of the fundraising mix for most nonprofits. Special events don't just raise money — they're often credited with raising friends along with funds. New donors, who don't know the organization, may come forward because the event itself sounds fun and interesting, because of who invites them, or because someone they admire is being honored. Special events, whether they're held in person or online only, can be wonderful catalysts for attracting support from businesses that like to be recognized when they make contributions or for attracting people who like to socialize and "be seen."

At their best, special events raise substantial amounts of money, draw attention to an organization's good work, and attract new volunteers. If fundraising is about cultivation, a special event can be a greenhouse for nurturing growth. You hope to create a special event that people look forward to, an annual tradition. Still, a special event, especially one held onsite, can be one of the most expensive ways to raise money; expenses may eat up half or even more of the gross event income. Putting together a special event draws upon all your nonprofit management skills and can drain staff and board time and energy away from other important activities.

Bottom line? Special events need careful planning. In this chapter, we show you how to put together the leadership, timeline, and budget that can lead to a successful special event — and steer clear of obstacles.

TIP

Check out File 16-1 at www.wiley.com/go/nonprofitkitfd6e for a list of web resources related to the topics we cover in this chapter.

Thinking through the Whole Event

If you think a special event is in your future, we recommend sitting down with staff and board members and raising such questions as these:

>> **What would our organization's followers enjoy and be comfortable doing, and how much would they pay to do it?** Not everyone enjoys listening to speaker after speaker while eating lunch or dinner at a fee-per-table fundraising event. After a while, each speaker becomes a blur. Sit down with your event planning team and ask them what type of event they would enjoy planning and what type of event they feel would appeal to the target audience. Different ideas are a good way to plan a more engaging fundraising event that offers a little bit of knowledge laced with mild appropriate entertainment, and perhaps a raffle for something donated by local merchants. Remember, the real decision-making in planning events is whether to have a live or online event depending on uncertain times.

>> **Whom does our organization know who can provide event elements?** Whether you decide to hold an in-person event or broadcast online, most events need donated goods, auction items, entertainment, and the like.

>> **Whom do we know who can be honored at the event or serve on an event committee?** The event leadership and volunteer committee are critically important to attracting donors to the occasion.

>> **When can we focus attention on a special event?** The last six weeks before an event are generally the most labor intensive. Look for a relatively clear six-week block of time in which you have no grant deadlines or other commitments.

>> **When can we hold an event without competing with our other fundraising drives?** If you hold annual fund drives in June and October, for example, why not plan your special event in the spring?

We offer some additional advice regarding these questions in the following sections.

Using your budget to guide decisions

Special events can be produced on bare-bones budgets, for princely prices, or for any amount in between. As with most kinds of investments, event planners expect a higher return in exchange for a higher investment. But don't exceed your means. In this section, we outline some ideas for tailoring an event to your organization's budget.

WARNING

When you're deciding on a type of event, we recommend avoiding ones that can make guests uncomfortable or deter them from attending, such as

>> Events that limit your guests' ability to come and go as they want — like a soiree on a boat in the middle of a lake.

>> Events at which your intended audience finds the attire, time, or place awkward.

>> Events designed to reach an audience that's completely unknown to your organization or its supporters. Do you like to go to a party where you don't know anybody?

TIP

After you've sketched out an idea for an event, go to your staff and board members and ask them directly: Would you attend this event? For this price? At this time of year? At this location? If your core followers and supporters aren't enthusiastic, the event won't raise money. If the idea excites them and they're willing to play a role in the event planning, you're on your way to success.

Low-budget special events

Most nonprofit organizations have a wealth of talent simply waiting for a showcase. Some of the following suggestions won't work for your organization, but they can get you thinking about similar events that would be perfect for your nonprofit:

>> **Sign up neighborhood children for a summer read-a-thon that benefits the library or an after-school literacy program.** By sending forms home to parents in advance, you can secure their permission and help with collecting pledges.

>> **Offer a bake sale with a distinctive theme celebrating a cultural group or holiday.** Organize your volunteers around three primary activities: setting up and pricing, selling, and taking down the sale. Plan in advance what to do with items that don't sell.

>> **Host a dinner party with a local well-known chef in a board member's home, and invite 15 to 20 potential donors who are friends and colleagues of the board member.** Although a dinner party for 15 people may not raise much money, don't rule out this idea. If every one of your board members signs up to host such a party over the course of a year, the cumulative amount raised may pleasantly surprise you.

>> **Convert high-cost, in-person events to virtual events.** Even after the pandemic, it's affordable to plan a virtual fundraising event. You don't need a special facility or caterer or all the other paraphernalia when you convert an in-person fundraiser to a virtual fundraiser. Deciding to have a virtual fundraiser can lower costs and increase revenue opportunities.

ALWAYS HAVE A PLAN B

When the pandemic abruptly interrupted all in-person fundraising events, we helped a chapter of a large national association convert three in-person events to a single virtual event. How did we do it? Well, it took all hands on deck at the organization as well as our team.

The first thing we did was notify all regional chapters that their annual in-person fundraisers for the association would convert to virtual events, for safety reasons. Everyone was onboard.

Then the hosting nonprofit association contacted the local television station to ask for their help in creating a livestreaming venue via YouTube. A well-known television news broadcaster stepped up and volunteered to be the master of ceremonies for interviewing program staff at the three locations. They also recorded interviews of many of the families and youths receiving services from the nonprofit.

Plans on the day of the event came together smoothly, considering that we had only six months to switch over to a virtual fundraising event.

On the plus side, the grant writer and development director at the nonprofit reached out to all past and current funders and asked them to pledge dollars or to fund grant requests for this annual-campaign virtual event. The nonprofit association forecasted, taking into account a volatile economy, raising $75,000 in total from the virtual event. When all was said and done, this virtual event ended up with $150,000 in donations. Cost: staff and staff time. Gain: Everything!

>> **Choose your virtual event's streaming platform.** If you expect less than 99 guests, you may be able to use a free or basic membership with a provider like Zoom. However, if you plan on having several hundred attendees at your virtual event, you will need to set a budget to pay for a streaming platform that has the bandwidth for larger groups of online attendees.

WARNING

Many nonprofit organizations produce raffles or prize drawings as low-cost activities to raise funds — if you plan to do so, proceed with caution. Such activities are defined as gambling or gaming in many states. Some states permit nonprofits to hold raffles, but in other states or jurisdictions, they may be illegal or may be presented only if you follow steps to secure a permit. You can find an overview of guidelines for hosting games of chance, raffles, and charitable auctions at the National Council of Nonprofits website (`www.councilofnonprofits. org`) and a quick guide to states' offices regulating nonprofits at the National Association of State Charity Officials (NASCO) website (`www.nasconet.org/ documents/u-s-charity-offices`).

Mid-budget special events

If you can afford a few more features in your special event, you may want to borrow or revise one of these ideas:

>> **Identify an up-and-coming performer and ask for a donation of a performance in exchange for the promotion that your event will bring.** The club or theater rental is likely to be your highest cost. If you choose an unusual site that's donated to you, make sure it can accommodate the performer's needs — acoustics, sound system, lighting, electrical outlets, and the like.

>> **Sponsor a daylong clean-up of a coastal area, park, or preserve.** Volunteers can be sponsored by having their friends sign up to pledge a certain gift amount to the organization for each pound or bag of trash they remove. Offer prizes for the most unusual refuse items found and the most sponsorship sign-ups.

>> **Produce an online auction.** Volunteers can help you reach out to friends to secure donations to be auctioned and draw attention to the event and auction items via social media. To build and hold interest in the auction, post regular updates and news about the event (with photos) on your website and social media pages. Don't forget that costs may include securing a seller's permit and remittance of sales taxes.

High-budget special events

If money is no object — at the front end, at least — these events may be of interest. All require more of an upfront investment:

>> **Hire a major speaker or entertainer from a lecture bureau or theatrical agency and make that person the focus of a dinner party or private concert.** Honor one or more business and community leaders at the event. Form an event committee of people who will invite their friends and people who may want to attend for the sake of the honorees.

>> **Present a dance featuring a live band.** Decorate festively. Make sure your crowd likes to dance and that your musicians' repertoire suits the moves that the crowd knows.

>> **Organize a celebrity athletic event.** Celebrity golf, bowling, and ping-pong — you name it — are all possible. Create teams pairing professional players with amateurs or local celebrities with donors. If you invite professional athletes, liberally handicap the amateurs so that everyone has a chance to win. Award trophies or certificates for many kinds of "achievements" — the longest drive, the bowling ball most often in the gutter, the quickest victory, and so on. Often these events end with celebratory dinners.

Sticking to your budget

The bottom line is simple: The total earnings from a special event must exceed its total cost — by a lot, you hope. But how do you get a handle on revenue and expenses? In this section, we offer some thoughts.

TIP

If you're staging an event for the first time, it's particularly important *early in the process* to ask core supporters — board, volunteers, and event leadership — how much they intend to give. Because these people are the most likely to give generously, knowing their intentions helps you forecast the overall results.

Sometimes fundraising events take several years to garner high-level support, so budget exactly how much you intend to make in years one, two, and three. It's not uncommon to break even the first year of an event or to have small net proceeds from your first venture.

Another way to estimate the fundraising potential of an event is to check with organizations that produce similar events. If they've presented a program year after year and yours is a first-time outing, ask them where their income levels began. Try to objectively weigh your event's assets against theirs. Are your boards equally well connected? Is your special guest equally well known?

TIP

Check out www.wiley.com/go/nonprofitkitfd6e for three sample special-events budgets — File 16-2 is a sample budget for a tribute dinner, File 16-3 is a sample budget for a concert or performance, and File 16-4 is a sample online auction budget.

Figuring the income side

Try to design your event so that it generates income in more than one way. A rummage sale may also include the sale of baked goods. An auction may add advertising to a printed program along with tickets to the event and the income generated from the sale of the auction items. This list presents standard event-income categories:

>> **Individual ticket sales**

>> **Table or group sales**

   Usually, for parties of eight or ten.

>> **Benefactor, patron, and sponsor donations**

   Donors receive special recognition in return for contributing higher amounts than a basic table or seat costs.

>> **Sponsorships of event participants**

   For instance, pledging to contribute a particular amount per mile run by a friend.

>> **Food and/or beverage sales**

>> **Sales of goods and/or services**

>> **Advertising sales**

   In printed programs or on banners, for example.

>> **Purchasing a chance**

   Raffle tickets or door prizes, for example.

Capturing expenses — expected and unexpected

Unless a wonderful sponsor has offered to cover all your expenses, your event will cost money to produce. These are the general categories:

>> **Building/facility/location:** Space rental, site use permits, security guards, portable toilets, tents, clean-up costs

>> **Advertising and promotion:** Save-the-date postcards, photography, posters, invitations, event programs, publicist costs, postage, event website with a ticket-purchase feature

>> **Production:** Lighting and sound equipment, technical labor, stage managers, auctioneers

>> **Travel and per diem:** For guest speakers, performers, or special guests

>> **Insurance:** For example, liability insurance in case someone gets hurt because of your organization's negligence, or shipping insurance to protect donated goods

>> **Food and beverages:** Permits for the sale or serving of alcohol, if necessary

>> **Décor:** Flowers, linens, fireworks, banners, rented tables and chairs

>> **Sales tax:** Varies by state, and collected by some states on food-and-beverage sales as well as on auction items and other goods sold

>> **Office expenses:** Letter-writing, mailing list and website management, detail coordination

>> **Miscellaneous:** Prizes, awards, talent treatment, name tags, signs, T-shirts

>> **All other staff expenses**

TIP

Always inquire about nonprofit pricing, and let vendors know that your organization is tax-exempt.

WARNING

In spite of your careful planning, certain expenses can appear unexpectedly and cause you to exceed your budget. If you plan to serve food at your event, keep these tips in mind to avoid surprise charges:

>> Confirm that all service and preparation charges are included in the catering budget.

>> If you need to add meals at the last minute, find out whether your caterer charges extra. If meals that you ordered aren't eaten, you probably still need to pay for them. Check your caterer's policy.

>> If some of the wine you've purchased isn't consumed, is the store willing to buy it back from you?

>> If wine has been donated to your event, find out whether your caterer charges corkage fees for opening and serving it.

Soliciting in-kind gifts for your event

When you think about what your event will cost and how you can pay for it, think about the business contacts that your board, staff, and outside supporters have. Often a business's contribution of *in-kind* (noncash) materials is more generous than any cash contribution to your event. You may need to be flexible about timing and willing to drop things off or pick things up, but don't overlook in-kind gifts. Donated auction items are one example. This list describes a few other examples:

>> Businesses in your community that have in-house printing equipment may be able to print your invitations and posters, saving you thousands of dollars.

>> A florist may contribute a roomful of valuable centerpieces in exchange for special recognition in the dinner program.

>> A donor may let you use their beautiful residence as your event site.

REMEMBER

You may not want or need all the in-kind gifts that are offered to you. In cases such as these, *do* look the gift horse in the mouth! Don't accept an in-kind contribution if it's not up to the standards you need for your event. Also, consider the implications of accepting the gift — both your need to honor any restrictions or conditions the donor places on the in-kind gift and the appropriateness of associating with the gift and its donor. For instance, if your agency helps young people recover from drug or alcohol addiction, don't accept a sponsorship from an alcoholic beverage company. If you're afraid of offending the donor or hurting a relationship, you can ask to use the gift in another context and acknowledge the donor publicly for their generosity.

TECHNICAL
STUFF

Donors will want to claim tax deductions for their in-kind contributions. It's their responsibility to tell the Internal Revenue Service if they're seeking charitable contribution deductions for the gifts, and it's your responsibility to acknowledge the donation in a prompt thank-you letter. If they make a contribution of noncash property worth more than $5,000, generally that item must be appraised before a value is assigned to it. For more information, see the IRS website at www.irs.gov.

Building your event committee

Strong volunteer leadership is the backbone of special-events fundraising. Some of the most important work you and your board will do as event organizers is to recruit a chair or cochairs for an event committee. Choose people who are well connected and who bring different contacts to their committee work — perhaps one community volunteer, one business executive, and one local athletic star. Many organizations place a board member on the event committee, but they also use the event as an opportunity to recruit beyond their boards, bringing in new, short-term volunteers.

TIP

Go-getter volunteers can make your event a great success, but they don't have the same responsibilities as your board and staff to protect your organization's financial well-being and reputation. Specify in writing who is ultimately responsible for making decisions (likely, your executive director, board, or board executive committee) and scheduling regular check-ins with volunteers to avoid poor decisions or misunderstandings.

We strongly recommend working closely with one or two volunteers who have planned fundraising events in the past and can help guide you and your committee through the process. Events are detail-heavy, and someone who has done this before can make sure that all details are addressed. Keep an event binder or shared online folder and document everything, including meeting notes, invoices, lists of tasks, timelines, budgets, and attendees.

Your cochairs' job is to build a network of support for the event. Usually they invite other well-connected people to join them as members of an event committee. Perhaps your board recruits three cochairs, and those cochairs recruit 25 event committee members. Your committee members and cochairs then send personalized letters, emails, and invitations and make phone calls urging people to support and attend the event. If each of them brings 20 people, you'll have quite a crowd!

TIP

Check out www.wiley.com/go/nonprofitkitfd6e for two related sample letters. File 16-5 is written by an event cochair, inviting someone to join an event committee. File 16-6 is written by a committee member to a potential donor.

Setting a date and location

You don't want to plan an event on Super Bowl Sunday or during your city's largest annual road marathon. Apart from avoiding holidays and other obvious dates when you would compete for your guests' attention, check around town to find out whether you're planning your event on the same date as one organized by another nonprofit agency. Be as thorough as possible in checking this date. Competing for the same audience on the same date — or even dates that are close to each other — hurts both organizations' results.

Though the idea isn't innovative, good hotels are generally excellent sites for special events. They often have several banquet rooms — and catering, podiums, sound systems, and parking valets are all available at the site. All these extras leave you with fewer details to manage.

Some of the best special events we've attended have been inside the nonprofit organizations they supported or in sites thematically linked to the cause being supported — such as a historic building or maritime museum. Outdoor locations such as vineyards, formal gardens, and mountaintops can be beautiful but require backup plans for variable weather, and climbing rocky pathways or crossing uneven lawns may make your event inaccessible to some of your hoped-for supporters.

Another creative angle on choosing a location is to match it to an event theme. We've put on a spooky Halloween party in a former mortuary.

TIP

If you're running short on ideas, ask your friends and colleagues about interesting places they've attended events, or hold a brainstorming session with your board. Make sure your constituents will feel comfortable going to the location you're considering.

Setting Up Your Timeline

Although events vary greatly in size and complexity, and although we've pulled off adequately successful events in two or three weeks, we recommend working against a six-month schedule. This section outlines a scheduling checklist for a gala dinner. You can easily modify it to fit other types of events. We also recommend a six-month schedule for planning or converting an in-person event to an online event.

The first three months

The first three-month period is, not surprisingly, the slowest part of event planning. You may wait several weeks to hear back from an invited celebrity, and you may need several more weeks to find a replacement if you're turned down. Here are the general steps:

» Develop the plan and recruit the event's leadership — we recommend two or three cochairs and an honoree.

» Secure entertainment and a location.

» Select a theme and a caterer.

» Send a save-the-date postcard and email announcement.

» Create an event web page and social networking site.

» Apply for any necessary permits (for charitable gaming, selling auction items, serving alcoholic beverages, street closures, and so on).

Months four and five

As the event draws nearer, you let others know about the upcoming event and begin contacting volunteers. Here are the general steps:

>> With the help of your event cochairs, recruit an event committee and/or a core group of volunteers.

>> Visit the site where the event will be held, checking out all the regulations and recommendations for its use.

>> Solicit in-kind contributions of materials you need for the event.

>> Send initial news releases announcing your speakers, celebrities, and/or event leadership. (See Chapter 13 for more details about a marketing and public relations program.)

>> Call all potential committee members.

>> Develop the invitation design. All text on the invitation should be ready for final design, printing, and online posting by six weeks before the event.

>> Select your menu and start working on decor ideas.

>> Personalize invitations with the help of committee members.

>> Mail and email the invitations.

Four weeks before the event

Spend the month before the event generating excitement and finalizing the details.

>> Build interest with frequent website and social media updates featuring photos and news bits.

>> Email a second batch of news releases.

>> Make phone calls to the media and to invitees to confirm coverage and travel plans.

>> Design the printed program to be passed out at the event.

>> Assist cochairs and honorees with their speeches (if necessary).

>> Gather the elements — baskets, banners, confetti, and other items — needed for decor.

In designing your event's promotional materials, you want the look of the invitation, program, event web page, signage, and audiovisual templates to be consistent. Schedule time to solicit logos from corporate sponsors and double-check the spelling of donors' names and how they want to be recognized.

The week before the event

Don't get too stressed in the days before the event. You should have only a few last-minute details to attend to, such as these:

» Confirm the number of guests you expect. A few days before the party, call *everyone* who has made a reservation and confirm their attendance. A few people will have changed their plans, and you don't want to pay for uneaten meals or run out of food. When ordering food from your caterer, assume that, under normal circumstances, 5 percent of your expected guests won't attend. If the event is free, 10 percent of them won't attend.

» Plan the table seating at the event (if necessary).

» Prepare place cards and table cards.

» Decorate the site.

TIP

Check out `www.wiley.com/go/nonprofitkitfd6e` for additional special-events timelines. File 16-7 is a sample timeline for a tribute dinner or luncheon, and File 16-8 is a sample timeline for a concert or performance.

WARNING

You may think that nobody can rain on your parade, but have emergency backup plans anyway. What if a performer is ill, a blizzard shuts down roadways, or permits aren't approved on time? You need to quickly move, replace, reschedule, or cancel your program. The faster you can communicate any changes, the better your constituents feel about sticking with you and your cause.

ISSUING A MEMORABLE INVITATION

Make the invitation one that potential guests will open and remember. If it's a physical invitation, addressing the envelope by hand and using stamps rather than metered postage makes it look more personal, and an intriguing phrase or logo on the outside may lead to its being opened.

What do recipients see first when they open your invitation? Most invitations are made up of an outer folded piece, a reply card, and a reply envelope. Want some more

(continued)

(continued)

attention? What if a compelling photograph slips out of the envelope? Or a small black cat, spider, or bat sticker falls out of your Halloween invitation?

In spite of our recommending these bells and whistles, we are firm believers in clarity. Make sure the reader of your invitation can easily see who's extending the invitation, what the event is, where and when it's being held, how much it costs, and how to respond to the invitation. If people have to search for these basics, the invitation will land in the recycling bin. And remember that people look forward to your event more if other people they know will be there. Make sure the names of the people on your event committee are clearly and prominently presented. Also list top sponsors (cash and in-kind) on the invitation so that invitees can see the businesses involved in the event. These tips are equally true for the electronic version of the invitation: Make it easy for your invitees to make reservations and send contributions.

Print the address, phone number, and/or website to which your guest should respond somewhere on the reply card, even though it's also printed on the reply envelope. Sometimes the pieces of an invitation become separated. You want your guests to readily know where to send their replies (and money!).

For informal and low-cost events, you may want to send only an e-invitation, using a service such as Eventbrite or Paperless Post, which distributes your invitation, collects reservations, sends reminders to your guests, and urges them to invite others via social media. If you have updated email lists of your donors and contacts, this approach can save you postage costs and reduce paper waste. A few disadvantages are that it can be challenging to include full credit to sponsors, and some people still find electronic invitations to be informal, making your event seem less important to recipients.

Spreading the Word

If the mantra of fundraising is "If you don't ask, you won't get," the mantra for special-events fundraising is "People won't come if they don't know about it." Your invitation list is likely the most valuable tool you have at hand for reaching out to event guests, but don't overlook the role that social media and traditional media can play.

Setting social media to blast

These days there are a plethora of social media options such as Facebook and YouTube that allow you to post information and updates about special events your nonprofit is hosting. First, your nonprofit will need to have a profile on your preferred social media sites. Here's a list of the top social media platforms for getting the word out about virtual and in-person events:

>> **Facebook:** 170 million subscribers

>> **Instagram:** 121 million users

>> **Twitter:** 81 million subscribers

>> **YouTube:** 30 million subscribers

In recruiting volunteer committee members, ask them which forms of social media they use, and arm them with tools to spread the word to their networks. For example, every time you create a post on the event's web page, email them and ask them to share it. You also can arm them with good photographs and background information and urge them to use the materials to blog or post social media updates.

REMEMBER

Good photographs are essential to your announcements being noticed on social media. Often we think of hiring a photographer for the event itself, but photographic work done before the gala may be even more important.

Finding a news angle

If your event has a newsworthy angle, send news releases to the media in the hope that they'll write about it or broadcast the news. (You can find information about writing news releases in Chapter 13.)

Think about all the angles you can exploit for publicity. Modify your basic news release to suit the content of appropriate newspaper and magazine section editors, producers of radio feature shows, and TV newsrooms. Follow up your emailed release with a phone call. These are a few possibilities:

>> **Entertainment section coverage of performers:** You may be able to arrange interviews between special guests and local entertainment reporters.

>> **Business section coverage of the event chair or honoree:** Many papers run a column highlighting the activities of local business and corporate leaders.

>> **Feature stories about the community improvements that your agency has helped to bring about or human interest stories about individuals who have benefited from its services**

>> **Food section coverage of your picnic lunch or the gourmet food trucks serving guests at your outdoor benefit concert**

- » **Health advice connected to your event:** If your organization is sponsoring a 10K run, what's the current advice about dietary preparation for long-distance running? If local celebrities or unusual teams (for example, six cousins, or all the elementary school's teachers) have signed up, a local paper or news station might interview them in advance.

- » **Society page coverage of your honorees, event committee members, or other guests at your event**

- » **Radio broadcast of your honoree or guest speaker's speech**

- » **Fashion page or television coverage of attire worn to your gala**

Getting a mention on radio or TV

The media needs great gobs of news, announcements, and other content every single day. You can snag some media exposure if, for example, you

- » Invite an anchor from the local news channel to serve as the emcee for the event and ask that person to promote the event and/or provide an on-air mention about it.

- » Prepare a prerecorded public service announcement (PSA) for broadcast by radio stations. (See Chapter 13 for guidelines on PSAs.)

- » Donate free event tickets to public television or radio stations to use as prizes of various kinds. If a station picks up on the idea, you gain a free mention — and maybe a number of free mentions.

- » Invite live weather or traffic reporters to cover conditions from your location. It can be a novel way to draw attention to your event.

After the Event is Over

By now, you and your team members are exhausted. You really want extra time off to recover from event planning, last-minute emergencies the day of the event, and several other issues with the event venue. Well, it's not time to rest yet. There's still a lot of work to do. Your donors came through with generous donations. Your fundraising goal was not only reached, but it was also exceeded! Don't make the mistake of waiting too long to start on the next steps of donor appreciation.

Write thank-you notes soon after the event to all committee members and volunteers, and make each letter as specific and personal as possible. The letter doesn't have to be long. Many people find handwritten notes of two or three lines to be much more sincere and memorable than boilerplate letters.

The thank-you letters you send to the attendees should clearly define how much money was donated and the cost of goods and services for the event. For example, if you host a dinner and the ticket cost is $100 per person and the food-and-beverage cost is $50 per person, the thank-you letter should thank the attendee for the $100 contribution and mention that the tax-deductible amount of the donation is $50. Thank-you letters for purchasing auction items should reference the amount paid for an item and the fair market value of the item as provided by the item's donor. It's a good idea to add language like this: "Please consult your tax advisor for specific tax advice." Event donations can be tricky, and this can keep you out of the business of providing tax advice.

Thank-you letters also should be sent to any person or business that made an in-kind contribution to the event. If you held an auction at the event, you can note that the auction generated $20,000 that wouldn't have been possible without the generous donation from the local historical society's gift shop.

TIP

Hold a brief gathering for key organizers and volunteers a week or two after the event. You can thank them personally again for their effort, though the real purpose is to gather their ideas about what worked, what needs to be improved, and what should happen in the future. You may want to invite a few attendees to this meeting and solicit feedback from their perspective. Good records of this wrap-up meeting are a jumping-off point for planning the following year's program.

Chapter **17**

Sleuthing for Grant Funding

Many people are familiar with the names of the nation's largest foundations. We can fantasize about receiving six- or even seven-figure grants from the likes of the WK Kellogg, Open Society, or Bill and Melinda Gates foundation. They have so much money — why wouldn't they support your nonprofit's work?

Foundations have missions, just like other nonprofits, and the most likely foundation to give you a grant may not be the largest in the land. Your task is to become a sleuth to identify the foundations whose priorities best match your nonprofit's goals. Spending time to write a good proposal matters — we discuss proposal writing in Chapter 18 — but finding a receptive audience for that proposal is just as important. It may be even more important.

This chapter shows you how to identify grant sources and figure out your approach to a grant giver.

TIP

Check out File 17-1 at www.wiley.com/go/nonprofitkitfd6e for a list of web resources related to the topics we cover in this chapter.

Assessing Your Nonprofit's Grant-Seeking Readiness

New nonprofit founders and boards are often under the impression that as soon as the ink dries on their IRS 501(c)(3) tax-exempt letter, a plethora of grants are just waiting for them to apply for immediately. That's not necessarily the case! If your nonprofit hasn't previously been awarded large-scale grants ($25,000 and more), your current operating budget is under $100,000, and your Form 990s haven't been filed on time, you need to reset your mindset to rely on your board to raise the funds — or request small amounts from potential local grant makers.

Here are some questions to test your nonprofit organization's readiness for plowing into applying for grants:

>> **What is the age of your nonprofit organization?** Age starts when you receive the tax-exempt approval letter from the IRS. Look at the date in the upper right corner of the letter — that's the approval date. (See Chapter 5.) New nonprofit organizations must not spin their wheels trying to apply for large-scale grants. It's time for your board to step up and raise some funds in different ways. Grants should be tabled until your nonprofit is at least two or three years old. Most potential grant makers aren't eager to take their chances on new nonprofit organizations.

>> **Who's on your board of directors?** Potential grant makers (foundations and corporations) look at the size of your board and who's on the board. (See Chapter 3.) Are your board members connected to the community that your nonprofit serves and where any grant awards will fund programs and services?

>> **Do your board members represent diversity in gender and equity?** Potential grant makers expect to see a board roster that includes the demographics of your board members. Grant makers are looking for diverse boards that represent the composition of your community and service populations. (See Chapter 3.)

>> **Are any of your board members related?** Did you know that potential grant makers view as suspicious any board rosters with very few members or related members (with the same last names)? Potential grant makers are looking for board members who can make objective decisions and not just go along with the founder or leader or the other relatives on the board.

>> **Do your board members contribute money (not just time) to your nonprofit annually?** Board service consists of more than the time spent sitting in a board meeting or on a committee — it means that every board member must be able to contribute an agreed-on amount annually to your nonprofit organization. Potential grant makers look for this board giving declaration in their grant application questions and emphasize the importance of having a financially contributing board of directors in their grant application deadlines. This is often referred to as a *give-or-get policy*.

>> **Does your nonprofit organization have an updated profile on GuideStar by Candid?** Potential grant makers expect reputable nonprofit organizations to have created profiles at this site. What are they looking for in your profile? If your nonprofit is a 501(c)(3), your mission statement, financials, contact information, and a copy of your most recent Form 990. If you're not in GuideStar by Candid, you likely will not be funded. There is no charge to set up your organization's profile. GuideStar works with the IRS to pull all of the Form 990's that can be retrieved to upload them to the GuideStar website.

>> **Does your nonprofit organization have collaborative partners?** These types of partnerships are bound by agreements and actions to share resources to accomplish a mutual goal. Collaborative partnerships rely on participation by at least two parties who agree to share resources, such as finances, knowledge, and staff. Potential grant makers want their successful grant applicants to have multiple community, regional, state, and, sometimes, national collaborative partners. Your partners can be other nonprofit organizations, licensing agencies, local, county, and state government agencies, national associations, and more.

Planning for a Foundation Grant Proposal

Grant sources can be grouped into two broad categories: private and public. Private sources are generally foundations and corporations, and public sources are based within some level of the government — city, county, state, or national. We write about public sources later in this chapter; here we provide the scoop on foundations and corporations.

When you look at the entire nonprofit sector, notice that gifts from individuals provide the largest portion (more than 70 percent) of private contributions. Because they play a smaller role, many foundations see themselves as providing resources for innovation or program improvement. They're a good place to turn to when your nonprofit has a new idea, wants to expand to a new location, or wants to compare and evaluate different methods. Generalizing is wrong, however. Some foundations provide flexible dollars — general operating support — that your nonprofit can use for any of its expenses. In fact, we've seen a gradual trend toward more funding for "gen op."

Learning about funding priorities

Sometimes foundations and government agencies actively seek grant proposals addressing particular regions or community needs. When doing so, they may issue a *request for proposals* (RFP) or a *program announcement.* Most foundations send their RFP announcements to the *Chronicle of Philanthropy* and *Philanthropy News Digest (PND).* At the *Chronicle*'s website (www.philanthropy.com), you can find these under Deadlines on the Fundraising menu, though the RFP newsletter released by *PND* started at the Foundation Center and now has its own PND by Candid website at https://philanthropynewsdigest.org. You can sign up to receive a weekly newsletter from PND that alerts you to these announcements.

Let us mention another noteworthy grant research website here: Instrumentl (www.instrumentl.com). Though it's relatively new on the scene, it has warp speed algorithms that do all the grant mining work for you. The company charges a fee for this service, but you can sign up for a free 14-day trial period on the site to look at funding priorities that you thought you'd never see for your grant research project. We believe that the site's content and ease of use is worth subscribing to the paid version after your trial period ends. Before you jump into checking out Instrumentl, go to LinkedIn and look for posts from grant writers that are affiliates of Instrumentl. When you use one of their links to access the site and you decide to subscribe, you will get $50 off of your first month's subscription.

More often, you have to find foundations that have the broad missions and stated preferences that seem to match your organization's work and convince them — after studying their guidelines — that the issues your nonprofit addresses are compelling and that your organization has devised a good approach for tackling them. That process of identifying a funding source generally has two phases: developing a broad list of prospects and then refining that list until you find the likeliest sources. We discuss both of these phases in this section.

TIP

Your time as a grant writer is best spent when you study the priorities and behaviors of the foundations you're approaching. *Shotgunning*, or sending the same proposal to a large number of foundations, is a waste of effort. *Targeting*, or focusing your attention on your most likely sources and writing to address their preferences, is much more effective.

Familiarizing yourself with types of foundations

Foundations are formed and governed in different ways. These differences may affect the way you address them as a grant seeker. The four basic kinds of foundations are independent, corporate, community, and operating. In this section, we describe how you can figure out which is which.

Independent foundations, large and small

Most foundations in the United States are classified as *independent* — also called *private* — foundations. Some of the country's largest foundations, such as the Bill and Melinda Gates Foundation, the Ford Foundation, and the Lilly Endowment, Inc., are independent foundations, but many small- and medium-size grant-making foundations also fall into this category.

Although they vary widely, these are the key characteristics that independent foundations share:

>> They're established with funds donated by individuals, families, or a small group of people.

>> Their purposes and modes of grant-making are set by their boards of directors, who may be family members (in which case, they're called *family foundations*) or their appointed representatives (*private operating foundations*).

>> Many (approximately 70 percent) of these foundations award grants primarily in the communities where they were formed, but others award grants in multiple locations.

>> They must file a 990-PF tax form with the Internal Revenue Service (IRS) each year.

TIP

A 990 is the type of tax form filled out by a 501(c)(3) nonprofit or public charity (such as a community foundation), and a 990-PF is the type of tax form completed by a 501(c)(3) private or independent foundation.

Corporate foundations and corporate giving

Corporations and businesses may support nonprofits by creating corporate foundations, or they may award money directly from their company budgets. Some do both!

Whether the business manages its giving through a foundation or directly from company coffers, the staff member who coordinates grant-making also may play another role within the corporation — such as public affairs director. You may notice that many corporate foundations and direct corporate-giving programs give away goods and services or provide technical assistance as well as cash grants.

These are the common characteristics of corporate foundations:

>> They're established with funds that come from a business or corporation.

>> Some of them maintain assets that they invest, and then they award grants from the money they earn on those investments. Many of them add to their grant-making budgets when their business is having a profitable year, but do not do so when business profits are weak. For this reason, their grant-making budgets can fluctuate dramatically.

>> Often they're governed by a board made up of company executives.

>> Most of them award grants in the communities where their employees live and work, and they see their grant giving as part of their role as good citizens.

>> Sometimes corporate foundations award grants to organizations where their employees volunteer or contribute or that their employees recommend to them.

>> As a type of private foundation, they must file a 990-PF with the IRS each year.

Companies' direct-giving programs share characteristics with corporate foundations, but they have a slightly different profile. Consider some of the following characteristics:

>> All funds available for grants come directly from company budgets and depend on the business's available resources. In lean years, the business may not support charitable causes.

>> Like corporate foundations, businesses with direct-giving programs tend to award grants in the communities where their employees live and work.

>> Many corporate-giving programs want to receive public recognition for their gifts. They justify their charitable giving to their owners or stockholders as good public relations.

>> Some companies are cautious about supporting controversial causes that might alienate their employees or stockholders.

>> Gathering information about grants awarded by these programs may be difficult because the businesses don't need to specify their support of charities in their financial statements.

TIP

Companies often want their gifts to be visible. So, for example, you may not want to accept a sponsorship from a whiskey distillery if you're managing a youth program.

TIP

Many corporate-giving programs match contributions that their employees make to nonprofit organizations. When seeking information about your individual donors, ask whether they work for a company that will match their gifts.

In your neck of the woods: Community foundations

The first community foundation, the Cleveland Foundation, was created in 1914. Today, more than 3,340 such foundations exist nationwide. Community foundations have a different, advantageous tax status from other kinds of foundations. The IRS classifies them as *public charities.* This list describes some other characteristics they share:

>> They're started with funds contributed by many sources, such as local trusts and individuals living in the communities they represent.

>> Community foundations focus their grant-making on the geographic areas in which they were established. Those areas may be as large as a state (Hawaii and Maine have community foundations), or they may be a county or city (Sonoma, California, or Chicago, Illinois).

>> They're governed by boards of directors made up of people who represent the communities they serve.

>> To keep their desirable public-charity tax status, they must raise money as well as give it away. For that reason, even a tiny community foundation has paid staff members.

>> Donors to community foundations may contribute to general grant-making programs or may create donor-advised funds and play a role in recommending how to award grants derived from their contributions. The number of donor-advised funds in the United States is growing rapidly.

TIP

When reviewing a grants list for a community foundation, if you see a grant that doesn't seem to fit within the foundation's published guidelines or geographic focus area, realize that it may have been awarded by a donor from an advised fund.

Operating foundations: Locked doors for grant seekers

Operating foundations generally don't award grants. They're formed to provide an ongoing source of support for a specific nonprofit institution — often a hospital or museum. When you come across an operating foundation, skip right over it!

Using the Foundation Directory Online to assemble a broad list of prospects

During the past 60 years, the public has gained increased access to information about funding sources. One milestone in this movement was the creation of the Foundation Center in 1956. Originally intended to collect information so that foundations could learn about one another, the Foundation Center quickly became a leading source of information for grant seekers. Today, the Foundation Center's grant research database has a new moniker: Foundation Directory Online (FDO) by Candid. We explain everything you need to know in the following sections.

Understanding the basics about FDO by Candid

TIP

FDO by Candid maintains databases of information on more than 235,000 grant maker profiles and grant-making public charities in the United States and a database of more than 22.7 million recent grants awarded. (Check out File 17-1 at www.wiley.com/go/nonprofitkitfd6e for a list of these sites.)

Candid Learning also provides data and news to classes, podcasts of public programs, webinars, and blogs. You can find a link to its website in File 17-1 at www.wiley.com/go/nonprofitkitfd6e.

Candid Learning's most popular research tool, the FDO, is available by subscription. Candid Learning has begun building an international database so that foundations worldwide can learn about one another's work and collaborate more effectively. A new aspect of the FDO illustrates maps of global giving, which is also useful for US organizations conducting international work.

Where does Candid Learning find its information? It compiles data from foundations' annual IRS 990 or a 990-PF tax forms, which include summaries of the foundations' major activities and lists of all their grants for the year reported. Candid Learning also surveys foundations annually, seeking more detailed information than sometimes appears on their tax forms. Increasingly, foundations are submitting their grants information electronically to Candid Learning as soon as those grants are approved — likely several times each year.

TIP

If you can't find a nearby funding information network, check with reference librarians at your local public library or nearby college and university libraries. These places may have licenses with Candid Learning to host their full searchable database of foundation profiles in the FDO.

The number of foundations in the United States grows and shrinks; as we write this book, the estimated number is 119,791. Reading profiles of all those grant makers is daunting (and a waste of your valuable time!). When using FDO by Candid to find the best options for your organization and project, you begin by asking whether a foundation satisfies the following four basic criteria:

>> **Geography:** Does this foundation award grants in the area where your nonprofit is based?

>> **Fields of interest:** Does this foundation award grants in the subject area of your organization's work?

>> **Type of support:** Does this foundation award the kind of grant you want?

>> **Application process:** Is this foundation open to reviewing proposals from grant seekers, or does it give only to preselected organizations? Some 72 percent of all US foundations don't accept applications.

If you answered yes to all four, good work! You've found an entry for your broad list of prospects. Strive to come up with a list of about 15 or 20 foundations.

TIP

If you have subscribed to FDO by Candid, you can note information about the foundations that interest you in Workspace and return to that dashboard to track deadlines and your progress toward applying.

If you find too few choices, broaden your search (for example, looking for grant makers in your *state* — not just in your city). If you find too many choices, narrow your options, perhaps by adding a keyword search. But, wait — we're jumping ahead in the process. First you need to become more familiar with these databases and search fields.

Discovering the center's directories and databases

FDO by Candid organizes its information in several databases. As you're creating your broad list of foundation prospects, you'll be most interested in four of them — all of which are available via FDO by Candid:

>> **Search Grantmakers:** Brief profiles of all US foundations, corporate-giving programs, and public charities, along with a growing number of non-US grant makers

>> **Search Companies:** Brief profiles of companies that sponsor giving programs — either through corporate foundations or directly from their company coffers

>> **Search Grants:** Indexes and brief descriptions of recently awarded grants

>> **Search 990s:** Foundations' 990 and 990-PF tax forms, which you can search using keywords

Another tool, Power Search, allows grant seekers to conduct keyword searches across all four databases listed here.

REMEMBER

The information contained in FDO by Candid is updated in real time.

TIP

Candid Learning's resources aren't your only options. The FoundationSearch (www.foundationsearch.com) commercial product features 100,000 foundation profiles for study, and NOZAsearch (www.grantsearch.com) offers an extensive database of charitable donations. You also can conduct an Internet search. Only about 10 percent of US-based foundations have websites, but many of the larger ones do. Some states and regions publish their own guides. Another research approach is to investigate who is funding other nonprofits in your area. Compile a list of organizations with a similar focus to yours, and investigate their donor lists in their annual reports, newsletters, and 990s.

Effectively searching the center's information

Here are a few pointers to help you make the best use of FDO by Candid's tools:

>> **Practice searching** using the free tutorials on the Candid Learning website:

```
https://learning.candid.org/training/search/format/
    on-demand/type/self-paced-learning.
```

>> **Take advantage of search options.** FDO by Candid offers options to search by grant maker location; fields of interest; transaction type (for example, scholarships, grants, or loans); geographic focus; trustees, officers, and donors; as well as keywords. If you're using the printed directories, you'll find indexes that allow you to search by similar fields.

>> **Use the indices.** FDO by Candid uses a consistent vocabulary in its databases. When filling in the search form, click the small word *index* so that you, too, are using this vocabulary. It greatly improves the effectiveness of your search.

>> **Eliminate the ones that reject unsolicited proposals.** More than 70 percent of US foundations don't open their doors and mailboxes to any applicant who chooses to apply. Instead, they study their fields of interest and go out and find grantees. One way to avoid wasting your time on these foundations is to select the check box that reads Exclude Grantmakers Not Accepting Applications when entering your search terms in FDO by Candid online.

TIP

You'll want to use FDO by Candid's controlled vocabulary for conducting your search. For many years, the FDO used the Internal Revenue Service's system for classifying nonprofits — something called the National Taxonomy of Exempt Entities. Not all grant seekers found those terms to be easy to understand, so the National Center for Charitable Statistics provides this classification system. You can find a link to the list of terms at the Center's website: We've included the link in File 17-1 at www.wiley.com/go/nonprofitkitfd6e.

>> **Determine whether you or your board members have any contacts who serve on foundation boards.** You can gather this information using the Trustees, Officers, and Donors search box in the Search Grantmakers section of FDO by Candid.

>> **Keep in mind that corporations also award grants.** FDO by Candid's top-level subscription gives you access to giving programs that are managed directly by corporations. Corporations frequently give in the communities where their employees live and work, and their profiles include information about where subsidiaries are located, as well as their corporate headquarters. Many companies award materials or services — often products they produce. You may find that these in-kind gifts are more valuable to your organization than the cash grants they also award.

TIP

You may want to consider how the company's policies and practices regarding such issues as domestic-partner benefits, staff diversity, energy consumption, or greenhouse gas emissions align with your nonprofit's values. The Search Companies profiles in FDO by Candid provide links to an array of these corporate social responsibility measures.

TIP

For a step-by-step guide to the foundation research process, check out File 17-2 at www.wiley.com/go/nonprofitkitfd6e. For each entry on your broad list, jot down notes and questions on a *foundation prospect evaluation sheet.* You can find a sample evaluation sheet in File 17-3.

If you now have your broad list of prospects in hand (or on your computer), it's time for cross-checking and deeper study that will help you to narrow your broad list to the five or six best potential sources.

Digging deeper to narrow your prospects

At this phase in your research, you truly become a sleuth, taking your broad list of prospects in hand and finding out more about each of them. See what you can discover from the following sources:

>> **Using Workspace:** If you're using the FDO by Candid grant research database, when you find a promising prospect, click Workspace in the upper right corner of the funder's profile. Workspace saves the foundation's information in a dashboard for you. Its assessment tool invites you to choose from a list of criteria to determine the strength of the match between your project and the foundation.

>> **Websites and annual reports:** Some foundations (approximately 10 percent of them) produce websites, and others publish printed annual reports with detailed information about their grant-making guidelines and grantees. These publications can be particularly helpful for grant seekers. They often include introductory letters from the foundation's leaders that provide insight into a foundation's philosophy or current direction. Foundation websites are easy to find with a simple Internet search. You can find announcements of new annual reports in *Chronicle of Philanthropy* (www.philanthropy.com), explore printed annual reports in some libraries, or call the foundations and ask to have the reports sent to you.

>> **Blogs and tweets:** Some foundation leaders post blogs or tweets about their work and grantees. Some have Facebook Pages. You can find their social media identities at their websites and follow or like them to receive ongoing updates.

>> **Form 990s:** Foundation 990 forms may be the only place to find a list of every single grant a particular foundation has awarded. Foundations are required to make their three most recent 990 or 990-PF reports available to the public. If they don't post them on their websites, you can find them at FDO by Candid (https://candid.org/research-and-verify-nonprofits/990-finder), NOZA 990-PF Database (www.grantsmart.com), and GuideStar by Candid (www.guidestar.org) websites. Some state agencies also provide online access to 990s.

TIP

Studying a foundation's 990 may intrigue you, but PDF files for the nation's largest foundations are enormous. We recommend against downloading a 990 from a large foundation that produces a website or an annual report containing grants lists. Reviewing 990s or 990-PFs is more useful when you're studying small foundations whose grants lists may not be readily available.

>> **The foundation's contact person:** If a foundation listing includes a contact person and phone number or an email address — and if it doesn't say you shouldn't call or write — feel free to contact that person to confirm information and ask any questions you may have. We recommend that you do so only after you've read as much as you can find about that foundation. This way, you can be focused, clear, and knowledgeable as you seek additional information.

Going for a Government Grant

Before you start daydreaming about massive state or federal funding, compare the pros and cons of private funding and public funding. Table 17-1 sorts things out for you.

TABLE 17-1   Comparing Private and Public Grant Sources

Private Sources	Public Sources
The purpose of the grant-giving entity is set by donors and trustees.	The purpose of the grant-giving agency is set by legislation.
Most foundations and corporations award grants to 501(c)(3) nonprofit organizations, some give to public agencies, and others give fellowships and awards to individuals.	Most agencies award grants, contracts, and loans to nonprofit and for-profit entities, to individuals, and to other government entities.
Most grants are awarded for one year, and grants are generally smaller than those awarded by public sources.	Many multiyear grants are awarded for large amounts of money.
The application process requires a limited number of contacts with individuals within the funding agency.	The application process is bureaucratic and may require applicants to work with staff at multiple levels of government.
Grants are sometimes awarded in response to simple two-page letters with backup materials.	Many proposals are lengthy (as long as 100 pages).
Agency files are private; applicants may not have access to reviewer comments or successful grant proposals submitted by other organizations. Review panels and board meetings may be closed to the public.	Agency records must be public. Applicants may visit many review panels; reviewer comments and successful proposals submitted by other nonprofits may be available.
Foundation and corporate priorities may change quickly according to trustees' interests.	Agency priorities may change abruptly when new legislation is passed or budgets are revised.
Developing personal contacts with trustees or with foundation staff may enhance your chances of securing a grant.	Developing personal contacts with congressional aides for state or national representatives may enhance your application's chances.
After accepting a grant, the recipient is usually required to file a brief final narrative and financial report.	After accepting a grant, the recipient may be required to follow specified contracting and hiring practices and bookkeeping and auditing procedures. It may have to prove other compliance with federal regulations. Grants can be relatively costly to manage.

If, after reviewing the info in Table 17-1, you decide that you're up to the task of seeking government grants, read on.

Federal grants

To pursue government funds, you need to study a different set of research guides from those that help you with foundations and corporations. The resource that's most likely to help you is online at www.grants.gov. This tool is more than a directory of information: At Grants.gov, you can both find and apply to federal grant programs.

Weighing the pros and cons of Grants.gov

Grants.gov is a perfect model of bureaucratic writing, and the site has so much information that it can overwhelm you. But the burden of this complexity is far outweighed by the tool's usefulness: Grants.gov is the only source you need for information about all federal grants. It incorporates more than a thousand programs representing $500 billion in annual grant awards. If you take the time to read the introductory information on the Learn Grants menu found on the home page, you'll find that the site is relatively easy to search.

Supplementing your search with the CFDA

Federal agencies provide 15 different types of funding, including program grants, insurance, loans, and "direct payments for specified use." For information about all 15 types of federal assistance, turn to another federal publication, *Catalog of Federal Domestic Assistance (CFDA)*, which can be found online at https://beta. sam.gov/content/assistance-listings. This website tends to be moved around by the government, so you may have to use a search engine to locate it.

We steer you to Grants.gov because, if grant support is what you're seeking, it's more tailored to your needs and, perhaps, less cumbersome. However, the CFDA website is a powerful tool that you also may want to explore. The two websites use the same catalog numbering system to identify funding opportunities.

Beginning your search with Grants.gov

REMEMBER

As you begin your search, pay attention to whether your organization is eligible to apply to a particular program. Some kinds of federal grants are available only to state and local governments, federally recognized Native American tribal governments, and other specified groups — not necessarily nonprofit organizations.

When opening the home page of Grants.gov, you're invited to search by

>> **Opportunity status:** Choose Posted, which means the funding program has been announced and is open for applications.

>> **Funding instrument type:** You're probably interested in a grant, but a few other forms of financial support are also listed.

>> **Eligibility:** This is the type of entity you represent — perhaps a nonprofit with 501(c)(3) status, a for-profit business, or a city or township.

>> **Category:** You choose among broad subject areas, such as agriculture or health, which is useful if you know you're interested in reviewing the programs offered by the Institute of Museum and Library Services, the Department of Homeland Security, or another specific agency.

>> **Keyword(s):** Within the Search Grants tab, you may use the basic search criteria, such as keyword, or faceted search to narrow your search results.

>> **Funding opportunity number and/or CFDA:** If you happen to know the number assigned to a program that interests you or the Catalog of Federal Domestic Assistance number assigned to it, you can enter that number and — *voilà!* — the program description appears.

Grants.gov can tell you which agencies and offices manage the funds for different grant opportunities. After identifying federal programs of interest, experienced grant seekers usually call, write, or email those offices to confirm the information. That's because even though Grants.gov information is updated frequently, it also ages quickly.

TIP

We outline more information about searching for federal grants and contracts and suggest further steps to take in your research in File 17-4 at www.wiley.com/go/nonprofitkitfd6e.

WARNING

Before you apply for a federal grant, you need to register with Grants.gov. The process, which involves several steps outlined in File 17-4, can take up to two weeks. Begin this process as soon as you decide to apply for federal funding so that delays don't cause you to miss a critical deadline.

Nonfederal government grants

Information about state, county, and municipal grants (for which state or local tax dollars generate money) can be trickier to find than those awarded by federal agencies. That's because the information isn't always compiled in resource guides. Some, but not all, state and city government offices do a good job of informing their constituents about funding opportunities.

During the research process, check the websites of state and local agencies related to your project (such as agencies overseeing education or child services) and visit with local government officials and congressional office staff members. Also, check to see whether your governor's website includes information about available grant programs.

Chapter **18**

Writing an Award-Winning Grant Proposal

E ven though grant-seeking is a highly competitive activity, writing a good grant proposal isn't particularly mysterious or difficult. First you identify a problem and make it compelling, and then you set goals for solving that problem, and, last, you propose a possible solution and a way to test the results. In the course of laying out the plan, you should also assert the special strengths of your organization and a sensible financial plan for the project — in the near term and later. You present your proposal in a readable form that tells a story and conveys your vision in terms both inspiring and practical.

Some proposals are quite long and elaborate. Some are just a few pages. Some are presented on paper, but most are submitted online in a text copy-and-paste format. Your research into funding sources (which we describe in Chapter 17) will uncover the preferences of different foundations and government programs, so you can figure out the best mode of presentation, level of detail, and method for submitting your proposal. You'll encounter many variations, but this chapter shows you the basics of how to write the grant proposal.

TIP

Check out File 18-1 at www.wiley.com/go/nonprofitkitfd6e for a list of web resources related to the topics we cover in this chapter.

Attending to Pre-Proposal Tasks

Generally, a grant writer develops a proposal by talking with staff members, volunteers, or the board about a project idea. Before setting fingers to keyboard, the writer should investigate the answers to these questions:

>> What is the demonstrated need in the community for the work you intend to do?

>> Who are the constituents who will benefit from your efforts? (Find out everything you can about them.)

>> What are others doing in this field?

>> Which particular strengths does your nonprofit bring to the project?

>> Specifically, what do you want to accomplish?

>> What will it cost to do it?

TIP

Sometimes a funding source announces a specific initiative for which it's inviting proposals — called a *request for proposals* (or *RFP*) or a program announcement. When you respond to an RFP, you're trying to convince the foundation or government agency that your nonprofit is the best one for the job.

Perfecting the letter of inquiry

Many funding sources screen proposal ideas before they invite extensive, detailed documents. This enables them to encourage only truly promising requests, saving both themselves and grant seekers the time and effort that is required when reviewing and writing longer proposals.

When you encounter a request for a *letter of inquiry (LOI)*, boil down the essence of the proposal (all eight areas covered in the later section "The Pitch: Writing a Competitive Grant Proposal") into a readable, compelling letter. The letter doesn't ask for a grant directly but, rather, asks for permission to submit more detailed information. Most letters of inquiry are two or three pages long. They may be made up of short answers to a foundation's online forms. Always follow the grant maker's stated preferences.

TIP

At www.wiley.com/go/nonprofitkitfd6e, File 18-2 is a sample letter of inquiry.

Passing the applicant eligibility screening questionnaire

Some funding agencies screen potential applicants by asking them to respond to short questionnaires that are found on the funders' websites. Questions often determine specific eligibility — such as whether the nonprofit organization serves a particular geographic area or the size of its budget. You may have to provide your nonprofit's federal employer identification number (EIN) so that the foundation can confirm with the Internal Revenue Service that you're a qualified 501(c)(3) nonprofit organization. In many cases, if you "pass" one of these surveys, you receive login information that permits you to submit more information — either a letter of inquiry or a full proposal. Usually, you've learned that you're eligible to apply, but you still don't know whether your application is a competitive one.

WARNING

Don't pass off the letter of inquiry or questionnaire as an inconsequential hurdle: First impressions can be lasting impressions.

The Pitch: Writing a Competitive Grant Proposal

Deep down, every good proposal is based on a well-considered plan, and designing that plan is a creative, even fun, part of the task. The differences from funder to funder lie in how to pitch that plan and the order in which its parts are assembled. But the parts themselves are fairly standard, as described in this list:

>> **Cover letter (when requested) and executive summary:** Provide a brief overview of the entire project and its costs, linking the project to the interests of the funding source. Most online applications don't invite cover letters, but they do ask for project summaries.

>> **Introduction or background:** Present the strengths and qualifications of the nonprofit organization.

>> **Statement of need:** Describe the situation that the proposed project will try to improve or eradicate. Convey the direness of the need by including statistics and sources to show evidence of need-supported research.

>> **Goals and measurable or SMART (*specific, measurable, attainable, realistic, and timebound*) objectives and outcomes:** Outline a vision for success in both the near future and the long term.

>> **Methods:** Describe the project activities, who will manage them, the time frame for the project, and the reason that the proposed approach is the best.

>> **Management plan:** List the names and qualifications of staff and/or contracted consultants that will help manage the funded project's implementation strategies.

>> **Evaluation:** Explain how the organization will measure completion of its objectives and outcomes.

>> **Budget:** Present the project's costs and sources of income.

>> **Sustainability or other funding:** Explain how additional funds will be raised if a grant is awarded but doesn't cover all costs. If the program is expected to continue beyond the grant period, how will future costs be covered?

Your proposal should be compelling to the foundation you're addressing, but be careful not to overstate what your nonprofit can and will do. If a grant is awarded, those promises can become binding in the foundation's grant agreement.

In this section, we cover each of these parts in detail.

Just like other nonprofit organizations, foundations have mission statements and goals. As a grant writer, you're working to convince your reader of a clear connection between the foundation's mission and your organization's work.

At www.wiley.com/go/nonprofitkitfd6e, check out Files 18-3 through 18-6 for samples of different types of full proposals.

Starting out with the cover letter and executive summary

Technically, the *cover letter* isn't part of the proposal narrative and may not even be requested by grant makers. When the cover letter is requested, it's attached to the top of the proposal (the first page of your grant proposal package), where it serves as an introduction to the document's primary points. One of its key roles is to convey how the proposal addresses the foundation's stated priorities. Cover letters often require a signature from the executive director and/or board president.

The letter mentions any contact the organization has had with the funding source. For example, you may say, "When we were introduced at the new teen center's ribbon-cutting ceremony last week, I was pleased to hear you talk about how important playing basketball was for you when you were growing up. Here at Backboard Nation, we're working to refurbish basketball courts in parks and playgrounds across the city."

Although you always want to lay out the basics of the request — how much money is needed and for what — you also can use the letter to say something about your personal connection to the cause. The letter should close with clear, specific information about the contact person to whom the funding source should direct any questions.

REMEMBER

Keep your cover letter to one page. Do not regress and make the letter look like a letter of inquiry.

The body of the actual grant proposal begins with an executive summary (similar to an abstract for a report), when requested, and contains an overview of its key ideas. You usually begin the Summary section with a one-sentence overview of the project and how much money is being requested in the proposal. Next you include the primary ideas from every section of the proposal (boiled down to one or two sentences per section). Finally, close the executive summary with the prognosis for future programming and funding for the program.

TIP

Don't use exactly the same wording to describe your project idea in the cover letter and in the project summary. You don't want to bore the reader, and you don't want to miss the opportunity to write in a more personal manner in the cover letter.

Introducing your organization and its operating history

Some proposals contain *introductions*. Others call this section *background information* or *organizational history.* However you label it, this part of the proposal describes the nonprofit organization that's seeking money.

Usually this section begins with a brief history of the nonprofit, its mission, and its major accomplishments. Then you describe the current programs as well as the constituents. After including these standard ingredients, you can draw on whatever other credentials recommend the organization for the work you're about to propose. Here are some areas you can mention:

>> Media coverage

>> Citations and awards

>> The credentials and/or experience of the nonprofit's leadership

>> Other agencies that refer clients to the nonprofit

>> Major grants received from other sources

>> Results of recent evaluations of your nonprofit's work

Although you're not yet describing the project idea, the items you introduce here should back up your nonprofit's qualifications to do the proposed work. Suppose that an after-school program for teenagers offers multiple programs — athletics, arts, and youth-led volunteer work. If the grant proposal seeks money to expand the volunteer program, the writer can tell the story of how that volunteer work began and evolved, where the teens have provided services, and who has praised their contributions.

TIP

If your organization is brand-new and you have no accomplishments or accolades to describe in this section, tell the story of how and why the organization was created, its mission and purpose, and the qualifications of its founders and board members.

If yours is the only organization that offers this program, mention it here. Funders like to know who else is addressing the same issues and how you differentiate yourself as an attractive source to receive financial support.

WARNING

You may be tempted to write on and on (and on and on and on) about an organization's history, philosophy, or mission — don't drag this section down by including too many details, using too much eloquent verbiage, or overstating the truth. One or two clear, factual paragraphs on these subjects is plenty.

Documenting the need for funding

A grant writer begins to shape the argument behind the proposal plan in a *statement of need* — sometimes called a *problem statement.*

This section brings forward the reasons behind the program for which your organization is seeking money (or behind all the organization's work if you're seeking general operating support). It does so by describing the needs of the constituents you will serve. It should incorporate substantial data to support the need for funding. All data or statistics incorporated in this section of your grant proposal's narrative should be cited (footnoted) or should include in-text references. And it should capture the funding decision-maker's attention — making them want to read on.

REMEMBER

You shouldn't describe your "need" as a lack of money but rather as a situation in the lives of your target service population, whether they're tree frogs, retired adults, or former racehorses. Don't start to solve the problem in your statement of need.

Setting goals, SMART objectives, and proposed outcomes

After you've described a need, the next step is to introduce what the nonprofit intends to achieve if it takes on the proposed project. You haven't yet described the project activities, but this section jumps ahead to show what can be accomplished if the project is a success. Why? First you pique the reader's interest and concern (in the statement of need), and then you demonstrate the possibility of a better future (in goals, objectives, and outcomes), and then you explain how to achieve that vision (in the Methods section).

Goals, objectives, and outcomes are related–but–different terms. You can find out more about them in Chapter 8, which discusses planning. The following list gives an overview of these terms:

>> *Goals* are broad, general results. They may be somewhat lofty. Goals start with verbs in the present tense, like *provide, develop, deliver, educate, empower, assist,* and *acquire.* Please do not add *ing* or *ed* (verb endings) to the root verb. Starting with a verb — instead of the words *Our goal is to. . .* or *The goal is to* — takes away from the dynamics of your goal statement(s) and uses up extra words, characters, and spaces in online copy-and-paste input-limited grant application templates.

>> *Objectives* should be SMART: *s*pecific, *m*easurable, *a*chievable (or attainable), *r*ealistic, and *t*imebound (or have a timeline for happening). What percentage (%) increase or decrease of change do you want to achieve and in which time frame, involving whom and where (tree frogs or racehorses in Atlanta), and by when (timeline)?

>> *Outcomes* are short-term, intermediate-term, and long-term. They relate to your SMART objectives, answering the question "What will our target population have achieved by the end of our grant funding?" What if you provide antismoking classes to students entering high school, reaching every first-year teen in four school districts? Your objective may be the percent of those teens who pass an exit test. Your short-term or intermediate-term outcomes may be *Increased gateway drug use resiliency*, demonstrating the social behavior changes as a result of the antismoking classes. The long-term outcome may be that, three years later, a lower-than-average percentage of the students who completed the classes begins smoking in high school.

REMEMBER

You want the outcomes to be significant, but you also have to be careful not to overstate how much the project can claim or measure. If a grant proposal says that a nonprofit intends to achieve a long–term outcome, the organization should be prepared to follow up with participants in the future.

Presenting (ta-da!) your project idea with evidence-based solutions

At last, it's time to explain the project idea. Who will do what to whom and over what period? If you're writing your proposal for a research project, generally this section is called *procedures.* For most other types of projects, it's called *methods* or *methodology.* Regardless of whether funders ask for methods or methodology or the *program design* or the plan of action, they are all the same item. You are being asked to write an in-depth description of how your nonprofit organization will solve the problems presented in the *needs* statement, or statement of the problem.

WARNING

Never write about problems in the statement of need that your grant award won't be able to solve or reduce, because your program design or methodology will have to address every need you've written about earlier.

Although the program design contains the idea that inspired the organization to seek funding, the writing should never be dull or mundane.

Your written response to the funder's questions should include heavily researched best practices, also known as *evidence-based solutions.* A *best practice,* as it relates to grant-writing, is a method or technique that has been generally accepted as superior to any alternatives because it produces results that are superior to those achieved by other means or because it has become a standard way of doing things. As the grant applicant, you can't just pull your solutions out of thin air or keep doing what you've already been doing or what you've seen other nonprofit organizations doing. No, you have to present solutions, trainings, programs, and services that have been implemented by larger, national government-funded grantees.

REMEMBER

When you search for evidence-based solutions, you need to make sure that your best practices come from either the creator of the best practice, for example, US Department of Education, or another reputable source. Wikipedia should not be your go-to for citing best practices. Trusted sources include government agencies, foundations, colleges and universities, and nationally known nonprofit organizations.

For example, if you search online for the phrase **best practices for designing a summer day care program for children with special needs,** here are just a couple of the helpful models you find:

>> This link takes you to a US General Services Administration PDF titled *Child Care Center Design Guide,* which provides info and insight obtained from multiple care researchers and practitioners: https://www.gsa.gov/cdnstatic/designguidesmall.pdf

>> This link takes you to a California Department of Education PDF titled *Inclusion Works! Creating Child Care Programs That Promote Belonging for Children with Disabilities,* 2nd Edition: www.cde.ca.gov/sp/cd/re/documents/inclusionworks2ed.pdf

TIP

A good program design section opens with an overview of the approach and then leads the reader through key phases in the project's development. It offers enough detail so that readers can imagine the project clearly but not so much that they sink into the daily grind. Another technique to preserve vitality is the use of charts or graphs to break up and complement the descriptive text.

Many projects require a few months of preparation before they can be launched. Factor in time for hiring and training staff, purchasing and installing equipment, identifying research subjects, or performing other necessary preliminary steps.

REMEMBER

Because this section contains all the project details, you may accidentally leave out or forget important information. These two topics are often overlooked:

>> **Hiring:** If you need to hire new staff to do the project work, be sure to discuss the hiring process, job descriptions, and qualifications. See Chapter 11 for ideas on hiring paid staff.

>> **Marketing:** Just because you create a fantastic proposal doesn't mean that anyone will show up to take advantage of it. Your proposal must explain how your organization plans to spread the word about this new project and inspire the target population to become involved. Chapter 13 provides tips on marketing your program to the public.

The proposal must explain what the organization will do and why the organization is taking that approach — the rationale. The reason may be that nobody has ever done it this way. The reason may be that the organization has tested the approach in a pilot program and knows that it works. The reason may be that another organization in another part of the country has tested this method.

Some funding sources ask you to fill out a table with columns in which you describe your goals, the *inputs* (resources you'll put into the project), strategies (also called *activities*), short-term objectives, intermediate-term outcomes, and long-term outcomes. These tables go by several names — often they're called *logic models.*

TIP

We introduce logic models in Chapter 9. Take a look at File 9-3 at www.wiley.com/go/nonprofitkitfd6e to see an example of a logic model.

WARNING

In an effort to raise as much money as possible, you may be tempted to change your programs to match a particular foundation's interests. Your board and management should carefully assess new project ideas to make sure they fit the organization's mission. Otherwise, the nonprofit may drift away from addressing its purpose.

Presenting the management plan

Funders want to know who will manage your grant-funded project. What are their job titles, past experience related to the grant-request subject area, how many hours per week (full-time equivalent) each position will work on the project, and, if the position is a new one made possible by the grant funding, what will the job description entail? This is not a lengthy part of the narrative; however, it must be addressed before writing your evaluation narrative.

Explaining how results will be measured

If you've carefully shaped the Goals, Objectives, and Outcomes section of the proposal, the desired project results are clear. The *Evaluation* section, then, explains how the organization will measure whether it met those goals, objectives, and outcomes.

This section says who will conduct the evaluation and why that person or consulting group is right for the job; what information is already known about the situation or population served; what instrument(s) will be used to measure the project's results; and how the finished report will be used.

Different kinds of evaluation are appropriate at different stages of a project. A nonprofit with a brand-new effort may want to spend the first year analyzing its internal efficiency, balance of responsibilities, and general productivity before beginning an in-depth study of whether outcomes are being achieved. In that first year, the most important question may be, "How can we make it run better?"

Some organizations evaluate all their projects with project staff. Who's better suited to understand the details and nuances of the work? Who else can grasp the goals and objectives of the project so quickly? Of course, the opposing view is that you get biased results by asking staff members whose ideas may have shaped the programs and whose livelihoods may depend on continuation of programs. Yet, outside consultants are more expensive, and they, too, are employed by the nonprofit organization and may bring some biases to the evaluation.

Here are some common questions addressed in evaluations (progressing from basic to complex):

>> What activities did you complete? Were project funds spent according to the proposal plan?

>> How many people are being served and by how many units of service (hours of counseling, copies of publications, and so on)?

>> How do consumers of the organization's services rate the quality of those services?

>> How does this organization's work compare to industry standards for effective work of this type?

>> What changes has the program made in the lives of the constituents served?

TIP

Often a nonprofit can discover a lot about the effectiveness of its work by analyzing information that it already gathers. For example, an organization may have on file intake and exit interviews with staff and clients, videotapes of activities, or comments submitted to its website.

If your organization plans to gather data from new sources (such as surveys, interviews, and focus groups), the proposal should explain what those sources are, who will design the instruments to be used, who will gather the information, and who will analyze the results.

Talking about the budget

It's time for your proposal to present information about project costs and the other funding that's available. If your organization offers only one service, the organization's budget is the same as the *program budget,* or *project budget.* If the proposal seeks funds for an activity that is one of many services the nonprofit provides, it's presented as a smaller piece of the overall budget.

TIP

Chapter 12 discusses how to compute the indirect costs that all programs within an organization share. Different foundations and government agencies have different attitudes about covering the indirect costs associated with projects. In late 2013, the federal Office of Management and Budget (OMB) issued an overhaul of federal grant policies that made it clear that nonprofits' indirect costs were legitimate and should be reimbursed. This OMB decision has been influential and appreciated by nonprofits. Check with the organization to which you're applying to see whether it limits how much can be charged to indirect costs or to management and fundraising expenses.

REMEMBER

If you have a federal grant, you have two options for the percentage of your indirect cost rate.

Option 1: Your organization will need to negotiate an appropriate indirect cost rate based on your nonprofit's size and structure. After you've negotiated a rate for your organization with the authorized federal cognizant agency (US Department of Health and Human Services, or HHS), the agreed-on rate applies to any government grant from any federal agency.

Option 2: In 2018, the federal government created a flat rate to streamline the negotiations and time involved in negotiating indirect cost rates with potential federal grant applicants. The OMB issued new rules that require governments at all levels — local, state, and federal — that contract with nonprofits via grant awards or competitive contract awards to reimburse those nonprofits for their reasonable indirect cost (often mistakenly called *overhead* or *administrative costs*) when federal dollars are part of the funding stream. The *de minimus* rate is applicable to federal grant application budgets submitted along with your grant applications to one of the 26 federal grant-making agencies — it's a flat rate of 10 percent. For more about the federal grant-seeking process, pick up a copy of *Grant Writing For Dummies*, 6th Edition, written by yours truly, Beverly Browning (Wiley).

Back to the project budget: Your budget should be clear, reasonable, and well considered. Keep a worksheet of budget assumptions with the grant file in case anyone asks months later how you computed the numbers it contains. Foundations don't want to believe that an organization is inflating the budget, nor do they want to think that the applicant is trying to make a proposal more competitive by requesting less than the true amount needed. Either approach — budgeting too high or too low in relationship to the cost of a project — can raise a red flag for funders.

Unless the foundation is willing to consider a proposal for 100 percent of the project costs, the proposal budget should include both income and expenses. Some foundations ask for the information in a particular format. For those foundations that don't require a special budget format, here are some general standards that apply to the presentation:

>> Income should head the budget, followed by expenses.

>> If the organization has multiple income sources, contributed sources should be listed apart from earned sources. Within contributed sources, a writer usually lists grants first, followed by corporate gifts and contributions from individuals.

>> All expenses related to personnel costs — salaries, benefits, and consulting fees — come first in the expense half of the budget. Usually, personnel costs are subtotaled.

>> Nonpersonnel costs — rent, printing, and materials and supplies, for example — follow the personnel costs and are also subtotaled.

>> Some kinds of project budgets allow for contingency funds of a certain percentage of the project's projected costs. These funds are usually listed last among expenses.

>> Budget footnotes can explain anything that may be difficult for a reader to understand.

REMEMBER

The budget resembles a spine for the rest of the proposal and supports every aspect of the plan. The costs of every activity in the Methods and Evaluation sections should be included.

Keep in mind that some project budgets seem simple and straightforward when, in reality, they're more complex. Say that an agency wants to purchase a piece of equipment. It researches the cost and writes it down as its one-and-only budget item. This approach may be foolhardy: Other costs may include shipping and installation, insurance, maintenance, supplies, and training of staff.

TIP

Check out Files 18-7 and 18-8 at www.wiley.com/go/nonprofitkitfd6e for sample foundation budget forms. You also can find sample proposals and their accompanying budgets at the same site.

Showing where the rest of the money comes from: The sustainability section

Willingness to cover the full cost of a project varies from foundation to foundation and from agency to agency. Some like to "own" a project and have their name strongly associated with it; therefore, they may be willing to cover full costs. Others like to be one of several supporters so that the nonprofit isn't entirely dependent on them. That way, the project can go on even if the funder can't continue to support it in a future year.

In Chapter 14, we introduce the age-old concept of not putting all your eggs in one basket. Between many foundations' reluctance to pay for 100 percent of a project's costs and their preference for offering short-term support, if you seek a grant for a new project, you want to know how you can cover the balance of the costs in the present and all the costs when the initial project grants have been spent. Foundations reviewing your grant proposals want to know the same information.

Your *sustainability plan* — addressing these needs for additional and future funding — should be clear and reasonable. Because a nonprofit can't assume it will receive every grant for which it applies, a foundation understands when a nonprofit has applied for more grant funding than the program costs. If a nonprofit lists another foundation as a possible source of income for a project, it doesn't necessarily have to have received that grant, but the prospect should be plausible. The size of the grant should be appropriate to others awarded by the agency, and the focus of the foundation should be aligned with the project request.

When listing sources of potential funding, note whether the funding is *proposed* (the application has been submitted), *committed* (the grant has been awarded or promised but funds have not been received), or *received* (the money is in hand). Funders like to have a general idea of where you are in the fundraising process.

WARNING

Foundation staff members talk with colleagues at other foundations. Never lie about having submitted a proposal or having received a grant from another foundation. That lie can undermine your request (and future requests, too)!

Generally, foundations hope to see nonprofit organizations growing less dependent on grants over time and are happy to see proposal budgets projecting future increases in earned revenue or individual contributions. Here are some possible sustaining sources you may describe in your proposal:

>> A government contract to continue a valuable service after it has been developed and tested

>> The sale of publications, recordings, or services based on the project

>> A membership drive

>> A major donor campaign

Some proposals don't need to address these concerns. They seek support for projects that begin and end in short periods. For example, a grant proposal may support the publication of a study of an agency's work. After the agency edits, designs, and posts the report on its website, future funding isn't needed. For certain other kinds of projects, future funding is vital. For example, you wouldn't want to start a recreation center for low-income youths and have to close it after a few years. The lack of program continuity can have a negative effect on clients.

Appending requested attachments

A proposal usually needs an appendix or attachments. Four key items that are routinely included in the appendix (and often identified by foundations as required enclosures) are

>> Proof of 501(c)(3) status from the IRS (in the form of a determination letter). (This may not be requested if you've provided an EIN in response to an online application questionnaire.)

>> List of the board of directors (and of any advisory boards)

>> Current year's organization budget

>> Prior year's financial statement (audited preferred)

Other common appendix items include

>> A list of major grants received in recent years

>> An organizational chart outlining staff and board roles

>> Copies of media clippings about the agency

>> Job descriptions and/or résumés of key staff

>> Samples of evaluations or reports

>> A copy of the strategic plan

>> Agency brochures and program announcements

>> Letters of commitment

WARNING Don't include attachments unless the grant instructions clearly ask for them. Funders receive many applications at a time and don't want to sort through information that isn't relevant to the proposal.

TIP At www.wiley.com/go/nonprofitkitfd6e, File 18-9 provides a list of steps to take for finishing and submitting your grant request.

Familiarizing Yourself with Other Types of Written Funding Requests

If you prepare a grant proposal following the format we describe in earlier sections, you'll have in hand a useful document, suitable for submission to many foundations. However, grant-writing isn't a field in which one size fits all or even one approach fits all. So, in the next few sections, we describe some common situations that call for variations on the basic proposal.

Trolling for corporate grants or sponsors

Proposals addressed to corporations and company-sponsored foundations are generally brief. A two-page letter or email is an excellent approach.

TIPS FOR ONLINE APPLICATIONS

More and more foundations are inviting or requiring applicants to apply online. Online application systems vary widely, so here are a few things to keep in mind:

- Well before any deadlines are due, check the funder's website to see whether you need to create an account before submitting a proposal. This procedure can take a few days.

- Online applications can be tricky. Some don't work on certain web browsers. Others get overloaded and time-out your submission.

- Plan ahead by gathering documents you want to include with your proposal and by setting up your electronic signature, if one is requested on the application.

- In the foundation's instructions for applicants, pay attention to whether you can save your work in the online system and come back to finish it later. If you can't, then draft, edit, and save your proposal before you start working on the foundation's online form.

- Check to see whether the funder specifies a word count or character count. Track the length of any drafts you write so that you don't have difficulty fitting the sections into the online form. And don't exceed the length! It may not be obvious to you as the applicant, but often the funder can't see any words or sentences that run longer than the prescribed length.

- Some online applications consist of a series of questions that aren't revealed until you've logged in to the system and begun filling out the form. When writing such a proposal, set aside a generous amount of time to concentrate on each answer. Don't skip a question just because you have answered it elsewhere. Either answer it again in a reworded response or type *This information is included in Section #.* Also, even though your prose is broken up by the system's form, read your answers carefully and in order, as if they were a continuous document. Paying attention to the flow of your prose will make your proposal more interesting and clearer.

- If the funder's online system allows you to upload a PDF of your proposal, we recommend that you do so. We've had problems with using the Track Changes function in Microsoft Word to mark edits, and — even if we've saved a final, clean version of the proposal — having those edits reappear when the document is uploaded.

- Always look back over your drafted proposal before pushing the Upload or Send button. If possible, save it for a day to read with fresh eyes. Some application systems allow you to save drafts online before submitting them.

- Submit the proposal at least 24 hours before it's due to allow time to address any technical difficulties. It's best to prepare ahead so that if you encounter difficulties, you still have time to try other approaches or to contact the funder for more information.

- Don't forget to press Send! Trust us — this happens. In most systems when it arises, the foundations are aware that you've prepared a document, but they can't read it.

Here's what to do in your proposal:

>> Ask for a specific contribution early in the letter. If you've already had contact with the funder, mention it.

>> If applicable, mention the involvement of any company employees on your board or volunteer committees.

>> Describe the need or problem to be addressed.

>> Explain what your organization plans to do if the grant is awarded.

>> Provide information about your nonprofit organization and its strengths and accomplishments.

>> Include appropriate budget data. If the budget is more than half a page long, include it as an attachment.

>> Discuss how the project will be sustained in the future.

>> Describe how your organization can acknowledge the gift publicly and provide visibility to the corporation.

>> Make a strong, compelling closing statement.

Some nonprofits seek sponsorships from corporations to help underwrite special programs, such as marathons, museum exhibitions, or beach clean-ups. Approaching a corporation about a sponsorship resembles proposing a business agreement.

Your organization may, for example, suggest to a local business that if it sponsors your charity's annual walk a thon, its name will be included on banners and T-shirts that will be seen by 50,000 people.

REMEMBER

In seeking sponsorships from corporations, keep in mind the difference between a qualified sponsorship and advertising. In a qualified sponsorship, an individual or a company makes a sponsorship payment to a 501(c)(3) nonprofit without an arrangement or expectation that the payer will receive a benefit in return. The nonprofit might acknowledge that sponsorship through use of the donor's name or logo or slogans, but may not specifically endorse that donor's products. The nonprofit also might provide goods or services of insubstantial value to the company in recognition of the gift. The sponsorship relationship is considered advertising when the nonprofit specifically endorses purchase of the company's products or services. Revenue to the nonprofit from advertising sales likely is unrelated business income and potentially subject to taxes on that income. The IRS website (www.irs.gov) provides additional details about such unrelated business income taxes (UBIT).

A sponsorship pitch usually starts with a phone call that is followed by a brief, confirming email. You can attach to that email a list of possible sponsorship benefits and the level of contribution expected for each.

At www.wiley.com/go/nonprofitkitfd6e, File 18-10 provides sample company foundation guidelines and File 18-11 shows a sample letter proposal to a corporation.

Seeking general operating support

If you're seeking funds for general operating support, your proposal needs to make an argument for the work of the entire nonprofit rather than for a specific project. In this type of request, some of the information about current activities, which is often included in the Introduction or Background Information sections, should be moved to the Methods section. The grant-making organization judges the application based on overall organizational strength and the nonprofit's role in its field.

If you're tailoring a proposal for general operating support, we recommend that you

>> Prepare an introduction that covers the agency's purpose, goals, and current programs. Describe its leadership (board and staff) and its history.

>> Describe, in the statement of need, current challenges the organization faces as it works to fulfill its mission.

>> When preparing the section on goals, objectives, and outcomes, address the external goals (how the nonprofit plans to serve its constituents) and internal goals (such as training the board of directors to fundraise).

>> Use the Methods section to describe the agency's planned activities for the year ahead.

>> In the Evaluation section, describe various means the agency uses to assess and improve its programs.

Asking for capacity building funding

The purpose of capacity building requests is to help your nonprofit build strengths in multiple areas of operation. These types of requests typically ask for funds to develop strategies for new programs; strengthen your fundraising, volunteer management, and accounting structures; or other consultant-providing services to build the capacity of your nonprofit organization. When the funding has been spent and all of the expert helpers leave your organization, it should be on solid ground in every area of consulting.

Grant makers that award capacity building grants typically publish the types of activities that can be funded. You can find them in grant research databases like the Foundation Directory Online (https://candid.org/find-funding) or Instrumentl (www.instrumentl.com?grsf=t2nrr3). Following is a list of areas within your nonprofit that can benefit from capacity building consulting. Every one of these areas is related to the operational framework of your nonprofit organization. Remember, solutions for strengthening your organization's capacity usually don't come from within (from staff and board members). Solutions come from paid consultants with decades of experience in each of these areas. Capacity building grant funding is intended to pay for the following areas of organizational improvement:

Organizational Development and Capacity Building

Capital campaign feasibility studies

Strategic planning

Board development

Executive transitions/succession planning

Program evaluation

Exploratory strategic alliances

Collaborative learning opportunities

Emergency and business continuity planning

Staff or board training and development

Conferences

Workshops/trainings

Consulting services

Program design

Volunteer recruitment and management

Board member recruitment

Endowment development planning

Marketing

Website and e-commerce development

Social media branding

Communications

Donor development efforts

Seed money: Proposing to form a new nonprofit

Some foundations specialize in seed funding for new projects and new organizations. A *seed funding proposal* has two key ingredients: careful assessment of the problem to be addressed and special qualifications its founders bring to its creation. Here's a quick outline of a proposal for a new endeavor:

>> Background information introduces the people who are creating the organization, their vision, the way they identified the idea, and steps they've taken to realize their vision.

>> The problem statement thoughtfully presents evidence that the founders have observed and learned about the needs to be addressed.

>> Although the goals may be lofty, stated objectives and outcomes should be reasonable considering the developing state of the organization.

>> Methods present plans for the first year or two of activities. They include discussion of how the organization will be structured and how services will be offered.

>> Evaluation plans may go easy during the organization's initial phases. Founders may be testing basic ideas for their feasibility and efficiency for a year or two before studying a program in depth.

>> The budget is likely to be the entire organizational budget. Some seed grant funders are willing to cover such start-up costs as equipment purchases or deposits for renting an office.

>> The Sustainability section should outline basic plans for supporting the nonprofit in the future (unless it addresses a discrete problem that may be solved within a few years).

TIP

The foundation may be willing to support a feasibility study that tests the viability of the seed project — how distinctive it is and who are its likeliest sources of support.

Following Through after Receiving Funding

As is true with any good fundraising, your grant proposal is part of a relationship that you want to develop and maintain over time. A funder who doesn't want to be bothered will generally tell you. In most cases, we recommend these actions:

>> **Thank them.** Thank the foundation at the time the grant is awarded, and acknowledge arrival of the check or wire transfer when the money shows up.

>> **Recognize the gift.** For most kinds of grant awards, list the funder in your printed materials. It's always a good practice to check with funders about whether and how they want to be listed, by sending them a brief letter or email with the text you plan to use. Some foundations tell you in their award letters how to acknowledge them.

>> **Keep them informed.** Your funder should hear from you at times when you're not requesting money. Don't overwhelm your funder, but sending someone a copy of good media coverage or inviting them to see your program in action are good ways to build a relationship.

>> **Let them hear bad news from you first.** If your organization is forced to move, a key staff member decides to leave, or you lose a contract you need in order to complete the project you proposed, make certain that your funder hears the bad news from you, not as a rumor. Let the funder know the steps you're taking to resolve the situation. Your organization's integrity is one of its most important assets.

>> **Prepare to submit reports on time.** Most grant awards will tell you when and how to submit interim and final reports. Schedule time in your calendar to gather the information you need and write that report as soon as you know the due date. The foundation will likely send a reminder as the due date approaches, but being prepared and submitting reports on time makes a good impression and sets the stage for a possible future grant request. When you fail to submit reports in a timely manner or do not submit any reports to the funder, you may eliminate the possibility of your organization being able to receive a grant from the funder in the future.

>> **Share what you've learned.** If your funder provides reporting guidelines, follow them. If not, look back at the goals, objectives, and outcomes you identified in your grant proposal and write about the steps you took to accomplish them and whether you were successful. Of course, you and the funder hope that the project has met its objectives, and initial outcomes are promising, but if it hasn't been successful, sharing what you learned — your thoughtful analysis of what went wrong and how you might adjust the program in the future — will be deeply appreciated.

In the beginning of this chapter we mention that foundations have missions just as other kinds of nonprofits do. Just remember, they can't fulfill their missions if they aren't learning alongside their grantees.

Chapter **19**

Capital Campaigns: Finding Lasting Resources

As a nonprofit organization matures, its staff and board may become eager to obtain resources that can stabilize the organization. One option is to raise *capital* — money to make specific, usually long-term, financial investments.

Some organizations raise capital funds for buying property or building facilities. Other raise such funds for *ventures* — money they put aside for major program innovations. Still others raise capital for cash reserves (funds available to grow and adapt in the future) or *endowments* — money they permanently invest, with the investment returns providing a source of annual income. If you're the director of a nonprofit taking on a capital campaign, imagine yourself as suddenly having two jobs: leading your organization and its programs and leading its capital project. Can you picture yourself wearing these two hats? Exhausting thought, isn't it? However, if the campaign project goes well, it can attract new donors and attention to your nonprofit. That benefit, combined with new resources to invest in your work, can make those two hats worth wearing.

Most capital campaigns, as varied as their purposes are, share a set of fundraising activities. Not every organization is positioned to make those strategies work. Read ahead and proceed cautiously before stepping onto the capital campaign trail.

Check out File 19-1 at `www.wiley.com/go/nonprofitkitfd6e` for a list of web resources related to the topics we cover in this chapter.

Beginning the Funding Plan

Suppose your adult literacy program wants to share its innovative teaching materials broadly through a series of books, but setting up an online publication-and-distribution program requires a big initial investment. Maybe your nonprofit school for children with hearing loss balances its budget each year, but it depends heavily on a small number of income sources. Having annual investment returns from an endowment may allow it to provide scholarships for children who can't pay full tuition rates. Or say you've found the building of your organization's dreams. It's just around the corner from where you currently serve clients, and it's bigger and better than your current building. Better yet, it's for sale at a reasonable price. You need money to buy it and money to make repairs.

If funds are contributed to your organization for an endowment, that money must be set aside and invested in accordance with state laws regarding endowments. It isn't liquid — if your nonprofit encounters cash flow problems, it should not borrow from the endowment to pay its bills.

In each of these cases, you need to raise a significant amount of money that's above and beyond your normal annual fundraising. Where do you begin? Capital fundraising, of course! However, keep in mind that it requires you to analyze your organization's situation and plan carefully and thoroughly. Not every organization is positioned to succeed at capital fundraising. You need to

>> **Preplan.** Gather information about technical assistance available to you, review your donor records, and create a rough campaign budget. If you're raising funds for an endowment, do you have access to good asset management advice that can ensure it's invested wisely?

>> **Develop your case.** Brainstorm with staff and board members.

>> **Test the project's feasibility.** Meet with a select group of potential contributors and gauge their interest. Consider the timing of your campaign: Will you compete with other campaigns?

>> **Evaluate the results.** Weigh the information from the interviews against your initial goal and then refine your goal and plan.

WARNING

An unsuccessful capital campaign can cost your organization money, hurt its reputation, and demoralize your staff and board. If your research suggests that you won't succeed, do *not* be foolhardy and forge ahead anyway.

Preplanning your campaign

After your board decides that it may want to raise funds for a capital project, seek outside assistance in the form of workshops, classes, or consulting. Convincing yourself that your capital campaign can work is easy, so test your vision on others. Here are some possible resources:

>> A program officer at a local foundation or staff in your city's economic development office or regional community loan fund may be able to suggest nearby resources.

>> The Nonprofit Finance Fund (www.nonprofitfinancefund.org) may offer programs in your area, including low-cost consultations, tools to analyze your financial position, workshops about raising capital, and loans for capital projects.

>> Your board may contain members with professional experience in financial lending and investing, architecture, construction, real estate, city government, and law — all can provide valuable assistance. If your board doesn't have such professional skills, its members may know professionals who do.

You need to begin raising funds from individuals and institutions that know your organization and care deeply about its work. Assess your organization's primary sources of contributed income. How detailed and accurate are your donor records? Who's been donating money to your cause and at what level? Critically important in this scan of supporters is identifying a person or a small team of people with resources, dedication, and good connections who would be willing to lead your campaign.

REMEMBER

When identifying possible resources for your capital campaign, don't overlook loans, which often play an important role in facility projects, both as standard mortgages and to help organizations complete projects on time. Often donors of large gifts don't write checks for the full amount of their pledges immediately, so organizations borrow some of the money they need to finish construction while waiting to receive those gifts.

If you're interested in loans, find the name of the federal community-development investment fund in your region. (Visit the Coalition of Community Development Financial Institutions at www.cdfi.org to view its list of members in all 50 states and the District of Columbia.) Also investigate whether any local foundations make program-related investments (low-interest loans) to nonprofits or guarantee bank loans for nonprofits.

Developing a rough budget

Before you test your project to find out whether it's feasible, you need assistance figuring out what it will cost. A common mistake organizations make is forgetting that raising money costs money. They need to dedicate staff time and invest in marketing materials and events. Often they hire outside consultants or new fundraising staff to assist them.

For example, if you want revenues from an endowment to cover five $10,000 scholarships, you need to raise at least $1 million. Your board may set a different policy, but most nonprofit organizations figure they can expect to earn between 3 percent and 5 percent on their endowments and spend at that rate each year without depleting the money they've put aside. When interest rates are very low, the board may decide to spend a smaller percentage earned on the endowment, which requires you to increase your fundraising goal, but we stick with the $1 million goal for this example. If you estimate that meeting that goal will take you a year-and-a-half, you may want to budget for

>> A skilled fundraising consultant who will spend an average of ten hours per week on your project

>> Printed materials and a project web page describing your organization and the fundraising campaign

>> Funds to cover the cost of meeting with prospective donors — travel and meals

>> Money to invest in recognizing and thanking donors, including a celebratory event at the culmination of the campaign

Budgeting for building projects is complex. If you identify a plot of land you want to build on or an existing building you want to renovate, you need to begin with rough estimates and develop a specific budget later — after you secure architectural drawings, construction permits from your city or county, and bids from contractors.

As you begin developing a budget, find out about the construction rules you need to follow. A local architect or city appraiser/inspector should be able to tell you which enhancements you're required to include in your building. For example, the Americans with Disabilities Act (ADA) establishes an important set of requirements. Buildings for public use must offer ramps and elevators for wheelchair users; appropriately placed plumbing, railings, and equipment; and large-print signs or audible signals. You may think to budget for the obvious, more-visible modifications that are needed, but an experienced professional can point out more subtle requirements that you may overlook.

REMEMBER

Just because a building is in use doesn't mean you can move right in and begin operating your programs there. Building codes are closely tied to the building's function. Rules for classrooms, for example, sometimes change according to the age of the children. And rooms in which large numbers of people gather are likely to have stricter safety requirements than those rooms used by individuals as offices. Building codes often change over time, and when a building changes hands or its use changes, it must then comply with the most recent requirements.

TIP

At www.wiley.com/go/nonprofitkitfd6e, you can find a checklist from the Nonprofit Finance Fund on hard and soft costs (see File 19-2), and three sample capital project budgets (see Files 19-3, 19-4, and 19-5).

Testing feasibility

Remember that tried-and-true method for buying a used car? The one where you circle the vehicle, kicking all the tires? An organization's capital campaign starts with that kind of tire-kicking, except that it's called a *feasibility study*, which is research that tests the hypothesis that you can raise the amount of money you need. Four feasibility study test points are

>> **Tire One:** How much money does this organization have the capacity to raise?

>> **Tire Two:** For this particular need?

>> **Tire Three:** At this location and at this time?

>> **Tire Four:** Is that enough money to meet the campaign's goals?

The accuracy of the feasibility study is important to the capital campaign. Whoever conducts it has to have enthusiasm for the project yet be able to listen carefully to the direct and indirect messages conveyed in the interviews. The person conducting the study must interview key leaders in the organization along with its current supporters and others whose support of the project would be critical to its success.

REMEMBER

Nonprofits often use a consultant for feasibility studies for this reason: The person is a step removed from the organization, and therefore interview subjects are more likely to be frank. However, if the consultant is not enthusiastic or doesn't think that the campaign is possible, the consultant can and should be discharged before they poison the process.

Leading the way with the board

Whether or not an organization's board includes wealthy individuals, all its members should contribute to the campaign. In fact, the full board's willingness to support the campaign is essential to its success. Potential donors who aren't board members are likely to ask whether you have 100 percent board participation.

REMEMBER

Board members are expected to lead the way. Their contributions may not be the largest, but they should be made in the campaign's earliest phases.

In addition, the size of a donor's gift (in relation to the amount the donor can afford) is some indication of enthusiasm. If a penniless playwright who serves on the board pledges $10,000 over five years toward a capital campaign for a theater, that person is making as clear a sign of enthusiasm as a wealthy banker on the board who makes a gift of $1 million. If the wealthy banker pledges $10,000 over five years, it suggests either that the board has a malcontent or that the project is unsupportable.

Conducting feasibility study interviews

A typical feasibility study interview opens with an overview of the proposed project, emphasizing why the nonprofit selected the project and how it can enhance the organization's programs and better serve its constituents. Next, the interviewer describes how much money the project needs and how, in general, the organization plans to raise it. If any major donors are already involved, the interviewer mentions their levels of support. Finally, the interviewer suggests a possible donation to the potential contributor and makes note of whether that person is likely to give to the campaign and how much the contribution may be.

The interview should be a conversation rather than a one-sided presentation. The more the interviewer can engage the interviewee in discussion, the more the interviewer finds out about how outsiders view the organization and about the fundraising potential.

In these conversations, most contributors aren't making promises, but they're suggesting their probable levels of support. The study, therefore, is important for two reasons:

>> It gathers information that helps the organization estimate whether its capital campaign goal is feasible.

>> It begins the process of cultivating contributions to, and leadership for, the campaign.

TIP

At www.wiley.com/go/nonprofitkitfd6e, you can find an example of feasibility study interview questions (see File 19-6) and an overview of the parts of a finished study (see File 19-7).

Analyzing the results of your study

To continue with the used-car metaphor, a feasibility study is like finding out — after talking to your parents, your spouse, or the bank — how much you can afford to pay for a car. Your parents may say that they'll give you money for a small sedan but not for a red sports car, and the same is true of a feasibility study. Board members, community leaders, and potential donors may tell you that they would support the venture or endowment if it were smaller, or the building if it didn't need a new foundation.

If the feasibility study suggests that you can't afford the champagne version of your plans, you may have to settle for a serviceable house wine edition. If your plans were already of the house wine variety, you may want to break the campaign into phases. If yours is a building renovation project, over the first two years you can make major safety and structural changes or renovate one of two floors. Then, maybe three or four years later, you can launch the second phase of a capital campaign to cover the upper-floor renovation costs or pay off the mortgage.

You may also find out that you need to wait. Perhaps your potential major donors recently gave to another campaign, and although they like your project, they aren't in a position to make a major gift to your organization. You may be able to come back to them in two years and receive major contributions. Or, maybe potential donors voiced concerns about your organization. Maybe your board has dwindled in size or your executive director just accepted another job. When you organize, recruit, and hire anew, your campaign can proceed.

And you may find out that undertaking the project isn't even a good idea. Period. At that point, it's time to start over and plan to address your goals in a different way.

Developing a Case Statement

In Chapter 15, on raising money from individuals, we outline steps for writing a case statement. A capital campaign cries out for a *case statement* — a brief, eloquently stated argument on behalf of the capital project. Sometimes these case statements are fancy brochures with profiles of scholarship recipients, drawings of a planned building, or stories about clients of the future. Sometimes they're just simple PDF statements.

A capital campaign case statement should incorporate the following elements:

>> A mission statement and brief history of the organization

>> A list of major accomplishments

>> Compelling information about the constituents served

>> A vision of how the mission can be served better as a result of the capital project

>> A vision for the results of the capital investment

>> The campaign's leadership and goals

>> Naming and giving opportunities

After you've put together your case statement, you can show it to prospective donors and use it to build your pyramid of gifts (see the next section).

Building the Pyramid of Gifts

You've sketched out a budget. You've set your sights on a reasonable goal. Your next most important need is to identify *campaign leadership* — a team or committee of volunteers who are willing to cheerlead on behalf of the campaign, make personal visits and calls, and sign letters asking for contributions. These leaders may be board members, but we recommend including some people from outside the board if appropriate enthusiasts can be identified. Their efforts not only ease your board's workload but their contacts also expand the pool of possible donors — and their involvement illustrates broader community support for the campaign.

Each campaign develops its own strategies, and each organization has distinctive strengths to call on, but most of them use the same diagram, which is based on conventional wisdom. It's a *gift table*, and it looks like a pyramid (see Figure 19-1).

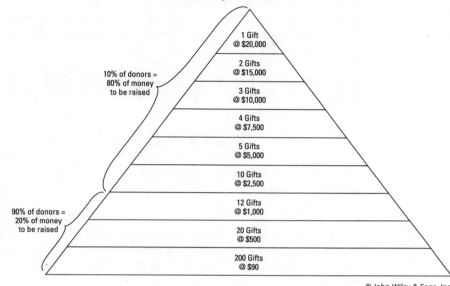

Campaign For $200,000
Sample Gift Table

1 Gift @ $20,000
2 Gifts @ $15,000
3 Gifts @ $10,000
4 Gifts @ $7,500
5 Gifts @ $5,000
10 Gifts @ $2,500
12 Gifts @ $1,000
20 Gifts @ $500
200 Gifts @ $90

10% of donors = 80% of money to be raised

90% of donors = 20% of money to be raised

FIGURE 19-1: A sample gift table, showing 80 percent of donations coming from 10 percent of donors.

© John Wiley & Sons, Inc.

Remember the old saying, "A handful of people do most of the work"? A capital campaign works that way. Only a few donors are able to contribute large gifts — they are placed at the top of the pyramid. Smaller gifts from many other donors fill in the lower levels as the campaign moves forward and the pyramid takes shape.

Starting at the top

We know you don't start at the top when building a pyramid, but that's where you begin with a capital campaign. Similarly, we structured the sample gift table in Figure 19-1 starting at the top, using the following scheme:

>> Ten percent or more of the money comes from a single gift, known as the *lead gift*. This large donation crowns the tip of the pyramid.

>> Fifteen percent of the money comes from the next two largest gifts.

>> Fifteen percent of the money comes from the next three largest gifts.

>> Overall, 80 percent of the money comes from 10 percent of the donors. In other words, if you receive 100 contributions, ten of those people will provide 80 percent of the money you must raise.

Say you're driving across town and pass the Janice Knickerbocker Symphony Hall, the Engin Uralman Medical Center, and the Jerome Kestenberg Museum of Natural History. What do Janice, Engin, and Jerome have in common? Generally, those people whose names adorn buildings made the contribution of 10 percent or more of the campaign total. They're called the *lead donors.*

REMEMBER

When you conduct your feasibility study, one thing you're trying to determine is the size of the campaign's largest gift and whether it totals 10 percent or more of the campaign total.

Your lead gift becomes one of your campaign's attractions. Some contributors may support a capital project because they like or admire the person after whom the scholarship fund or building is named, even if they have little connection to the cause or organization.

TIP

Many times, the lead donors want to be part of something new and transformative and are looking for an opportunity for recognition. However, always clarify with your lead donor prospects whether naming opportunities and public recognition are important to them. Sometimes a lead donor wants to be anonymous — you'll want to honor that request.

After the lead gift is in place, your organization begins seeking the other major gifts that make up the first one-third of the funds to be raised. (In our example in Figure 19-1, just six contributions make up 40 percent of the goal.) Individuals usually pledge these lead gifts during personal visits from nonprofit staff and board members. (See Chapter 15 for more about raising money from individuals.)

Continuing down the pyramid's structure to the widening middle, an organization usually moves beyond board members and major donors to seek grants from foundations and corporations.

Applying for grants as part of your capital campaign

Grant proposals for capital projects follow the general outline of a standard grant proposal (see Chapter 18) with some variations and additions. The grant writer needs to describe the organization's goals and activities and its constituents' needs, and convincingly describe how a stronger organization with stronger capital assets will better serve the organization's goals and clients. Although your proposal may focus on any kind of capital investment project, we discuss a standard building project in the following outline of a campaign grant proposal:

>> The introduction includes general information about current facilities and leads up to a discussion of the need for a new or renovated building.

>> The problem statement describes the needs of clients or potential clients and how the organization's current building (or lack of a building) hinders their satisfaction of those needs.

>> The Goals and Outcomes section discusses aspirations that the organization holds for serving its clients and its goals for the capital project (the building's dimensions and amenities).

>> The Methods section briefly touches on how you're delivering services but primarily focuses on how you're conducting the capital campaign, how construction will proceed, and the activities you're undertaking to connect current and future clients to the building. Organizations often include a discussion of the results of the feasibility study in this section as a rationale for how they set goals and how they planned the campaign.

>> The Evaluation section focuses on whether the building project will meet its goals (such as achieving all city fire and safety code standards) and on how the improved building serves clients.

>> The budget usually includes two major sections: hard costs (for land or building purchase or construction) and soft costs (for financing, fundraising, or promotion).

>> The Sustainability section discusses how the capital campaign is progressing and where the organization anticipates raising the necessary funds to complete it. This section also provides information about how the finished project will affect the organization's operating costs and how any additional expenses will be covered in the future. It may include a statement that completing the building project will help ensure the organization's future stability.

Ending the quiet phase and moving into the public phase

Early on, when you're conducting the capital campaign among trustees, close friends of the nonprofit, past donors, and foundations, the campaign is in what's called the *quiet phase*. When the organization has raised 75 percent to 80 percent of the money it needs, the fundraising style changes. The managers are growing confident that the campaign can succeed, and they announce it to the general public at a press conference, tour, gala party, or cornerstone-setting event.

This is the time to seek smaller donations from lots of people — neighbors, friends of friends, and grandparents. You can often raise these contributions from special events, mailings to individuals, and proposals addressed to smaller foundations and businesses.

Smaller gifts from many people construct the base of the pyramid. Don't discount these gifts. They're important financially to close out the campaign and also to build a feeling of participation among all your donors.

Other focused fundraising drives are structured along the gift-table pattern. Whether you're raising money for your child's school, an election, or a community fair, a gift table can help shape your plans.

TIP

Check out File 19-8 at www.wiley.com/go/nonprofitkitfd6e for a sample capital campaign gift table.

REMEMBER

Funds raised for a capital campaign must be used for the purposes described in the solicitation — whether it's a case statement or grant proposal. Many people don't recognize that the capital contributions can't just be treated as unrestricted funds if not enough money is raised to engage in the capital project.

Realizing the Benefits and Risks of Capital Campaigns

Although you may describe your request for capital support as a one-time need to potential supporters, many campaign donors continue to give after you finish the campaign project. They've been introduced to the agency, they've left their names in its lobby or attached to a scholarship fund, and they want to be sure that it succeeds over time. In the best situations, capital campaigns strengthen the nonprofit organization's programs by enabling it to improve services and by broadening its donor base. A capital project also can benefit staff morale because it improves working conditions.

In recent years, some thoughtful foundations, service organizations, and consulting groups have advocated for better "capitalization" of nonprofit organizations. Their point is that donors — particularly foundations — have encouraged nonprofits to come up with break-even financial results year after year. Although breaking even is much better than going into debt, emphasizing it as a virtue means that nonprofit organizations rarely put money aside for an unexpected crisis or infrastructure investment.

No for-profit business would thrive under these circumstances. And nonprofit organizations, many of which are formed to tackle important social and educational needs, should be just as innovative as businesses — maybe even more so. A campaign to raise, in effect, working capital for your nonprofit that you can use to innovate or to weather a financial shortfall may be harder to explain to donors than a campaign to build a building, but it may be just as important to your organization's vitality.

TIP

At www.wiley.com/go/nonprofitkitfd6e, we include links in File 19-1 to some key papers about capitalization that may help your nonprofit make the case for a campaign to raise working capital.

Although capital projects are meant to enhance your organization's programs and vitality, capital campaigns also have their drawbacks:

>> Capital campaigns may detract from an organization's fundraising for operations. If you ask a donor to contribute to a building project, that person may not contribute to the organization's ongoing programs in the same year.

>> Capital campaigns may double, triple, or quadruple an organization's fundraising expenses while they're being conducted.

>> Campaigns that don't succeed or that drag on for a long time can damage an organization's reputation. Because buildings tend to be visible entities, the public may be more aware of an organization's slow-moving construction project than of a problem with its programs or services. If the campaign doesn't succeed, it's important to discuss the situation with its donors, and, of course, honor the terms under which the gifts were made. Donors may want their contributions to be returned, or — if taking the tax deduction is important to them — they may choose to alter the terms and purposes of their gifts.

>> Organizations often have turnover in their fundraising staffs after a capital campaign. Employees may stick around to achieve the campaign goal, but a heavy workload may cause burnout.

In short, capital projects offer opportunities and pitfalls, buy-in and burnout, and new donor development and loss of current annual fund donors. But when completed, they often pay for concrete, lasting benefits and are worthy of celebration.

4

The Part of Tens

Chapter 20

Ten Tips for Pivoting in Times of Uncertainty

You'll likely come across problems in the course of managing your nonprofit organization. Everyone does. But sometimes those problems are so severe that you must change the way you do your work to address them.

You may face a catastrophe — a natural disaster, a pandemic, the destruction of a venue, or the serious illness or death of a staff or board member. Or shifts in legislation or foundation policies may cause you to lose important grants or contracts. Although some crises are sudden and fierce, others may build gradually. Several modest deficits may add up to significant debt. The needs of your constituents may change. A competitor may win away your clients or staff members.

The choices you make in challenging circumstances depend, in part, on how much time you have to plan. Is the change you're facing sudden, or has it been gradual? Is it long-term or temporary? Thinking about a crisis or dry spell when you're currently successful isn't fun, but it's necessary in order to survive. So, in this chapter, we provide ten tips for making choices in tough times.

REMEMBER

Transforming or even closing a nonprofit in hard times draws on the same courage, leadership, and resourcefulness you used to create it. You need to be clear and decisive; include others in making and executing your plans; ask for help when needed; and base your decisions on accurate information.

Create an Emergency Operations Plan

Recognizing a sudden crisis is easy, but often the most difficult aspect of managing a nonprofit is seeing a gradual decline and the need to change. Likely, you work so hard and feel such dedication that you can't believe your organization is floundering.

REMEMBER

Financial problems have clear consequences (so be on the lookout for them): When deficits exceed 10 percent of an operating budget, the organization will have trouble paying bills within 30 or 60 days. When the deficit exceeds 20 percent of the budget, the pressure intensifies. The inability to make payroll or timely tax payments signals severe problems.

A loan or an emergency fundraising drive may solve a short-term problem, but an organization must consider whether its business model is working. Do programs consistently cost more money than the organization's earned income and fundraising capacity? It can't keep borrowing funds or crying out for help without alienating its friends and supporters.

Before there is a sign of trouble that may or will result in an interruption of your programs and services, this is the time to rally together your board of directors. Why? They, along with the founder and/or executive director, need to sit down and create an emergency operations plan (EOP). The EOP addresses response procedures, organizational and staff capabilities, and how to handle the financial impact of the nonprofit. For example, when will employees be allowed to work from home? Have you written out the list of emergency resources to keep delivering services at even a minimal level? What is the communication plan for letting your stakeholders and the greater community know of your situation and limitations and whom to contact with questions?

Communicate When Making Hard Decisions

A colleague of ours once asked, "What do you mean by 'hard decisions'? Are they hard because they're unpopular? Or are they hard because we must choose among options and the best choice is unclear?" The answer is both.

If you're facing an unpopular decision — laying off staff, for example — communicate clearly and move forward decisively. The longer you delay, the greater harm you may do to your organization and to those employees. In most cases, that communication should be both internal (to board and staff) and external (to donors and constituents). If the change will affect your scale of operations, you may even want to announce it to the press.

Step Back and Regroup

The appropriate first action when you recognize that your organization faces a crisis may be to step back and take a breath. You need to ask which programs best address your mission and are of the highest quality, which are the most expensive, and which are the best at earning revenue or attracting contributions. That analysis requires time and effort on the part of the staff and board. You can make small adjustments, such as reducing the hours that a program operates or cutting back on costlier activities. You may even consider suspending all programs temporarily to give yourself time to plan. Not every nonprofit can do so without harming constituents, but many can. A hiatus can allow you to focus full attention on your options while reducing overhead costs.

REMEMBER

If you do take a break, communicate your reasons to your members, clients, and funders, and keep everyone informed of your progress. It's critical to your long-term health as a nonprofit that your supporters know you care about them. Also, even if your income and expenses are negligible, be sure to file your Form 990 with the IRS.

Set a Manageable Fundraising Goal

When raising money, you want to present an upbeat story and can-do attitude, right? And when challenges arise, you may feel the need to hide from donors. When a financial shortfall is creating the organization's crisis, sometimes people stop fundraising. But if donors care about your nonprofit (and why would they have given you money in the first place if they didn't care?), many will still care when times are tough.

We recommend setting a fundraising goal for a concrete amount — perhaps for two months of office rent or finishing a youth basketball tournament. Make that goal realistic yet meaningful, ask for help with meeting it, and report back on your progress. When you meet that goal, it gives you a positive story to share that helps rebuild your confidence and enthusiasm among your supporters.

Collaborate with Others in Your Field

If the field in which you work has seen a decline in funding or an increase in competition for staff or clients, it may be time to identify others who provide similar programs and begin to work together. Who shares your organization's values and approach? Can you serve clients better by combining services?

Collaboration enables you to bring different strengths, resources, and knowledge to a task. It assumes that you can work with greater depth and understanding by way of a partnership. You also may save some money.

TIP

We recommend that you try a temporary, modest project with your partner before launching a large-scale combination of services. Shared goals and values and shared fields of interest matter, but personal compatibility is important as well. Also, as you step into a partnership arrangement, make sure that more than one leader in each organization is participating in the conversations and negotiations. Collaborations often falter if the key contact person at one of the two organizations leaves. A team can ensure continuity.

Share a Back Office

Maybe program collaboration won't work for your organization, but other types of collaboration may be successful. For example, why not approach another non-profit about sharing a staff member? By hiring together, you may be able to offer a stable, full-time job with a competitive salary rather than a part-time gig. In turn, your organizations can engage more experienced and qualified employees.

Of course, you'll want to be careful in setting up this arrangement. Two organizations hiring the same person half-time may diminish that person's benefits. One way around this problem is for one of the organizations to serve as the paymaster, with the other one contributing to the cost of the employee, but this strategy works only if clear lines are drawn that specify when the person is working for which organization. Talk to an employment attorney to devise a clear shared-employee arrangement that benefits all parties.

REMEMBER

When sharing an employee, both organizations need to give that person clear direction about setting priorities and balancing attention between them.

Sharing things instead of people also can reduce your operating costs. Consider whether you can save money by purchasing equipment, securing office space, or combining supply orders with others. And don't assume that you can share these things only with organizations that resemble yours. In a study of nonprofits in the Puget Sound region, researchers found that some of the best shared-space experiences were among unlike nonprofit organizations, such as a theater school that operated in the late afternoons and evenings and a day care center that operated early in the day.

Place a Program within Another Agency

One question you should continually ask is how to best meet the needs of the people you serve. Your clients are your reason for existence, after all. If your nonprofit is stretched too thin to achieve everything it's trying to do, why not spin off a program, placing it within another reputable organization that shares your values? You may find that another organization, operating at a different scale or involving people with different skills and knowledge, is positioned to do a better job of managing that program.

We understand that it's difficult to give up a piece of your agency's work, but making this choice is the responsible thing to do for your clients. Plus, it may enable you to focus on the services that best address your nonprofit's mission. Of course, placing a program with another agency also will likely reduce your costs.

Merge with Another Nonprofit

One challenging but responsible choice for your nonprofit may be to merge with another organization. Mergers in nonprofits are similar to those in the business world. Generally, in a merger, one organization dominates the other.

Mergers require thoughtful planning that involves teams of people from both nonprofits. Plan in two phases: First, thoroughly discuss your missions, goals, and program philosophies. If those aren't aligned, the merger won't work. Keep those goals foremost in mind as you move into the second phase of planning, which involves choosing a name, selecting staff, consolidating boards, and arranging a new structure. If problems arise in the second phase of planning, return to the primary conversation and ask whether your missions are aligned and your constituents will be well served by the merger.

TIP

We strongly recommend that, when executing a merger, you have a facilitator lead you through the plans and decisions, and work with an attorney to determine questions to be raised and risks assessed before agreeing to a merger. That same attorney can draw up your final agreements if the merger is prudent. Also be open to the idea of bringing in new staff and board members who will be committed to the merged organization without loyalties to either of the original entities.

Close with Dignity If Necessary

Nonprofit organizations generally resist closure, maybe because they're usually founded by people with a vision and a desire to serve the public. Yet sometimes, closing is the right choice.

REMEMBER

If your nonprofit's financial health fails and its program quality declines, accept the idea of closure before it's a last-gasp necessity. Shutting down a nonprofit involves several stages — some of them formally defined and some of them merely good practices. We suggest that you do the following:

>> **Take care of your employees.** Warn them about the impending closure and, if possible, provide them with job counseling and severance pay.

>> **Take care of your clients.** Work with other agencies to make sure that client needs will be met in the future. If you have subscribers or members, offer refunds or work with other nonprofits to honor their benefits.

>> **Tell your donors and professional partners.** They should hear about your planned closure from you rather than by way of rumor or the media. Clear communication of your story must be presented before rumors begin.

>> **Pay your debts or negotiate settlements of your obligations before closing.** Doing so protects your reputation and the reputation of your board members and also engenders trust in nonprofits as good business partners.

>> **Document your work.** What's your nonprofit's legacy of services to the field? What has it learned? How can your knowledge benefit others? We recommend gathering your information and placing it in a library, school, historical society, or online archive.

>> **Celebrate and recognize your staff, board, and volunteers.** The people who have contributed their time, labor, and expertise to your nonprofit deserve applause and thanks.

Complete the Government's Closing Paperwork

If you decide to close your nonprofit, it isn't enough to lock your doors and hang a Closed for Good sign. You also need to take a few formal steps. One of the first is to hold a board meeting at which the board votes to dissolve the organization and records that decision in the board minutes. Another is to take an inventory of all your assets — money, furniture, client lists, web domains, costumes, fish tanks, and so on — and pass them on, sell them, or return them appropriately, honoring your donors' intentions if some items were contributed for specific purposes. If you have assets to distribute, you must pass them on to a nonprofit with a similar mission. You may also need to file closing notification with your state's nonprofit filing division. This is the division where you first filed your articles of incorporation and also where you filed your annual report each year to earn a certificate of good standing.

You'll likely want some technical assistance from a consultant or an attorney to complete the paperwork because you have certain state and federal requirements to meet:

>> **State requirements:** Procedures and documents vary by state. For example, in California you need to make an initial filing related to the planned dissolution with the attorney general. After the attorney general issues a waiver of objections to the dissolution plan, you file a certificate of dissolution with the secretary of state. Check with the state agency through which you incorporated on the appropriate steps to take.

>> **Federal requirements:** Just as you turned to the Internal Revenue Service (IRS) to create your nonprofit, you return to the IRS to shut it down. You must file a final Form 990 tax return (see Chapter 6 for details about the 990) within four months and 15 days of your organization's formal dissolution date. As you do so, check the Terminated box in Part B on the first page of the return. You also need to answer yes in Part IV, Line 31, about whether the organization is terminated, liquidated, or dissolved, and then file Schedule N, which asks for a list of assets, their value, and where they were distributed.

Chapter **21**

Ten Tips for Raising Seed Money

R aising money is essential to managing a successful nonprofit organization. In fact, nothing is easier than knowing you should be raising money — and nothing is more difficult than asking for it. This chapter contains our top ten tips for that all-important task of raising funds.

Ask

One of fundraising's oldest adages is, "If you don't ask, you won't get."

Developing fundraising plans, compiling lists of names and email addresses for potential donors, and designing invitations to fundraising events are labor-intensive tasks. But those tasks aren't the ones that slow you down in fundraising. Instead, many people pause when picking up the telephone or ringing the doorbell — in other words, when it comes to asking for money. Then, when it's a little too late for the prospective donor to make a decision, write a check, or forward a proposal to a board meeting, these fundraisers make their move and stumble over their own procrastination.

We repeat: "If you don't ask (and ask at the right time), you won't get."

Hit Up People You Know

Some fundraisers believe that the entire money-raising game is in knowing people with money and power and working those contacts — charming them to bend their wills and write those checks. To be honest, if yours is a good cause, that approach isn't bad.

But what if you don't know wealthy people? Does that mean you can't raise money? No, it doesn't. Begin with people you know. Don't be afraid to ask your friends and associates. From a donor's point of view, saying no to someone you know is more difficult than saying no to a stranger.

REMEMBER

Often, people who can afford to give don't look like they have money. They might drive older cars, live in lower-income neighborhoods, or wear secondhand clothing. That's why they have money — they have either inherited, earned, won, or invested it *and* lived way below their means. Don't judge a book by its cover or by the type of shelf it's sitting on.

Tell Your Story and Don't Ramble

The best way to write an effective fundraising letter or make a successful presentation to potential donors is to tell a story. You don't have to explain how your organization was founded and everything it has done since then (although that history may be worth a brief mention). Instead, the best stories and presentations focus on the constituents you serve and how they benefit from your efforts. Such stories are hopeful. They paint a picture of a better future and describe what "better" looks like in clear, specific terms.

REMEMBER

Pace the story so that it has a bit of drama (but don't stoop to melodrama or hyperbole). Focus on facts — clear evidence of your success. Recognize and discuss the complexity of the field in which you work, but don't drone on and on about technical matters that will cause your audience to zone out. In your mind, before you start rambling, pull up your elevator speech. It works! (Chapter 15 provides you guidance on creating an elevator speech).

Show How You're Improving Lives

In grant-writing terms, the piece of advice in this section's heading would be worded as "clearly describe your outcomes." Keep in mind that outcomes are different from outputs. *Outputs* is the word used for the quantity of work a nonprofit organization produces — the number of meals served, shelter beds offered, workshops led, miles covered, or acres planted. *Outcomes* is the word used for the changes that occurred as a result of those outputs. Well-defined outcomes are the hallmark of a good grant proposal, fundraising letter, web page, or pitch.

In other words, providing training about nutrition to a group of 50 seniors isn't going to result in your desired outcomes if those seniors don't change their eating patterns and live longer, healthier lives. Removing toxins from a lake isn't enough if its fish population and ecosystem aren't revived. Exposing 500 children to formal music lessons isn't enough if none of them can read a simple score later. Don't leave potential donors thinking, "Sounds nice, but so what?"

Use Numbers to Convey Urgency and Compassion

Effective requests for money include information about how much is needed to achieve change or test an idea. Make sure to present in clear terms any data you cite. In most cases, telling your reader or listener how much a needed change costs — the cost per child to participate in a special classroom for a year, the cost per injured sea mammal rescued, the cost per well in a remote village — helps to make your point.

REMEMBER

Nothing undermines a well-written proposal or case statement faster or more thoroughly than a confusing budget or a muddled financial statement. Double-check your presentation to make sure every activity in your proposal is represented in the budget and that every item in your budget can be traced easily to the work outlined in your proposal. If some items may be confusing to your reader, include budget notes. In all cases, check your math.

Research, Research, Research

Earlier in this chapter, we tell you to ask people you know for money. We're not taking back that advice, but at some point you need to move beyond your immediate circle of acquaintances. That's where doing your homework pays off.

Before you send a fundraising letter, submit a proposal, or visit with a corporate-giving director, find out as much as you can about the prospective contributor. Do you have anything in common on a personal level? Maybe the foundation director you're meeting recently published an article. If you read it, you have a conversation topic to break the ice. This advice holds true even when your approach is a membership mailing or an email appeal: You want to know as much as you can about the people whose names are on the lists you develop, borrow, or purchase.

More important, you want to find out as much as you can about your potential donor's giving behavior. Does this person give small amounts of money to a wide array of organizations or give generous gifts to a few selected agencies? Does the foundation like to be the only contributor to a given project, or does it prefer to support an activity along with others? Does the corporate-giving program prefer a low-key style, or does it like to have the company's involvement highlighted?

TIP

You can turn to many sources for this information; just be sure to make research a habit. For instance, you can do any of the following:

>> Refer to Candid Learning's online resources (`https://learning.candid.org`). Don't overlook its *Philanthropy News Digest* (*PND* on its website), which announces research published and grants awarded by foundations and their grantees.

>> Look up the foundation at the Council on Foundations' website (`www.cof.org`) to see whether it has recently issued a report or been featured in an article.

>> For personal information about individuals, conduct an Internet search; look at LinkedIn bios (`www.linkedin.com`); peruse local newspapers; and contact college alumni associations.

>> Follow business and social news along with obituaries to keep track of people's families, professional developments, and affiliations.

>> Pay close attention to contributor lists when you attend events at other nonprofit organizations.

Know Your Donors' Point of View

Have you ever heard the old saying, "To catch a trout, think like a trout"? Well, this saying also applies to raising money for your nonprofit. The point of conducting research is to be able to talk or write about your organization in ways that are compelling to your listener or reader. You don't want to warp your message or change your mission, but you do want to think about it (and talk or write about it) in ways that respect your audience's point of view. To do so, you need to think about your organization as if you were a prospective donor yourself.

Donors have different personal giving styles, so you need to put yourself in donors' shoes when deciding how to raise money from particular individuals or companies. You don't want to offer to host a tribute dinner in honor of someone who prefers to contribute anonymously, for instance. And you don't want to downplay a gift from a contributor who relishes public acknowledgment. Some donors prefer the sociability of supporting a cause via a special event, others respond to email appeals, and still others like to see as much of their money as possible directly support the service being provided. (If possible, let them see that service with their own eyes!)

TIP

Whenever possible, ask donors how they prefer to be recognized, and also ask them why they donate to your organization. Their answers may surprise you — and will help you craft your future message and approach.

Many people forget that foundations are nonprofit organizations with mission statements and that their job is to support proposals that further their missions. Your job as a grant seeker is to measure how your goals align with their purposes. For example, many corporate-giving programs and company-sponsored foundations work to improve the communities in which their employees live and work. When these organizations discover that their employees are involved in or contribute to a given cause, they may be more inclined to support that cause.

Government grant-making programs are created by way of state and federal legislation. If you find a program that seems well suited to your organization's work, reviewing the legislation or, when possible, attending public hearings about the program is worth your time. Doing so helps you fully understand the program's context and intentions.

Build a Donor Pyramid

Earlier in this chapter, we suggest starting by asking people you know. Imagine your fundraising approach as starting with those people at the peak of a pyramid and working your way down to the broader base. After asking people you know, try to enlist those donors in asking their contacts to support your organization as well. Some are likely to respond (in part because people they know also are contributors). Then ask those new donors to ask their friends. If each contributor leads you to two additional contributors, you steadily build your pyramid.

Distributed fundraising platforms such as www.causes.com are one easy way for your donors to raise money for you. (See Chapter 15 for more about distributed fundraising.)

Make It Easy to Respond

You've written a brilliant appeal letter. You've created a compelling website. You've delivered a stirring speech to a roomful of prospective donors. You've got them hooked. They want to contribute. But they're glancing around the room with confused looks on their faces. You blew it. You didn't give them an easy way to respond.

REMEMBER

Always suggest a specific amount for donors to consider contributing. Connect that amount to what you need and to their potential giving levels (which you can estimate from your research). And always make immediate giving easy for them: Distribute an addressed envelope and reply card with each mailing, enable a reader to click through your email to the Donate Now button on your website, or set up a labeled box by the exit where donors can leave contributions. Give potential donors pens, stamps, email addresses, pledge cards, and any other tools to help them respond when you have their attention. Also, if you're targeting donors in multiple states, remember to register to fundraise in each state that requires it.

Keep Good Records

After you begin attracting contributors, your donor records become your most valuable fundraising tools. Individuals who give to your organization once are likely to continue giving for three or more years. If you thank them, address them as if they're part of your organization, and generally treat them well, the size of their gifts is likely to increase over time.

Working with foundations, corporations, and government sources is a different story. In their case, you want to keep clear records of your original project goals and outcomes, project budget, and due dates for any required reports. Although these sources may not be willing or able to support your organization year after year, their future support is more likely if you're a conscientious grantee who submits reports on time and keeps clear records.

You can create a simple database by recording names, addresses, phone numbers, email addresses, patterns of giving, and personal information (such as whether a donor knows one of your board members or whether they're married and have children). Consider investing in *donor management software.* Several good ones are available. Some are pricey, others are free. Find out more about donor software that's right for your organization by searching articles on Idealware's website (www.idealware.org). Or check out Givelify (www.givelify.com), which allows donors to contribute monthly.

REMEMBER

However you keep it, guard your donor database carefully and invest the time necessary to keep it up to date. It's one of your organization's most valuable resources.

Chapter **22**

Ten Tips for Protecting Your Nonprofit

Protecting your nonprofit organization encompasses tasks that can range from purchasing sandbags to filing government forms. These activities should be driven by an ongoing, thoughtful assessment of your organization's risks.

Some risks that nonprofits face vary according to where they're based and what they do. Is your office on the banks of a river or in tornado country? Do you work with preschool-age children or with injured raptors? Other items are universal: protecting the safety of staff and clients, protecting the organization's assets, protecting its tax-exempt status, and protecting its reputation. Although no nonprofit manager can anticipate every problem that arises, it's wise to put systems and precautions in place.

TIP

Check out File 22-1 at www.wiley.com/go/nonprofitkitfd6e for a list of web resources related to the topics we cover in this chapter.

Assessing Your Risks

Evaluating risks should be a routine part of your planning and operations. We recommend that you begin with a big-picture analysis of your nonprofit and its potential vulnerabilities. Your list should include these factors:

>> Location and facility

>> Activities and programs

>> Beneficiaries of your programs

>> Management and financial systems

>> Contracts and collaborations

>> Employees

>> Board members and volunteers

>> Communications and reputation

You may note that your organization works with young children and uses organization-owned vans to transport them; its board has limited financial management knowledge; its employees and programs must be licensed; and its computer systems are old and prone to crashing. Each of these observations makes the organization vulnerable.

Planning for Emergencies

Blizzard belt, floodplain, earthquake fault line, hurricane path, gas leak: Likely all the nation's nonprofits are vulnerable to some kind of natural or human-made disaster. Your emergency plan should have these three elements:

>> Preventing problems by eliminating as many potential risks as possible.

>> Preparing for emergencies by devising procedures and assigning roles for enacting them.

>> Training everyone on your staff to respond to several scenarios. Drill and practice your responses.

We recommend that your nonprofit put together an emergency planning team of three or four volunteers, staff, and board members. Include people on the committee who represent different kinds of expertise and who would be level-headed in an emergency. Sketch out different response scenarios. Three common options are evacuation, lockdown, and shelter-in-place.

Your emergency team should

>> **Prepare to ensure the whereabouts and safety of staff members and their families.** Phone lists that include information for staff members, their local family members, and an out-of-state contact should be kept up to date and in a safe place. The same kind of information should be kept current for clients.

>> **Plan evacuation routes, identifying nearby shelters, fire stations, or hazards.** Put up posters with maps showing how to safely exit your building via the steps (never the elevator, which could fail if the electricity goes out), and post a list of nearby facilities considered safe places for people seeking refuge.

>> **Collect and store emergency supplies — sufficient food and water for 72 hours along with flashlights, batteries, a radio, and a first-aid kit.** Remember that cellphones may not work in an emergency. Encourage staff members to keep on hand a few days' worth of prescription drugs (if you must stay in place) and a pair of comfortable shoes at work (if you must evacuate).

>> **Safeguard your records.** Are your computers backed up regularly? If you depend on data collection, do you send it away regularly to a safe location? Also, if your accounting system is online, you may want to lock away some checks that can be handwritten in an emergency.

>> **Plan to take action.** How will your board take action to respond to an emergency if calling a meeting and securing a quorum is difficult? Some states permit nonprofits to add allowances to their bylaws that outline how decisions can be made under emergency circumstances.

TIP

You can find useful tools for emergency planning at www.ready.gov (the federal government's all-hazards approach to planning). San Francisco CARD (www.sfcard.org) offers a template for an emergency plan that focuses on the San Francisco Bay Area but is adaptable to other settings.

Filing Annual Federal Forms

Each year, the federal government requires 501(c)(3) nonprofit organizations to submit a *Return of Organization Exempt from Income Tax*, commonly known as Form 990. The complexity of this document varies according to the size of your organization:

>> **The 990-N or e-postcard** is for organizations with gross receipts that normally are $50,000 or less.

>> **The 990 Short Form or 990-EZ** is for organizations that normally have annual gross receipts above $50,000 but less than $200,000 and total assets of less than $500,000.

>> **The 990** is for organizations that are larger than those permitted to file the 990-N or the 990-EZ. Smaller organizations that qualify to file the 990-N or 990-EZ may choose to make the greater disclosures required and file the 990.

REMEMBER

Your 990 tax form needs to be postmarked or filed electronically on the 15th day of the fifth month after the close of your financial year unless it falls on a weekend or holiday. You may request an extension if needed. Failing to file can jeopardize your nonprofit status.

Filing Annual State Forms

Each state has its own laws and regulations for how and when a nonprofit must report its activities. In some states, your nonprofit will receive a sales-tax exemption. To find your state laws, visit the directory of state offices on the IRS website at www.irs.gov/charities-non-profits/state-links.

If you change your articles of incorporation or bylaws during the year, you need to follow the laws of your state (in the case of articles of incorporation) or the rules described in your bylaws to register the change.

Furthermore, as of this writing, 36 states, the District of Columbia, and some local governments require nonprofits to register and pay an annual fee if they are fundraising in the state. The number of states requiring this fundraising registration changes from time to time. See www.multistatefiling.org for updated information. Also, many Secretary of State's offices have annual forms to be filled out and returned (business forms and annual filings). Contact your Secretary of State's office for filing requirements.

Paying Employment Taxes

Although nonprofit organizations don't need to pay federal taxes on revenue related to their exempt purpose, and — in some states and jurisdictions — don't need to pay local property taxes or sales taxes, they must pay employment taxes, including the employer's portion of employment and social security taxes and unemployment insurance. In most cases, these taxes are paid quarterly to state tax boards and the Internal Revenue Service. Not every state requires nonprofits to pay unemployment taxes, but every nonprofit must pay federal unemployment taxes. Failing to pay these taxes leads to stiff penalties and interest charges. Unpaid employment taxes are one of the few nonprofit liabilities for which the organization's board members may be personally liable. Check with your local state unemployment office or department of revenue for filing and payment requirements for your state.

Reporting Payments to Consultants

If your organization hires a consultant to design its website, conduct an evaluation, or manage other specialized tasks, and if that consultant is paid $600 or more during a single year, your nonprofit must report these payments by filing the IRS Form 1099 shortly after the end of each calendar year. Some states also require that this information be reported. You can find more information at www.irs.gov/charities-non-profits/state-links.

Maintaining Transparency

Transparency is a buzzword in the nonprofit arena these days, and although it may sound like jargon, it represents an important set of standards — namely, nonprofits should be aboveboard and honest in their personnel matters, fundraising, finances, and delivery of services. One smart thing to do is to review the IRS rules for public disclosure by visiting www.irs.gov. Also, you should review the recommended principles and practices for nonprofits in 27 different states, compiled by the National Council of Nonprofits at www.councilofnonprofits.org/tools-resources/principles-and-practices-where-can-you-find-best-practices-nonprofits.

The council also has summarized a set of standards for excellence. Here are its recommended transparency practices:

>> Be honest with donors about how their contributions are used, and offer them the opportunity to opt out of being identified as contributors, apart from being listed on Schedule B of the 501(c)(3) nonprofit's Form 990.

>> Initiate a conflict-of-interest policy for staff and board members.

>> Make your IRS Form 1023 exemption application available for disclosure upon request.

>> Develop a sexual harassment policy and process.

>> Post your most recent Form 990 or a related financial statement on your website.

>> Adopt an internal complaint and whistleblower policy in accordance with laws in your state.

Responding to Negative Press

Even good, conscientious nonprofit organizations can draw negative media attention. The negative coverage may be based on accurate or inaccurate information, but even untrue accusations can be damaging. When bad press arises, follow these guidelines:

>> **Wait to speak to the media or members of the public *after* you have fully investigated the complaint or critique and are ready to provide a clear statement.** You don't want to delay a response for a long time, because your silence can appear to be an admission of guilt, but neither do you want to retract an initial statement. It's fine to say, "We are issuing a statement on Friday morning" when asked to comment.

>> **Choose a small number of people (perhaps your executive director and board chair) who are authorized to speak to the media.** Don't permit others to comment. You *must* present a clear, consistent message.

>> **Answer the media's questions directly and truthfully.** Also be sure to insert a positive message about how you're rectifying the situation, whether the complaint is valid, or how much value your organization's work has.

>> **Acknowledge and address the controversy on your website.** You can do it in a press release, and — if it's a major concern — in a letter to your funders and donors. In all communications, indicate that you're taking the criticism seriously.

Protecting Your Online Reputation

Information reported online is important to your organization's reputation. Negative comments collected on your website or social media pages can be damaging because of how quickly and easily they can be transmitted to many people.

If someone is disappointed with your services, apologize (if appropriate) and invite them to try again, either for no charge or at a discounted fee. In doing so, be careful of an admission of responsibility and liability, especially if the organization wasn't responsible and should not be liable. Sometimes people may offer what they consider to be constructive criticism. Treat these comments with respect and thank them for their advice. Generally, you should ignore angry, vengeful comments. Responding often makes it worse.

Determining Insurance Needs

A nonprofit's insurance needs vary according to whether it

>> Offers services within its own (or a rented) piece of property

>> Has employees (We discuss employee benefits in Chapter 11.)

>> Makes use of volunteers (See Chapter 10.)

>> Makes direct contact with clients, students, patients, or audiences and the nature of that direct contact

>> Involves professional services

>> Creates and publishes materials

>> Transports clients, especially children

Most of the claims reported by nonprofit organizations are accidents and injuries related to falls at nonprofit locations or special events or are related to the use of automobiles. All nonprofit organizations should purchase general liability (sometimes called *slip-and-fall*) insurance. You need to purchase specialized kinds of liability insurance if your organization has significant direct client contact that involves a potential risk. Health clinics and therapy programs need such insurance to protect them if a client is hurt or handled inappropriately. So do programs offering activities with possible physical dangers, such as rock climbing, sailing, or horseback riding.

If your organization occasionally produces events or conducts work in locations other than its central office or building, double-check to make sure you're covered for these offsite events. You may need to purchase a rider to your regular liability insurance policy to cover such situations.

You should also purchase a type of auto insurance known as *non-owned/hired* in case an employee or volunteer is involved in an automobile accident.

In most states, workers compensation insurance is required by law. If an employee is injured in the course of performing their job, this insurance helps protect both the employee and the employer. The cost of your workers compensation insurance is calculated according to the number of employees, the number of hours they spend on the job, and the nature of the work they do.

Here's a list of a few other kinds of insurance to consider:

» Property insurance for damage to property and equipment owned or leased by the nonprofit

» Employee dishonesty insurance or fidelity bonds to protect against embezzlement

» Directors and officers (D&O) insurance to protect the personal assets of directors, officers, and employees from lawsuits against the nonprofit organization. Corporate laws vary by state, but in most cases directors and officers are protected (even without insurance) if they're providing reasonable oversight of the nonprofit. That "reasonable" oversight involves attending meetings, asking questions, keeping well informed about the organization, and acting in good faith in the best interests of the organization. However, D&O insurance generally covers the cost of a legal defense against lawsuits. We encourage nonprofits to shop around among different insurance companies because D&O insurance products vary widely.

5

Appendixes

The nonprofit world has its own lingo. Flip to the glossary whenever you encounter an unfamiliar word.

The website that supplements this book offers many helpful documents and links to useful websites. Appendix B lists the ones available online.

Appendix A

Glossary

annual report: A report published by a nonprofit organization, foundation, or corporation describing its activities and providing an overview of its finances. A foundation's annual report usually lists the year's grants. Many states require a 501(c)(3) nonprofit to provide an annual financial report to members or board members.

articles of incorporation: A document filed with an appropriate state office by persons establishing a corporation. Generally, this filing is the first legal step in forming a nonprofit corporation.

board of directors: Individuals recruited, nominated, and elected to serve on a nonprofit organization's governing board. The board is responsible for overseeing the nonprofit's activities. Boards meet frequently and vote on the affairs of the nonprofit and are financially responsible for the nonprofit's funds on deposit and any irregularities in financial reporting.

bylaws: Rules governing a nonprofit organization's operation. Bylaws often outline the methods for selecting directors, forming committees, and conducting meetings.

capacity building: A general term used to describe activities that help a nonprofit organization strengthen its internal operations so that it can do its job better. Examples include staff and board training, computer and financial-management systems upgrades, and consultant assistance for planning.

capital campaign: An organized drive to raise funds to finance an organization's capital needs — buildings, equipment, renovation projects, land acquisitions, or endowments.

capital support: Funds provided to a capital project.

case statement: A brief, compelling document about an organization's plans, accomplishments, and vision.

challenge grant: A grant made on the condition that other funds must be secured before it will be paid — usually on a matching basis and within a defined period.

charitable contribution: A gift of goods, money, or property to a nonprofit organization.

charity: A word encompassing religion, education, assistance to the government, promotion of health and the arts, relief from poverty, and other purposes benefiting the community. Nonprofit organizations formed to further one of these purposes generally are recognized as exempt from federal income taxes under Section 501(c)(3) of the Internal Revenue Code.

community foundation: A grant-making organization receiving its funds from multiple public sources, focusing its giving on a defined geographic area, and being managed by an appointed, representative board of directors; technically classified by the Internal Revenue Service as a public charity, not a private foundation.

community fund: An organized community program making annual appeals to the general public for funds that are usually disbursed to charitable organizations rather than retained in an endowment. Sometimes called a federated giving program.

corporate foundation: A private foundation that derives its grant-making funds primarily from the contributions of a profit-making business.

corporate-giving program: A grant-making program established and managed by a profit-making company. Unlike a corporate foundation's grant-making, a corporate-giving program's gifts of money, goods, and services go directly from the company to grantees.

demonstration grant: A grant made to experiment with an innovative project or program that may serve as a model for others.

donor-advised fund: A fund held by a community foundation or another charitable organization for which the donor, or a committee appointed by the donor, reasonably expects to have advisory privileges over the distribution or investments of the assets — including by awarding grants and contributions to 501(c)(3) nonprofit organizations.

donor-designated fund: A restricted fund — often held at a community foundation — for which the donor has specified how the proceeds from the fund will be used.

endowment fund: A fund generally invested to provide income for the long-term (or sometimes permanent) operation of an organization.

excise tax: An annual tax of net investment income that private foundations must pay to the Internal Revenue Service.

family foundation: Not a legal term, but commonly used to describe foundations that are managed by family members related to the person or persons from whom the foundation's funds were derived.

federated campaign or federated giving program: A plan to raise funds for an organization that will redistribute them as grants to nonprofit organizations, often led by volunteer groups within clubs and workplaces (such as United Way and Combined Federal Campaign).

fiduciary: The fiduciary duty of board members is the responsibility to act in the interests of the nonprofit, those it serves, and those donating funds for operations, as opposed to their own self-interest.

fiscal sponsor: A nonprofit 501(c)(3) organization that formally agrees to sponsor a project led by an individual or a group from outside the organization that does not have nonprofit status. If the outside individual or group receives grants or contributions to conduct an activity, those funds are accepted, on behalf of the project, by the fiscal sponsor.

501(c)(3) nonprofit: A term describing the Internal Revenue Service's designation for organizations whose income isn't used for the benefit or private gain of stockholders, directors, or other owners. A nonprofit organization's income is used to support its operations and further its stated mission. It may sometimes be referred to as a nonprofit organization (NPO).

foundation: A nongovernmental, nonprofit organization with funds and a program managed by its own trustees and directors, established to further social, educational, religious, or charitable activities by making grants. A private foundation may receive its funds from an individual, family, corporation, or another group consisting of a limited number of members.

fundraising: The seeking of financial support for a charity or a cause or another enterprise.

gift table: A structured plan for the number and size of contributions needed to meet a fundraising campaign's goals.

grantee: An individual or organization receiving a grant.

grantor: An individual or organization awarding a grant.

independent sector: The portion of the economy that includes all 501(c)(3) and 501(c)(4) tax-exempt organizations as defined by the Internal Revenue Service, all religious institutions, all social-responsibility programs of corporations, and all people who give time and money to serve charitable purposes. It's also called the voluntary sector, the charitable sector, the third sector, or the nonprofit sector.

in-kind contribution: A donation of goods or services (not of money).

lobbying: Efforts to influence legislation by shaping the opinions of legislators, legislative staff, and government administrators directly involved in drafting legislative policies. The Internal Revenue Code sets limits on lobbying by organizations that are exempt from tax under Section 501(c)(3).

logic model: A graphical illustration that outlines the resources, activities, outputs, and outcomes of an organization or a program and shows, thereby, how it intends to achieve change. Sometimes called a theory of change.

matching gifts program: A grant or contributions program that matches employees' or directors' gifts made to qualifying nonprofit organizations. Each employer or foundation sets specific guidelines.

matching grant: A grant or gift made with the understanding that the amount contributed will be matched with revenues from another source on a one-for-one basis or according to another defined formula.

mission statement: A succinct statement of the purpose and key activities of a nonprofit organization.

objective: A measurable statement about how goals will be achieved, often referred to as a *s*pecific, *m*easurable, *a*ttainable, *r*ealistic, and *t*imebound (SMART) objective.

outcome evaluation: An assessment of whether a project achieved the desired long-term results.

program officer: A staff member of a foundation or corporate-giving program who may review grant requests, recommend policy, manage a budget, or process applications for review by a board or committee. Other titles, such as program director or program consultant, also are used.

program-related investment: A low-interest loan or another investment made by a foundation or corporate-giving program to another organization for a project that would accomplish one of the foundation's exempt purposes.

proposal: A written application, often with supporting documents, submitted to a foundation or corporate-giving program when requesting a grant.

public charity: A type of organization, classified under Section 501(c)(3) of the Internal Revenue Code, that normally receives a substantial part of its income from the general public or government. The public support of a public charity must be fairly broad and not limited to a few families or individuals.

restricted funds: Assets or income whose use is restricted by a donor for a specific purpose or activity.

strategic planning: An organizational process of defining its strategy, or direction, and making decisions about allocating its resources to pursue this strategy, including the board's creation of mission and vision statements, goals, objectives, timelines, action plans for achieving objectives, and who within the organization will be responsible for carrying out each part of the action plan.

tax-exempt: A classification granted by the Internal Revenue Service to qualified non-profit organizations that frees them from the requirement of paying taxes on their income. Private foundations, including endowed company foundations, are tax-exempt; however, they must pay a modest excise tax on net investment income. All 501(c)(3) and 501(c)(4) organizations are tax-exempt, but only contributions to a 501(c)(3) are tax-deductible to the donor.

unrelated business income: Income from a trade or business, regularly carried on, and not substantially related to furthering the exempt purpose of the organization. Such income may, therefore, be taxable.

unsolicited proposal: A proposal sent to a foundation without the foundation's invitation or prior knowledge. Some foundations decline unsolicited proposals.

Appendix **B**

About the Online Content

Throughout this book, we refer to specific files that help you set up and run your nonprofit organization. We've placed those files at www.wiley.com/ go/nonprofitkitfd6e. The following list summarizes the files that you'll find on the website:

» **File 1-1:** Chapter 1 Web Resources

» **File 1-2:** Nonprofit Activity Types

» **File 2-1:** Chapter 2 Web Resources

» **File 2-2:** Sample Fiscal Sponsorship Contract

» **File 3-1:** Chapter 3 Web Resources

» **File 3-2:** Sample Grid for Planning Board Recruitment

» **File 3-3:** Board Officer Position Descriptions

» **File 3-4:** Sample Board Contract

» **File 3-5:** Sample Outline of Board Meeting Minutes

» **File 3-6:** Sample Board Meeting Agenda, Simple

» **File 3-7:** Sample Board Meeting Agenda, Formal

>> **File 4-1:** Chapter 4 Web Resources

>> **File 5-1:** Chapter 5 Web Resources

>> **File 5-2:** Checklist for Forming a 501(c)3 Nonprofit Organization

>> **File 5-3:** Writing Organizational Bylaws

>> **File 6-1:** Chapter 6 Web Resources

>> **File 7-1:** Chapter 7 Web Resources

>> **File 8-1:** Chapter 8 Web Resources

>> **File 8-2:** Sample Planning Retreat Agenda

>> **File 8-3:** Sample SWOT Analysis

>> **File 8-4:** Sample Matrix Map: A Tool for Bottom-Line Decision-Making (included with permission from Jeanne Bell, CEO, CompassPoint Nonprofit Services, www.compasspoint.org)

>> **File 8-5:** Sample Outline of a Strategic Plan

>> **File 8-6:** Theory of Change for Program Planning Worksheet

>> **File 8-7:** Theory of Change Narrative (included with permission from © The Global Partnership for Sustainable Development Data)

>> **File 8-8:** Sample Needs Assessment Questionnaire

>> **File 8-9:** Planned Change and Facilities (included with permission from the Nonprofit Finance Fund, © Nonprofit Finance Fund, www.nonprofitfinancefund.org. All rights reserved.)

>> **File 8-10:** List of Required Spaces (included with permission from the Nonprofit Finance Fund, © Nonprofit Finance Fund, www.nonprofitfinancefund.org. All rights reserved.)

>> **File 9-1:** Chapter 9 Web Resources

>> **File 9-2:** Evaluation: Some Definitions of Terms

>> **File 9-3:** Sample Logic Model (included with permission from Harvard Family Research Center, © 1999 President and Fellows of Harvard College. Published by Harvard Family Research Project, Harvard Graduate School of Education. All rights reserved. No part of this publication may be reproduced without permission of the publisher. Since 1983, HFRP has helped stakeholders develop and evaluate strategies to promote the well-being of children, youth, families, and communities. HFRP's work focuses on early childhood education, out-of-school time programming, family and community support in education, complementary learning, and evaluation. Visit www.hfrp.org to access hundreds of resources with practical information for evaluators, practitioners, researchers, and policymakers.)

>> **File 12-14:** Tips for Reading an Audit

>> **File 13-1:** Chapter 13 Web Resources

>> **File 13-2:** Sample Audience Survey Form: Mercer County Home Healthcare Services

>> **File 13-3:** Sample Survery of Participants and Volunteers

>> **File 13-4:** Sample News Release (modified version, included with permission from Carla Befera)

>> **File 13-5:** Sample Media Alert

>> **File 13-6:** Sample Calendar Release

>> **File 13-7:** Sample Photo Caption

>> **File 13-8:** Sample Form for Photography or Video Permission

>> **File 13-9:** Sample Public Service Announcement

>> **File 14-1:** Chapter 14 Web Resources

>> **File 14-2:** Sample Fundraising Plan: High School Music Awards Program

>> **File 14-3:** Sample Fundraising Plan: Neighborhood Park Coalition

>> **File 14-4:** Sample Fundraising Budget: High School Music Awards Program

>> **File 14-5:** Sample Fundraising Budget: Neighborhood Park Coalition

>> **File 15-1:** Chapter 15 Web Resources

>> **File 15-2:** Sample Donor Acknowledgement Letter: Contribution of $250 or More, No Good or Service Provided

>> **File 15-3:** Sample Donor Acknowledgement Letter: Contribution of $250 or More, Good or Service Provided

>> **File 15-4:** Sample Solicitation Letter

>> **File 15-5:** Sample Newsletter (reprinted with permission from Graywolf Press, Minneapolis, MN, www.graywolfpress.org)

>> **File 15-6:** Sample Newsletter (reprinted with permission from Graywolf Press, Minneapolis, MN, www.graywolfpress.org)

>> **File 15-7:** Sample Email for Building a Potential Donor Relationship

>> **File 15-8:** Using Social Media and Your Website to Enrich Your Fundraising Appeal

>> **File 15-9:** Telemarketing Do's and Don'ts and Sample Telemarketing Scripts

>> **File 16-1:** Chapter 16 Web Resources

>> **File 16-2:** Sample Budget for a Tribute Dinner

>> **File 16-3:** Sample Special-Events Budget for a Concert or Performance

>> **File 16-4:** Sample Online Auction Budget

>> **File 16-5:** Sample Special-Events Committee Invitation Letter

>> **File 16-6:** Sample Special-Events Solicitation Letter

>> **File 16-7:** Sample Special-Events Timeline: Tribute Dinner or Luncheon

>> **File 16-8:** Sample Special-Events Timeline: Concert or Performance

>> **File 17-1:** Chapter 17 Web Resources

>> **File 17-2:** Foundation Research Overview

>> **File 17-3:** Foundation Prospect Evaluation and Tracking Sheet

>> **File 17-4:** Federal Grants Research

>> **File 18-1:** Chapter 18 Web Resources

>> **File 18-2:** Sample Letter of Inquiry (included with permission from the San Francisco Mime Troupe)

>> **File 18-3:** Sample Letter Proposal

>> **File 18-4:** Cover Letter and Sample Proposal Addressed to the Randall A. Wolf Family Foundation Requesting Support for Tri-City Hot Meals' new program (included with permission from Kristie Kwong)

>> **File 18-5:** Sample Full Proposal Submitted to the Walter & Elise Haas Fund for Dancers' Group Presents and Bay Area Dance Week (included with permission from Dancers' Group and grant writer Julie Kanter)

>> **File 18-6:** Sample Federal Grant Request for Operating Support (included with permission from UCSF AIDS Health Project)

>> **File 18-7:** Sample Project Budget Submitted to the Walter & Elise Haas Fund for Dancers' Group Presents and Bay Area Dance Week (included with permission from Dancers' Group and grant writer Julie Kanter)

>> **File 18-8:** Sample Foundation Budget Form

>> **File 18-9:** Steps for Finishing and Submitting a Grant Request

>> **File 18-10:** Sample Company-Sponsored Foundation Guidelines and Application Information

>> **File 18-11:** Sample Letter Proposal to a Company-Sponsored Foundation

>> **File 19-1:** Chapter 19 Web Resources

Index

employees beneficiary associations [591(c)(9)], 28

Employer Identification Number (EIN), 80–81

employment taxes, 405

endowment fund, 412

endowments, 369

entrepreneur, 31

EOP (emergency operations plan), 386

equity, in board of directors, 44–45

establishing

  public charity status, 85–86

  salary levels, 187–188

estimating

  costs of moving, 145

  fundraising contributions, 273–274

eTapestry, 278

evaluations

  about, 147–148

  analyzing results, 156–159

  choosing evaluators, 154–155

  conducting, 155–156

  employee progress, 195

  expenses, 210–211

  grant proposal, 350, 356–357

  importance of, 148

  management responsibility of, 197

  methods of, 152–154

  organizational capability, 141

  planning process, 149–155

  responsibility of independent contractor, 203

  selecting, 149–150

  staff capability, 141

event committee, 319–320

ex officio board members, 40, 116

examining

  income, 208–210

  references, 192

excessive compensation, 26

excise tax, 26, 85, 412

executive committees, 49

executive directors, 41, 118–119

executive summary (grant proposal), 349, 350–351

expenses

  evaluating, 210–211

  special event, 317–318

external factors of planning, 126–127

F

Facebook, 258–259

Facebook For Dummies (Abram and Karasavas), 259

facilities, planning, 142–146

family foundation, 412

Farris, Sharon (author)

  Nonprofit Bookkeeping & Accounting For Dummies, 224, 226

feasibility study, 146, 373–375

federal grants, 343–344

federal requirements for closing paperwork, 390

Federal tax forms, 404

federated campaign, 412

federated giving program, 412

fee income, 208–209

fees

  evaluating for budgets, 210

  Form 1023, 90

  independent contractor, 205

fidelity bonds, 408

fiduciary, 39, 412

financial information management, 88–89

financial reports

  accounting, 224–226

  conducting audits, 227–229

  managing financial systems, 232–233

  preparing, 226–227

  reading, 229–232

financial systems, 232–233

finding

  fiscal sponsors, 36

  funding, 21–22

  help, 20–21

  independent contractors, 203

  members for board of directors, 43–51

  resources, 14–15

  volunteers, 169–173

R

About the Authors

Dr. Beverly A. Browning: Bev was introduced to nonprofits when she was elected to the board of directors to a small volunteer center in Flint, Michigan. As the youngest board member, Bev found herself naïve and unprepared to make informed decisions on fiduciary and other governance matters under the board's authority. So she quickly started asking questions and studying nonprofit organizations. She has been a consultant for nonprofits from start-ups to development office assessments and board member training for over 40 years. Bev, who is the author of 44 publications, manages a nonprofit foundation and a for-profit corporation. She holds degrees in organizational development, public administration, and business management. She has been developing and teaching grant-writing courses for Cengage Learning (ed2go) for 20 years.

Stan Hutton: Stan became involved in the nonprofit world after cofounding a nonprofit organization in San Francisco. Since that time, he has worked as a nonprofit manager, fundraiser, consultant, and writer. He served as executive director of the Easter Seals Society of San Francisco and a fundraiser for Cogswell College. For five years, he wrote for and managed a website about nonprofits for About.com. He has worked at the San Francisco Study Center and the Executive Service Corps of San Francisco. He is now a senior program officer at the Clarence E. Heller Charitable Foundation.

Frances N. Phillips: Frances is program director for the Arts and the Creative Work Fund at the Walter and Elise Haas Fund in San Francisco. She also teaches creative writing at San Francisco State University, and taught grant-writing at SFSU for more than 25 years. Previously, Frances worked as executive director of Intersection for the Arts and of the Poetry Center and American Poetry Archives at San Francisco State University, and as a partner in the public relations and fundraising firm Horne, McClatchy & Associates. Frances is an advisory board member for Kelsey Street Press, and a policy council member of the California Alliance for Arts Education. She also is co-editor of the *Grantmakers in the Arts Reader*.

Dedication

Bev: To Aaliyah and the universe of nonprofit organizations

Stan and Frances: To Alice, Tristan, and Isaac

Authors' Acknowledgments

Bev: To the entire team at John Wiley & Sons, Inc., including Tracy Boggier and the entire editing team. I am grateful for your trust in me and guidance in updating this book. I'd like to give a shoutout to Margot Maley Hutchison, my literary agent at Waterside Productions. Margot, you've changed my life and made it possible for me to live my best life. Thank you!

Stan and Frances: This book started with our agent, Marina Watts, who had the idea and approached us to write it. Many thanks to her, to project editor Elizabeth Kuball (5th edition), to acquisitions editor Tracy Boggier, and to technical editor Gene Takagi (5th edition), who guided us through shaping and revising our manuscript. We also thank our colleagues who gave us permission to include examples of their work on the website that accompanies this book. Finally, we are grateful to the staff at Foundation Center West (particularly, Michele Ragland Dilworth, Natasha Isajlovic, and Sarah Jo Neubauer); Marcelle Hinand, president of M. Hinand Consulting; Julie Taylor, formerly of Chitresh Das Dance Company; and Jennifer Wong, of the California Alliance for Arts Education for their advice.

We owe much of our knowledge of the nonprofit sector to a remarkable array of professionals with whom we have worked. It is impossible to list everyone who has helped and inspired us, but we would be remiss not to name a few. Lori Horne, Jean McClatchy, and Ginny Rubin showed Frances the satisfaction of raising money for good causes. She is grateful to the boards of the Poetry Center at San Francisco State and Intersection for the Arts, for giving her the chance to be a nonprofit executive director, and to her current and past colleagues at the Walter and Elise Haas Fund — particularly, Bruce Sievers and Pamela David. Stan wants to add his thanks to Arthur Compton, Louise Brown, Neil Housewright, John Darby, Jan Masaoka, and Bruce Hirsch, all of whom have given him opportunities to work in the nonprofit sector and provided guidance along the way.

Publisher's Acknowledgments

Senior Acquisitions Editor: Tracy Boggier
Project Editor: Alissa Schwipps
Copy Editor: Becky Whitney
Technical Editor: Mary A. Byrne

Production Editor: Tamilmani Varadharaj
Cover Image: © garagestock/Shutterstock

Leverage the power

Dummies is the global leader in the reference category and one of the most trusted and highly regarded brands in the world. No longer just focused on books, customers now have access to the dummies content they need in the format they want. Together we'll craft a solution that engages your customers, stands out from the competition, and helps you meet your goals.

Advertising & Sponsorships

Connect with an engaged audience on a powerful multimedia site, and position your message alongside expert how-to content. Dummies.com is a one-stop shop for free, online information and know-how curated by a team of experts.

- Targeted ads
- Video
- Email Marketing
- Microsites
- Sweepstakes sponsorship

20 MILLION
PAGE VIEWS
EVERY SINGLE MONTH

15
MILLION
UNIQUE
VISITORS PER MONTH

43%
OF ALL VISITORS
ACCESS THE SITE
VIA THEIR MOBILE DEVICES

700,000 NEWSLETTER
SUBSCRIPTIONS
TO THE INBOXES OF
300,000 UNIQUE INDIVIDUALS
EVERY WEEK

# of dummies

Custom Publishing

Reach a global audience in any language by creating a solution that will differentiate you from competitors, amplify your message, and encourage customers to make a buying decision.

- Apps
- Books
- eBooks
- Video
- Audio
- Webinars

Brand Licensing & Content

Leverage the strength of the world's most popular reference brand to reach new audiences and channels of distribution.

For more information, visit dummies.com/biz

PERSONAL ENRICHMENT

     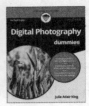

Staying Sharp
9781119187790
USA $26.00
CAN $31.99
UK £19.99

Facebook
9781119179030
USA $21.99
CAN $25.99
UK £16.99

Guitar
9781119293354
USA $24.99
CAN $29.99
UK £17.99

Investing
9781119293347
USA $22.99
CAN $27.99
UK £16.99

Beekeeping
9781119310068
USA $22.99
CAN $27.99
UK £16.99

Digital Photography
9781119235606
USA $24.99
CAN $29.99
UK £17.99

Meditation
9781119251163
USA $24.99
CAN $29.99
UK £17.99

Pregnancy
9781119235491
USA $26.99
CAN $31.99
UK £19.99

Samsung Galaxy S7
9781119279952
USA $24.99
CAN $29.99
UK £17.99

iPhone
9781119283133
USA $24.99
CAN $29.99
UK £17.99

Crocheting
9781119287117
USA $24.99
CAN $29.99
UK £16.99

Nutrition
9781119130246
USA $22.99
CAN $27.99
UK £16.99

PROFESSIONAL DEVELOPMENT

Windows 10
9781119311041
USA $24.99
CAN $29.99
UK £17.99

AutoCAD
9781119255796
USA $39.99
CAN $47.99
UK £27.99

Excel 2016
9781119293439
USA $26.99
CAN $31.99
UK £19.99

QuickBooks 2017
9781119281467
USA $26.99
CAN $31.99
UK £19.99

macOS Sierra
9781119280651
USA $29.99
CAN $35.99
UK £21.99

LinkedIn
9781119251132
USA $24.99
CAN $29.99
UK £17.99

Windows 10 All-in-One
9781119310563
USA $34.00
CAN $41.99
UK £24.99

SharePoint 2016
9781119181705
USA $29.99
CAN $35.99
UK £21.99

Fundamental Analysis
9781119263593
USA $26.99
CAN $31.99
UK £19.99

Networking
9781119257769
USA $29.99
CAN $35.99
UK £21.99

Office 2016
9781119293477
USA $26.99
CAN $31.99
UK £19.99

Office 365
9781119265313
USA $24.99
CAN $29.99
UK £17.99

Salesforce.com
9781119239314
USA $29.99
CAN $35.99
UK £21.99

Coding
9781119293323
USA $29.99
CAN $35.99
UK £21.99

dummies.com

dummies®
A Wiley Brand

Learning Made Easy

ACADEMIC

Algebra I dummies

Mary Jane Sterling

9781119293576
USA $19.99
CAN $23.99
UK £15.99

Basic Math & Pre-Algebra dummies

Mark Zegarelli

9781119293637
USA $19.99
CAN $23.99
UK £15.99

Calculus dummies

Mark Ryan

9781119293491
USA $19.99
CAN $23.99
UK £15.99

Chemistry dummies

John T. Moore, EdD

9781119293460
USA $19.99
CAN $23.99
UK £15.99

Physics I dummies

Steven Holzner, PhD

9781119293590
USA $19.99
CAN $23.99
UK £15.99

1,001 Practice Questions SAT dummies

Ron Woldoff

9781119215844
USA $26.99
CAN $31.99
UK £19.99

Organic Chemistry I dummies

Arthur Winter

9781119293378
USA $22.99
CAN $27.99
UK £16.99

Statistics dummies

Deborah J. Rumsey, PhD

9781119293521
USA $19.99
CAN $23.99
UK £15.99

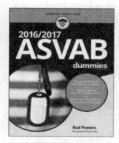

2016/2017 ASVAB dummies

Rod Powers

9781119239178
USA $18.99
CAN $22.99
UK £14.99

1,001 Practice Questions Praxis Core dummies

Carla Kirkland
Chan Cleveland

9781119263883
USA $26.99
CAN $31.99
UK £19.99

Available Everywhere Books Are Sold

Small books for big imaginations

GETTING STARTED WITH Coding
Get Creative with Code!
Camille McCue, PhD

9781119177173
USA $9.99
CAN $9.99
UK £8.99

MODDING Minecraft
Build Your Own Minecraft Mods!
Sarah Guthals, PhD
Stephen Foster, PhD
Lindsey Handley, PhD

9781119177272
USA $9.99
CAN $9.99
UK £8.99

MAKING YouTube VIDEOS
Star in Your Own Video!
Nick Willoughby

9781119177241
USA $9.99
CAN $9.99
UK £8.99

DESIGNING Digital Games
Create Games with Scratch!
Derek Breen

9781119177210
USA $9.99
CAN $9.99
UK £8.99

GETTING STARTED WITH Raspberry Pi
Program Your Raspberry Pi!
Richard Wentk

9781119262657
USA $9.99
CAN $9.99
UK £6.99

EXPERIMENTING WITH Science
Think, Test, and Learn!
Mark J. Gellis, PhD

9781119291336
USA $9.99
CAN $9.99
UK £6.99

CREATING Digital Animations
Animate Stories with Scratch!
Derek Breen

9781119233527
USA $9.99
CAN $9.99
UK £6.99

GETTING STARTED WITH Engineering
Think Like an Engineer!
Camille McCue, PhD

9781119291220
USA $9.99
CAN $9.99
UK £6.99

WRITING Computer Code
Learn the Language of Computers!
Chris Minnick and Eva Holland

9781119177302
USA $9.99
CAN $9.99
UK £8.99

Unleash Their Creativity

dummies.com

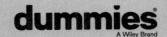